WILLIAM BLAKE IN CONTEXT

William Blake, poet and artist, is a figure often understood to have 'created his own system'. Combining close readings and detailed analysis of a range of Blake's work, from lyrical songs to later myth, from writing to visual art, this collection of thirty-eight lively and authoritative essays examines what Blake had in common with his contemporaries, the writers who influenced him, and those he influenced in turn. Chapters from an international team of leading scholars also attend to his wider contexts: material, formal, cultural, and historical, to enrich our understanding of, and engagement with, Blake's work. Accessibly written, incisive, and informed by original research, *William Blake in Context* enables readers to appreciate Blake anew, from both within and outside of his own idiom.

SARAH HAGGARTY is Lecturer in the Faculty of English and Fellow of Queens' College, at the University of Cambridge. She has published three previous books about Blake: *Blake's Gifts: Poetry and the Politics of Exchange* (Cambridge, 2010); *William Blake: Songs of Innocence and of Experience (1794)* (with Jon Mee, 2013); and *Blake and Conflict* (with Jon Mee, 2009).

WILLIAM BLAKE IN CONTEXT

Edited by
SARAH HAGGARTY
University of Cambridge

CAMBRIDGE
UNIVERSITY PRESS

University Printing House, Cambridge CB2 8BS, United Kingdom

One Liberty Plaza, 20th Floor, New York, NY 10006, USA

477 Williamstown Road, Port Melbourne, VIC 3207, Australia

314–321, 3rd Floor, Plot 3, Splendor Forum, Jasola District Centre, New Delhi – 110025, India

79 Anson Road, #06–04/06, Singapore 079906

Cambridge University Press is part of the University of Cambridge.

It furthers the University's mission by disseminating knowledge in the pursuit of education, learning, and research at the highest international levels of excellence.

www.cambridge.org
Information on this title: www.cambridge.org/9781107144910
DOI: 10.1017/9781316534946

© Cambridge University Press 2019

This publication is in copyright. Subject to statutory exception and to the provisions of relevant collective licensing agreements, no reproduction of any part may take place without the written permission of Cambridge University Press.

First published 2019

A catalogue record for this publication is available from the British Library.

Library of Congress Cataloging-in-Publication Data
NAMES: Haggarty, Sarah, editor.
TITLE: William Blake in context / edited by Sarah Haggarty.
DESCRIPTION: New York : Cambridge University Press, 2019. | SERIES: Literature in context | Includes bibliographical references and index.
IDENTIFIERS: LCCN 2018049854 | ISBN 9781107144910 (hardback)
SUBJECTS: LCSH: Blake, William, 1757–1827 – Criticism and interpretation. | Literature and society – England – History – 18th century. | Literature and society – England – History – 19th century. | Art and literature – England – History – 18th century. | Art and literature – England – History – 19th century. | BISAC: LITERARY CRITICISM / European / English, Irish, Scottish, Welsh.
CLASSIFICATION: LCC PR4147 .W475 2019 | DDC 821/.7–dc23
LC record available at https://lccn.loc.gov/2018049854

ISBN 978-1-107-14491-0 Hardback

Cambridge University Press has no responsibility for the persistence or accuracy of URLs for external or third-party internet websites referred to in this publication and does not guarantee that any content on such websites is, or will remain, accurate or appropriate.

Contents

List of Illustrations	page ix
Notes on Contributors	xi
Acknowledgements	xx
List of Abbreviations	xxi
Introduction *Sarah Haggarty*	1
PART I: LIFE, WORKS, AND RECEPTION	5
1 Life *Leo Damrosch*	7
2 Networks *Jon Mee*	15
3 Engraving *Mark Crosby*	23
4 Illuminated Books *David Worrall*	35
5 Manuscripts *Sarah Haggarty*	43
6 Book Illustration *Luisa Calè*	56
7 Painting *Martin Myrone*	70
8 Early Reception *Sibylle Erle and Keri Davies*	79

9	Late Reception *Jason Whittaker*	87
10	Editing and Editions *Morris Eaves*	94

PART II: FORM, GENRE, AND MODE — 103

11	Comedy *Fred Parker*	105
12	Prophecy *Ian Balfour*	113
13	Rhythm *Derek Attridge*	120
14	Songs *Steve Newman*	129
15	Sound *Michael D. Hurley*	139
16	Sublimity *David Baulch*	147
17	System, Myth, and Symbol *Tilottama Rajan*	155

PART III: CREATIVE CROSS-CURRENTS — 163

18	The Bible *Stephen Prickett*	165
19	Chaucer, Spenser, and Shakespeare *David Fuller*	173
20	Milton *G. A. Rosso*	184
21	The Eighteenth Century and Romanticism *David Duff*	192
22	Byron *Jerome McGann*	200

23	Pre-Raphaelites and Aesthetes *Elizabeth Helsinger*	211
24	Yeats, Eliot, and Auden *Edward Larrissy*	219
25	Whitman, Crane, and the Beats *Linda Freedman*	227

PART IV: HISTORY, SOCIETY, AND CULTURE — 235

26	Animals *Kurt Fosso*	237
27	Antiquarianism *Noah Heringman*	245
28	Education and Childhood *Louise Joy*	254
29	Empiricism *Nicholas M. Williams*	262
30	Life Sciences *Denise Gigante*	270
31	London *Saree Makdisi*	277
32	Money *Matthew Rowlinson*	286
33	Moravianism *Alexander Regier*	293
34	Mysticism *Laura Quinney*	301
35	Nationalism and Imperialism *Julia M. Wright*	309
36	Sex, Sexuality, and Gender *Susan Matthews*	317
37	War and Revolution *Andrew Lincoln*	325

38	(Without) Sympathy *Steven Goldsmith*	333

Further Reading   345
Index   364

Illustrations

3.1 W. Blake, *Joseph of Arimathea among the Rocks of Albion*,   page 26
first state, 1773, engraving, black carbon ink on paper,
© Fitzwilliam Museum, Cambridge

3.2 W. Blake, *The Canterbury Pilgrims*, fourth state, 1810,   29
engraving, Collection of R. N. Essick

3.3 J. Basire, *The Field of the Cloth of Gold*, 1774, engraving,   31
Collection of M. Crosby

3.4 W. Blake, *Job* separate plate, second state, c. 1804 or later,   32
engraving, Collection of R. N. Essick

6.1 W. Blake, *Edward Young, Night Thoughts* [1797], *Copy 1:*   59
electronic edition, Object 25, 2007, etching and engraving,
William Blake Archive (Collection of R. N. Essick)

6.2 W. Blake, *The Descent of Man into the Vale of Death*, c. 1805,   60
pen and grey ink and grey wash, with watercolour,
© The Trustees of the British Museum, London

6.3 W. Blake, *Christ Descending into the Grave*, 1808, in *Robert*   62
Blair, The Grave: electronic edition, Object 3, 2007, etching
and engraving, William Blake Archive

6.4 W. Blake, *The Messengers Tell Job of His Misfortunes*, 1823–6,   63
in *Illustrations of the Book of Job: electronic edition*, Object 6,
2002, intaglio engraving, William Blake Archive (Collection
of R. N. Essick)

6.5 W. Blake, *When the Morning Stars Sang Together*, 1823–6, in   65
Illustrations of the Book of Job: electronic edition, Object 16,
2002, intaglio engraving, William Blake Archive (Collection
of R. N. Essick)

6.6 W. Blake, *The Mission of Virgil*, 1824–7, watercolour over   67
pencil, pen and ink, and scratching out, Birmingham
Museums and Art Gallery

7.1	W. Blake, *The Spiritual Form of Nelson Guiding Leviathan*, c. 1805–9, The Picture Art Collection/Alamy Stock Photo	72
7.2	W. Blake, *The Spiritual Form of Pitt Guiding Behemoth*, c. 1805, The Picture Art Collection/Alamy Stock Photo	73
19.1	W. Blake, *Characters from Spenser's Faery Queen*, c. 1825, watercolour, Petworth House and Park, West Sussex, © National Trust Images/John Hammond	177
19.2	W. Blake, *As if an Angel Dropped Down from the Clouds*, 1809, Art Collection 2/Alamy Stock Photo	180
19.3	W. Blake, *Pity*, c. 1795, Art Collection 2/Alamy Stock Photo	182
20.1	W. Blake, *Michael Foretelling the Crucifixion to Adam*, 1808, pen and ink and watercolour, Museum of Fine Arts, Boston	190
38.1	W. Blake, *The Belvedere Torso [verso]*, c. 1779/80, graphite on two joined sheets, Rosenwald Collection, National Gallery, Washington	334
38.2	W. Blake, *Moses Staying the Plague (?) [recto]*, c. 1780/85, graphite on two joined sheets, Rosenwald Collection, National Gallery, Washington	335
38.3	W. Blake, *The Angel Rolling the Stone Away from the Sepulchre*, c. 1808, pen and ink and watercolour, Victoria and Albert Museum, London	337
38.4	W. Blake, *Milton a Poem*, Copy B, Plate 15, 1811, relief and white-line etching with hand colouring, Huntington Library and Art Gallery, California	343

Notes on Contributors

DEREK ATTRIDGE is Emeritus Professor at the University of York, UK, and the author of books on poetic form, literary theory, South African writing, and James Joyce. His books on poetry include *Well-weighed Syllables: Elizabethan Verse in Classical Metres* (1974); *The Rhythms of English Poetry* (1982); *Poetic Rhythm: An Introduction* (1998); *Meter and Meaning* (with Thomas Carper, 2003); *Moving Words: Forms of English Poetry* (2013); *The Craft of Poetry: Dialogues on Minimal Interpretation* (with Henry Staten, 2015); and *The Experience of Poetry: From Homer's Listeners to Shakespeare's Readers* (2019).

IAN BALFOUR is Professor of English at York University, Canada. He is the author of *The Rhetoric of Romantic Prophecy* (2002) and *Northrop Frye* (1988). He has published numerous essays on Romantic poetry, British and German, as well as on Godwin, Inchbald, Austen, Mary Shelley, and De Quincey. He co-curated an exhibition at Tate Britain on William Hazlitt. He is at work completing a book on the theory and practice of the sublime.

DAVID BAULCH is Associate Professor of English at the University of West Florida. His topics of research include Romantic poetics, psychoanalysis, post-structuralism, and non-human theory. He is currently revising a book manuscript entitled *Being at the Limit: William Blake Difference and Repetition* for SUNY Press. He has edited Thomas Lovell Beddoes's *The Brides' Tragedy* for *Romantic Circles* (2007), and his articles have appeared in journals such as *European Romantic Review, Studies in Romanticism, The Wordsworth Circle, The Coleridge Bulletin,* and *Romantic Circles Praxis Series.*

LUISA CALÈ (Birkbeck, University of London) has written on the intersections between reading, viewing, and collecting in the Romantic period. Her publications include *Fuseli's Milton Gallery: 'Turning*

Readers into Spectators', and co-edited special issues on 'The Disorder of Things' (*Eighteenth-Century Studies*) and 'Literature and Sculpture at the Fin de Siècle' (*Word and Image*). Her current project is entitled *The Book Unbound*, with chapters on Walpole, Blake, and Dickens.

MARK CROSBY is Associate Professor of English and Director of the Digital Humanities Center at Kansas State University. He has co-authored, with Robert N. Essick, a book on Blake's Genesis Manuscript (2012); co-edited *Re-envisioning Blake* (2012), and edited a special issue of *Huntington Library Quarterly* (Fall 2017) on Blake's manuscripts. He is currently working on a book about Blake's often fractious engagements with the patronage system.

LEO DAMROSCH has taught at the universities of Virginia and Maryland and at Harvard, where he is now an emeritus professor. In addition to books on various eighteenth-century topics, he has published biographies of Rousseau and Swift and two books on Blake, *Symbol and Truth in Blake's Myth* (1980) and *Eternity's Sunrise: The Imaginative World of William Blake* (2015). *The Club: Johnson, Boswell, and the Friends Who Shaped an Age* will be published in 2019.

KERI DAVIES, an independent scholar, is Vice-President of the Blake Society. He has written on William Blake's parents (particularly his mother's links to the Moravian Church), and on the social and intellectual milieu of early Blake collectors, and other friends and acquaintances of the painter-poet.

DAVID DUFF is Professor of Romanticism at Queen Mary University of London and founder-director of the London–Paris Romanticism Seminar. His publications include *Romance and Revolution: Shelley and the Politics of a Genre* (1994), *Romanticism and the Uses of Genre* (2009), and three edited books: *Modern Genre Theory* (2000), *Scotland, Ireland, and the Romantic Aesthetic* (2007, co-edited with Catherine Jones), and *The Oxford Handbook of British Romanticism* (2018). He is currently editing *The Oxford Anthology of Romanticism* and writing a literary history of the Romantic prospectus.

MORRIS EAVES is Professor of English, Turner Professor of Humanities, and director of the A. W. Mellon Graduate Programme in the Digital Humanities at the University of Rochester, New York. He is author of *William Blake's Theory of Art* (1982) and *The Counter-Arts Conspiracy* (1992), and many essays on romanticism, media history, and editorial theory; and co-editor of *William Blake: The Early Illuminated Books* (1993), *Blake / An Illustrated Quarterly* (1967–present), and the *William Blake Archive* (1996–present). His book in progress, *Posterity*, views editing as an everyday, multisensory human activity.

SIBYLLE ERLE, FRSA, is Reader in English Literature at Bishop Grosseteste University in Lincoln, UK. She is the author of *Blake, Lavater and Physiognomy* (2010) and chapters and articles on Blake, Fuseli, Lavater, Tennyson, Ludwig Meidner, and *Frankenstein*. She co-curated with Philippa Simpson the display 'Blake and Physiognomy' (2010–11) at Tate Britain, co-edited (and contributed to) with Laurie Garrison the special issue *Science, Technology and the Senses* (*RaVoN*, 2008), and co-edited with Laurie Garrison, Verity Hunt, Phoebe Putnam, and Peter West *Panoramas, 1787–1900: Texts and Contexts*, 5 vols. (2012). She is co-editing with Morton D. Paley *The Reception of William Blake in Europe* (2019).

KURT FOSSO is Professor of English at Lewis & Clark College in Portland, Oregon, and the author of *Buried Communities: Wordsworth and the Bonds of Mourning* (2004). His recent work focuses on animality and depictions of animals in the Romantic period, and includes essays in *European Romantic Review* (2014) and *Beastly Blake*, edited by Helen P. Bruder and Tristanne Connolly (2018).

LINDA FREEDMAN is Lecturer in English and American Literature at University College London. She is the author of *Emily Dickinson and the Religious Imagination* (2011) and *William Blake and the Myth of America: From the Abolitionists to the Counterculture* (2018). Her research and teaching interests are transatlantic and interdisciplinary, ranging from the Romantic period to the present and focusing on the relationship between literature, religion, politics, and the visual arts. She has contributed numerous articles and essays on such topics to journals and edited collections, and is currently writing a cultural history of the Book of Genesis.

DAVID FULLER is Emeritus Professor of English at the University of Durham, UK, author of monographs on Blake, Joyce, Shakespeare, and (co-authored) literary treatments of the sacraments, editor of texts by Marlowe (Clarendon) and Blake (Longman Annotated Texts), and of two co-edited collections (Oxford, Palgrave). He has written on a range of poetry, drama, and novels from Medieval to contemporary, on editorial theory, on opera, and on dance. His *Shakespeare and the*

Romantics is forthcoming in the series 'Oxford Shakespeare Topics' (2019). His other current work is for a Wellcome Trust-funded project, the Life of Breath, on structures of poetry related to breathing, and the performance of poetry.

DENISE GIGANTE is Professor of English at Stanford University and the author of several books on Romantic literature and poetry, including, most recently, *The Keats Brothers: The Life of John and George* (2011) and *Life: Organic Form and Romanticism* (2009). She is currently working on a book about Blake and Italian iconography called *The Mental Traveller*.

STEVEN GOLDSMITH is Professor of English at the University of California, Berkeley. He is the author of *Unbuilding Jerusalem: Apocalypse and Romantic Representation* (1993) and *Blake's Agitation: Criticism and the Emotions* (2013). His current project is a study of mere materialism in Rembrandt, Melville, and Schwitters.

SARAH HAGGARTY is Lecturer in the Faculty of English, and Fellow of Queens' College, University of Cambridge. Her publications include the books *Blake's Gifts: Poetry and the Politics of Exchange* (2010) and *William Blake: Songs of Innocence and of Experience (1794)* (with Jon Mee, 2013), and essays about William Cowper and letter-writing, and Blake, Isaac Newton, and geometry. Her next book, part-funded by a Leverhulme Trust Research Fellowship, will be about practice-based theories of time in religious writings of the late eighteenth century.

ELIZABETH HELSINGER is John Matthews Manly Distinguished Service Professor Emerita of English and Art History at the University of Chicago. Her monographs include *Ruskin and the Art of the Beholder* (1982), *Rural Scenes and National Representation* (1997), *Poetry and the Pre-Raphaelite Arts* (2008), and *Poetry and the Thought of Song* (2015). She has also edited *The Writing of Modern Life: The Etching Revival in France, Britain, and America* (2009) and co-edited *The Woman Question: Britain and America, 1837–1883* (1983); she is an editor of *Critical Inquiry*.

NOAH HERINGMAN teaches English at the University of Missouri. His publications include two edited volumes and two monographs, *Romantic Rocks, Aesthetic Geology* (2004) and *Sciences of Antiquity: Romantic Antiquarianism, Natural History, and Knowledge Work* (2013). He has also published numerous articles on poets such as Blake, Keats, and Charlotte Smith and on topics ranging from the history of geology to the Anthropocene. In addition to editing the print series *Vetusta Monumenta*, he is presently completing a monograph on the history of deep time, which includes a chapter on Blake.

MICHAEL D. HURLEY teaches English at the University of Cambridge, where he is a University Lecturer and a Fellow of St Catharine's College. He is the author of *Faith in Poetry: Verse Style as a Mode of Religious Belief* (2017) and *G. K. Chesterton* (2012), co-author of *Poetic Form* (with Michael O'Neill, 2012), editor of *The Complete Father Brown Stories* (Penguin Classics), and co-editor of *Thinking through Style: Non-Fiction Prose of the Long Nineteenth Century* (with Marcus Waithe, 2018).

LOUISE JOY is Fellow and Director of Studies in English at Homerton College, University of Cambridge. She has co-edited two volumes of essays, *The Aesthetics of Children's Poetry* (2017), and *Poetry and Childhood* (2010). Her work on eighteenth-century literature has appeared in *Studies in Romanticism, European Romantic Review, History of European Ideas, Literature and Theology,* and *Philosophy and Literature*. Her monograph, *Literature's Children: The Critical Child and the Art of Idealisation*, will be published later this year.

EDWARD LARRISSY is Emeritus Professor of Queen's University, Belfast. He is the author of *William Blake* (1985), *Reading Twentieth-Century Poetry: The Language of Gender and Objects* (1990), *Yeats the Poet: The Measures of Difference* (1994), *Blake and Modern Literature* (2006), and *The Blind and Blindness in Literature of the Romantic Period* (2007). He has edited *Romanticism and Postmodernism* (1997), *W. B. Yeats: The Major Works* (2001), *The First Yeats: Poems by W. B. Yeats 1889–1899* (2010), and *The Cambridge Companion to British Poetry 1945–2010* (2015). He is a Member of the Royal Irish Academy.

ANDREW LINCOLN is Professor Emeritus of the English Department, Queen Mary University of London. His publications include the Blake Trust edition of William Blake's *Songs of Innocence and of Experience* (1992), *Spiritual History: A Reading of William Blake's The Four Zoas* (1995), *Walter Scott and Modernity* (2007), and numerous articles on Blake and Scott. He is currently working on the culture of war in Britain during the long eighteenth century.

SAREE MAKDISI is Professor of English and Comparative Literature at the University of California, Los Angeles. He is the author of *Reading William Blake* (2015), *Making England Western* (2014), *Palestine Inside*

Out: An Everyday Occupation (2010), *William Blake and the Impossible History of the 1790s* (2003), and *Romantic Imperialism* (1998).

SUSAN MATTHEWS is Senior Research Fellow at University of Roehampton and the author of *Blake, Sexuality and Bourgeois Politeness* (2011).

JEROME MCGANN is John Stewart Bryan University Professor, University of Virginia and Visiting Research Professor, University of California, Berkeley. He is completing a study of Colonial American literature, *American Literature before American Literature*, as well as a series of studies of Romantic and post-Romantic prosody.

JON MEE is Professor of Eighteenth-Century Studies at the University of York, UK. He has written widely on Blake, most recently a guide to criticism on *Songs of Innocence and of Experience* with Sarah Haggarty. He is currently writing a book on networks of improvement in the commercial towns of the early industrial revolution focused particularly on medico-literary ideas of imagination, genius, and materialism.

MARTIN MYRONE is Senior Curator at Tate Britain, London, specialising in eighteenth- and early nineteenth-century British art. He is the author of monographs on William Blake, Henry Fuseli, and George Stubbs, and of *Bodybuilding: Reforming Masculinities in British Art 1750–1810* (2005). He has curated a range of exhibitions and display projects at Tate Britain, including *Gothic Nightmares: Fuseli, Blake and the Romantic Imagination* (2006), *John Martin: Apocalypse* (2012), and *British Folk Art* (2014).

STEVE NEWMAN is Associate Professor of English at Temple University, Pennsylvania. He is the author of *Ballad Collection, Lyric, and the Canon: The Call of the Popular from the Restoration to the New Criticism* (2007) as well as articles on Shakespeare and song, Scottish Romanticism, and other topics. He is the editor of *The Gentle Shepherd* for the forthcoming *Collected Works of Allan Ramsay* (Edinburgh University Press), and is currently heading up a digital humanities project on *The Beggar's Opera* and working on a monograph, *Time for the Humanities: Competing Narratives of Value from the Scottish Enlightenment to the 21st Century Academy*.

FRED PARKER is Senior Lecturer in English at the University of Cambridge and a Fellow of Clare College; his research interests lie mainly in the long eighteenth century. He is author of *Johnson's Shakespeare* (1989), *Scepticism and Literature: An Essay on Pope, Hume, Sterne, and Johnson*

(2003), and *The Devil as Muse: Blake, Byron, and the Adversary* (2011). His most recent book, just completed, has the provisional title *On Declaring Love: From Richardson to Austen*.

STEPHEN PRICKETT is Regius Professor Emeritus of English at Glasgow University and Honorary Professor at the University of Kent, UK. A Fellow of the Australian Academy of the Humanities, former Chairman of the UK Higher Education Foundation, he has published two novels, nine monographs, seven edited volumes, and over one hundred articles on Romanticism, Victorian Studies, literature, and theology.

LAURA QUINNEY is Professor of English at Brandeis University, Massachusetts. She is the author of three books of criticism, including most recently *William Blake on Self and Soul* (2009), and two books of poetry, *Corridor* (2008) and *New Ghosts* (2016). She is currently working on a scholarly book about subjectivity and existential alienation.

TILOTTAMA RAJAN is Canada Research Chair and Distinguished University Professor at the University of Western Ontario, where she has also been Director of the Centre for Theory and Criticism. She is the author of over a hundred articles on Romantic literature and/or philosophy and contemporary theory, and has published four books, including *Dark Interpreter: The Discourse of Romanticism* (1980), *Deconstruction and the Remainders of Phenomenology* (2002), and *Romantic Narrative: Shelley, Hays, Godwin, Wollstonecraft* (2010). She has also edited seven collections and scholarly editions, most recently Godwin's *Mandeville* (2015). She is currently working on encyclopaedic (dis)organisations of knowledge from German Idealism to deconstruction, with a particular emphasis on the pressure that the life sciences bring to bear on philosophy, and also on the eighteenth-century physiological theorist John Hunter.

ALEXANDER REGIER is Associate Professor of English at Rice University, Texas, and editor of the scholarly journal *SEL Studies in English Literature 1500–1900*. He is the author of *Fracture and Fragmentation in British Romanticism* (2010), the co-editor of *Wordsworth's Poetic Theory: Knowledge, Language, Experience* (2010), and has edited special journal issues on 'Mobilities' and 'Genealogies' (both *SEL*). His articles on Romanticism, rhetoric, William Wordsworth, Walter Benjamin, ruins, contemporary poetry, the aesthetics of sport, and other topics have appeared in a wide variety of journals. His book *Exorbitant*

Enlightenment: Blake, Hamann, and Anglo-German Constellations is scheduled to be published later this year.

G. A. ROSSO is Professor of English at Southern Connecticut State University. He has published a number of books and essays on Blake, the most recent a study of Blake's three long poems titled *The Religion of Empire: Political Theology in Blake's Prophetic Symbolism* (2016). He currently is working on a study of Blake and Methodism, concentrating on the influence of eighteenth-century British Revival hymnody on Blake's religious myth.

MATTHEW ROWLINSON is Professor of English and a member of the core faculty in the Centre for Theory and Criticism at Western University, in London, Ontario. He is the author of *Real Money and Romanticism* (2010) and *Tennyson's Fixations: Psychoanalysis and the Topics of the Early Poetry* (1994), as well as articles and reviews on literature of the Victorian and Romantic periods. Recent and forthcoming publications include an edition of Tennyson's *In Memoriam* (2014), and essays on Charles Darwin and on animal sounds in poetry.

JASON WHITTAKER is Professor of English and Head of the School of English and Journalism at the University of Lincoln, UK. His publications include *William Blake and the Myths of Britain* (1999), *Radical Blake: Influence and Afterlife from 1827* (with Shirley Dent, 2002), and *Blake 2.0: William Blake in Twentieth Century Art, Music, Culture* (edited with Steve Clark and Tristanne Connolly). He is currently completing a monograph on the first hundred years of the hymn 'Jerusalem'.

NICHOLAS M. WILLIAMS is Associate Professor of English at Indiana University, Bloomington. He is the author of *Ideology and Utopia in the Poetry of William Blake* (1998) and editor of *Palgrave Advances in William Blake Studies* (2005). His current research focuses on embodiment in texts of the Romantic period and its connection to theories of motion.

DAVID WORRALL is Professor Emeritus in English at Nottingham Trent University, UK. He has published widely on William Blake, editing *William Blake, The Urizen Books* for the William Blake Trust (1995) and co-editing, with Steve Clark, *Historicizing Blake* (1994), *Blake in the Nineties* (1999), and *Blake, Nation and Empire* (2006). He has also led two research projects on Blake, the first (with Keri Davies) on Blake and

Moravians (AHRC, 2004–6) and the second (with Nancy Jiwhon Cho) on Dorothy Gott, the female prophet Blake met in 1789 (Panacea Society, 2008–10).

JULIA M. WRIGHT is Professor of English and University Research Professor at Dalhousie University, Canada. She is the author of four monographs, including *Blake, Nationalism, and the Politics of Alienation* (2004) and *Representing the National Landscape in Irish Romanticism* (2014), and the editor of *Irish Literature, 1750–1900: An Anthology* (2008), two of Lady Morgan's novels, and the two-volume *Companion to Irish Literature* (2010). She has also co-edited a number of collections of essays, including *A Handbook to Romanticism Studies* (with Joel Faflak, 2012) and *Reading the Nation in English Literature* (with Elizabeth Sauer, 2009), and her essays have appeared in such journals as *European Romantic Review* and *Studies in Romanticism*.

Acknowledgements

I am grateful to Linda Bree at CUP for commissioning this book, to her successor, Bethany Thomas, for managing the final stages of the project, and to their editorial assistants, Isobel Cowper-Coles and Tim Mason, for their support. I am also grateful to Jan Baiton, Mathi Mareesan, and Sarah Starkey for shepherding the book through production. The contributors to this book have been an absolute pleasure to work with: I am particularly thankful for their expertise, for their saying 'yes' to begin with, and for their patience and good humour during the long-drawn-out progress to print. Several collectors have been most generous in allowing us to reproduce Blake's or associated artwork gratis. I am also delighted to be able to use Dennis Creffield's remarkable *Improvisation on the Life Cast of William Blake (5)* on the book's cover: many thanks to the collector, to Mr Creffield's family, and to Philip Dodd for making this possible.

Finally, some notice of late arrivals and departures: Beatrice and Imogen, Fazlul and Kate – my love to you all.

Abbreviations

Unless indicated otherwise, all textual references are to Erdman's edition, listed below (E). In accordance with Erdman's practice, when citing Blake's writing we tend to reference plate and line numbers (e.g. 22: 5), although sometimes plate (pl.) or line (l.) numbers alone suffice. For the heavily revised manuscript *VALA / The Four Zoas*, we reference 'Night' (N), page (p.), and line (l.) numbers. In all cases, we adopt the conventional 'E' to signify page numbers in Erdman's edition. Erdman's text is also available to view and search online: erdman.blakearchive.org

The William Blake Archive, again listed below (WBA), offers unparalleled access to images of Blake's works, referred to within its electronic editions as 'objects' (obj.). There is a yet greater range of Blake's art available in Butlin's two-volume *Paintings and Drawings*; references here are to numbered catalogue entries in the first, *Text*, volume (Butlin) – note that Vol. II, *Images*, is organised differently.

BB	G. E. Bentley, Jr, *Blake Books* (Oxford: Clarendon Press, 1977)
BR	G. E. Bentley, Jr, *Blake Records*, 2nd edn (New Haven; London: Yale University Press for the Paul Mellon Centre for Studies in British Art, 2004)
Butlin	M. Butlin, *The Paintings and Drawings of William Blake*, 2 vols. (Yale: Paul Mellon Centre for Studies in British Art, 1981), I: *Text*
E	D. V. Erdman (ed.), *The Complete Poetry and Prose of William Blake*, commentary by H. Bloom, rev. edn (Berkeley, CA: University of California Press, 1982, and repr.)
Gilchrist	A. Gilchrist, *Life of William Blake, 'Pictor Ignotus': With Selections from His Poems and Other Writings*, 2 vols. (London and Cambridge: Macmillan, 1863), I

Stranger	G. E. Bentley, Jr, *The Stranger from Paradise: A Biography of William Blake* (New Haven: Yale University Press, 2001)
Viscomi	J. Viscomi, *Blake and the Idea of the Book* (Princeton: Princeton University Press, 1993)
WBA	M. Eaves, R. Essick, and J. Viscomi (eds.), The William Blake Archive, www.blakearchive.org

Introduction
Sarah Haggarty

> In this Picture, believing with Milton, the ancient British History, Mr. B. has done, as all the ancients did, and as all the moderns, who are worthy of fame, given the historical fact in its poetical vigour; so as it always happens, and not in that dull way that some Historians pretend, who being weakly organized themselves, cannot see either miracle or prodigy; all is to them a full round of probabilities and possibilities; but the history of all times and places, is nothing else but improbabilities and impossibilities; what we should say, was impossible if we did not see it always before our eyes.
> – William Blake, *Descriptive Catalogue* (1809), E 543

Whether it is the cussedness of Blake, or the cussedness of some of us who write about him, he does not feel immediately like the most obvious candidate for a series about 'writers in context'. For a start, Blake was not just a writer, but also an artist practising in a range of media – writing, drawing, etching, engraving, printmaking, and painting. His earliest audience knew him as a visual artist, and if – thinking of the 'sister arts' of painting and poetry – we had to choose one sister over another, it would seem to be the visual arts that make him the more historically legible, embedded and affiliated as he was by education, friends and patrons, and professional practice. Some of the guiding terms from Blake's aesthetics (particular vs general; invention vs execution; outline) make most sense in a visual cultural context, as do his governing metaphors for artistic production (drawing; printmaking).[1] The reach of this language in Blake's usage, though, was across the sister arts, yoking visual and verbal together. Writing alongside engraving bookended his career, and his most celebrated creative achievement would seem for most people nowadays to be the 'composite art' of the illuminated books.[2] While conceiving of Blake purely as a writer can make it appear that he virtually failed to secure a contemporary audience, furthermore, looking at his work in the round suggests a degree of (admittedly still modest) success. The entire print run of illuminated books, if one can put it like this, numbered fewer than two hundred copies, but '[w]hile the numbers are small compared to commercial book and print publications, they are considerable when compared to the press runs of original prints of Gainsborough, Barry, [and] Stubbs'.[3] Blake also made and sold engravings and book illustrations to commercial publishers, and produced single and serial drawings, engravings, prints, paintings, and manuscripts for private patrons, notably Thomas Butts and John Linnell. Necessarily, therefore, chapters in the first part of this book engage with Blake's productions across a range of media, and reassess their reception, attending both to the networks within which they moved and to the motivations of some of their earliest collectors. Chapters throughout the book also regularly invoke visual as well as verbal examples, not least as Blake often figures his responses to fellow writers, including biblical writers, Spenser, Shakespeare, Milton, Robert Blair, Thomas Gray, and Edward Young in visual images. If we are unable to include quite as many illustrations as we would have liked in these pages, we hope by being precise in our references to point readers on.

Blake was not just a writer, then. For various reasons, he might also seem like one peculiarly out of step with his own times (the 1750s to the 1820s). What widespread fame Blake has is posthumous, catalysed by his 'discovery' in the 1860s by the Rossettis and Gilchrists, who produced the first full-length biography and textual editions. Blake may not have willed this belatedness, insofar as aspects of his class position contrived to set him apart from polite culture – or better, to strand him between cultures: 'little' and 'great', artisan and intellectual, antinomian and rationalist.[4] Blake's autodidacticism has also counted against him, insofar as it has been interpreted to mean that he existed outside culture (specifically scholarly, or Enlightenment cultures), proceeding instead by 'unguided reading and accidental encounter' to assemble some homespun version of his own.[5] There are other features of Blake's work, beliefs, and behaviours yet more difficult to assimilate, his strong claim to vision, not least. This not only vexed Blake's contemporaries, but may also vex the possibility of contemporaneousness – of Blake's works fitting into any context other than that which they themselves have created. So compelling is Blake's emphasis on the visionary imagination, so vivid are his depictions of what he sees, 'Really & Truly', so populated and intricate are the myths he creates or elaborates (especially in his later work, from the late 1790s), that he issues a challenge to 'historical and chronological evidence' as the sole guarantee of truth (E 658, 618). There is also the matter of Blake's contrariety – rhetorical, intellectual, and temperamental – which can seem perpetually at risk of freewheeling.[6] Whatever the 'happy state of Agreement', it might appear that William Blake 'for One [would] not Agree' (E 783).

Context, whether historical, genealogical, textual, or otherwise, is a lot about making things fit. Rees's *Cyclopaedia* (1819), for instance, defined *contexture* as the 'disposition and union of the constituent parts' of 'works of nature and art' – a 'union' liable to be dismantled and denaturalised immediately by one such as Blake who denied the premises of Newtonian physics.[7] We need not endeavour only to read writers in the way we think they would like to be read, of course. But it seems important to acknowledge at the outset of a book such as this that Blake is a figure who at the very least prompts us to think carefully about what we mean by 'context'.

By and large this is not a debate we engage in explicitly over the course of the chapters that follow. The tendency of authors has rather been to strip away anything that obstructs a direct and accessible discussion of their topic. Each of the book's four sections implies a different slant on context, to be sure: Part I emphasises biography and the histories of media and reception; Part II is attentive to form, genre, and mode (and is relatively unusual in treating Blake's lyric, and mythic or epic, works together); Part III is interested in allusion and influence, and in creative conversations that cut across, or gather, time as well as ramify within particular periods; and Part IV examines issues of history, society, and culture, giving the last word to a chapter whose placement is at once accidental (by virtue of alphabetical ordering) and entirely appropriate to the spirit of this volume. Authors have, however, carved out their topics, and made decisions about what counts as context, independently, which has led to a diversity of approach across the volume, and even within each of its parts. Equally, we have ensured that each chapter stands alone, to enable readers to follow their own interests. The brief 'Further Reading' lists at the very end of the volume are designed both to help prioritise and to supplement suggestions for extra reading provided by the chapters' notes. The 'List of Abbreviations' shows our main sources of reference, and further reading specified for the 'Introduction' operates as a general bibliography of sorts.

It is Blake's character Los who resolves to 'Create a System' lest he 'be enslav'd by another Mans' (*Jerusalem* 10: 20, E 153). *William Blake in Context* would have it not both ways, but neither. Not in thrall to Blake's idiom, but with an ear always to its resonance, coming at man, myth, and works from without as well as within them, we accept the inevitable otherness of our contextualising approach. We also hope by its means to sound Blake anew.

Notes

1. On 'drawing', see Viscomi, Ch. 4, 32–44; on 'printmaking', see J. Viscomi, 'In the Caves of Heaven and Hell: Swedenborg and Printmaking in Blake's *Marriage*', in S. Clark and D. Worrall (eds.), *Blake in the Nineties* (Basingstoke: Palgrave Macmillan, 1999), pp. 27–60.
2. Introduced in the mid-twentieth century by Jean Hagstrum, the term 'composite art' was glossed by Northrop Frye as a 'radical form of mixed art' which must be read as a unity. See W. T. J. Mitchell, *Composite Art* (Princeton: Princeton University Press, 1978), p. 3 and n.
3. Viscomi, 338.
4. See J. Mee, *Dangerous Enthusiasm: William Blake and the Culture of Radicalism in the 1790s* (Oxford: Clarendon Press, 1992), esp. 'Conclusion: A Radical without an Audience?', pp. 214–26, and E. P. Thompson, *Witness Against the Beast: William Blake and the Moral Law* (Cambridge: Cambridge University Press, 1993), esp. 'Introduction', pp. xv–xxv, and 'Anti-hegemony', pp. 106–14. Thompson borrows the idea of '"great" (or polite)' and '"little" (or popular) tradition[s] of culture' from the anthropologist Robert Redfield (p. xxii), and in part develops it as a model of diversity opposed to the exclusive emphasis on Blake's affiliation to '"The Tradition" of neo-Platonic and hermetic thought' (p. 33) that he finds in K. Raine, *Blake and Tradition*, 2 vols. (Princeton: Princeton University Press, 1968). See further N. Heringman's discussion in Chapter 27 of this volume, suggesting Blake's knowledge of both practical and scholarly traditions of antiquarianism.
5. P. Bourdieu, 'Education and the Autodidact', in *Distinction: A Social Critique of the Judgment of Taste*, trans. R. Nice (London: Routledge, 2013), pp. 328–31 (p. 329). T. S. Eliot recognised the artisanal character of Blake's autodidacticism (his 'ingenious' and 'home-made [philosophy] [...] put together out of the odds and ends about the house'), but did not credit it; for him, Blake 'lacked' tradition, 'indulging in a philosophy of his own' (Eliot, 'Blake', in *The Sacred Wood: Essays on Poetry and Criticism* (London: Faber & Faber, 1997), pp. 128–34 (pp. 132–3, 134)). E. P. Thompson reminds us that '[a]lternative intellectual traditions' were available: not only Rational Dissent, but also yet more marginal, specifically anti-rationalist groupings (*Witness*, pp. xviii–xix).
6. See J. Mee and S. Haggarty, 'Introduction', in *Blake and Conflict* (Basingstoke: Palgrave Macmillan, 2009), pp. 1–11 (pp. 1–5).
7. A. Rees, *The Cyclopaedia; or, Universal Dictionary of Arts, Sciences, and Literature*, 39 vols. (London: 1819), Vol. IX.

PART I

Life, Works, and Reception

CHAPTER I

Life

Leo Damrosch

Two things are especially worth knowing about Blake's life, and neither has been properly appreciated until recently. One is how hard he worked, for very little remuneration, at an exacting craft that was widely regarded as mere manual labour, even by artists in more prestigious genres such as oil painting and sculpture. The other is how tragically undervalued he was during his entire lifetime, with a humble reputation as an engraver (usually of other people's designs), and no reputation whatsoever as a poet. His magnificent achievements, in not just one art but two, represent a heroic victory against terrible odds.

There were few remarkable external events in Blake's life, apart from a shocking trial for alleged sedition. Biographers have had to fill out their pages with descriptions of the contemporary art world, of fellow artists who left reminiscences, of political radicals with whom Blake may or may not have associated personally, and of the London he knew intimately and allegorised as Jerusalem and its antitype Babylon.

Blake's great myth, which developed and deepened over the years, was intended to embody the experience of all human beings, and also of the sociopolitical structures they enslave themselves to. He never wanted to write anything like Wordsworth's *Prelude*, yet in his own way he is as personal as Wordsworth – perhaps even more so, if one thinks of the 'Wordsworth' in *Tintern Abbey* or the *Prelude* as an idealised simulacrum, projected by the egotistical sublime. Blake is often sublime, but his self-scrutiny is anguished and questing, not egotistical. His poems are filled with lived experience that is sometimes ecstatic, sometimes close to despairing, but he was determined to recast that experience in symbolic forms that would have universal application.

Blake was born in London in 1757, to a Dissenting family, though he was baptised in an Anglican church. His father kept a hosiery or haberdashery shop in Broad Street (now Broadway Street) in Soho. An older brother, James, would take over the business after their father's death. There were also two younger brothers, John and Robert, and a sister, Catherine. Robert was William's closest companion until he died from tuberculosis in 1787, when he was just twenty-four. In the prophetic poem *Milton*, he appears as William's alter ego in eternity.

Blake never belonged to any church, apart from a brief episode of interest in Swedenborgianism, but he always considered himself a disciple of Jesus though not of Jehovah. In time he would feel a vocation in the line of prophets that began with Isaiah and Ezekiel and came down through John of Patmos and most recently John Milton. As he wrote to a friend when he was composing *Milton*, 'I am under the direction of Messengers from Heaven Daily & Nightly' (Blake to Butts, 10 January 1803, E 724).

In early childhood, according to his own later account, Blake experienced startling visions – angels in the fields among the haymakers (the countryside was still close by) and the face of God at a window. In modern terms these were eidetic visions: not hallucinations, but images perceived as vividly as if they were real. For him they *were* real, windows into the realm of the spirit. Yet he was never an otherworldly mystic; he wanted to inspire readers and viewers to enter into the fullness of eternity right here and now:

> To see a World in a Grain of Sand
> And a Heaven in a Wild Flower
> Hold Infinity in the palm of your hand
> And Eternity in an hour.
>
> ('Auguries of Innocence', ll. 1–4, E 490)

Blake learned to read and write at home and never attended any ordinary school. Long afterward he said that his parents recognised his rebellious temperament and feared that he would be flogged. But from an early age he showed artistic talent, and in 1768 was enrolled in Henry Pars's drawing school in the Strand, whose mission was to prepare graphic artists for commercial employment. Four years after that, he began a seven-year apprenticeship with the engraver James Basire, living in Basire's house in Great Queen Street, not far from Lincoln's Inn. These and other London sites recur frequently in Blake's later work. He also studied briefly at the Royal Academy of Arts, felt undervalued there, and nurtured a lifelong resentment of its president, Sir Joshua Reynolds.

In 1782 Blake married Catherine Boucher, five years younger than himself, who was probably a servant and was barely literate. In due course he taught her to read. Catherine became a valued partner in the production and colouring of Blake's prints, and also an invaluable emotional mainstay.

Friends who knew the couple late in their lives tended to sentimentalise their relationship, but it is known that there had been severe tensions in earlier days, and some unpublished manuscript poems represent marriage as a stifling prison:

> To a lovely mirtle bound
> Blossoms showring all around
> O how sick & weary I
> Underneath my mirtle lie
> Why should I be bound to thee
> O my lovely mirtle tree. ('To My Mirtle', E 469)

Like many London artisans at the time, Blake was inspired by the French Revolution and hoped for a British one, though well aware that radicals were going to jail for alleged sedition. Little is known about the details of his life in those days, but he does not seem to have engaged in direct political action. Indeed, after the excitement during the 1790s, he later expressed disillusionment with politics, and created a visionary critique of the social order far more profound than any programme of political reform.

During the last decade of the eighteenth century, the Blakes lived in Lambeth on the south bank of the Thames, and for a time he secured an adequate income engraving images for books. In these he executed conventional techniques with great skill, but meanwhile he was developing a startlingly different symbolic art of his own, for which he developed a technique of 'relief etching' that is described elsewhere in this volume (Chapter 4).

The images were two-dimensional and iconic, resembling the style of medieval illuminated manuscripts that Blake had seen during his time with Basire, and in a series of these 'illuminated books' he combined words and images with inspiring originality. The process of etching, printing, and hand-colouring with watercolours required much time and patience, and the money they brought in barely made up for the cost of materials, let alone labour.[1] Nor did they lead to much recognition. Near the end of Blake's life, Henry Crabb Robinson showed the great *Songs of Innocence and of Experience* to Wordsworth and Coleridge, who thought some of the lyrics quite good, but made no attempt to cultivate their author. They are not known to have commented on the images that accompany the texts.

The five years from 1789 to 1794 were a time of extraordinary creative fertility. In 1789 *Songs of Innocence* was first issued, a collection of eloquent lyrics intended to be read (or sung) to small children, conveying a message of trust and love. (The Blakes never had children of their own.) In 1794 a complementary set of *Songs of Experience* was added; purchasers could buy either volume separately, or as a combined volume whose title page describes the poems as 'Shewing the Two Contrary States of the Human Soul'.

In *Europe: A Prophecy* and *The Book of Urizen*, also in 1794, Blake began to develop his remarkable personal myth. By then two other notable works had already appeared: the 1793 *Visions of the Daughters of Albion* and *America: A Prophecy*. Even earlier Blake probably began working on the spectacular medley of prophecy, proverbs, and satire called *The Marriage of Heaven and Hell*, which may have been first printed in 1790. Its fundamental idea would remain central to his thinking for the rest of his life: that a dynamic of opposing forces is essential to the existence at every level, from the cosmic to the personal. Orthodox morality, he charged, privileged passive 'goodness' and denigrated energy as 'evil', but both are necessary and should interact like partners in a marriage: 'Without Contraries is no progression.' To put it another way, reason is necessary, but not at the expense of energy.

These illuminated books were relatively short, ranging from eight plates for *Visions* to twenty-eight for *Urizen*. After producing several copies of each in an initial printing, further copies were made only when ordered by individual customers, and that did not happen often. Consequently, most are exceedingly rare today. Nearly three dozen copies of the *Songs* are known to exist, but only thirteen of *Visions*, nine of the *Marriage*, and eight of *Urizen*. Having been hand-coloured, each copy is unique.

The works from this period represent the culmination of Blake's 'composite art', as it is sometimes called – texts accompanied by images that are not so much illustrations as alternative perspectives, or even critiques. (In the later, longer poems, many plates that are dense with verse have no images at all.)

In 1795 Blake issued a series of twelve large colour prints that rank among his finest work. These incorporate ideas that could not have been obvious to viewers at the time. *Newton*, for example, shows the great physicist not as a Cambridge don but as a naked athlete at the bottom of the sea, trapped by his mathematical rationalism beneath the suffocating water of materiality. And *Elohim Creating Adam* depicts a God who is more like a Gnostic demiurge than like the orthodox deity, pressing down heavily on a staring and helpless Adam who is still being moulded out of clay.

In 1800 the Blakes gratefully accepted the invitation of a wealthy dilettante, William Hayley, to settle in the Sussex village of Felpham, not far from Chichester and with a view of the sea. The plan was for Blake to turn out portraits and other works for Hayley's circle of friends, and at first the rural setting and sense of freedom were intoxicating. However it soon became clear that the well-intentioned Hayley was a fussy meddler and had not the slightest appreciation of Blake's original work.

During these years, Blake was elaborating a long manuscript prophecy, or symbolic epic, originally entitled *Vala* and later *The Four Zoas: The Torments of Love & Jealousy in The Death and Judgement of Albion the Ancient Man*. In this work he developed a brilliant but increasingly complicated myth of the divided self, distributed into four faculties or modes of experience, whom he called the Zoas, and their corresponding female Emanations.

By this time, Blake's deepest preoccupations were fully embodied in symbolic form. Inspired by Neoplatonic writers and by visionaries such as Jacob Boehme, he greatly elaborated the critique of empiricist rationalism, and of patriarchal authority, that he had begun as long ago as 1788. This poem and its successors are also haunted by sexual anxieties and jealousy, as the subtitle of *The Four Zoas* testifies. When separated from the male Zoas, a rupture that is treated as disastrous, the Emanations are at once tauntingly erotic and cruelly domineering. An ominous principle called the Female Will also plays an increasingly significant role, the implications of which are still fiercely debated.

Each of the three great prophecies – *The Four Zoas, Milton*, and *Jerusalem* – ends with an apocalyptic breakthrough, after which harrowing anguish is to be followed by a restoration of a unified self and world, figured as the universal man Albion. An older generation of critics used to represent this apocalypse as a fully realised victory; more recently the persistence of intractable conflict has struck critics as most apparent. Undoubtedly all these preoccupations reflect Blake's personal experience, but exactly how they do so can only be guessed at.

In 1803 came the unexpected crisis, when a drunken soldier in Felpham called John Scolfield accused Blake of making seditious statements, a capital offence if convicted. Hayley engaged an excellent lawyer, who called convincing character witnesses, and Blake was acquitted. Enclosed in a letter to his friend Thomas Butts is a wrenchingly painful poem acknowledging that his troubles may have been brought on by his own idiosyncratic temperament:

> O why was I born with a different face
> Why was I not born like the rest of my race
> When I look each one starts! when I speak I offend
> Then I'm silent & passive & lose every Friend.
>
> (16 August 1803, E 733)

The trauma of the sedition trial continued to haunt Blake; it surfaces from time to time in the late prophecies. Each of these ambitious poems – *Milton* was printed in fifty plates, *Jerusalem* in a hundred – incorporates material from the unpublished *Four Zoas* and much else as well. *Milton* also contains, in a long introductory 'Bard's Song', a heavily allegorised version of the spiritual conflict with Hayley – a conflict that took place in Blake's mind and was probably unknown to Hayley himself. After the acquittal Blake sent him grateful thanks, and reported, 'O Glory! and O Delight! I have entirely reduced that spectrous Fiend to his station, whose annoyance has been the ruin of my labours for the last passed twenty years of my life' (23 October 1804, E 756). The immediate context was an exhibition of paintings at the Truchsessian Gallery that inspired a recovery of Blake's personal vision, after years of struggling to work in styles that were not really his own.[2] But the statement undoubtedly reflects liberation from profound psychic distress as well. It seems clear that he suffered from schizoid tendencies, and possibly bipolar disorder. His closest friends, however, were all in agreement that he was in no sense 'mad'.[3]

Blake's life back in London, from 1803 until his death in 1827, was marked by few incidents. Work for publishers dried up, and he had no success in attempts to make a name with tempera and watercolour paintings. His one public (and solo) exhibition was rather quixotically mounted in his brother's haberdashery shop in 1809. It included a painting illustrating the *Canterbury Tales* that is still much admired, but otherwise a group of strange symbolic pieces that may not have shown his genius to best advantage. The one mention of the exhibition in print was a vicious review in the *Examiner* by Robert Hunt, who described the paintings and accompanying *Descriptive Catalogue* as the work of 'an unfortunate lunatic [. . .] the wild effusions of a distempered brain' (*BR* 283). Together with his brother Leigh – and the soldier Scolfield – Robert Hunt would subsequently appear as a villain in Blake's poems.

After much revising and enlarging, *Milton* was finally published in 1811, and *Jerusalem* in 1820. Only four copies of *Milton* are known to survive, and five of *Jerusalem*. Just one of the latter was coloured, though very brilliantly; Blake seems to have resigned himself by then to seeking customers who wanted his works as art objects, not as poems.

There were periods of deep depression, but most of the time Blake seems to have been contented in his simple life, at various London addresses. He maintained close friendships with a number of artists, particularly John Flaxman and Henry Fuseli, whose imaginative paintings have a good deal in common with his. Thomas Butts was a civil servant who not only bought many of Blake's paintings, but also understood his ideas unusually well; some of Blake's most memorable observations occur in his correspondence with Butts.

During the 1820s the Blakes' final residence was a small flat in Fountain Court, just off the Strand, from which the Thames could be glimpsed. A group of young disciples now gathered around, notably the teenaged Samuel Palmer who would go on to a distinguished artistic career of his own. Blake also took regular walks out to Hampstead where the painter John Linnell was living. Much of what we know about his life, during this period and earlier as well, comes from reminiscences by these friends that were collected years later by Alexander Gilchrist in the first important biography.

In these last years Blake concentrated his efforts in visual art rather than poetry, beginning an ambitious series of illustrations to Dante's *Divine Comedy*, and publishing a magnificent set of engravings for the Book of Job. Characteristically, the images and accompanying scriptural texts embody a trenchant critique of the orthodox message of Job, suggesting that a God who could authorise Satan to torment a good man must be satanic himself.

Blake died in 1827, possibly as a result of lifelong contact with copper dust and nitric acid fumes.[4] Catherine survived him by four years, greatly helped during that time by their friend Frederick Tatham, and was interred next to him in Bunhill Fields, the Dissenters' burial ground. At some time after that Tatham, who had fallen under the influence of a self-styled prophet and faith healer called Edward Irving, destroyed great masses of Blake's works as being morally objectionable. No one today knows what was lost.

A generation later, the brothers Dante Gabriel and William Michael Rossetti became Blake enthusiasts, and acquired the precious manuscript that is known as the Rossetti Notebook. They also helped Gilchrist's widow Anne to include a generous selection of poems in a supplementary volume to the 1863 *Life of William Blake*, 'Pictor Ignotus' – 'unknown artist'. In 1893 the first comprehensive edition of *The Works of William Blake* appeared, edited by William Butler Yeats in collaboration with Edwin J. Ellis.

During the twentieth century, following the lead of S. Foster Damon and Northrop Frye, Blake's canonical status became secure, and he is conventionally grouped with five of his contemporaries as the great English Romantic poets. But it is important to remember that in his own time he felt isolated and ignored, and that a wounding sense of social alienation helped to generate his magnificently imaginative myth:

> What is the price of Experience do men buy it for a song
> Or wisdom for a dance in the street? No it is bought with the price
> Of all that a man hath his house his wife his children
> Wisdom is sold in the desolate market where none come to buy
> And in the witherd field where the farmer plows for bread in vain.
> <div style="text-align: right;">(<i>VALA/Four Zoas</i> N2, p. 35, ll. 11–15, E 325)</div>

Notes

1. See G. E. Bentley, Jr, 'What Is the Price of Experience? William Blake and the Economics of Illuminated Printing', *University of Toronto Quarterly*, 68 (1999), 617–41.
2. See M. D. Paley, 'The Truchsessian Gallery Revisited', *Studies in Romanticism*, 16 (1977), 265–77.
3. A number of leading scholars have concluded that Blake did indeed suffer from what R. N. Essick calls 'a mild form of schizophrenia': see '*Jerusalem* and Blake's Final Works', in M. Eaves (ed.), *The Cambridge Companion to William Blake* (Cambridge: Cambridge University Press, 2003), pp. 251–71 (p. 257).
4. See L. Robson and J. Viscomi, 'Blake's Death', *Blake / An Illustrated Quarterly*, 30.1 (Summer 1996), 36–49.

CHAPTER 2

Networks

Jon Mee

Blake is the visionary, alienated from this world, who spoke to angels. Blake was in this world 'manly and independent'.[1] From neither perspective does there seem to be much room for thinking about Blake and networks. Nevertheless he spent most of his working life in the heavily networked domain of London's art and publishing circles, caught in a prolonged period of transition between systems of patronage and the commercial marketplace for books. Blake's illuminated books brought into being networks of readers who sustained him through his life. Their commissions were conceived not just in terms of business transactions, but also as arbiters of friendship that brought complex rewards and obligations for those involved. Distinctive to Blake, however, is the way these networks are understood to include a traffic between the physical and the spiritual world that brings together angels with the laborious activities of the engraver's burin.

   Blake's career was involved in a sequence of overlapping relationships with patrons who brought him into their circles and encouraged him to produce his art. These relationships were never simple. Blake slotted into no round hole, although it would be naïve to think that any of the period's networks ever functioned as smooth pathways of circulation between stable points. John Keats, for instance, struggled with the obligations he felt towards Leigh Hunt and Percy Shelley, not least where literary influence blurred into patronage. At the beginning of his career, Blake's poetry seems to have been performed – and quite probably sung – at the conversazione of Harriet Mathews and her husband the Reverend A. S. Mathews, satirised in his conversation piece *An Island in the Moon*. The Reverend Mathews provided a preface to Blake's privately printed letterpress *Poetical Sketches* (1783), although their relationship seems to have broken up by late 1784. J. T. Smith placed the blame squarely on Blake's 'unbending deportment, or what his adherents are pleased to call his manly firmness of opinion, which certainly was not at all times considered pleasing by every one'.² If Blake was conversable, it was often after the pattern of what he called 'Mental Fight', whereby the collision of mind with mind was valued over artificial manners (*Milton* 1[i]: 13, E 95). But he was quite capable of adapting himself to those he found supportive, at least for a time, and far from unversed in the culture of polite sociability and literary sensibility, as Susan Matthews has shown.³

At the time Blake frequented the Mathews salon, the bookseller Joseph Johnson was employing him as an engraver. Johnson was responsible for most of Blake's commissions from 1779 to 1786, and continued to employ him up to 1801. The relationship with Johnson may seem more purely commercial than his association with the Mathews circle, but it did involve some degree of sociable engagement, even if not with the intimacy that seems to have defined Johnson's involvement with the writers he published, including authors such as William Godwin, Thomas Paine, and Mary Wollstonecraft, not to mention Blake's friend the painter Henry Fuseli.⁴ Whether Blake was intimate with Johnson's inner circle or not, the bookseller certainly regularly drew on his services as an engraver, and sometimes even used him as a go-between with his writers, as was the case with John Gabriel Stedman, author of *Narrative, of a Five Years' Expedition, Against the Revolted Negroes of Surinam* (1796). Blake acted as a mollifying mediator between Johnson and Stedman for several years over the mid-1790s. Beyond employing Blake as an engraver, Johnson at least entertained the idea of supporting Blake sufficiently to print up proofs of the unpublished long poem *The French Revolution* in 1790.⁵

By 1799, Blake seems to have felt that Johnson was not doing all he could for him. 'Johnson may be very honest and very generous too', wrote Blake to the poet William Hayley in 1804, 'where his own interest is concerned' (E 750). Whether this assessment of Johnson's character was reasonable or not, it played its part in Blake's departure from London for Sussex, where he joined Hayley's circle in 1800, although in truth the two worlds overlapped intriguingly, as Hayley himself was a Johnson author. Hayley was someone for whom poetry and networking were intimately bound together. 'Much of the man's literary career had its foundation in the simple exchange of favours and sonnets', writes Reggie Allen, who notes the way Hayley maintained the cohesion of his group through donating and receiving verses in praise.⁶ Among other things Blake's position within Hayley's literary network opened him up – whether he knew it or not – to continual commentary from other members. Charlotte Smith thought Blake ungrateful in his refusal to be 'any thing than an engraver' (*BR* 224). Lady Harriet Hesketh wrote to another member of Hayley's circle, the Reverend John Johnson, to report her fears over the friendship: 'My hair stands on end to think that Hayley & Blake are as dear friends as ever!' She even imagined Blake would 'set fire to all his papers, & poor Hayley will consume in his own fires'. Hayley responded to these fears by representing Blake as part of a spiritual network that included her cousin 'our dear angelic [William] Cowper' (ibid. 204, 205). Hayley had employed Blake to engrave the poet's portrait by George Romney for his *Life of Cowper* (1802), another Joseph Johnson publication. George Romney had been part of the same circle until his death in 1802 and Blake helped Hayley with his *Life of Romney* (1809), locating works by the painter, and eventually supplying engravings for the published biography. Other fruits of this network for Blake were a working collaboration with the printer Joseph Seagrave in Chichester, and, perhaps most importantly, the defence provided by Hayley's friend Samuel Rose when he was tried for libel in 1804 (see *BR* 198–201).

Blake found that friendship at Felpham seemed to tend towards a network of patronage that mired him in the same 'drudgery of business' he told Thomas Butts he had found in the employment of Joseph Johnson (E 724). Out of this experience, Blake seems to have developed his creative opposition between spiritual and corporeal friendship. Rejecting Hayley's prior poetic account of 'Friendship!' as 'Thou Sweet subduer of mental strife', Blake increasingly presented friction as a necessary component of creativity.[7] Nevertheless, returning to London after the Felpham debacle, Blake was to remain dependent on contacts Hayley provided for him over several years, as well as two older relationships that lasted throughout his career, those with Thomas Butts and George Cumberland. For five years from 1806 commissions from Butts were virtually Blake's sole source of support, with the dubious effect that he was freed from the judgement of others (see *BR* 222–3). The association with Cumberland had stretched back to the time when they were both young artists in 1780, but included collaborations on *Thoughts on Outline* (1796) and various attempts to win commissions on Blake's behalf until the very end of his life. At his death, Blake left an unfinished plate for a calling card that Cumberland wished to use 'to spread my old friends fame and promote his wife's Interest – by making him thus the subject of conversation and his works' (ibid. 67–8, 483).

Perhaps the most sustaining relationship of Blake's later life was with the landscape and portrait painter John Linnell, introduced to Blake by Cumberland's son in 1818. Linnell employed Blake on work he was doing for a portrait of the Baptist minister James Upton. From this point on,

Linnell played an important role in securing commissions for Blake, buying his works, and even influencing his style, not least in the luminosity of the late paintings that each of them were to share with the group of young painters known as the Shoreham Ancients. Linnell also introduced Blake to Eliza Aders, to whom Blake sent a copy of *Songs* after showing her specimens at a dinner party. Henry Crabb Robinson, who was at the same party, visited Blake socially several times between December 1825 and February 1827. This connection put Blake's work into circulation with other major poets he was never to meet in person, including Dorothy and William Wordsworth and Samuel Taylor Coleridge.

Most of these circles were brought into being as networks by the circulation of Blake's illuminated books and his other engraved and painted works. The books created, as Sarah Haggarty puts it, 'enduring bonds between persons: treating sales like presents; transforming readers into members of a religious republic; crafting divinity into humanity'.[8] The relatively few illuminated books sold cemented a personal relationship between Blake and the purchasers, to the point that transaction could shape the form of the book before and after its creation.[9] As these gifts circulated, they formed networks that Blake often wished to understand as defined in 'spiritual' rather than narrowly contractual terms. Blake frequently cast these networks in terms of a traffic with Eternity: 'You O Dear Flaxman are a Sublime Archangel My Friend & Companion from Eternity in the Divine bosom is our Dwelling place I look back into the regions of Reminiscence & behold our ancient days before this Earth appeared in its vegetated mortality to my mortal vegetated Eyes' (Blake to Flaxman, 21 September 1800, E 710). In *The Marriage of Heaven and Hell*, he had earlier imagined a conversazione with Isaiah and Ezekiel, possibly parodying Isaac Watts's careful repudiation of such enthusiasm.[10] By the end of his life, he represented himself fully in conversation with sources of inspiration from Milton to Jesus.

Contemporary thinking about networks by Bruno Latour and Tim Ingold among others would push us to consider networks as constituted not just by human agents, but also by the things that pass along and through them as 'actants'. In relation to Blake, this step would involve thinking of each of Blake's books, paintings, prints as an 'actant' in a network, something that could wield its own agency to bring its readers into relation or even close them off from each other. Thinking of Blake's works only as 'arbiters' between human agents risks underestimating their role as participants in networks they actively brought into being, creating and transforming and not just confirming human-to-human relations. In this regard, also, the illuminated books might even be seen as networks in themselves, or, to use Ingold's preferred term, 'meshworks' of paper, ink, paint, copper plates, and all the other materials that participated in the process of production.[11] Blake constantly represents creation as the meshworking of affective things, as in the building of Golgonooza in *Jerusalem*, part of a ceaseless process of becoming that anticipates Ingold's account of human culture and its relation with things as '*working with* materials and not just *doing to* them, and of bringing form into being rather than merely translating from the virtual to the actual'.[12] Within Blake's own verbal and visual universe, books are usually figured in negative terms, as with Urizen's 'book of iron' that effectively separates creation from Eternity (see *VALA/Four Zoas* N7, p. 78, l. 2, E 353f.). Implicitly, however, Blake understands his own work as chapters in 'the Book of Life' greeted with exultation in his description of his design for the Last Judgement to Ozias Humphry (E 553). Blake's books are conceived not as closed off points in a network, turned in upon themselves in a Urizenic form of creation, but open to their readers in what Saree Makdisi describes as a 'virtual network'. The virtuality of these networks is partly a product of the complex relations between the verbal and the visual, for instance, in editions of the *Songs*, and the multiplicity of inter-textual possibilities they generate for readers. The network of the illuminated book, for Makdisi, is '*virtual* because it is not always necessarily activated and, even when it is, not always activated in the same way'.[13] Each reader that encounters the illuminated books realises this network in their own way, perhaps to the extent that each new reader of Blake joins a network that stretches to infinity to form 'an audience that literally did not exist, that no longer existed – or that does not yet exist'.[14]

From another point of view, this textualist approach is in danger of underplaying the way the illuminated books are meshworks of materials, print, ink, paper, and so on, materials which exerted their own pushback as part of the creative process, rather than just passively succumbing to the human agency of the artist. Joseph Viscomi's work has played an important role in showing how the medium of the illuminated book 'evolved and was conceived through production' (Viscomi xxv). Blake's post-production processes allowed him to experiment with different page orders, so no two copies, for instance, of the separately printed *Innocence* are the same. Blake's illuminated books are also 'virtual' in the sense that they remained open to being physically reconfigured. Those who received them sometimes intervened to reshape the materials of the network.

George Cumberland, for instance, incorporated his own work into the books he received from Blake more than once. Several other copies were extra-illustrated by their owners as Luisa Calè has shown.[15] Strikingly, within the books, creation is often described as a process whereby materials form an affective network:

> The stones are pity, and the bricks, well wrought affections:
> Enameld with love & kindness, & the tiles engraven gold
> Labour of merciful hands: the beams and rafters are forgiveness:
> The mortar & cement of the work, tears of honesty: the nails:
> And the screws & iron braces, are well wrought blandishments,
> And well contrived words, firm, fixing, never forgotten,
> Always comforting the remembrance: the floors, humility,
> The cielings, devotion: the hearths, thanksgiving.
>
> (Jerusalem 12: 30–7, E 155)

This account understands a network as a constant act of renovation, 'more an act', as Steven Vine describes Golgonooza, 'than an object, more a verb than noun – a build*ing*'.[16]

Representations of creation within the illuminated books as an open-ended material process may have functioned as an invitation that helps explain why they have inspired other artists and performers since Blake's time to reimagine them across different media. Ironically, as the online Blake archive has made the illuminated books newly accessible to their readers in their complex mediality, so they have encouraged others to think about reconstituting them for new contexts. The very idea of the book may be constraining if it militates against the re-use of the illuminated books. In this regard, Jon Saklofske has suggested they might more properly be understood as a Local Area Network open to be reordered, reconfigured, and reimagined by readers in ways that live up to Blake's resistance to the standard logic of the forms of production available to him in his own time.[17] Blake's resistance to these forms involved him in productive struggle with and in the materials of his art. Certainly many network theorists today, Ingold and Latour among them, would object to any idea of virtuality that underplayed the material autonomy of the objects Blake produced in their many different forms.[18]

Notes

1. A. Cunningham, 'William Blake', in *Lives of the Most Eminent British Painters, Sculptors, and Architects*, 6 vols. (London: 1830), II, 147–79, 487–8.
2. J. T. Smith, *Nollekens and His Times*, 2 vols. (London: 1828), II, 457.

3. See S. Matthews, *Blake, Sexuality and Bourgeois Politeness* (Cambridge: Cambridge University Press, 2011), and J. Mee, '"A Little Less Conversation, A Little More Action": Mutuality, Converse, and Mental Fight', in S. Haggarty and J. Mee (eds.), *Blake and Conflict* (Basingstoke: Palgrave Macmillan, 2008), pp. 126–43.
4. Blake had a complicated relationship with the Johnson circle. Alexander Gilchrist claimed that Johnson was 'friendly' towards Blake, 'and tried to help him as far as he could help so unmarketable a talent' (Gilchrist 92). As well as employing Blake as an engraver, Johnson seems also to have displayed some of the illuminated books at his shop: see K. Davies, 'Mrs. Bliss: A Blake Collector of 1794', in S. Clark and D. Worrall (eds.), *Blake in the Nineties* (Basingstoke: Palgrave Macmillan, 1999), pp. 212–30 (p. 216). However there were serious differences in the ethos of the publisher's circles and Blake's visionary enthusiasm. See the discussions, for instance, in J. Mee, *Dangerous Enthusiasm: William Blake and the Culture of Radicalism in the 1790s* (Oxford: Oxford University Press, 1992), pp. 220–3, and R. N. Essick, 'William Blake, Thomas Paine, and Biblical Revolution', *Studies in Romanticism*, 30.2 (1991), 189–212.
5. See *Stranger* 113–17 on the relationship between Blake and Stedman. The published plates are dated from December 1792 to December 1794, although Stedman's book was not finally published until 1796.
6. R. Allen, 'The Sonnets of William Hayley and Gift Exchange', *European Romantic Review*, 13 (2002), 383–92 (p. 384).
7. W. Hayley, *An Essay on Epic Poetry; In Five Epistles to the Revd. Mr. Mason* (London: 1782), l. 425, p. 23. The phrase 'mental strife' appears in several of Hayley poems from his *Epistle to a Friend, On the Death of John Thornton, Esq.* (London: 1780) onwards, always negatively.
8. S. Haggarty, *Blake's Gifts: Poetry and the Politics of Exchange* (Cambridge: Cambridge University Press, 2010), p. 1.
9. M. Phillips, *William Blake: The Creation of the Songs from Manuscript to Illuminated Printing* (London: The British Library, 2000), p. 111.
10. See the discussion of this point in Mee, '"A Little Less Conversation"', pp. 134–5.
11. T. Ingold, *Being Alive: Essays on Movement, Knowledge and Description* (Abingdon: Routledge, 2011), p. 64.
12. Ibid., p. 10.
13. S. Makdisi, *William Blake and the Impossible History of the 1790s* (Chicago and London: University of Chicago Press, 2003), p. 166.
14. Ibid., p. 324.
15. L. Calè, 'Gendering the Margins of Gray: William Blake, Classical Visual Culture, and the Alternative Bodies of Ann Flaxman's Book', in H. Bruder and T. J. Connolly (eds.), *The Body, Gender and Culture* (London: Pickering and Chatto, 2010), pp. 133–43.
16. S. Vine, 'Blake's Material Sublime', *Studies in Romanticism*, 41 (2002), 237–57 (p. 255).

17. J. Saklofske, 'Remediating William Blake: Unbinding the Network Architectures of Blake's Songs', *European Romantic Review*, 22 (2011), 381–8.
18. See Graham Harman's opposition to talk of 'potential' and 'virtual' networks. He insists on Latour's notion of actants 'as always fully deployed in the networks of the world' (*Prince of Networks: Bruno Latour and Metaphysics* (Melbourne: Re.press, 2009), p. 28).

CHAPTER 3

Engraving

Mark Crosby

For much of his adult life Blake earned his living as a professional engraver, creating a range of prints that run the gamut of the craft, from portrait frontispieces to illustrations of Wedgewood's porcelain, Chaucer's pilgrims to the experimental relief-etched plates of the illuminated books. During a career that spanned the end of his apprenticeship in 1779 to his death in 1827, Blake produced in excess of 430 prints. The majority were reproductive book illustrations, with around fifty separate plates, and while his contemporaries regarded him as a more than competent copy engraver, Blake is now acknowledged as one of Britain's finest original printmakers, creating such masterpieces as the *Illustrations to the Book of Job*. This chapter surveys Blake's professional career as an engraver, tracing the development of his style as he mastered the graphic techniques of his trade.

After four years studying at Henry Pars's drawing school on the Strand, Blake embarked on an apprenticeship that would define his professional career and profoundly influence his aesthetic credo. According to Frederick Tatham, a close friend of Blake's during his last years, Blake's father (a hosier) was so impressed by his son's artistic ability that a 'painter of Eminence' was sought to tutor the precocious teenager (*BR* 665). The high cost of this proposed tutelage led the young Blake to request instead that he learn the less prestigious, and significantly less expensive, trade of engraving. After first approaching William Wynn Ryland, a successful engraver who had popularised the French chalk or stipple manner of engraving, the highly regarded traditional line engraver, James Basire, was settled upon.[1] On 4 August 1772, a few weeks shy of his fifteenth birthday, Blake was apprenticed to Basire for the sum of £52. 3s (*BR* 12–13).

The son of an engraver, James Basire studied the rudiments of engraving under Richard William Seale before spending time with the engraver and antiquarian Richard Dalton in Rome, sketching designs after Raphael and Michelangelo.[2] As an apprentice, Basire was taught the repertoire of engraving and etching techniques that enabled the replication of form, tone, and depth onto copperplates so as to reproduce printed impressions of an image. During the period of Basire's apprenticeship, the English School of engraving was dominated by line engravers such as George Vertue who cut or etched lines into the surface of the copperplate – a process known as intaglio – using an array of tools to create linear patterns such as dot and lozenge, hatching and cross-hatching. These linear techniques were influenced by Continental practice and the circulation and translation of Abraham Bosse's *De la manière de graver à l'eau forte et au burin* (1645). By the end of Basire's apprenticeship, a more painterly approach to engraving had become fashionable in England that employed a different set of techniques such as stippling and mezzotint. This painterly style produced a softer aesthetic and was typically used in portraiture and decorative prints, such as landscapes. Under Dalton's tutelage Basire mastered both the linear and the painterly styles, enabling him to work successfully in the three dominant pictorial genres of the eighteenth century: historical subjects, landscapes, and portraiture. On 3 December 1752 Basire completed his apprenticeship, was granted the freedom of the Company of Stationers, and established a copy engraving business at 31 Great Queen Street where he tutored apprentices.

As a reproductive copy engraver, Basire made his living translating images created by other artists in different media onto copperplates. Basire's command of the techniques required to reproduce linear and painterly styles is evident in the range of prints he executed throughout his career. He was also a specialist in executing large-scale prints after paintings, such as *Le Champ de drap d'or, or the Interview between Henry VIII and Francis I 1520* and *The Distribution of His Majesty's Maundy*, which were both executed during Blake's apprenticeship. The majority of prints issuing from Basire's workshop during Blake's time were line engravings executed using the mixed method of preliminary etching followed by engraving. Line engraving demanded time and skill both to master and to accomplish. It was Basire's ability to provide accurate reproductions using a firm, linear technique that came to define his style and that of his apprentices.[3] Basire's skill in line engraving also led to his succeeding Vertue as the official engraver to the Society of Antiquaries in 1755 and his later appointment as official engraver to the Royal Society in 1770, making him, at the time of Blake's apprenticeship, one of the most respected and highly valued line engravers of the period.

Under Basire's tutelage, Blake learnt the mixed method of etching and engraving and around the dozen or so linear patterns necessary to create a visual syntax capable of reproducing images onto copperplates. The first reliable example we have of Blake's ability as an engraver is the separate plate that he later entitled *Joseph of Arimathea among the Rocks of Albion* (Fig. 3.1). On the only known impression of the first state he inscribed in black ink, 'Engraved when I was a beginner at Basires from a drawing by Salviati after Michael Angelo.' Blake heavily reworked the plate sometime after 1820 and together with the title added an inscription that begins 'Engraved by W Blake 1773 from an old Italian drawing.' In the inscription on both states Blake acknowledges that the drawing of the figure was after the original painted by 'Michael Angelo', almost certainly Michelangelo's fresco in the Pauline Chapel in Rome of *The Crucifixion of St Peter* (1541). The background, however, appears to be of Blake's own composition.[4] If this was an exercise set by Basire, it is possible that the choice of subject was encouraged or even suggested by him, recalling the drawings after Michelangelo's frescos that he made in Rome during his own apprenticeship.

Carried out sometime during the second year of his apprenticeship, the first state of *Joseph of Arimathea* offers the only certain example of Blake's skill as a line engraver during the early stages of his seven-year apprenticeship. Blake's ability to use a variety of linear patterns to achieve form and tone is clearly evident, including hatching, cross-hatching, and dot and lozenge. Yet, while Blake seems to have learnt the basic visual syntax of the reproductive line engraver, he has not yet mastered all the linear techniques. In his hatching and cross-hatching Blake uses only two thicknesses of lines, which offers little variation in tone. The spaces between lines are similar if not equal, which produces a flatness in the overall design. This is most noticeable in the cliffs behind the figure and in the ground beneath his feet. Blake's use of hatching in both areas is so similar that any sense of distance is lost. By the time he completed his apprenticeship, on or around 4 August 1779, Blake had greater command of these linear techniques and, after the necessary step of becoming a freeman of the Stationers's Company so that he could practise his trade in London, entered what he later describes as 'the ocean of business' (E 704).

Blake's career as a commercial engraver and printmaker can be split into three phases: during the early phase he established his professional reputation as a copy engraver, purchased a copperplate rolling press, and took his own apprentice; during the mid-phase Blake created book illustrations after his own designs for one of the most popular graveyard poems of the eighteenth century, Edward Young's *Night Thoughts or, The Complaint and The Consolation*, and published his Canterbury Pilgrims print. In the

Fig. 3.1: W. Blake, *Joseph of Arimathea among the Rocks of Albion*, first state, 1773, engraving, black carbon ink on paper, © Fitzwilliam Museum, Cambridge

final phase, he produced the Virgil woodcuts and *Job* and *Dante* series that mark the pinnacle of his achievement as a line engraver.

During the early phase, Blake's main employers were the booksellers clustered around St Paul's Churchyard. The linear visual syntax associated with Basire can be seen in Blake's early reproductive prints of architectural designs, Bible illustrations, portrait frontispieces, and a variety of vignettes for natural philosophy books. In 1782 Blake modified this visual syntax in two pastoral scenes after Jean-Antoine Watteau, combining short lines, flicks, and stippling. With James Parker, a fellow apprentice under Basire, Blake established a short-lived printshop at 27 Broad Street in 1784. Two extant separate plates from this endeavour, the *Zephyrus and Flora* and *Calisto*, evince a similar development in Blake's visual syntax with the use of short lines and stippling and, taken together, indicate an attempt to broaden his commercial appeal beyond book illustration.[5] These engravings also mark the beginning of Blake's long association with the artist Thomas Stothard, the most important book illustrator of the period.

For book illustrations, Blake was paid by the plate, with the smaller format prints earning him between 2 guineas and £5. There was also payment for reclamation work, where the engraver reworked the original copperplates usually after they became worn from repeated printing. For the larger separate plates Blake was paid considerably more. For example, in 1788 the doyen of the British print-selling industry, John Boydell, commissioned Blake to engrave Hogarth's painting of the scene of Macheath's trial from John Gay's *The Beggar's Opera*. This was Blake's largest reproductive engraving after another artist and evinces a range of cross-hatching and delicate stippling to achieve variety in tone and texture, depth and shadow, and while there is no extant evidence to indicate how much he was paid for the commission, Boydell paid several hundred pounds for comparable engravings. The same year, the liberal bookseller Joseph Johnson employed Blake for the first time. This was to be one of Blake's longest and most important professional relationships, with Johnson providing much of Blake's reproductive engraving work in the form of book illustrations for the next decade.

On 10 July 1788, Blake took on an apprentice, Thomas Owen, for a fee of £52.10.[6] The money Blake received from the Hogarth commission together with Owen's apprentice fees afforded a move to a larger home south of the Thames and time to develop his illuminated printing process – a process of relief-etching that enabled direct composition of text and design on the same matrix – and between 1788 and 1795 Blake published thirteen original illuminated books and the intaglio *For the Children: The Gates of Paradise*

(1793).[7] During the same period, Blake produced book illustrations for Johnson, although some of these may have been the work of Owen, possibly the plates for C. G. Salzmann's *Elements of Morality* (1791).[8] While apprenticeships typically lasted seven years, it appears that Owen and Blake parted ways within a year or two. By the mid-1790s, Blake was experimenting with planographically printed large colour drawing, engraved plates after his own designs for an edition of John Gay's *Fables* (1793), and copy engravings illustrating John Gabriel Stedman's influential account of the brutalities of the slave trade, *Narrative, of a Five Years' Expedition, against the Revolted Negroes of Surinam* (1796). Blake also produced a number of separate plates after his own designs, notably the companion *Job* (1793) and *Ezekiel* (1794) prints. In 1795 Blake was also approached by the publisher Richard Edwards to create a series of designs illustrating Young's *Night Thoughts*. In terms of scope and format, this was perhaps Blake's most ambitious commercial venture. Blake produced 537 watercolour designs on large folio sheets, with the designs surrounding a central text panel, of which forty-three were engraved and published with the first four Nights of Young's poem in 1797. Blake's illustrations are notable for their literal interpretations of Young's metaphors and a visual syntax that harkens back to Basire's linear style, with firm line work and extensive use of un-etched areas of the copperplate to achieve form. Unfortunately for Blake, the first volume of a proposed multi-volume edition of *Night Thoughts* was a financial failure and marks the beginning of a downturn in his fortunes as a commercial engraver.

Due to the paucity of commissions from London booksellers, Blake moved to the Sussex coast in 1800 to work with the poet and biographer William Hayley. While many of Blake's engravings for Hayley are reproductive book illustrations, perhaps of most interest in terms of technique is one of the first jobs for his new patron, the broadside ballad *Little Tom the Sailor* where Blake white-line etches his designs and relief etches Hayley's text. After returning to London in September 1803, Blake continued to produce reproductive book illustrations for Hayley and around 1805 began work on a large painting of Chaucer's Canterbury Pilgrims. Exhibited in his 1809 one-man exhibition, Blake followed the commercial strategy set out by Boydell in the late 1780s by using the painting as a marketing tool for a large-scale engraving.

Blake was also in competition with the engraver-turned publisher Robert Cromek, who around the same time commissioned Stothard to paint the same subject. As it turned out, Blake managed to get his print onto the market before Cromek and it was the largest integral copperplate

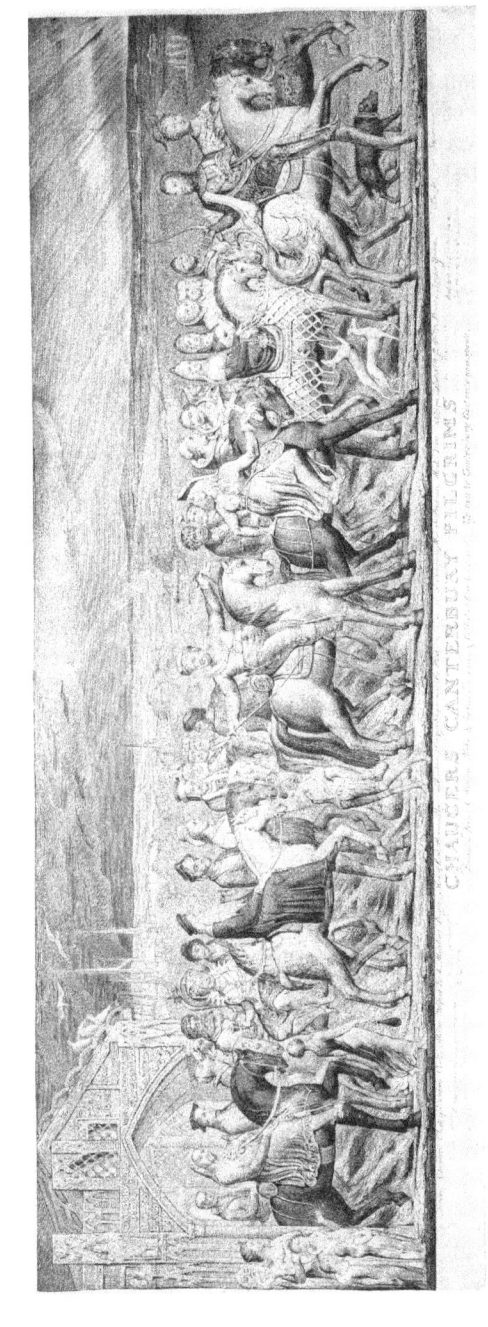

Fig. 3.2: W. Blake, *The Canterbury Pilgrims*, fourth state, 1810, engraving, Collection of R. N. Essick

Blake produced (Fig. 3.2). In the Prospectus for the engraving, Blake advertises the forthcoming print as:

> a correct and finished Line manner of Engraving, similar to those original Copper Plates of Albert Durer [...] and the old original Engravers, who were great Masters in Painting and Designing, whose method, alone, can delineate Character as it is. (E 567)

For Blake, Chaucer's pilgrims were character archetypes. To delineate such archetypes he favours the linear techniques associated with Basire, Durer, and the 'old original Engravers' rather than more illusionistic techniques used to reproduce pictorial works in oils. In the first state of the Canterbury Pilgrims print, Blake deploys a combination of firm outline and short and long lines typical of Basire. For instance, the foreground, middle-distance trees, and the Tabarde Inne are delineated with short strokes while long, gently curving strokes are used for the pilgrims, their costumes, and the horses. Such contrasts between short and long linear strokes can be seen in Basire's engraving *The Field of the Cloth of Gold* (Fig. 3.3). We also know that Blake had *The Field of the Cloth of Gold* in mind for he follows the left-to-right compositional arrangement of the Royal procession from Guion with Chaucer's Host in Blake's engraving assuming the central, outward-facing position of Henry VIII surrounded by his retinue. Blake also includes the two hunting dogs in similar positions to those in Basire's engraving.

The final phase of Blake's professional engraving career was largely influenced by one of his most important friends and patrons, John Linnell. An artist and engraver of considerable merit, Linnell provided Blake with financial assistance through engraving commissions and by purchasing his works, including illuminated books. They met in 1818 and immediately began working together on a portrait engraving of the Baptist minister James Upton. Linnell also introduced Blake to the Linnell family physician, Robert Thornton, whose 1821 edition of the *Pastorals of Virgil* was illustrated with a series of woodcut engravings by Blake. Unlike the mixed method of etching and engraving Blake had used for his earlier book illustrations, woodcut engravings print from the surface of the woodblock and any area of the surface that has been cut away appears as white. Like the relief-etching method Blake used to produce his illuminated books, woodcut engraving is a relief process that requires the engraver to think in positive and negative terms. Blake's experience of relief etching clearly helped with the Virgil woodcuts, where the image was conceptualised and executed in negative and utilises the contrast between light and dark to

Fig. 3.3: J. Basire, *The Field of the Cloth of Gold*, 1774, engraving, Collection of M. Crosby

Fig. 3.4: W. Blake, *Job* separate plate, second state, *c.* 1804 or later, engraving, Collection of R. N. Essick

depict form, depth, and tone. Using a mixture of short lines and flicks cut into the surface of the woodblock, Blake delineates figures, landscapes, and buildings and evokes brilliant light from the sun and moon, and shadows and daylight on fields and roads. Blake's reliance on lines and the contrast between the paper support and black ink significantly influenced his final engraving commissions beginning with his greatest achievement in line engraving, the *Illustrations to the Book of Job*.

In 1823, Linnell commissioned Blake 'to Engrave the Set of Plates from his own Designs of Job's Captivity' (*BR* 386). These twenty-two plates are masterpieces of intaglio engraving and certainly the finest examples of Blake's ability as an interpreter, designer, and engraver. To create these plates, Blake reduced his watercolour designs of Job in a sketchbook and then transferred the reduced design onto the copperplate with a steel etching needle or a stipple burin. As Linnell observed, Blake 'cut with the graver entirely on copper without the Aid of Aqua fortis' (*BR* 318). Eschewing the mixed method that had been the mainstay of his professional career, the Job plates are pure line engravings. The existence of proof prints and repoussage (hammering the reverse of the copperplate to flatten the engraved lines) reveal that Blake altered the design at various stages of the engraving process. As with the Virgil woodcuts, Blake relies on the contrast between the black ink and the surface of the paper to delineate form, depth, and tone. We can also see the influence of this technique in the second state of the Job (*c.* 1820–7) separate plate and the later states of the Canterbury Pilgrims print where burnishing has been used to accentuate the dark and light areas of the image. Indeed, a notable feature of these late engravings is the concentration on dramatic lighting as a key component of the images, such as the insertion of the lightning bolt in the Job separate plate (Fig. 3.4).

During the final year of his life, Blake produced a series of large-scale engravings illustrating Dante after his own watercolour drawings, which Linnell had commissioned in 1824. Of the 104 watercolours, seven were selected from the Inferno to engrave. As with the Job plates, Blake employed pure line engraving for the Dante plates (for an example, see Fig. 6.6). Yet, rather than a stipple burin, Blake initially used a drypoint needle followed by a graver, allowing himself considerable freedom as he sketched directly into the surface of the copper. While these plates were unfinished at Blake's death, they evince the aesthetic and conceptual development of the linear style he had learnt as an apprentice.[9] In the *Descriptive Catalogue* (1809) Blake sets out his artistic credo, stating that the 'golden rule of art, as well as of life, is this: That the more distinct, sharp, and wirey the bounding line, the more perfect the work of art' (E 550). In his commentary on the Canterbury Pilgrims he observes 'Every Line is the Line of Beauty' (E 575). During the mid-phase of his professional career, Blake refined his aesthetic by reducing Basire's house style to its most basic function and, influenced by the younger Linnell, sought to recuperate line engraving from being considered merely a mechanical technique of reproductive illustration. In his final series of prints, Blake succeeded in this endeavour, transforming pure line engraving into a mode of original invention.

Notes

1. Two Victorian biographies suggest that Blake was so 'horrified by' Ryland's 'countenance that he would not be' apprenticed to him. See *BR* 665 fn, 729.
2. Basire was apprenticed to Seale on 8 October 1747 and then to Dalton on 3 June 1748. See National Archives, Register of Duties Paid for Apprentices' Indentures, IR 1: 18.

3. According to Richard Gough, 'Mr James Basire['s] burin will do credit to every individual or body of men who employ it'. See J. Nichols, *Literary Anecdotes of the Eighteenth Century*, 9 vols. (London: 1812–16), II, 586.
4. Blake could have modelled his backdrop on the high rocky cliff, shoreline, and seascape pictured in Sir Joshua Reynolds's portrait of Commodore Keppel, painted in 1754.
5. The same combination of line and stipple is seen in the two companion prints after George Morland, *The Idle Laundress* and *The Industrious Cottagers*, both from 1788.
6. See M. Phillips, *William Blake Apprentice and Master* (Oxford: Ashmolean, 2014), p. 84, and G. E. Bentley, *William Blake in the Desolate Market* (Toronto: McGill-Queen's University Press 2014), pp. 218–19.
7. Of the thirteen illuminated books, *The Book of Ahania* and *The Book of Los* are not strictly relief etched. The text is intaglio etched and the designs are planographically printed.
8. The attribution of the forty-five unsigned plates in Salzmann to Blake is detailed in R. N. Essick, *William Blake's Commercial Book Illustrations* (Oxford: Clarendon Press, 1991), p. 50.
9. Linnell printed the Dante plates in 1838.

CHAPTER 4

Illuminated Books

David Worrall

David V. Erdman's *The Complete Poetry and Prose of William Blake* (1982) would have been unrecognisable to Blake. This is because Erdman's edition was printed in letterpress, the moveable metal type (now digitised) introduced by William Caxton in 1476 where individual letters could be rearranged to form entirely new works. During his lifetime, only one of Blake's poems, *The French Revolution* (1791), was printed in letterpress. The medium Blake preferred to use for his poetry was to etch his verse onto copper plates, along with integrated visual designs, in what Blake called 'Illuminated Books' (E 693). The illuminated books, in their order of printing, began with *Songs of Innocence* (1789) and go through to *Jerusalem the Emanation of the Giant Albion* (1804–20).[1] The greatest parts of these works were produced using a specialist technique known as relief-etching. Grasping the ontology of the materiality of the illuminated books is the first step towards situating them amid Blake's overall creativity.

The illuminated books were a development of printmaking skills Blake learned when he was apprenticed as an engraver from age fourteen in 1772 until 1779. The core skills he acquired fitted him to become an engraver of commercial book illustrations. Initially seeking such a career, his ownership of a printing press (a wooden apparatus with a large spoked wheel to impress the dampened paper onto the plate, one at a time) also enabled him to control their means of production.

There are a number of aspects of the illuminated books which, particularly in a digital age, are technically challenging not only on account of the intractability of the medium but also on account of the perceptual, motor, and cognitive dexterities required to make them. From the reader's point of view, the pictures and verse appear seamlessly to merge. These appearances mask a daunting reality. Today combining image and text is unremarkable. In the eighteenth century, visual images, without exception, had to be made by hand as a single physical entity on metal or wood with little or no capability for subsequent modification. The basis for all pre-photographically reproduced image making was the laborious creation of a series of lines (sometimes finely granulated so as to appear as tones) which deceived the eye into thinking the viewer was observing a solid object, whether that object was a face, a building, or a landscape.

All visual images, including captioning texts, had first to be formed upon a strong, impermeable printing surface from which prints could be taken when impressed with ink. The printing surface Blake used for the illuminated books was the copper plate. All printmaking on such surfaces required the physical removal of metal. This could be done either by engraving (using a sharpened tool to chisel out copper grooves to fill with ink) or by etching, which is a technology based on using acid to remove copper. The variant of etching Blake predominantly used in the illuminated books was relief etching. In relief etching, a varnish-laden brush is used to paint words and images onto the copper plate. The varnish acts as a resist which allows the acid to eat around it, revealing the image or text highlighted as a low relief plateau of unbitten copper (hence, relief etching). This low relief outline can then be inked for printing.

Text in the illuminated books was written in mirror-image. That is, Blake started on the right hand side of the copper plate and wrote leftwards. His patron, John Linnell, recalled his 'extraordinary facility [...] in writing backwards' (*BR* 609). One of the problems of writing backwards is ensuring a consistent slope for the characters. Blake's gradually developing facility with mirror writing can be witnessed in the tiny *All Religions Are One* and *There Is No Natural Religion*, both usually assigned to 1788 (but not certainly printed until 1794). Mirror writing occurs naturally in children but is suppressed in adulthood.[2] Since many *Songs of Innocence* are concerned with identifying and relocating childhood sensibilities, it is possible his increased encounter with mirror writing (the perceptual process is emblematised on the title page of *The Book of Urizen*, 1794) included a contemplation of a relocation of this ability.

The technicalities of the production of the illuminated books and their bibliographical history are complex.[3] For example, they were, in part, co-produced. His wife, Catherine, probably did some of their colouring (constituting major interventions into their presentation and perceived meaning), particularly in those works where watercolour was added (such as *Songs of Innocence*). Her presence would have been essential at the printing stage to provide a clean pair of hands to William's dirtied with ink. Probably the closest cognate for Blake's illuminated books are limited editions of prints produced by artist printmakers. In that world, the smaller the print run, the greater their exclusivity and the higher their perceived value. However, as seems to be the case with Blake, 'value' does not necessarily equate with financial reward or success. Rather, his intermittent excursions into producing illuminated books may have been straightforwardly conceived as a visual artist's alternative way of reaching new patrons or purchasers, or even simply satisfying pre-existing friends and clients.

In short, Blake produced extremely limited editions. For example, *The Book of Los* (1795) and *The Book of Ahania* (1795) were only printed in two copies each (referred to as Copies A and B). For both titles, only Copy A exists. To give a quick caution as to the ease of predicting the range of processes he employed, despite relief-etching being the predominant process, the texts of *The Book of Los* and *The Book of Ahania* are intaglio etched (the technique of contemporary caricature printmakers such as James Gillray). Demonstrating or showcasing his command over several high-class skills in printmaking may have been as much as a determinant of what he produced as the artistic or poetic expressive decisions he made within them.

Allied to relief etching, Blake also developed a process of colour printing. Colour printing, where it was done at all, was previously restricted to using multiple, accurately registered, plates each carrying a different colour. Blake's method took advantage of very small print runs which limited the danger of colours merging. This gave some works a second lease of life and, although the editions were small anyway, it also increased their rarity.

Although the printmakers' methods Blake employed implies few buyers were sought, there was an intriguing moment, at the height of his productivity, when his illuminated books might have become better known. The bibliophile Richard Twiss, writing in September 1794, told a friend there are 'several more of Blakes books at Johnsons in St. P^s Ch. Y$^{d'}$.[4] Joseph Johnson was London's leading publisher for liberal writers such as Mary Wollstonecraft, Erasmus Darwin, and Joseph Priestley. Twiss eventually acquired a copy of the tiny uncoloured, intaglio etched *For Children: The Gates of Paradise* (1793). While Johnson is not known to have ever sold any of 'Blakes books', their availability in his bookshop may mark an attempt by Blake to reach his target market of affluent, politically progressive bibliophiles.[5]

In order initially to grasp Blake's lifetime production cycle of illuminated books, the single most important modern document is a tabulated Appendix printed in Joseph Viscomi's *Blake and the Idea of the Book* (1993, pp. 376–81). Although difficult and occasionally frustrating to read,

Viscomi's book has been hugely influential. He conclusively demonstrated that Blake produced his illuminated books in editions, that is, in single sessions of printings only occasionally supplemented by printings in subsequent years. He showed that their production (not just their composition) clustered in the years 1789–90 and 1793–5. After those dates, there were big gaps only intermittently filled with occasional printing sessions of pre-existing titles (in 1804 Blake printed just three more copies of *Songs of Innocence*, for example). He then printed three copies of his newly composed *Milton a Poem* in 1811, produced some early proofs of (a short) *Jerusalem* in 1807 but did not print a complete set until 1820. Blake's final illuminated books, *On Homers Poetry* [and] *On Virgil* (1822) and *The Ghost of Abel* (1822), were both relief etched, but as one plate comprised the entirety of the former and two plates the latter, they were conceived on a very reduced scale.

The date ranges of composition and production into print for *Milton a Poem* and *Jerusalem the Emanation of the Giant Albion* are unusually long. *Milton* was produced (in the sense of composed and first printed) 1804–11 and *Jerusalem* 1804–20. At the very least, this suggests Blake was giving increased attention to works other than the illuminated books. His 1809 private exhibition off Oxford Street would be one such activity. Strikingly, neither *Milton* nor *Jerusalem* employs the colour-printing techniques he had developed so carefully in the 1790s. Emphasising their status as limited editions, *Milton* had fifty-two plates prepared and four copies printed while *Jerusalem* had one hundred plates and five copies printed (a sixth was left uncollated). Again, the correlates suggest high-class printmaking rather than books of poetry.

The intermittency of this output needs to be contrasted with Blake's work in other areas (on which see Chapters 3, 5, 6, and 7 of the present volume). The twin influences of the professionalisation of English studies in universities coupled with the contrasting vacating of Blake studies by art historians (although not museum curatorial teams) have worked to privilege the illuminated books, distorting our appreciation of the scale of his productivity as a visual artist. It is in this wider artistic context, and more specifically in the context of printmaking, that we might best understand the materiality of the illuminated books. Not least, the illuminated books exist within Blake's other types of printmaking output. The most obvious of these are his commercial book illustrations where he used the so-called mixed-method technique common to his contemporaries in the trade, combining engraving (for the faces, hands, etc.) with etching (for the landscape, buildings, etc.). A third category of print comprises the

Separate Plates which were occasional or experimental prints but which included works such as *The Approach of Doom* (*c.* 1792) and *Albion Rose* (*c.* 1793/1804).

Blake's illuminated books are saturated with references to printmaking. This is at its most extreme in *The Marriage of Heaven and Hell* (1790). *The Marriage*'s editors write, 'Blake's graphic processes take over the allegory at least twice in the *Marriage*, on plates 6–7 and 14–15, and perhaps more (it is sometimes hard to tell, simply because the terminology of printing tools, materials, and processes is so extensive).'[6] These metaphors have received sustained analysis.[7] One of the simpler allusions is that *The Marriage*'s 'devil' characters are elaborations of 'printer's devil', the nickname for the apprentice or youngest employee in a printing office.

With the illuminated books, technology is a powerful influence on meaning. The individual copper plate, and not the complete work, is the primary unit of expression. Blake is extremely clear about this. After almost a lifetime practising his profession, in one of his last relief-etched illuminated books (in this case, strictly, a print), *On Homer's Poetry* (which shares the same plate as *On Virgil*, both assigned to 1822), he wrote that 'when a Work has Unity it is as much in a Part as in the Whole' (E 269). Ascribing meaning to sequences of text in the illuminated books is highly problematic unless one can take account of, at least, their sequential variability not to mention their differences in presentation and dates of printing.

Although Blake clearly exploited these technologies to their full, it is important to realise how their limitations may affect interpretation. A primary flexibility (or inflexibility) arising from writing narrative poems onto copper is that the only viable means of modification or amendment is the addition or subtraction of plates. With difficulty, individual letters or words can be mended by burnishing (rubbing) the plate or, as a last resort, altering with pen after printing. For the literary critic, this has the attraction of apparently conferring an enormous coherence of authorial (or readerly) intention on each plate. However, narrative sequences may not always be what they seem.

It is feasible, for example, that Blake conceived *The Marriage* as a four-page anti-Swedenborgian pamphlet starting at plate 21 ('I have always found that Angels') and ending with 'One Law for the Lion & Ox is Oppression'. From that core he then added plates, sophisticating its narrative and multiplying its generic identities (like *Song* lyrics, the 'Proverbs of Hell' are perfect for copper plates). However, even then one needs to be wary. Although Copy B was printed in 1790 it was prefixed with a frontispiece titled *Our End Is Come*, an intaglio print unambiguously dated by Blake as 'June 5: 1793'. It is one of his most remarkable images, certainly suitable to a revolutionary moment and potentially amplifying the three-plate 'Song of Liberty', which also seems to have been a supplementary addition to *The Marriage*. Alternatively, more mundanely, *Our End Is Come* could have been posthumously added to Copy B before 1834.[8]

Such bibliographic issues, which magnify problems of interpretation, abound. Perhaps the most startling of these is *The Book of Urizen*, printed in 1794 with single additional printings in 1795 and 1818. No two copies share the same sequence of plates. In the cases of Copies A, B, E, and F, there are also variant orders of text.[9] This includes the entire exclusion in some copies (D, E, F, G, J) of plate 4, which is the only plate where Urizen speaks (about his 'books formd of metals'), amounting to the subtraction of some 10 per cent of the poem's textual length.

The physical flexibilities (and limitations) of Blake's production methods impact upon reader reception in ways with few parallels in letterpress or manuscript expression. Even arranging them into books is fraught with bibliographical challenges. For example, while some illuminated books were printed on both the recto and the verso sides of the paper, others were printed on one side only (like prints). For the three collections known as *A Large Book of Designs* and *A Small Book of Designs* (the latter extant as two copies comprising different compilations), which drew from the repertoire of Blake's most inventive visual images from the early 1790s illuminated books, other precedents demand consideration. The *Designs* impressions were printed *c*. 1796 but not entirely collated until *c*. 1818 (some of them probably for Dawson Turner). Strikingly, Blake seems to have been requested to completely mask out any poetry integrated with the designs by covering up the text with paper to prevent it from printing. In the case of an impression in Tate Britain of Plate 6 of *The Book of Urizen*, he obliterated nine lines of his own relief-etched poetry when he printed it out but, *c*. 1818, he newly captioned it in pen, 'I sought Pleasure & found Pain' / 'Unutterable'. The print was not discovered until it surfaced in Glasgow in 2002 so it is not included in Erdman's *Complete Poetry and Prose*. Today, however, surely it requires to be afforded the status of an authorised hermeneutical direction for any interpretation of *The Book of Urizen*? Is this, because it has a text, also part of *The Book of Urizen*? Or, is it a captioned print in another *Book* (of *Designs*)?

In face of these complexities, it is insufficient simply to aggregate Blake's writings indiscriminately, as may be the tendency of literary criticism. It is also unhelpful to elide the historical intermittence of composition and printing, as if the illuminated books were 'dervish-like placeholders for the real, ahistorical moment that is the present'.¹⁰ Instead, we need a methodology consistent with the material individuality of plates and printings, including their sequencing and status. Perhaps the closest correlates for the illuminated books are Blake's Large Colour Prints of 1795/1804. On account of the way they were printed and finished in editions of no more than three impressions, not only is each one unique (technically each one is also a different state), they also look immediately different to the casual glance. While no one would argue anything other than that they form a series, no one would bother to argue that they also form a single sequence.

Notes

1. I have taken *Songs of Innocence* as the first book in illuminated printing since this work (along with *The Book of Thel*) has a firmly etched date of '1789'. J. Viscomi believes two other works, *All Religions Are One* and *There Is No Natural Religion* (which do not have etched dates), can be securely antedated a year earlier, to 1788: see 'Blake's Invention of Illuminated Printing, 1788', [undated] *Branch: British, Representation, and Nineteenth-Century History*, www.branchcollective.org/?ps_articles=joseph-viscomi-blakes-invention-of-illuminated-printing-1788 However, *All Religions Are One* (which exists in a single copy) includes a leaf (plate 6) unambiguously watermarked '1794 / I Taylor'. Since *All Religions Are One* and *There Is No Natural Religion* were printed from the same set of papers (where watermarks exist on these two books, they are to 'Taylor' or 'I Taylor'), neither can be firmly dated before 1794.
2. G. D. Schott, 'Mirror Writing: Neurological Reflections on an Unusual Phenomenon', *Journal of Neurology, Neurosurgery and Psychiatry*, 78 (2007), 5–13.
3. Only one small fragment of one relief-etched copper plate (for *America*, 1793) exists, now in the National Gallery of Art, Washington, DC. All theories of the production of the illuminated books rely absolutely on forensic reconstructions based on the paper prints, so to a degree are hypothetical, although Viscomi's *Blake and the Idea of the Book* may be taken to be foundational.
4. K. Davies, 'Mrs Bliss: A Blake Collector of 1794', in S. Clark and D. Worrall (eds.), *Blake in the Nineties* (Basingstoke: Palgrave Macmillan, 1999), pp. 212–30; G. P. Tyson, *Joseph Johnson: A Liberal Publisher* (Iowa City: University of Iowa Press, 1979).
5. The editors of the blakearchive.org allude to a possible 'erased imprint' of the publisher J. Dodsley on Copy A of *For Children: The Gates of Paradise* (1793) in the Library of Congress. Even with the Library of Congress reading room magnifier, I have not been able to confirm this erasure: www.blakearchive.org/exist/blake/archive/work.xq?workid=gates-child&java=no

6. M. Eaves, R. N. Essick, and J. Viscomi (eds.), *William Blake: The Early Illuminated Books* (London: Tate for the Blake Trust, 1998), p. 124.
7. See, for example, J. Viscomi, 'The Evolution of *The Marriage of Heaven and Hell*', *Huntington Library Quarterly*, 58 (1996), 281–344, and 'In the Caves of Heaven and Hell: Swedenborg and Printmaking in Blake's *Marriage*', in Clark and Worrall, *Blake in the Nineties*, pp. 27–60.
8. R. N. Essick, *The Separate Plates of William Blake* (Princeton: Princeton University Press, 1983), pp. 30–7.
9. The founding insight is that of J. J. McGann, 'The Idea of an Indeterminate Text: Blake's Bible of Hell and Dr. Alexander Geddes', *Studies in Romanticism*, 25 (1986), 303–24.
10. A. M. Cooper, *William Blake and the Productions of Time* (Farnham: Ashgate, 2013), p. 1.

CHAPTER 5

Manuscripts

Sarah Haggarty

Blake wrote far more in manuscript than the material that we know of today: pages missing from extant works, fair copies presumed not to be *sui generis*, and overlapping contemporary testimonies tell us that. This paper stuff, handwritten and unprinted, seems always to have been at risk of imminent extinction. Blake himself, apparently, was 'tempted to burn [his] MSS', and his young artist friend, Frederick Tatham, stands accused of destroying 'a large number' of Blake's 'designs, poems, notebooks' following Catherine's death in 1831 ('enact[ing] the holocaust of Blake manuscripts – not designs, I think, as I have heard from his own lips', according to Anne Gilchrist).[1] What non-printed papers remain have endured in the shadow of Blake's illuminated books, held by many over the past one-and-a-half centuries to have been his greatest achievement. Yet even as we might recognise the peculiarly scriptorial and sketchy character of these books – these '"printed manuscript[s]"'; these 'fair cop[ies]' of chirographic texts and 'freely drawn' designs that appear to have come together as composite only on the copper plate – we risk diluting our attention to Blake's manuscripts proper.[2] Blake's work in manuscript is 'diverse', 'significant', and as yet 'understudied'.[3] Granted, our knowledge of it benefits from an ongoing history of editorial intervention, which has focused on describing, interpreting, and remediating individual manuscripts or works. But there is still no systematic study of Blake's manuscripts *in toto* (for instance, his habits of note-taking, his practices of composition and revision, his work within and across particular genres), and little discussion about how to define the contours of such an enquiry. This chapter makes some such preliminary effort, asking: what are Blake's manuscripts? How do they cohere? What is their relationship to scribal and print cultures at large? And how might we account for their peculiar power – for the intimate access they seem to promise to Blake's working methods, his habits of mind, the movement of his thought?

Among Blake's manuscript materials still extant are one notebook, two sketchbooks,[4] and four once-stitched-together, (almost) standalone works (*An Island in the Moon*, *Tiriel*, *VALA / The Four Zoas*, and *Genesis*), in various states of finish, with certain leaves missing, added, disordered, or reordered. There are some ninety-four letters;[5] there are accounts and receipts; there are at least fifteen annotated books;[6] and there is an entry to a manuscript autograph album. There are also fugitive pieces loose, and scraps never bound. Lines of writing, in pen or pencil, singly or in clutches, can be tidy, inserted, altered, scribbled out, or erased entirely; drawings can be washed in colour, ink-outlined, emergent from a series of pencilled alternatives, or faint and wavering. Revision is the rule: there are few of Blake's manuscripts unmarked by it. And determining what in Blake's manuscripts was deleted or added, bound or ordered, when, and by whom, has been a perennial problem for manuscript editors.

How we now identify, describe, and categorise Blake's manuscripts is inconsistent, and indeed subject to ongoing questions about methodology that bedevil writers about manuscript culture more broadly. Two of the handiest overviews of what Blake's manuscript materials actually comprise – both worth consulting – take different tacks. The 'Contents' list of Erdman's *Complete Poetry and Prose*, structured by theme ('Satiric verse and epigrams') and prejudicially – as it favours the illuminated books – by medium ('Prophetic works, unengraved'), makes no explicit mention of manuscripts, although the volume's 'Textual notes' enable readers to single out the titles of most of Blake's manuscript writings, albeit piecemeal, and with 'the literary work', and associated ideals of integrity, as a primary taxonomic principle. Thus, for example, Blake's main notebook is dismembered, its tissues rent and scattered. Material on art and artists entangled physically, thematically, and chronologically is disaggregated (or at least, tacitly disassembled then reassembled) into a selection of pieces posthumously titled *Public Address, Vision of the Last Judgment*, and several shorter verses.[7] The remediation of manuscript in letterpress also inevitably entails distortion. Layout, for instance, is significant in notebooks, and even more important in marginalia, with '[d]ifferent functions [. . .] assigned to different spaces' in a book. Blake may mark a note as summary simply by virtue of its placement at the head of a page, something we need to see in order to understand that note's significance.[8] The Blake Archive, in contrast to Erdman's edition, offers us photographs and hypertext transcriptions. It also prioritises to a greater extent some of the material determinations of the manuscript form, such as the cohesion conferred by a common binding. Still, one must look to the British Library website for

Blake's main notebook, and to printed facsimiles for the annotations (all included, however partially, by Erdman). The originals themselves also continue to hold surprises, and can be found in libraries' special collections and archives, mainly in the UK and North America.

The cohesion of particular Blakean manuscripts is signalled by a variety of means. Draft title-pages drawn by Blake identify two works: the illustrated, prophetic poem *VALA*, a title he cancelled in favour of *The Four Zoas* (Fitzwilliam Museum; composed *c.* 1796–1807), and *Genesis*, an illuminated transcription of the biblical verses, with some minor but telling alterations (Huntington Library; composed 1827).[9] *Ideas of Good and Evil*, written in 'a dim broad scrawl of pencil [...] on the reverse page of the second MS. leaf' of the *Notebook*, was also read as a general title-page of sorts by Swinburne and W. M. Rossetti.[10] More decidedly a third work, a poem, with a set of separate, but associated, illustrations, has the title *Tiriel* written in Blake's hand on its paper wrapper (British Library; composed *c.* 1789); and a fourth, a burlesque, written originally on a single quire of paper, is conventionally called 'An Island in the Moon', a title culled by later editors from its opening line (Fitzwilliam Museum; composed *c.* 1784–5).[11] All these works are in different ways incomplete: *Island* is missing two or more pages; *Genesis* has two alternative title pages, its colouring gradually falls away, and its text halts at Gen. 4:15; and *Tiriel* has lines 'left unfinished' (although, in truth, its alleged incompleteness has less to do with what it lacks materially, in itself, than with how it may be supposed not to measure up to later permutations of Blake's mythography and techniques of page design and printing).[12] The senses in which a manuscript might be incomplete ramify further in the case of *VALA / The Four Zoas*, the order of whose pages, let alone of the sequence of revisions made to most of them, is a matter of editorial reconstruction: some clutches of pages were once stitched together, but by the 1890s, when it was first made public, the manuscript was '"unpaged and unsorted"'. With its accretion of scripts, many textual interpolations, designs of varying determinacy, and diversity of paper support, the manuscript 'at several stages [...] was evidently finished, while at no stage was [Blake] ever done with it'. Despite the finality of its last words, 'End of the Dream' (E 407), *VALA / The Four Zoas* is host to an array of 'unresolved complications', including, most notoriously, two versions of 'Night VII'.[13]

Whether Blake intended these several works to remain unprinted, and how those intentions might have evolved, is on the existing evidence impossible to determine. Perhaps the highly wrought *Genesis*, touched by gold leaf, and *Island*, neatly copied for the most part, and supposedly exclusive in its implied address to a coterie audience, were designed to remain in manuscript?[14] Perhaps the opening of *VALA*, in its careful, copperplate hand, discloses Blake's initial intention of having it etched or engraved, an intention afterwards abandoned, or modified?[15] Perhaps the separate text and design elements of *Tiriel* were once destined to be reconciled, the designs engraved, and set at regular intervals into a letterpress text, in the manner of contemporary illustrated books such as Boydell's edition of Shakespeare's *Dramatic Works* (1791–1805)?[16]

Others of Blake's verses and critical writings extant only in manuscript are more widely diffused, and, historically, have been more variously categorised. *The Pickering Manuscript* (Morgan Library and Museum, transcribed *c.* 1807), its name granted haphazardly by its ownership in the mid-nineteenth century by B. M. Pickering, is a collection of ten poems, seven of them (including 'Auguries of Innocence' and 'The Mental Traveller') surviving only in this source. The collection is unillustrated, has no title-page, and its earliest reception is unknown. However, the manuscript has a clear integrity: it is (unusually for Blake's surviving manuscripts) a sustained fair copy – clearly written, neatly arranged, scarcely changed – which suggests 'a specific occasion for the collection'. Perhaps it was 'made for some friend or patron'?[17] Far more diverse in content is Blake's main notebook, known as 'the *Notebook*' (British Library, *c.* 1787–1847), although it seems Blake utilised several more such volumes over the course of his career.[18] This main, 'not very large' notebook, originally used as a sketchbook by Blake's younger brother Robert, was kept 'near at hand all his life' by Blake following Robert's death in 1787.[19] The *Notebook* is also sometimes known by an alternative title, *The Rossetti Manuscript*, which refers not only to the *Notebook* proper, but also to D. G. Rossetti's transcription of some of its verses, which he appended to, and had bound with, Blake's book after acquiring it in 1847. The *Notebook* is primarily a site of original composition, containing both working drafts and fair copies, both fragmentary or indeterminate sketches and more detailed drawings, although it also includes some few commonplaces and journalary notes: factual 'Memorand[a]' of engraving techniques appearing beneath precise evocations of mental state ('Tuesday Jan^{ry}. 20. 1807. between Two & Seven in the Evening – Despair', N 4); notes taken from newspapers (N 59, 96–7). Some of the original material is extant only in this source: shorter verses; a large part of 'The Everlasting Gospel' (1818 or later); and various writings on art and artists – much of which emerges sporadically, even on non-consecutive pages, with later compositions jostling to fill whatever space is left by earlier ones.

The *Notebook* also contains numerous drafts, notably of emblems reworked in *The Gates of Paradise* (*For Children*, 1793; *For the Sexes*, 1818) and elsewhere, and of poems adjusted to fit *Songs of Experience*.

The survival of drafts, and the recognition that writing extant only in fair copy was most probably preceded by rougher, preliminary material prompts us to think further about the relationship of manuscript and print.[20] Some of Blake's manuscript writings made their way to the press during his lifetime, as we have just seen. Numerous poems printed in *Songs* (1794), indeed, have manuscript precursors: a version of *Innocence*'s 'Laughing Song' was handwritten in a copy of the typeset *Poetical Sketches* (1783), and versions of 'Holy Thursday', 'Nurses Song', and 'The Little Boy Lost' appear in *An Island in the Moon* (1784). The *Notebook* hosts drafts of eighteen poems later printed in *Experience* (see E 790–1), with some (but arbitrarily, not all) of these struck through with 'a vertical line indicating some form of selection', perhaps '[marking] those that had been copied on to copper plate for relief etching'.[21] By one way of looking at it, then, these draft materials are in a sense cancelled, redundant because superseded by a better technology. It is striking that this is also what Joseph Viscomi seems to suggest of the 'drafts' he presumes would once have existed for other illuminated books. A triumph of Viscomi's study of Blake's illuminated printing is its vindication of the copperplate as a compositional medium, and of etching as an inventive, rather than reproductive, technique, primarily through the similarity of etching to drawing.[22] Viscomi does not deny that 'rough sketches' and 'text[s]' or 'portions of a manuscript in progress' existed prior to Blake taking brush to copper. However, '[i]ndependent of one another, they were merely raw material for designs'. What matters to Viscomi is page design, and given the 'near-complete absence' of preliminary whole-page paper mock-ups extant, he can justify his claim that this is inaugurated on the copper.[23] Manuscripts, then, supply both material and metaphor, before being 'replace[d]' by 'print'.[24]

But print was not necessarily writing's destiny, even within Blake's lifetime. The advent of the printing press in mid-fifteenth-century Europe is now understood by scholars not to have effected an 'epistemic rupture', but an 'ongoing negotiation of meaning' between manuscript and print.[25] Practices such as scribal publication did not die out, but persisted, prompting us to revisit the supposition that manuscripts, while unprinted, are also necessarily unpublished. More heavily revised and miscellaneous writing of Blake's, such as in the *Notebook*, has been assumed to be private, and even fair or 'largely fair' copies, such as the *Pickering* and

Island manuscripts, may be viewed dimly for their assumed circumscription of audience.[26] Yet as Harold Love has argued, in late seventeenth-century Britain, scribal publication was 'more than the chrysalis stage of an intended print publication'. Scribal transmission meant (in a weak sense) that handwritten texts could move beyond private possession, and even (in a strong sense) become publicly available.[27] Such scribal practices persisted into the eighteenth century and beyond, as important studies by Margaret Ezell, H. J. Jackson, Michelle Levy, Ann Blair, David Allan, and Tessa Whitehouse have shown.

To situate Blake in such scribal contexts should therefore be unremarkable – and we need not be diverted by any lament about his failure to reach a contemporary audience. Letters, for example, especially letters to patrons, were still in Blake's lifetime '[a form] of "social commerce"'.[28] They might have multiple authors (as Hayley's hand shares space with Flaxman's or Blake's in letters of October 1801), and multiple addressees (as Blake answers verses sent by Butts with verses to both him and his wife, Eliza, in October 1800). They might also circulate beyond this (as Ozias Humphry forwards Blake's carefully drafted, gilt-edged manuscript description of his 'Design of the Last Judgment' to the Earl of Buchan in January 1808, or as Cromek transcribes Blake's 'dedication' to the *Grave* in a letter of April 1807 to James Montgomery, warning him not to copy it in turn).[29] It was equally common in a period when 'reading was more often than not a *social* activity' for friends to exchange annotated books, and indeed for annotators to write with such an audience in mind (marginalia were more widely published in the periodical press only from the early nineteenth century).[30] In some of his earliest annotations, to J. C. Lavater's *Aphorisms on Man* (Huntington Library, 1788), Blake clearly responds to the author's invitation to 'interline' and 'mark' his printed text, 'then shew your copy to whom you please' – the book is marked by notes in other hands, albeit of uncertain provenance (E 583, 883). There are also clear signs of annotation as shared experience, or anticipated exhibition, in others of Blake's notes, including those he made in Robinson's copy of Wordsworth's *Poems* (1815) (*BB* 701) – as indeed there are in one of the Wordsworth family commonplace books (The Wordsworth Trust, DCMS 26), in which appear extracts from many writers transcribed in various hands, including four of Blake's poems copied by William and Mary from Malkin's *Memoirs* (1806).[31]

If at the time Blake was writing there was a border between manuscript and print, then, it was not one that need be crossed once and for all, and indeed not one that could be crossed only one way. The early modern codex was a flexible form, jointly occupied by the written hand and type.[32] Even at the close of the eighteenth century, print continued to invite, or incite, handwritten script, most evidently in practices of note-taking, whether within the covers of printed books or separately.[33] Blake's marginalia, for example, are enabled by the conventions of the printed codex even as they also 'challenge' them, as for example Blake responds to both the function and the blank spaces left on the printed title-page when he inserts his own name above Sir Joshua's in Reynolds's *Works* (British Library, 1798), asserting a rival authorship ('This is the opinion of Will Blake', E 635).[34] Material could also work its way out of print, and into manuscript. Take the printed text of Young's *Night Thoughts*, which became a support for Blake's water-coloured drawings as he illustrated the poem, and the printed proofs of Blake's engravings for *Night Thoughts*, which were transformed in turn into pages of the manuscript *VALA / The Four Zoas*.[35] Paper was precious, of course, especially as it rose in cost from the 1780s and 1790s.[36] Frugality and periods of poverty made Blake a prolific recycler, reclaiming 'scrap paper', and repurposing proofs from a whole host of works.[37] Such recycling undoubtedly has a certain accidentality, and its effects may be felicitous. Yet the patterns that emerge deserve to be looked at more carefully if we are ever to attend to what Paul Mann called 'the ontology of [. . .] manuscript' – to manuscript as it is, rather than as it might have been.[38]

Even as scribal cultures persisted, manuscripts – within Blake's lifetime, and with increasing intensity – were credited with a peculiar power. This owes much to changing understandings of drawing and the sketch, which since the Renaissance (paradigmatically in Giorgio Vasari's *Lives of the Most Eminent Painters, Sculptors, and Architects*) had been said to reveal more of an artist's skill than a more finished painting. In eighteenth-century Britain, the 'unfinished sketc[h]' was supposed by both Burke's aesthetics of sublimity, and Gilpin's, of the picturesque, to promise 'something more' to the imagination, thus giving pleasure 'beyond the best finishing'.[39] The revelatory potential attributed to drawings – their potential to reveal an artist's skill, their mind, their working methods – thus carried an affective charge. Likewise, the apparent unfinishedness or conditionality of all but the neatest of writers' manuscripts, their processual quality, their ostensible disclosures, tended from the eighteenth century (and still do tend) to be understood to arouse a range of feelings that print did not – not just pleasure, but prurience or discomfort. '[I]nterlined, corrected', and '[in]determinate' in its 'written hand', the manuscript of Milton's 'Lycidas' seemed 'repugnant' to Charles Lamb when he saw it in a Cambridge library. 'Print settles' such indeterminacy, Lamb decided, resolving 'never [to] go into the work shop of any great artist again'.[40] By contrast, A. C. Swinburne was initially drawn to Blake by 'the great mass of more disorderly writing' in the *Notebook*, 'the mass of floating verse and prose [in which] there is absolutely no hint of order whatever', which nonetheless was 'the great source and treasure-house' of most of Blake's 'fresh[est]' verse and prose, and 'among the most important relics left of Blake'.[41] For all his interest in the *Notebook*'s 'short sweet songs', Swinburne is no anthologist – no purist, and no bowdleriser. He repeatedly refers to the materiality of the manuscript, its 'close rough handwriting', its 'mass of huddled notes jotted down in a series of hints, on stray sides and corners of leaves, crammed into holes and byways out of sight or reach'.[42] Formless such a floating mass of materials may be, but as some of Swinburne's metaphors imply – transporting us from the material assemblage of the *Notebook* to the metaphysics of versification – such formlessness could be generative of a lyric verse, like Blake's, that 'pauses and musters and falls always as a wave does, with the same patience of gathering form'.[43]

Swinburne also relishes what the clutter of the Notebook's few more mundane entries reveal of the Blakes' 'daily habit of life and tone of thought': their dabbling in bibliomancy, for instance, when one Sunday in August 1807 'My Wife was told by a Spirit to look for her fortune by opening by chance a book which she had in her hand it was Bysshes Art of Poetry [...] I was so well pleased with her Luck that I thought I would try my Own' (E 696).[44] In some ways, this entry is atypical of Blake's note-taking: not only does he rarely date *Notebook* entries, but he also seems to have seldom transcribed works by other writers, as here he transcribes extracts from Behn and Dryden. But in other ways, the entry is entirely characteristic: of Blake, in its embrace of felicity and enthusiasm (bibliomancy was associated at the time with Methodist and Moravian communities), and of the notebook as a genre, hospitable to traditions of commonplacing (preserving favoured parts of texts; manufacturing a personal copy).[45] However revelatory it may be to learn about them, Blake's habits are neither singular nor idiosyncratic, but rooted in shared cultural practices.

The same can be said of his annotations, whose liveliness is witness to the kind of critical reading advocated within Dissenting culture. 'Deal freely with every Author you read', writes Isaac Watts, in *The Improvement of the Mind* (1741), 'mark the Faults or Defects, and endeavour to do it better [...] in the Margin of your Book'.[46] But to Gilchrist, reading in the

1860s, Blake's annotations to Lavater facilitate a more intimate access: 'To me they seem mentally physiognomic [...]. We, as through a casually open window, glance into the artist's room, and see him meditating at his work, graver in hand' (Gilchrist 67).[47] Gilchrist's remark is in line with Lavater's own, influential, argument that 'hand-writings [...] are so many expressions, so many emanations, of the character of the Writer', something 'not amenable to disguise or falsification'.[48] Lavater's ideas fed into the appetite for autograph-collecting, and correlative fetishisation of the written hand – whether in manuscript, or engraved reproduction – that swept Europe from early modernity, peaking in the nineteenth century.[49] Autographs functioned like relics (recalling Swinburne's vocabulary), conducting historical readers back to a process of inscription forever new. As one commentator put it in 1829: 'To hold in our hand the lines which some celebrated man has written, is to stand with him on the same point of time, to be present with him while he thinks and counsels, and this relic which is left of his thoughts and feelings, makes them as visible to us now, as they were five hundred years ago'.[50]

Blake himself professed to be sceptical about autographs, which tended to be written 'helter skelter like a hog upon a rope or a Man who walks without Considering [what] he shall run against'. This, he fancies, was why an attentive artist might be incapable of writing one. But write one he did, in William Upcott's album *Reliques of My Contemporaries* (1820–33), producing something that was 'in some measure', he thought, '[a Work] of Art & not of Nature or Chance' (E 698). Blake's autograph gathers together many of the threads drawn out in this chapter. It shows the sociability of manuscript culture, putting Blake in the 'good Company' of George Cruikshank, William Hone, John Thelwall, Sydney Morgan, John Clare, Amelia Opie, Charles Lamb, Coleridge, and many other signatories (E 698).[51] It testifies to a fascination with the written hand that helped later in the century to foster the recuperative interest of Swinburne, Gilchrist, and the Rossettis. It also, finally, shows Blake's twofold understanding of composition as both craft and mental activity, manifest alike in his theory and practice.[52] Even the 'firm, determinate outline, struck at once' might emerge from the process of its execution ('to invent is to find', writes Blake's artist friend Henry Fuseli: 'to find something presupposes its existence somewhere, implicitly or explicitly, scattered or in a mass') (E 693).[53] Widely dispersed, sometimes thick with revision, subject to subsequent thoughts and readings as well as first ones: Blake's manuscripts are a central and defining example of his inventive achievement.

Notes

1. *BR* 435; W. M. Rossetti, *Some Reminiscences of William Michael Rossetti*, 2 vols. (London: Brown Langham & Co, 1906), II, 307; A. Gilchrist to W. M. Rossetti, letter of 9 November 1862, in *Anne Gilchrist: Her Life and Writings*, ed. H. H. Gilchrist, pref. note by W. M. Rossetti (London: T. Fisher Unwin, 1887), p. 129. On the possible extent of Blake's composition in manuscript, see *BR* 435–6, 660, 680.
2. R. N. Essick, *Blake and the Language of Adam* (Oxford: Clarendon Press, 1989), p. 170; Viscomi 25, 385 n. 2.
3. M. Crosby, 'Introduction', in *HLQ, Special issue: William Blake's Manuscripts*, ed. Crosby, 80.3 (2017), 361–4 (pp. 362–3).
4. Still intact are the so-called 'Blake-Varley Sketchbook' (1819) and a sketchbook containing drawings for *Job* (1823); others recorded are now disbanded or missing (see *BB* 630 on Virgil; Butlin 692 on Varley; Gilchrist 332 and *BR* 401 on Dante; and *BR* 416). See further n. 18 below, on notebooks.
5. On the number of letters extant, note Crosby, 'Introduction', p. 362.
6. On Blake's annotated books, see *BB* Part V; E 670 (cf. *BB* 702); and P. J. Cardinale and J. R. Cardinale, 'A Newly Discovered Blake Book: William Blake's Copy of Thomas Taylor's *The Mystical Initiations; or, Hymns of Orpheus* (Bodleian Library; 1787)', *Blake / An Illustrated Quarterly*, 44.3 (2010–11), 84–102. Blake himself identifies three further sets of annotations not now extant (E 660).
7. See D. V. Erdman (ed.), with D. K. Moore, *The Notebook of William Blake: A Photographic and Typographic Facsimile* (Oxford: Clarendon Press, 1973), p. 13. References to pages in the *Notebook* (N) will henceforth appear in the main text.
8. H. J. Jackson, *Marginalia: Readers Writing in Books* (New Haven, CN: Yale University Press, 2001), p. 27, and pp. 18–43, passim. Blake's annotation 'Paine has not attacked Christianity. Watson has defended Antichrist' at the head of the Preface recto of Watson's *Apology for the Bible* (Huntington Library; 1797), for instance, indicts the whole book, rather than responding merely to the underlined words 'christian states', as Erdman's text suggests (E 612).
9. See M. Crosby and R. N. Essick, 'Commentary by the Editors', in *Genesis: William Blake's Last Illuminated Work* (San Marino, CA: Huntington Library, 2012), pp. 23–46.
10. A. C. Swinburne, *William Blake: A Critical Essay* (London: J. C. Hotten, 1868), p. 112. On the title's link to *For Children: The Gates of Paradise* (1793) see ibid., p. 182n., and Erdman, *Notebook*, p. 7.
11. M. Phillips, 'Introduction', in *An Island in the Moon: A Facsimile of the Manuscript* (Cambridge: Cambridge University Press, 1987), pp. 3–26 (pp. 3–4).
12. See G. E. Bentley, Jr, 'Introduction', in *Tiriel* (Oxford: Clarendon Press, 1967), pp. 1–55 (esp. pp. 20–1, 25–6).

13. W. Blake, *Vala or The Four Zoas*, ed. G. E. Bentley, Jr (Oxford: Clarendon, 1963), pp. 193, 197; C. T. Magno and D. V. Erdman, 'Introduction', in *The Four Zoas* (Lewisburgh: Bucknell University Press; London and Toronto: Associated University Presses, 1987), pp. 13–21 (p. 14).
14. Phillips, *Island*, p. 6.
15. Blake's projected intentions for *VALA / The Four Zoas* have been much debated. Was it to have been engraved? (See Bentley, *Vala*, p. 157.) Was its text to have been set in type? (See P. Mann, 'Editing *The Four Zoas*', *Pacific Coast Philology*, 16.1 (1981), 49–56 (p. 51).) Or was it to have been fully realised as 'a unique Illuminated Manuscript? (See D. V. Erdman, 'The Binding (et cetera) of Vala', Library, 5th series, 19 (1964[1968]), 112–29 (p. 125).)
16. See R. N. Essick, 'The Altering Eye: Blake's Vision in the *Tiriel* Designs', in *William Blake: Essays in Honour of Sir Geoffrey Keynes*, ed. M. D. Paley and M. Phillips (Oxford: Clarendon, 1973), pp. 50–65 (p. 50).
17. www.blakearchive.org/work/bb203; E 859. Note also the case Bentley makes for an alternative title, *The Ballads Manuscript*: see 'The Date of Blake's Pickering Manuscript or the Way of a Poet with Paper', Studies in Bibliography, 19 (1966), 232–43 (p. 243).
18. See Bentley, *Vala*, pp. 160, 191, on the 'notebook' paper used at pp. 143–4 of the *VALA/Four Zoas* manuscript, and Erdman, *Notebook*, p. 93, on smaller 'notebook' pages appended, pp. 117–20.
19. Erdman, *Notebook*, pp. 1–2.
20. See Bentley, *Vala*, p. 157; Viscomi 30; and M. Phillips, *William Blake: The Creation of the Songs: From Manuscript to Illuminated Printing* (London: British Library, 2000), p. 87.
21. Phillips, *William Blake*, p. 87.
22. Viscomi 29–30, 31. On the different movements of Blake's hand in engraving, etching, and drawing, see A. S. Gourlay, 'Blake Writes Backward', *HLQ*, 80.3 (2017), 403–21.
23. Viscomi 28, 30. Exceptions, as Viscomi acknowledges, are from *Thel*, and perhaps *America* and *Visions* (pp. 26–8).
24. Ibid., p. 385 n. 2.
25. L. Gitelman, *Always Already New: Media, History, and the Data of Culture* (Cambridge, MA and London: MIT Press, 2006), p. 6.
26. Phillips, *Island*, 6.
27. H. Love, *Scribal Publication in Seventeenth-Century England* (Oxford: Clarendon Press, 1993), pp. 35–6.
28. S. E. Whyman, *Sociability and Power in Late-Start England: The Cultural World of the Verneys, 1660–1720* (Oxford: Oxford University Press, 1999), p. 4; see also C. Brant, *Eighteenth-Century Letters and British Culture* (Basingstoke: Palgrave, 2006) on writers' '[play] with a public-private divide' (p. 52). On Blake's letters, see S. Haggarty, *Blake's Gifts: Poetry and the Politics of Exchange* (Cambridge: Cambridge University Press, 2010), esp. pp. 76–80.
29. G. Keynes (ed.), *Letters of William Blake: With Related Documents*, 3rd edn (Oxford: Clarendon, 1980), §34, §36, §25, §110, §101.

30. See Jackson, *Marginalia*, p. 65, and *Romantic Readers: The Evidence of Marginalia* (New Haven, CN: Yale University Press, 2005), pp. 156–7, 300.
31. See M. Moorman, 'Wordsworth's Commonplace Book', *Notes and Queries* (September 1957), 400–5, and the relevant page in the Wordsworth Trust online Collections Search.
32. See J. T. Knight, 'Organizing Manuscript and Print: From Compilatio to Compilation', in T. Johnston and M. Van Dussen (eds.), *The Medieval Manuscript Book: Cultural Approaches* (Cambridge: Cambridge University Press, 2015), pp. 77–95.
33. Jackson, *Romantic Readers*, p. 33.
34. See J. Snart, *The Torn Book: Unreading William Blake's Marginalia* (Selinsgrove, PA: Susquehanna University Press, 2006), pp. 21–2, 167.
35. See L. Calè, 'Blake, Young, and the Poetics of the Composite Page', *HLQ*, 80.3 (2017), 453–79.
36. D. C. Coleman, *The British Paper Industry, 1495–1860: A Study in Industrial Growth* (Oxford: Clarendon Press, 1958), pp. 174, 203; Bentley, 'The Date of Blake's Pickering Manuscript', p. 243.
37. See Blake to Maria Denman, 18 [14] March 1827, E 783.
38. P. Mann, 'The Final State of *The Four Zoas*', *BiQ*, 18.4 (Spring 1985), 204–15 (p. 208). His hopes are realised by such fine readings as Calè's, which shows how the proof pages of *Night Thoughts* 'inscribe in the [*VALA/Four Zoas*] manuscript the memory and alternative possibilities of their earlier book articulations' ('Blake, Young', p. 466).
39. E. Burke, *A Philosophical Enquiry into the Origin of Our Ideas of the Sublime and Beautiful* (London: 1757), §XIII, 'Infinity in Pleasing Objects', p. 59; see also Viscomi 33.
40. C. Lamb, 'Oxford at the Vacation', *London Magazine* (October 1820), 365–9.
41. Swinburne, *William Blake*, pp. 112, 130–1. On Swinburne's initial exposure to Blake, see R. Rooksby, *A. C. Swinburne: A Poet's Life* (Aldershot: Scolar Press, 1997), p. 60.
42. Swinburne, *William Blake*, pp. 132, 152n., 160.
43. Ibid., p. 134. On the 'fluid and formless mass' of Swinburne's sea, 'given structure by the rhythms of the waves', see J. A. Walsh, '"Quivering Web of Living Thought": Conceptual Networks in Swinburne's Songs of the Springtides', in *A. C. Swinburne and the Singing Word: New Perspectives on the Mature Work*, ed. Y. Levin (Farnham: Ashgate, 2010), pp. 29–54 (p. 51).
44. Swinburne, *William Blake*, pp. 127, 130–1n.
45. See D. Allan, *Commonplace Books and Reading in Georgian England* (Cambridge: Cambridge University Press, 2010), pp. 255, 258.
46. I. Watts, *The Improvement of the Mind*, 2nd edn (London, 1741), pp. 63–4.
47. Gilchrist's choice of the word 'graver' (an engraver's tool) here summons the chirographic aspect of the illuminated books even as it is embedded in a discussion of Blake's handwritten marginalia. On the double work of writing, both 'by the Hand' and 'by a Graving or Carving Tool, or Instrument', see D. Defoe, *An Essay upon Literature* (1726), cited and

discussed by A. Douglas, *Work in Hand: Script, Print, and Writing, 1690–1840* (Oxford: Oxford University Press, 2017), p. 5 and passim.
48. J. C. Lavater, 'Of Design, Colouring, and Writing', in *Essays on Physiognomy*, trans. H. Hunter, 3 vols. (London: 1789), III, 253–62 (p. 258); Douglas, *Work in Hand*, p. 29.
49. See A. N. L. Munby, *The Cult of the Autograph Letter in England* (London: Athlone Press, 1962).
50. Review of J. G. Nichols, *Autographs of Royal, Noble, Learned, and Remarkable Personages* (1829), *Monthly Review* (October 1829), 212–21 (pp. 213–14).
51. See D. V. Erdman, 'Reliques of the Contemporaries of William Upcott, "Emperor of Autographs"', *Bulletin of the New York Public Library*, 64.11 (November 1960), 581–7.
52. On activity of mind and hand, see Haggarty, *Blake's Gifts*, Ch. 4. See also L. Gurton-Wachter's brilliant reading of Blakean 'counter-attention' in *Watchwords: Romanticism and the Poetics of Attention* (Stanford, CA: Stanford University Press, 2016), p. 52 and passim.
53. H. Fuseli, *Lectures on Painting* (1801), cited by Viscomi 40. Viscomi's discussion of drawing (Ch. 4) is exemplary and foundational for any study of Blake's manuscripts.

CHAPTER 6

Book Illustration

Luisa Calè

Blake's career as a poet and artist coincides with the emergence of 'illustration'. Since the end of perpetual copyright in 1774, engravings became a common bibliographic element of cheap reprints of British poets.[1] Before the current visual meaning of 'illustration' was crystallised in the 1810s (as 'pictorial elucidation', whether of 'any subject', or 'a literary or scientific article, book, etc.'), it was recorded in book titles through terms such as 'embellished with superb engravings', 'etchings', or 'figures'.[2] This terminology emphasises the composite nature of the book, pointing to the separate processes involved in producing different book parts: illustrations were pulled in different printing workshops and added to the book later. Blake's corpus challenges this division of labour, its distinctions between the classical writer and the modern artist, and between invention and reproduction.

In his 1793 prospectus 'To the Public', Blake advocated relief etching as a 'method of Printing both Letter-press and Engraving in a style more ornamental, uniform, and grand, than any before discovered, [...] a method of Printing which combines the Painter and the Poet' (E 692–3). To distinguish his productions from reproductive engravings and emphasise the connection between writing, miniature, and the medieval aesthetic of the illuminated manuscript, Blake called this method 'illuminated printing'. Blake's prospectus lists each item by title, genre ('a prophecy', 'a poem', *Songs*), mode of production, and size. His works 'in illuminated printing' are entered 'with' the number of designs; yet, unlike commercial illustrated editions, this bibliographic detail does not identify something superadded to the letterpress, for the number of 'designs' correspond to the number of pages; in other words, the illuminated books are identified as visual productions and the texts subsumed under the designs. The corpus of the painter and poet is unified through the engraver's book productions, sandwiched between two subjects presented as 'Historical Engraving', and the final two items tagged 'a small book of Engravings' (E 693). However, in his commissions to illustrate the works of other poets Blake moved away from the uniform poetics of illuminated printing. This chapter explores Blake's approaches to book illustration, focusing on his visual responses to Edward Young's *Night Thoughts* (1796–7), Robert Blair's *The Grave* (1808), *The Book of Job* (1805–6, 1821–7), and Dante's *Commedia* (1824–7).

Blake's illustrations to Edward Young's *Night Thoughts* (1796–7) and Thomas Gray's *Poems* (1798) emphasise the division of labour between writer, artist, and publisher through a book composite that staged the separation of media and modes of production. In early 1796 the publisher Richard Edwards disbound the pages of first and second editions of Young's *Night Thoughts* (1742–5), and 'inserted the letterpress close cut' into large sheets of paper, so that Blake could illustrate the wide margins in watercolours.[3] Blake illustrated Young's nine Nights page by page, producing 537 watercolours around the letterpress. Out of his two volumes of watercolours, forty-three designs were chosen to be engraved in an edition of the first four Nights published by Edwards in 1797.[4] The watercolour volumes can be considered as interim objects comparable to the altered books used in preparing a new edition of a work, where expanded margins allowed authors and editors more space to write around the text. Collectors also used such extended pages to obtain more space on which to paste prints, drawings, watercolours, and other extraneous materials, hence the term 'extra-illustration'. Although Blake's *Night Thoughts* watercolours share the process of customising books with the practice of extra-illustration, they are quite different because of their consistent intervention on each page and the uniform choice of medium. Blake's process of illustration emphasises the tension between text and image. Some of his designs enhance the volumetric effects of the page by placing sleeping figures on top of the text panel or drawing decorative frames around it that call attention to the point where the page of letterpress meets the illustrated margin. However, other compositions fail to accommodate the text and seem to compete for the centre of the page. In such cases, Young's text seems to have been superadded: the text panels seem to have been cut through the designs to insert the letterpress in the middle of Blake's designs, and the illustration reclaims primacy over the words. However, the pages of letterpress inserted into the centre of the designs also remind the reader that a book has been dismantled in order to recycle its pages and cover the holes in the book of watercolours. By contrast, in the 1797 edition the text seems superimposed on the engraving, and the reader is encouraged to imagine the composition continuing beneath the page of letterpress.

Blake's illustrations to Young are an act of parody in the literal sense of a composition that is placed next to Young's poem. Sometimes literalising Young's allegories, sometimes extending or amplifying his metaphors and similes into actions and episodes, Blake creates a cast of characters out of Young's abstractions and produces a counter-poem in the margin of the page. Asterisks penciled in the margins of the text identify the illustration's textual source. For instance, in Night III Young identifies night as his poetic domain, inviting bards to take the sun for themselves, inebriated by a 'wilderness of joy; / Where *Sense* runs Savage, broke from *Reason*'s chain' (p. 46; Fig. 6.1). Blake's surround illustration inverts the negative connotations of Young's text: joy is embodied in the figure of a naked woman advancing with arms held up; her unchained anklet suggests that she stands for emancipation, hailing the reader to break loose from Reason's chain, associated with slavery. Hovering above her a personification of Night represented as a faceless blind figure with disproportionately big masculine hands lifts a dark mantle ready to capture and hide her in darkness. While the impending action evokes the rape of Proserpine, its meaning is inverted. Blake's personification of sensual joy will not be suppressed. Against Young's call to reject pleasure, her body can transform the dark world under the mantle of Night into an implausibly radiant realm of light. This arresting image offers an alternative to Young's Miltonic poetics of blindness.

How to represent literary texts in visual form was a pressing problem for eighteenth-century theorists, who contrasted painting, the art of placing bodies one next to the other in space, to writing, which represents the development of actions in time. Yet illustration complicates the distinction between verbal and visual media, as it embodies abstract notions of painting and poetry in the form of the book as a support for reading and viewing. As a tool for ordering and turning pages, the book has the potential to become a pre-cinematic medium. Blake experimented with the book's capacity to convey the impression of movement by illustrating a body represented in different moments of an action. In his illustrations to Young, the reader sees impending actions develop as the elongated figure of Time strides across a page opening and encircles the letterpress upon turning the page (pp. 25–6; see WBA, Copy 1, obj. 15–16). More conventional approaches to illustration involve selecting one action isolated in its pregnant moment; bringing together multiple scenes in one composition known as a poly-scenic narrative; or producing a series of illustrations.

Fig. 6.1: W. Blake, *Edward Young, Night Thoughts* [1797], *Copy 1: electronic edition*, Object 25, 2007, etching and engraving, William Blake Archive (Collection of R. N. Essick)

Blake's illustrations to Robert Blair's *The Grave*, from a watercolour drawing produced for Thomas Butts to the series of designs engraved by Luigi Schiavonetti for Robert Cromek's edition of *The Grave: A Poem. Illustrated by Twelve Etchings executed from Original Designs* (1808), present

Fig. 6.2: W. Blake, *The Descent of Man into the Vale of Death*, c. 1805, pen and grey ink and grey wash, with watercolour, © The Trustees of the British Museum, London

different solutions to the problem of visual narrative. In the watercolour drawing, Blair's metaphor of life as a journey offers the narrative device to impart linear form on a miscellany of episodes, as a downward path subsumes the polyscenic composition of episodes set in caves opening out on the sides (Fig. 6.2). No lateral scenes are found in the corresponding illustration published in the 1808 volume, where some of those scenes are developed into independent illustrations (p. 21; see WBA Copy 1, obj. 8). A page number on the top right margin of the plate identifies the facing page of letterpress, and a short quotation is added in the caption at the bottom: ''Tis here we all meet!' Instead of being anchored to the text, the illustration reveals the extent of Blake's 'invention': no steps or caves can be found in the facing letterpress, which focuses on 'this world / [...] a spacious burial-field unwall'd, / Strew'd with Death's spoils, the spoils of animals.'[5] The short title *The Valley of Death* inscribed as a caption under the etching alludes to Psalms 23:4, a source of Blake's invention also not found in Blair's text; the longer title *The Descent of Man in the Vale of Death* listed in the paratext adds the downward trajectory.[6] These added layers reveal the creative work of titling in reinventing a subject or revealing its field of allusions.

Moving from the polyscenic watercolour to the illustrated edition of Blair's poem, Blake isolates key turns or episodes in the text as cues for visual inventions. Opening the volume the reader finds to the left of the first page a frontal image, with a caption including the title *Christ Descending into the Grave* and lines from the facing text: 'Eternal King! Whose potent Arm sustains / the Keys of Hell and Death' (Fig. 6.3). The exclamation mark turns the identifying words into an invocation, although the authorial element that precedes them in the text ('Thy succours I implore') is left out, thus repurposing the words to fit the composition.[7] Its perspective from below places the reader among the damned in the flames of hell. The position at the beginning of the poem suggests that Christ, whose eyes are averted sideways, needs to be invoked by the reader: his arms thrust open and slightly forward, bearing the keys of salvation, offer proleptic hope and a way up towards the illuminated space behind him. Since the image faces the beginning of the poem at the beginning of the book, we can take this illuminated space as an allegory for the space of reading. Representing the reader as *Viator* is a frequent device in Blake's works from *Night Thoughts* to *Jerusalem*, where the traveller is seen from behind entering a door leading to a dark interior. Here we are invited to think of the reading experience as an exit to the journey of life, prepared by the deathbed scenes, which multiply the one found in the polyscenic watercolour into a series of illustrations placed in interiors punctuating the reading experience.

Other ways of translating poetic actions in visual form are exemplified by Blake's illustrations to Job, a repeated effort that produced two series of watercolours, the Butts set (*c.* 1805–6, 1821–7) and the Linnell set (1821); reduced versions in a sketchbook (1823); and finally *Illustrations of the Book of Job, in Twenty-one Plates, Invented and Engraved by William Blake* (1826). Blake's Job combines experiments in the episodic rhythm of the series with polyscenic compositions that capture different temporal layers within individual plates. The first and last plates share the setting, characters, and broad composition, so they can be read as a pair. The viewer is

Fig. 6.3: W. Blake, *Christ Descending into the Grave*, 1808, in Robert Blair, *The Grave: electronic edition*, Object 3, 2007, etching and engraving, William Blake Archive

encouraged to apply the logic of before and after and infer the action occurring between the point of time captured by each plate, noticing the changes that visually sum up the narrative from beginning to end. In the fourth illustration, a messenger is fast approaching Job and his wife seated in the foreground, while a smaller messenger can be seen approaching

Fig. 6.4: W. Blake, *The Messengers Tell Job of His Misfortunes*, 1823–6, in *Illustrations of the Book of Job: electronic edition*, Object 6, 2002, intaglio engraving, William Blake Archive (Collection of R. N. Essick)

in the background (Fig. 6.4). These messengers seem to be different instantiations of the same figure captured in different moments of the same action, while perspective provides a structure that conveys the temporal arc of the story from the past foreshortened in the background to the present moment at the centre. However, the text inscribed under the 1826 engraving contradicts this visual impression. The first line, presented in larger font, reads 'And I only am escaped alone to tell thee' (Job 1:15); below it in smaller font Blake excerpts the subsequent line 'while he *was* yet speaking / there came also another' (Job 1:16). The text added around the illustration clarifies that the two figures represent different messengers and perspective is used to arrange two actions in the same illustration. What the first messenger has to say is written in yet smaller font above the illustration. In the Job plates, Blake inverts the page layout explored in the Young illustrations, where the design encircles a rectangle of letterpress. Here the composition of text and image on the page is shaped by the visual logic of the engraver. The expectation of uniform lines of letterpress arranged in a rectangular panel is subverted by the variation in font size, irregular spacing, and curved lines as the text is broken up into captions arranged around the illustration, turned into elements of design. The reader's eye is attracted to the dark mass of the illustration at the centre of the page, then invited to read the line beneath the image first, and probably follow down the page, before turning back up to the top. Blake's visual syntax breaks linear habits of reading.

In *Illustrations of the Book of Job*, biblical excerpts and additional scenes from different biblical sources are used to illustrate the actions presented in the engravings in the centre of the page, while sentences from the text of Job are arranged in new sequences interspersed with quotations from other books of the Bible. This practice of composition evokes biblical exegesis engaged in reading the life of Jesus combining sentences taken from different books of the Gospels, or allegorical reading practices training the reader to interpret Old Testament episodes as foreshadowing events in the New Testament. Blake's illustrations translate these reading practices into adventurous polyscenic compositions. Consider plate 14 (Fig. 6.5), a composition that divides the engraving into three parts with a Urizenic image of God the father as master of the elements in the centre, seated on a cloud-shaped frame, marking the bound of the horizon above Job and his family. The Lord's head is inscribed in the Sun and above him the reader can visualise the time 'When the morning Stars sang together, & all the Sons of God shouted for joy' (Job 38:7). The Lord's outstretched arms structure the composition, providing two more partitions for additional scenes, and pointing to a further layer of narrative outside the main composition. In the framing border the story of the days of creation is presented in

Fig. 6.5: W. Blake, *When the Morning Stars Sang Together*, 1823–6, in *Illustrations of the Book of Job: electronic edition*, Object 16, 2002, intaglio engraving, William Blake Archive (Collection of R. N. Essick)

roundel illustrations and excerpts from Genesis. These roundels evoke the Introduction to *Songs of Innocence*, and the page layout of parallel Old and New Testament scenes in the *Bible Moralisée*.[8] This device is here used to convey elements in the speech of the Lord answering Job out of the whirlwind (featured in pl. 13; see WBA Copy 1, obj. 15), asking him where he was at the time of Creation. The outstretched arms posture returns in pl. 20 (WBA Copy 1, obj. 22), where Job takes on the Lord's Urizenic stance to point at miniaturised episodes of his story hanging on the walls around him, including a small version of the Lord answering Job in a whirlwind (pl. 13) placed right behind him to mark the lesson learned and the change undergone. From being the suffering subject of a hermeneutic drama, Job has mastered and appropriated the Lord's visionary power. It is his turn to frame the narrative.[9] In this powerful self-reflexive engraving, Blake recreates a classic polyscenic device, which consisted in the architectural arrangement of key moments in a story captured in pictures hung along the walls of a gallery or a church.

In the early eighteen hundreds, Blake produced series of watercolour illustrations without any textual reference. Chief among them are two series illustrating the *Paradise Lost* for Butts and Joseph Thomas (1807–8), and the Dante illustrations for John Linnell (1824–27), which he left unfinished at his death. Linnell gave Blake 'a folio volume of a hundred pages', in which he sketched 102 illustrations (Gilchrist 332). Unlike the typographical layout arranging the text at the centre of the page in the *Night Thoughts* watercolours, Blake's Dante has the horizontal layout of a 'book of drawings' (E 778). The literary source is limited to a notation of the relevant Canto in the corner of the page. Freed from the words on the facing page and the partitions of the book that shaped the encounter with Young and Blair, Blake has more scope to reinvent and rearrange Dante's inventions, revealing his interests through an uneven selection of subjects (seventy-two for Inferno, twenty for Purgatorio, ten for Paradiso). Illustrating Canto I of the Inferno, Blake frames the wood and the allegorical beasts as a picturesque margin in the foreground, and redirects the eye towards the dynamic blue-sky encounter with Virgil (WBA obj. 1). His political connotations as the apologist of the Roman empire, and the historical coordinates of Dante's writing are moved to Canto II, compressed in a powerful Urizenic portal framed by the temporal power of God and empire above and two captive giants on the sides (obj. 2; Fig. 6.6). This framing brings to view allusions to empire from a range of places in Dante's work to mark the oppressive bound of the horizon that the reader has to negotiate before entering the door to hell in Canto III (obj. 3). Metamorphosis and the boundaries of the human form provide the greatest artistic challenge in a series of eight illustrations dedicated to the punishment of thieves transformed into serpents and back in Inferno

Fig. 6.6: W. Blake, *The Mission of Virgil*, 1824–7, watercolour over pencil, pen and ink, and scratching out, Birmingham Museums and Art Gallery

xxiv–v (obj. 49–57). Blake's response to Dante's scenes of metamorphosis reveals the fundamental approach of the artist interested in literature as a testing ground for the possibilities and limits of visual invention.

Focus on the materiality of the book restores Blake's illustrations to a wider context of Romantic print culture. In addition to patterns of reiteration and reuse of iconographical motifs across illuminated books and commercial illustrations,[10] the alternative sequencing of full plate illustrations in the illuminated books has its correlative in the mobility of illustration within commercial editions even when page numbers prescribe an illustration's specific position facing a relevant page of text. An alternative sequence is proposed at the back of the 1808 edition of *The Grave*, where the designs are declared 'of themselves a most interesting Poem' (p. 33), suggesting they may be detached and enjoyed as a portfolio of prints. Alternatively, they can be repurposed as illustrations to other books, revealing additional or independent iconographies. Blake's illustrations to Blair and Job were inserted in extra-illustrated Bibles alongside reproductive engravings of the Old Masters and Romantic period print series.[11] Placed alongside reproductive engravings that miniaturised frescoes and historical paintings into the hand-held format that could be inserted into a book, Blake's illustrations connect writing to painting, and the order of books to the field of art.

Notes

1. W. St Clair, *The Reading Nation in the Romantic Period* (Cambridge: Cambridge University Press, 2004), p. 134; F. Bonnell, *The Most Disreputable Trade: Publishing the Classics of English Poetry 1765–1810* (Oxford: Oxford University Press, 2008). On the shifting semantics of 'illustration', see I. Haywood and S. Matthews, 'Romanticism and Illustration: Introduction', in Haywood and Matthews (eds.), *Romanticism and Illustration* (Cambridge: Cambridge University Press, forthcoming 2019).
2. 'illustration, n.', *OED Online*, Oxford University Press, June 2017, www.oed.com/view/Entry/91580
3. A. Flaxman, 16 March 1796, British Library, Flaxman Papers, Add. MS 39780, fol. 212r–v; L. Calè, 'Blake, Young, and the Poetics of the Composite Page', *Huntington Library Quarterly*, 80.3 (2017), 453–79. For the watercolours, see British Museum, Department of Prints and Drawings, 1929, 0713.1–270.
4. E. Young, *The Complaint, and the Consolation; or, Night Thoughts, by Edward Young* (London: Edwards, 1797). All Young references will be quoted from this edition, and page numbers entered in the text.
5. R. Blair, *The Grave: A Poem. Illustrated by Twelve Etchings Executed from Original Designs* (London, 1808), p. 21.

6. R. N. Essick and M. D. Paley, *Robert's Blair's* The Grave *Illustrated by William Blake: A Study with Facsimile* (London: Scolar, 1982), pp. 64, 62.
7. See Blair, *The Grave*, p. 1.
8. On the *Bible Moralisée* and the Introduction to *Songs of Innocence*, see M. Phillips, *William Blake: Apprentice and Master* (Oxford: Ashmolean, 2014), pp. III, 260.
9. H. Fish, *The Biblical Presence in Shakespeare, Milton, and Blake* (Oxford: Oxford University Press, 1999), p. 317; M. D. Paley, *The Traveller in the Evening: The Last Works of William Blake* (Oxford: Oxford University Press, 2003), pp. 256–8.
10. Consider *Death's Door*, from Blake's *America* (1793) to his illustration of Robert Blair's *The Grave* (1808), discussed in S. Makdisi, *William Blake and the Impossible History of the 1790s* (Chicago: University of Chicago Press, 2003), pp. 181–4.
11. Plates from Blake's Grave and Job illustrations extra-illustrated in the Kitto and Douai Bibles, now at the Huntington Library, are catalogued by R. N. Essick, *The Works of William Blake in the Huntington Collections: A Complete Catalogue* (San Marino, CA: Huntington Library, Art Collections, Botanical Gardens, 1985).

CHAPTER 7

Painting

Martin Myrone

Recent scholarship has ensured that we can consider Blake as a more completely visual artist than has often been the case in the past. The 'visual turn' in Blake studies has involved both focusing on the imagery he produced and seeing even the textual elements of his illuminated book as themselves visual. The different aspects of Blake's output as a visual artist, in watercolour, tempera painting, conventional print media, relief printing, and monotype, have not though been treated evenly. If the 1978 Tate exhibition offered a strong representation of temperas and watercolours (surely in part reflecting the final stages of the preparation of a magisterial catalogue raisonné by the show's curator, Martin Butlin), this emphasis on Blake as a kind of art-historical Old Master has not been followed through in exhibitions culture.[1] The most recent exhibitions, in London in 2001, Paris in 2009 and Oxford 2014, have focused productively on Blake's printmaking, with particular attention to the turbulent 1790s.[2]

This focus on Blake's printmaking might be said to match contemporary understanding of him as an artist and, to a degree, his self-perception. When on 8 October 1779 Blake had registered as a student at the Royal Academy's drawing schools, he elected to be designated as an 'engraver'.[3] If that statement reflected the reality of his training to that point, it may have also marked a sense of destiny.[4] Blake certainly went on to become well regarded as a professional engraver, and it is this guise, rather than as a painter or certainly as a poet, that he was usually known. In the diary of Joseph Farington he was 'Blake the Engraver' and when the poet William Hayley took up his cause in 1801, he referred to him as 'an excellent Enthusiastic creature [. . .] by profession an Engraver'.[5] As G. E. Bentley's carefully complied figures suggest, it was commercial printmaking which always provided the most dependable source of income for the artist, despite the patronage of a few individuals interested in his paintings and watercolours around the turn of the century (most significantly, the civil servant Thomas Butts).[6]

But Blake made repeated attempts to achieve recognition as a painter. He exhibited at the Royal Academy on six occasions between 1780 and 1808, a total of twelve paintings, mainly of biblical subjects. This may not be a prolific record of exhibition, but any one of these paintings could in principle have been seen by tens of thousands of people during the run of the exhibitions in the spring of those years, and most of his contemporaries from the Academy schools showed much less.[7] But the exhibitions were also sites of sometimes aggressive professional rivalry between artists.[8] Those working on a modest scale or in the medium of watercolour felt especially vulnerable to being overshadowed, leading to the creation of separate exhibiting societies. It was this situation that Blake alluded to when he complained in 1809: 'The execution of my Designs, being all in Water-colours (that is in Fresco), are regularly refused to be exhibited by the *Royal Academy*' ('[Advertisement of the Exhibition]', E 527).[9]

Like some other artists of the time, Blake sought to overcome these challenges by setting up his own one-man exhibition, although in his case in the rather unpromising setting of the upstairs rooms of his brother's haberdashery shop in Golden Square, Soho. The show included sixteen paintings, and was accompanied by quite a substantial *Descriptive Catalogue*.[10] For all the esoteric qualities of Blake's imagery, this was an attempt to gain public attention as a painter and, more than that, engage people's interest and reform their tastes. *The Bard, from Gray* (Tate) drew from the poet Thomas Gray, with a subject treated by other, far more conventionally minded artists such as Benjamin West; Blake's *Canterbury Pilgrims* (Pollok House, Glasgow) was in competition with a version of the same subject by Thomas Stothard. *The Spiritual Form of Nelson* and *The Spiritual Form of Pitt* (tempera on canvas; Tate Gallery, London) are something else, though (Figs. 7.1 and 7.2). These mind-bogglingly dense images represent these national heroes as, respectively, a Christ-like figure with a halo, and a classical athlete, each directing a gigantic monster of war. Nelson directs the actions of Leviathan, the massive serpent, Pitt of Behemoth, the monster who represents war on land. It may be possible to interpret these in entirely idiosyncratic terms, confirming our perception of Blake's eccentricity. But in combining allegorical and symbolic figures with an idealised rendering of a known individual in a cosmically abstracted setting, they are not so far removed from precisely contemporaneous efforts elaborately to memorialise Nelson and Pitt in stone in Westminster Abbey and the Guildhall. One could also recall Benjamin West's attempt to apotheosise Nelson in paint (Yale Center for British Art, New Haven), or even James Gillray's more

Fig. 7.1: W. Blake, *The Spiritual Form of Nelson Guiding Leviathan*, c. 1805–9, The Picture Art Collection/Alamy Stock Photo

phantasmagorical political satires from the time.[11] Given this context, it was not unreasonable of Blake to expect some public attention.

The most important picture in Blake's exhibition was *The Ancient Britons*, now lost, but apparently painted on an imposing scale with multiple figures larger than life, like the most ambitious of contemporary history paintings, such as those produced for John Boydell's 'Shakespeare Gallery' in the 1790s. The long catalogue entry that Blake produced about this picture is one of the clearest statements from the artist about how his images should be interpreted, but the sheer visual impact of the canvas can only be guessed at (see *Descriptive Catalogue*, E 542–5). Many years later the artist Seymour Kirkup recalled seeing the picture in the exhibition, and

Fig. 7.2: W. Blake, *The Spiritual Form of Pitt Guiding Behemoth*, c. 1805, The Picture Art Collection/Alamy Stock Photo

described it as 'too Greek', with the figures resembling classical sculptures. But he was full of admiration for the picture as a whole, noting 'There is a great propriety in its academic character, for the Britons went naked – I am not sure if he gave them a sort of bathing-drawer, to make them decent' (*BR* 289). If it had survived, our view of Blake as a painter would be quite different.

The exhibition was a dismal failure. A sole contemporary comment appeared in print from the art critic of *The Examiner*, Robert Hunt, which infamously dismissed the exhibits as the 'wild effusions of a distempered brain' (*BR* 283). It was in the context of these terrible disappointments that Blake wrote his most venomous statements about the state of the art, scribbling his wild accusations in the margins of his copy of Joshua Reynolds's *Discourses* and fulminating in the 'Public Address'. After 1809, Blake exhibited in a public show only once more, when, in 1812, his works were included in the annual exhibition of the Associated Painters in Water Colours. Blake submitted the *Pitt* and *Nelson* and the painting of Chaucer's pilgrims from the 1809 solo exhibition, but also 'Detached specimens of an original illuminated Poem, entitled "*Jerusalem the Emanation of the Giant Albion*"' (BR 312).[12]

The presence of proof plates from *Jerusalem* in the 1812 exhibition points to the equality Blake projected between the media of print and different painting techniques, especially clear in his routine use of the term 'fresco' to refer equally to water colour painting, colour printmaking, and tempera. Blake repeatedly put the medium of printmaking under pressure in ways which were intended to yield more painterly images. In 1795 Blake conceived his group of twelve 'large colour prints' on a uniform format, some inscribed with the word 'fresco', but all printed using a sort of monotype technique (printing from a tacky painted surface, creating textured, densely coloured surfaces).[13] In the case of the *Jerusalem* 'specimens' shown in 1812, Blake may have coloured his prints especially heavily to effect some degree of intentional deceit: '[p]erhaps', conjectures Robert N. Essick, 'the organizers [of the watercolour exhibition] did not even recognise that these were prints because of the thoroughness of the hand colouring.'[14]

What might be considered 'true' fresco meant painting with pigments onto a wet plaster surface and completing the painting with water-based paints as the surface dried, but the term was used to refer to all wall-paintings. It conjured associations with the heroic endeavours on a grand scale of the painters of the Renaissance, and the values of grandeur, intellectual mastery and technical perfection. As Reynolds had noted, 'The principal works of modern art are in *Fresco*, a mode of painting which excludes attention to minute elegancies: yet these works in Fresco, are the productions on which the fame of the greatest masters depends.'[15] It was generally understood, though, that the damp and cold climate combined with a lack of patronage meant that true fresco could never be practised successfully in Britain. There was, then, an apparent irony: the greatest achievements of art to be recommended to the students of the Academy were in a medium and on a scale that would never likely be achieved in Britain. Reynolds's solution was to present an idea of the 'Grand Manner' or 'Great Style' as consisting of an ethos, rather than a technique or in subject matter. The modern artist in Britain could emulate the great fresco painters by painting broad and ideal forms, but with a disciplined precision in drawing and technique, even if he was painting in oils, and even if he was painting a portrait or a scene from everyday life rather than noble allegory or complex narrative.

Blake follows Reynolds in principle, elevating 'fresco' as the supreme artistic medium, but also, idiosyncratically, in practice. He envisaged that he would paint his designs on a vast scale, on the walls of churches and public buildings. Of the Pitt and Nelson pictures, he wrote of his wish of 'having a national commission to execute these two Pictures on a scale that is suitable to the grandeur of the nation, who is the parent of his heroes, in high finished fresco, where the colours would be as pure and as permanent as precious stones though the figures were one hundred feet in height' (*Descriptive Catalogue*, E 531). In reality they were almost always on a small scale. Morton D. Paley suggests these can properly be considered as 'portable frescos', both modellos for never-to-be realised grand projects, and in effect surrogates for those projects.[16] The very density and intensity of Blake's individual painted or colour-printed designs often centred on a single figure but were nonetheless rich in allusion and imagery, registers of a form of over-investment, a desire to make these small pictures carry greater meaning and impact than their format might comfortably permit.[17]

The tempera paintings, and the heavily textured use of specially mixed printing inks or paints in the 'large colour prints', were an attempt to emulate the characteristic textures, and more importantly, the stringent technical restrictions, of fresco. While oil paint could be manipulated and reworked, entirely obscuring or transforming the original drawn design, the rhetoric surrounding Blake's use of 'fresco' was that each colour needed to be laid on purely, following precisely a linear design. Blake's use of the medium was fundamentally as a means of giving colour to tonal and linear designs executed in diluted ink or earth colours.[18] Importantly, he tended not to mix these colours on the palette, but applied them pure, using the whiteness of the paper to lend a sense of intensity and brightness to his transparent colours. Blake's method was aimed at ensuring the purity of individual colours and the primacy of the drawn design. Although watercolour painting itself was eschewed in high art theory, because of its associations with routinely commercial coloured prints and topographical landscapes and its use by amateurs and women, deployed in this way it could be interpreted as conforming to the esteemed productions of the fresco painters of the Renaissance.

Bentley has noted recently that while Blake's 'vocation was as a commercial engraver [. . .] [h]is avocation – and his passion – was as a painter in watercolours'.[19] Thus, in considering a topic somewhat marginalised in

Blake studies, we come to central questions about Blake, his identity, and his place in art history. When he exhibited at the Academy in 1800 (his tempera of the *Miracle of the Loaves and the Fishes*, Robert N. Essick Collection), he did so as an 'Honorary' exhibitor, a designation generally reserved for genteel individuals exhibiting for pleasure rather than seeking profit.[20] When he referred to himself as a painter in a letter of 1799, his words suggested that he undertook this work as a side-line, without the expectation of becoming professionally established: 'If I am a Painter it is not to be attributed to Seeking after' (Blake to Trusler, 23 August 1799, E 703). Noting to Hayley the news that his friend Jonathan Spilsbury had given up art, he wrote: 'I concieve that he may be a much better Painter if he practises secretly & for amusement.' Blake, seeking to pursue painting for the sake of (in his terms) 'True Art', but in the context of a market-driven culture, became a deeply conflicted figure (Blake to Hayley, 28 September 1804, E 755). If this interminable struggle between domineering market and struggling self is a sign of 'Romantic' culture, it also has present-day resonance. It is surely this aspect of Blake the painter, with his disposition to 'work like an artist', passionately, in the ambiguous spaces between public and private, leisure time and work hours, without any real hope of sustained material or critical reward, a manageable career structure or any promise of state support, which should speak to us most urgently now.[21]

Notes

1. M. Butlin, *William Blake* (London: Tate Gallery, 1978); M. Butlin, *The Paintings and Drawings of William Blake*, 2 vols. (New Haven and London: Yale University Press, 1981). On the presentation of Blake as an Old Master in the 1978 exhibition see D. Bindman, 'William Blake – an Exhibition and a Book', *The Burlington Magazine*, 120.903 (June 1978), 418–21.
2. R. Hamlyn and M. Phillips, *William Blake* (London: Tate Publishing, 2001); M. Phillips (ed.), *William Blake (1757–1827): Le génie visionnaire du romantisme anglais* (Paris: Paris musées, 2009); M. Phillips, *William Blake: Apprentice and Master* (Oxford: Ashmolean, 2014).
3. See A. Ward, '"Sr Joshua and His Gang": William Blake and the Royal Academy', *Huntington Library Quarterly*, 52.1 (Winter 1989), 75–95.
4. Among Blake's close contemporaries, for instance, William Bond registered as a student in sculpture though trained by Bartolozzi and going on to become established as a stipple-engraver; Robert Fagan, another pupil of Bartolozzi, registered as a painter (in which field he had some success living in Italy); Edward Dayes, though apprenticed to the mezzotint printmaker William Pether, registered as a painter.

5. K. Garlick and A. Macintyre (eds.), *The Diary of Joseph Farington*, 16 vols. (New Haven, CN, and London: Yale University Press, 1978), 11, 497; *BR* 104.
6. See G. E. Bentley, Jr, *William Blake in the Desolate Market* (Montreal and Kingston: McGill-Queen's University Press, 2014), p. 105, for a summary chart of lifetime earnings which shows that Blake's income from commercial engraving work far outweighed income from painting and illuminated printing. Only for a brief period (1800–9) did income from painting at all approach that from engraving (£460 compared to £640).
7. Ward calculated that the entire cohort of Blake's 'classmates', who also registered at the Schools on 8 October 1779, exhibited a total of twenty-five works between 1780 and 1785, mainly portraits and architectural designs, and only one literary picture, while Blake's seven exhibits from the same period were all on serious biblical and historical themes. See Ward, '"Sr Joshua and His Gang"', pp. 78, 89 n. 20.
8. On exhibitions culture see D. H. Solkin (ed.), *Art on the Line: The Royal Academy Exhibitions at Somerset House, 1780–1836* (New Haven, CN, and London: Yale University Press, 2001).
9. For the context see G. Smith, *The Emergence of the Professional Watercolourist: Contentions and Alliances in the Artistic Domain, 1760–1824* (Aldershot: Ashgate, 2002).
10. See T. Patenaude, '"The Glory of a Nation": Recovering William Blake's 1809 Exhibition', *The British Art Journal*, 4.1 (2003), 52–63. See also the papers published online in *Tate Papers*, 14 (Autumn 2010), www.tate.org.uk/research/publications/tate-papers/14
11. See M. Myrone (ed.), *Gothic Nightmares: Fuseli, Blake and the Romantic Imagination* (London: Tate Publishing, 2006), pp. 204–5.
12. See R. N. Essick, 'Blake's 1812 Exhibition', *Blake / An Illustrated Quarterly*, 27.2 (1993), 36–41.
13. N. Cahaner McManus and J. H. Townsend, 'The Large Colour Prints: Methods and Materials', in J. H. Townsend (ed.), *William Blake: The Painter at Work* (London: Tate Publishing, 2002), pp. 82–99.
14. Essick, 'Blake's 1812 Exhibition', p. 40.
15. J. Reynolds, *Discourses on Art*, ed. R. N. Wark (New Haven, CN, and London: Yale University Press, 1975), p. 81.
16. M. D. Paley, 'William Blake's "Portable Fresco"', *European Romantic Review*, 24 (2013), 271–7.
17. The over-investment in single-figure compositions is a more general characteristic of academically ambitious contemporary art in Britain and France, and this provides an under-explored context for Blake's distinctive picture-making. See T. Crow, *Emulation: David, Drouais, and Girodet in the Art of Revolutionary France*, rev. edn (New Haven, CN, and London: Yale University Press, 2006), and M. Myrone, *Bodybuilding: Reforming Masculinities in British Art, 1750–1810* (New Haven, CN, and London: Yale University Press, 2005). For a recent account, see also S. Caviglia, 'Life

Drawing and the Crisis of *Historia* in French Eighteenth-Century Painting', *Art History*, 39 (2016), 40–69.
18. N. Cahaner McManus and J. H. Townsend, 'Watercolour Methods', in Townsend (ed.), *William Blake: The Painter at Work*, pp. 61–79.
19. Bentley, *Desolate Market*, p. 45.
20. Bentley's assertion that this status question arose because of reforms at the Schools is not correct; these changes concerned attendance at the drawing schools, and did not influence the right to submit works for exhibition (see *BR* 89n.).
21. The phrase and the point outlined here derive from a reading of A. McRobbie's eye-opening *Be Creative: Making a Living in the New Culture Industries* (Cambridge: Polity, 2016).

CHAPTER 8

Early Reception

Sibylle Erle and Keri Davies

The accepted version of Blake's early reception is that before the publication of Alexander and Anne Gilchrist's *Life of William Blake: 'Pictor Ignotus'* (1863), Blake was known only as a book-illustrator, completing new editions of Edward Young's *Night Thoughts* (1797), Robert Blair's *The Grave* (1808), and *The Illustrations of the Book of Job* (1826). Opinion about Blake was influenced by Allan Cunningham's ambivalent evaluation in *Lives of the Most Eminent British Painters, Sculptors, and Architects* (1830–2): a pleasant person, an independent thinker, and quite mad. The received account resurfaces in comments by Hazlitt, Wordsworth, Coleridge, and Henry Crabb Robinson.[1] Another trend, which continued well into the twentieth century, is the notion that Blake as an enthusiast chiefly appealed to (male) Dissenters.[2] Already during his lifetime Blake had a following and particularly, as this chapter will show, a female as well as genteel audience.[3]

Most of the early female collectors were spinsters and women of independent means.[4] After assessing the sweep of Blake's early reputation more broadly, this chapter will focus on four early collectors of his works: Rebekah Bliss (1747–1819), a wealthy bibliophile linked to the 'polite dissent' of the Independent Chapel at Carey Street New Court, and the earliest Blake collector; Eliza Aders (1785–1857), the illegitimate daughter of the painter and mezzotint engraver John Raphael Smith (1751–1812); Sophia Chichester (1795–1847), the third wife of Colonel Chichester of Arlington Court; and Anne Gilchrist (1828–85), the widow of Alexander. We shall seek to contribute to the existing research on early collectors by teasing out their social situations as well as their intellectual and aesthetic motives for collecting Blake. The value of such cultural contexts is that they shed light on the perception of Blake as a spiritual guide in the context of particularly spiritual collections. As well as looking into Blake's personal connections with his early female collectors and their leanings towards mysticism and Swedenborgianism, this chapter will draw attention to the material interests of early collectors. It will embed the four case studies amid detail of other collectors.

The picture of Blake as an eccentric outsider has long since been revised, especially in work on Blake's early reception.[5] In tracing the provenance of Blake's works, Martin Butlin and G. E. Bentley Jr have identified most of the early collectors.[6] In the Appendix to *William Blake in the Desolate Market* (2014), Bentley has collected a long list of Blake enthusiasts, including the 693 subscribers to Robert Blair's *The Grave* (1808) and the forty-seven to *Illustrations of the Book of Job* (1826). There is no space in this chapter to discuss the circulation of Blake's works among male collectors. The most important collection was that of Thomas Butts who owned 'the largest Blake collection ever assembled'.[7] Also significant in the forming of Blake's early reputation would have been Blake's brother James, who offered his shop for the 1809 exhibition, George Cumberland (1754–1848), and 'The Ancients', Blake's disciples (including Frederick Tatham, Samuel Palmer, George Richmond, Edward Calvert, and by association, John Linnell). We do not know if William Beckford shared his copies but Isaac D'Israeli certainly showed off his Blakes to visitors (*BR* 328n.). If Thomas Butts (1757–1845) owned the majority of Blake's paintings, nevertheless there are some female collectors who owned paintings or drawings, though many of these early collectors cannot be identified beyond their names. Subscribers to Blair's *The Grave* include Mary Anne Schimmelpenninck (1778–1856), a member of the long-established Moravian community in Bristol. Blake's *Job* was purchased by Sarah Austin (1793–1867), a Unitarian.[8] Elizabeth Iremonger, another Unitarian, owned the *Songs* that introduced Robinson to Blake's poetry.[9] Euphrasia Fanny Haworth (1802–83), a spiritualist and Swedenborgian, and friend of Browning, owned copy M of *Thel* (*BB* 129). This evidence, which does not include the posthumous collectors who bought from Catherine Blake and Frederick Tatham, shows that the mission of the Gilchrists' *Life* to defend and rehabilitate Blake as 'pictor ignotus', or 'unknown painter', is built on a myth.

Rebekah Bliss owned two copies of the *Songs* as well as *For Children: The Gates of Paradise*, both a coloured and an uncoloured copy of Young's *Night Thoughts* (1797), and a copy of Blair's *The Grave* (1808).[10] Known for her Dissenting background, Bliss also took an interest in the materiality of Blake's works. She owned copy G of the *Songs*, one of the three surviving colour-printed copies, and showed it to Richard Twiss.[11] Rebekah's tastes for illuminated manuscripts meant that she collected Blake alongside expensively bound books or prints. She left her cousin, Ebenezer

Maitland, 'Sir Wm Hamiltons Roman and Grecian Antiquities', a publication of very great importance in the development of neoclassical design and Blake must have seen it, because the British Museum has two sheets of drawings by Blake which are careful copies of designs in this book. In view of the rarity of these volumes, their presence in Bliss's library represents strong evidence that William Blake knew Mrs Bliss and copied these designs from the book in her possession.[12]

Now to Eliza Aders, who owned a number of works by Blake, acquired directly from the poet-printer. Eliza married, possibly bigamously, her third husband, the wealthy German merchant and collector Charles (Karl) Aders, in Paris in 1820.[13] Eliza, who was an amateur miniature painter exhibiting her work at the Royal Academy in 1839 and 1841, was it seems the dominant partner in the collecting: she had the expertise, while her husband provided the finance.[14] The Aderses were friends with John Flaxman, Thomas Lawrence, Robinson, Wordsworth, Coleridge, and Lamb. Their home on 11 Euston Square in London was a magnet for artists because of its pioneering collection of late fifteenth- and early sixteenth-century German and Netherlandish religious paintings, including works then attributed to Hans Memling and Jan van Eyck, of which English audiences were still unaware. Their most prized possession, a copy of the Ghent altarpiece *The Adoration of the Lamb*, they were 'characteristically eager to show'.[15] Had Blake viewed the Aders's collection, it would have been as overwhelming to him as the Truchsessian Gallery had been a few years earlier.[16]

When Dorfman discusses the Aderses, she talks about Mrs Aders's salon, emphasising the opportunities there for viewing Blake's works.[17] Eliza was a beautiful and sociable person.[18] She knew Linnell, who visited with Blake who later sold her his *Songs* (copy AA).[19] Eliza also subscribed to *Job*.[20] Robinson, who first met Blake on 10 December 1825, the very day Blake delivered Eliza's *Songs*, brought with him prospective buyers of Blake's works, such as the German painter Jakob Götzenberger, and entertained Eliza's guests by reciting 'The Tyger'.[21] Robinson recorded: '[Blake] was shewn soon after he entered the room some compositions of Mrs. Aders' which he cordially praised And [sic] he brought with him an engraving of his Canterbury pilgrims for Aders.'[22] Robinson, whose 'William Blake, Künstler, Dichter und religiöser Schwärmer', published in Perthes's *Vaterländisches Museum* (1811), had introduced Blake to German readers, also introduced Blake's works to Wordsworth who read Blake's poetry in Malkin's *A Father's Memoirs of His Child* (1806).

Blake's personal connections with early collectors are important. Elizabeth Butts (1770–1851), wife of Thomas, owned a manuscript and may have employed Blake as a painting instructor.[23] Blake presented *Poetical Sketches* (1783) to his friends,[24] may have made Hayley's *Little Tom the Sailor* (1800) gratis for Widow Spicer, and gave a copy of Percy's *Reliques* (1765) to Mary Ann Linnell (1796–1865).[25] Devalle Varley, wife of John, owned various works, including plate 20 of *Marriage*.[26] Another salon Blake had contact with is, of course, that of Harriet Mathew (1743–1815), wife of the Rev. A. S. Mathew (1734–1824). The Mathews sponsored the publication of *Poetical Sketches* (1783) but are not known to have owned any Blakes.[27] The family were Swedenborgian sympathisers; their daughter, Harriet (1766–98), married Göran Ulrik Silfverhjelm (1762–1819), Swedenborg's great-nephew.[28] Thus Blake had Swedenborgian patrons from the very start of his artistic career. The first posthumous edition of Blake's *Songs of Innocence and of Experience* (1839) was issued by J. J. Garth Wilkinson, a Swedenborgian and homoeopath. Wilkinson borrowed the *Songs* (copy J) from Charles Augustus Tulk, another Swedenborgian, when preparing his edition.[29] Tulk was happy to lend; he also lent his copy to Coleridge in 1818. Tulk's wife Susannah herself owned plate 1 of *All Religions Are One* and *There Is No Natural Religion* (*BB* 82, 446). More Swedenborgian friendship and family relations can be traced to and through the Flaxman circle. Maria Denman (1766–1861), Flaxman's sister-in-law, owned *Songs* (copy O), which she later gave to Nancy Flaxman (1760?–1820), who also owned *Innocence* (copy D). The Swedenborgians, in short, owned a substantial number of early works, and Wilkinson could have had access to all of them.

Interest in 'mystical Blake' leads us to Colonel John Palmer Chichester (1769–1823), who owned *The Sea of Time and Space*, otherwise the Arlington Court Picture, a mysterious work apparently incorporating alchemical imagery (Butlin 803).[30] Writing about 'a possible association' between Blake and Chichester, Jacqueline E. M. Lathan suggests that it was most likely his much younger wife Sophia who asked for the painting to be purchased.[31] On Monday 8 May 1820, Linnell took Blake to visit the painter Henry Wyatt (1794–1840) and then on to see Lady Ford. It is possible that Sophia, her still unmarried daughter, might have been present to make the acquaintance of Mr Blake the visionary painter (*BR* 370). Sophia Chichester (née Ford) married in 1822 but was disinherited the following year. The painting, which dates from 1821, arrived at Arlington Court in 1823, the year of Colonel Chichester's death. While the Aderses collected Blake's works for their beauty and perhaps for the naturalism of the devotional topics which they so admired in early German and Dutch art,[32] it seems that Sophia Chichester was drawn in by Blake's mystical imagination. Latham argues that Sophia, like Blake, was disillusioned with the established church, emphasising her interest in mystical thinking and Swedenborg. Before her marriage, Sophia befriended James Pierrepont Greaves (1777–1842), a socialist and mystic, as well as John 'Zion' Ward (1781–1837), preacher and successor of the prophetess Joanna Southcott. Sophia also financially supported radical preachers, such as James 'Shepherd' Smith (1801–57), another millenarian, and Richard Carlile (1790–1843), a Paineite-turned-Christian agitator.[33]

We come finally to Anne Gilchrist, whose opinions of Blake diverge in some important respects from her better-known husband's. Anne married in 1851, one year before the first sale from the Butts collection, and lived next to the Carlyles in Chelsea until her husband's premature death in 1861. Having worked with her husband, Anne, a mother of four children, decided to finish the biography. In her memoir, edited and published by her son Herbert Harlakenden, Anne shows determination and scholarly acumen in her planning of the final stages of the book, which involved increased support from the Rossettis.[34] They agreed that the biography was 'practically completed, but not in every detail'.[35] However, when Anne writes to William Michael on 22 May 1862 it seems that she disagreed with her husband: 'I find blanks left in the MS. where should follow some brief description of *The Marriage of Heaven and Hell, The Book of Ahania, The Song of Los, Asia*, and *Africa*. The kind helpfulness and thoroughness with which you have hitherto met my requests makes me bold to ask that you would furnish me with a brief general description of each of these.'[36] Anne identified the biography's weak point, namely the lack of any substantial discussion of the prophetic books, remedied much later in Swinburne's *William Blake: A Critical Essay* (1868) (for more on which see Chapter 23).

Anne, no doubt, was an independent spirit and decided not to rely on the Rossettis. Trying to fill the gaps left for the prophetic books herself, she writes: 'And then to begin with, was the grand difficulty of how to get sight of these, some not even in the British Museum. At length after much letter writing, I got Mr. Monckton Milnes to lend me [...] his magnificent copies of some of these; but they were to be fetched and returned by hand, and only to be lent for a week.'[37] Monckton Milnes (Lord Houghton), who owned *Jerusalem* as well as the only surviving copy of *Ahania* but never published anything on Blake, was a generous lender who also showed his book collection during breakfast parties at Upper Brook Street.[38]

Swinburne, who used this collection and was left to his own devices, apologised for accidently taking the 'Blake MS. Book' with him. Swinburne also had access to Anne's copies of the illuminated books.[39] John Linnell, on the other hand, was not a happy lender. Anne did her best to avoid him.[40] She was aware too of 'Mrs Aders's collection', saying that she could not trace it. Charles Aders had been declared bankrupt on 31 December 1832.[41] Anne's own role as collector is emphasised by her creation of a Blake room at Brookbank; according to her memoir, Tennyson studied the large colour print *God Judging Adam* there in 1866; and when George Eliot stayed at the cottage in 1781 'a cloud of Blake-drawings and engravings graced the walls'.[42] Tennyson, whom Anne had sent a copy of the *Life*, visited while house-hunting and Eliot was permitted to rent the cottage with George Henry Lewis for several weeks so that she could finish *Middlemarch*.[43]

The bustle of collecting activity we have described in this chapter shows that Blake was not as 'unknown' as the Gilchrists would have it – an opinion, in fact, that may have been more Alexander's than Anne's. What many of Blake's early collectors had in common was a keen interest in Blake's working processes as well as affinities with mystical or Swedenborgian thinking. What stands out is that they most likely knew Blake personally and were, therefore, aware of the material condition of his works.

Notes

1. For comments on 'mad Blake' see M. Bottral (ed.), *William Blake, Songs of Innocence and of Experience: A Casebook* (London: Macmillan, 1970). Excerpts of Cunningham's commentary can be found, together with materials about Blake by B. H. Malkin, H. C. Robinson, J. T. Smith, and F. Tatham, in *BR* Appendix 1, 561–732.
2. See, for example, J. Mee, *Dangerous Enthusiasm: William Blake and the Culture of Radicalism in the 1790s* (Oxford: Clarendon Press, 1992).
3. A. Whitehead, '"Mrs Chetwynd & Her Brother" and "Mr. Chetwynd"', *Blake/An Illustrated Quarterly*, 42.2 (2008), 75–8.
4. K. Davies, '"My Little Cane Sofa and the Bust of Sappho": Elizabeth Iremonger and the Female World of Book-Collecting', in H. Bruder and T. Connolly (eds.), *Queer Blake* (Basingstoke: Palgrave, 2010), pp. 221–35.
5. See, for example, D. Dorfman, *Blake in the Nineteenth Century: His Reception as a Poet from Gilchrist to Yeats* (New Haven: Yale University Press, 1969), and C. Trodd, *Visions of Blake: William Blake in the Art World 1830–1930* (Liverpool: Liverpool University Press, 2012).

6. M. Butlin, *The Paintings and Drawings of William Blake*, 2 vols. (New Haven: Yale University Press, 1981); Bentley, *Blake Books*, and its *Supplement* (Oxford: Clarendon, 1995).
7. M. L. Johnson, 'Catalogue of Some of Blake's Pictures at "The Salterns": Captain Butts as Exhibitor, Litigator, and Co-Heir (with His Sister Blanche)', *University of Toronto Quarterly*, 80.4 (2011), p. 893.
8. B. Bryant, 'The Job Designs: A Documentary and Bibliographical Record', in D. Bindman (ed.), *William Blake's Illustrations of the Book of Job*, 2 vols. and 4 portfolios in 2 boxes (London: William Blake Trust, 1987), Text vol., p. 134.
9. G. E. Bentley, Jr, *William Blake in the Desolate Market* (Montreal and Kingston: McGill-Queen's University Press, 2014), p. 148.
10. K. Davies, 'Mrs. Bliss: A Blake Collector of 1794', in S. Clark and D. Worrall (eds.), *Blake in the Nineties* (New York: St Martin's, 1999), pp. 212–30.
11. Davies, 'Mrs. Bliss', pp. 214–15.
12. K. Davies, 'Rebekah Bliss: Collector of William Blake and Oriental books', in S. Clark and M. Suzuki (eds.), *The Reception of Blake in the Orient* (London and New York: Continuum, 2006), pp. 38–62 (pp. 41–2).
13. For Eliza's complicated marital history see Ed Pope's website: edpopehistory.co.uk/content/3-wives-3-husbands-living
14. See L. Campbell, *The Fifteenth Century Netherlandish Schools* (London: National Gallery, 1998), p. 12.
15. For the Aders's collection see M. D. Paley, *Samuel Taylor Coleridge and the Fine Arts* (Oxford: Oxford University Press, 2008), p. 87.
16. A. Blunt, 'Blake's Pictorial Imagination', *Journal of the Warburg and Courtauld Institutes*, 6 (1943), 190–212; M. D. Paley, 'The Art of "The Ancients"', *The Huntington Library Quarterly*, 52.1 (Winter 1989), 97–124.
17. Dorfman, *Blake in the Nineteenth Century*, pp. 18, 22, 52.
18. A.T. Story, *The Life of John Linnell*, 2 vols. (London: Richard Bentley and Son, 1892), I, 224.
19. Bentley, *Blake Books Supplement*, p. 127.
20. Bentley, *Desolate Market*, p. 108.
21. E. J. Morley (ed.), *Henry Crabb Robinson on Books and Their Writers*, 3 vols. (London: Dent, 1938), I, 324; Story, *Life of John Linnell*, I, 223.
22. H. C. Robinson, *Blake, Coleridge, Wordsworth, Lamb, Etc.*, ed. E. J. Morley (Manchester: Manchester University Press, 1922), p. 2.
23. Bentley, *Desolate Market*, p. 118. See also J. Viscomi, 'William Blake's "The Phoenix / to Mrs Butts" Redux', *Blake / An Illustrated Quarterly*, 29.1 (Summer 1995), 12–15.
24. For the copy given to Tulk see G. Keynes, *A Bibliography of William Blake* (New York: Grolier Club, 1929), pp. 78, 80.
25. Bentley, *Desolate Market*, pp. 179, 155.
26. Bentley, *Blake Books Supplement*, pp. 99–100.
27. Bentley, *Desolate Market*, p. 160.

28. M. D. Paley, '"A New Heaven Is Begun": William Blake and Swedenborgianism', *Blake / An Illustrated Quarterly*, 13.2 (Fall 1979), 64–87. Silfverhjelm was the grandson of Swedenborg's sister Catharina (1693–1770). He married Harriet Matthew at St Pancras Old Church, 26 May 1794.
29. Dorfman, *Blake in the Nineteenth Century*, 20.
30. On the imagery, see C. Heppner, *Reading Blake's Designs* (Cambridge: Cambridge University Press, 1995), pp. 237–77.
31. J. E. M. Latham, 'The Arlington Court Picture', *Blake / An Illustrated Quarterly*, 29.1 (Summer 1995), 24.
32. Paley, *Coleridge*, pp. 83–92.
33. Latham, 'The Arlington Court Picture', p. 24.
34. H. H. Gilchrist, *Anne Gilchrist, Her Life and Writings, with a Prefatory Note by William Michael Rossetti* (London: T. Fisher Unwin, 1887), pp. 94, 97, 104, 113.
35. W. M. Rossetti, *Rossetti Papers 1862 to 1870* (London: Sands and Co., 1903), p. 5.
36. Ibid., 6.
37. Gilchrist, *Anne Gilchrist*, p. 125.
38. J. Pope-Hennessy, *Monckton Milnes: The Flight of Youth 1851–1885* (London: Constable, 1951), pp. 38–39, 65, 151.
39. C. Y. Lang, *The Swinburne Letters*, 6 vols. (New Haven: Yale University Press, 1959–62), I (1959), 61–63, 86, 90.
40. Rossetti, *Rossetti Papers*, p. 27; Gilchrist, *Anne Gilchrist*, pp. 123, 132–3.
41. 'W. Jameson. Charles Aders. W. K. Jameson', *London Gazette* (1833), 37.
42. Gilchrist, *Anne Gilchrist*, pp. 168, 218–19.
43. For Anne's collection and friendship with Tennyson see S. Erle, *Tennyson and Blake: Beamin Jowett's Copy of Blake's Illustrations of the Book of Job on the Isle of Wight, Tennyson Research Bulletin* (Lincoln: The Tennyson Society, 2016).

CHAPTER 9

Late Reception

Jason Whittaker

During the interwar period and the middle of the twentieth century, academic critics such as S. Foster Damon, David Erdman, and Northrop Frye established Blake as a writer and artist of significance, one whose intellectual and cultural impact on Britain was also recognised by institutions such as the Tate (later Tate Britain), which increasingly devoted space to Blake's works.[1] Yet by the turn of the millennium Blake was frequently treated as a special category by Romanticists who tended to view him as separate to his contemporaries.[2] It is not that the academic study of Blake has gone into decline – far from it – more that it has sometimes felt in the past quarter century to have become an eccentric offshoot of the main tree of Romanticism. Such shifts of academic reputation are impelled by the vagaries of Blake's chronology: while his most famous works fall within the time frame of the Romantic period, many of his literary and aesthetic sentiments belong to an earlier generation. Yet the influence of Blake outside of universities has rarely been stronger than in the first decades of the twenty-first century. To give one example, between 1927 and 1999 there were just over fifty separate recordings of the hymn 'Jerusalem' (leaving aside those emerging in the late 1950s from the inclusion of the Blake–Parry hymn as part of 'Last Night of the Proms'), whereas from 2000 to 2016 there have been nearly 150 versions (again, ignoring Proms recordings). At the same time, such popularity is not itself a guarantee of success with the custodians of academic culture. In the words of Michael Kimmelman's review of the 2001 exhibition of Blake's work at the Metropolitan Museum of Modern Art, New York: 'you can't help noticing how he [Blake] has suffered in recent decades – or benefited, depending on your orientation – from association with a long line of colourful admirers'.[3] This chapter is concerned with two waves of popular reception of Blake since the Second World War: the first, in the late 1960 and 1970s, linked to the rise of a political and social counter-culture; the second, from the 1970s onwards, manifest as a more diffuse and frequently less political popular appropriation.

Perhaps the most important first phase of popular post-war reception was the adoption of Blake into the counter-culture from the 1960s onwards. In the simplest version of this reception history, Blake rises to prominence as the prophet of (self) liberation who preaches that everyone must create a system or be enslaved to another man's (or, more accurately, *The* Man's). In popular music, The Fugs, Bob Dylan, and, of course, The Doors invoked a Blake who was the emblem of a desire to tune in, turn on, and drop out; similarly, seeing his visions of angels and devils as political acts, poetical and cultural harbingers such as Allen Ginsberg, Timothy Leary, and Aldous Huxley used him to explain their own rebellion against the Cold War status quo. In some cases, this appropriation of Blake operated in only the vaguest terms: for all that he name-dropped Blake, there is little evidence that Jim Morrison read much of his poetry, whereas Ginsberg returned to Blake's verse again and again throughout his life. Throughout the post-war period, there are responses that arise from a detailed and thoughtful reaction to Blake's art and writings, while others simply respond to a rather vague notion of what Blake should represent.

This revolution in Blake's reception did not take place overnight. Thus, for example, in the 1940s and 1950s the art historian, literary critic, and anarchist Herbert Read frequently referred to Blake as a political as well as an artistic outsider, one who could help explain the new forces in Modernist art that were slowly becoming accepted in Britain after the Second World War. Similarly, Joyce Cary presented the Blakean protagonist of his novel *The Horse's Mouth* (1944) as part of a modernist resistance to fascism. Edward Larrissy sees Cary's novel as 'a plausible point of entry into the postmodern', dealing as it does with the disjunction of a sage who represents an ideal against the actual chaos of experience.[4] Figures such as Read and Cary seemed to work in isolation at this time, however, as did another post-war poet who was inspired to write after experiencing a vision of Blake in 1948. Reading 'Ah! Sun-Flower', Allen Ginsberg heard what he felt to be 'the voice of Blake himself' and experienced a vision over the roofs of East Harlem, becoming convinced from that moment on that he was a 'chosen, blessed, sacred poet' (on Ginsberg's response to Blake, see further Chapter 25).[5]

At this point, the Beats were not yet a movement and neither Ginsberg nor his friends could anticipate the events of the 1960s. One of the most significant means by which Blake was linked to the counter-culture was via the decision by Aldous Huxley to title his influential 1954 essay detailing his experiences of mescaline, *The Doors of Perception*, after a quotation from

The Marriage of Heaven and Hell, introducing a later generation of psychedelics to the works of Blake. Wayne Glausser has argued that Huxley treated Blake's visions 'as evidence of an unusual neuropsychological condition', a channel to exalted perceptions that were only usually available to a few artists.[6] But by the 1960s the experiences of LSD appeared to make such exalted perceptions available to the masses as never before, including to many who were less interested in the political aspects of the counterculture and more concerned with music and hedonism. Ironically, considering how little contact Blake had with drugs in the late eighteenth and early nineteenth centuries (one biographer describes Blake's most dangerous vice as a daily pint of porter),[7] the art and poetry of William Blake was to become thoroughly enmeshed in the drug culture of the 1960s, his art encapsulating the trippy experiences of psychedelia in a way that appealed greatly to those seeking some kind of expression of their interior landscapes. In the work of Ginsberg in particular, as well as other Beats such as William Burroughs and Michael McClure, Blake offered a sense of spiritual connection through art that conventional Western religion appeared to have lost. In 'Sunflower Sutra', sitting with Jack Kerouac and seeing a 'dead gray shadow' of a sunflower against abandoned, rusting machinery, Ginsberg is reminded of his visions of Blake in Harlem and, snatching up the dead sunflower, preaches his sermon of inner illumination, a moment of satori by which Blake appeared to have more in common with the religions of the east than dead, grey Judeao-Christianity.

Larrissy observes that both Ginsberg and Robert Duncan (whose 1970 collection, *Roots and Branches*, harnesses many elements of Blake's poetry) yoke Blake to a 'late Romantic agenda of their own', one greatly influenced by Modernists such as Ezra Pound and William Carlos Williams.[8] By drawing on jazz in particular, Ginsberg with fellow Beats, notably Kerouac, sought to appeal to a wider, more popular readership. Yet far more effective in reaching this wider audience, as Ginsberg himself appreciated, were new forms of pop music. Ginsberg may have had a role to play in introducing a young Bob Dylan to Blake, though as Clark and Keery argue his influence never went beyond the early lyrics.[9] Another intersection with popular culture came via The Doors, with Ginsberg and Jim Morrison knowing each other's work. As Tristanne Connolly points out, Jim Morrison's actual knowledge of Blake may not have been especially comprehensive, but through him, together with Dylan, and indeed Huxley, a particular version of Blake that presented him as a freewheeling, rebellious, and romantic spirit was refracted to a much wider popular culture than would have been possible through Ginsberg's poetry alone.[10]

By the time Ginsberg joined Michael Horovitz and Adrian Mitchell at the Royal Albert Hall as part of the International Poetry Incarnation in 1965, some seven thousand people attended to watch them recite poetry as part of a happening. In 1969, Horovitz edited a collection *Children of Albion: Poetry of the 'Underground' in Britain*, complete with a cover of *Albion Rose*, previously known as 'Glad Day' on the front cover. James Keery argues that Horovitz's collection reflects 'a sentimental image of Blake', particularly as its title is a misinterpretation of the sinister role of the Children of Albion in the later prophecies.[11] Such sentimentality (or blithe misprision) was not the key note of other poets such as Iain Sinclair, whose *Lud Heat* (1975) and *Suicide Bridge* (1979) are replete with the darker echoes of Blake's visions of London. In these complex, shifting poems Sinclair parodies not so much Blake as those who believe uncritically in his occult influences. Larrissy identifies these texts as clear signs of a shift to a postmodern aesthetic, in particular as they are influenced as much by the work of William Burroughs as by Blake.[12]

Sinclair's poetry marks a possible sign of things to come in the reception of Blake's work, but more generally the 1970s saw a continuation of counter-cultural idealisation, as in Mitchell's *Tyger: A Celebration Based on the Life and Works of William Blake* (1971), and Theodore Roszak's *Where the Wasteland Ends: Politics and Transcendence in Postindustrial Society* (1972). Yet throughout the decade – recalling Blake's earlier treatment in the wake of Pre-Raphaelitism and Aestheticism – there was something of a backlash:[13] when punk emerged onto the scene, for example, it was this very connection to the Beats and counter-culture that counted against the Romantic poet. Derek Jarman – whose uses of Blake later in his career were profound – restricted himself to mocking the hymn 'Jerusalem' in his punk film *Jubilee* (1978). Oppositional readings of Blake were starting to appear elsewhere in popular culture, as in Angela Carter's 1978 article, 'Little Lamb Get Lost', for *New Statesman*. Carter, however, as Larrissy points out, was engaged in a dialogue with Blake, just as Blake was in dialogue with Milton,[14] and this position as a 'friendly enemy' offers contrary readings as a sign of true friendship in works such as *The Passion of New Eve* (1977) and the short story 'The Tiger's Bride' (1979).[15]

From the 1980s on, Blake's reception began to fragment so that he was no longer just the prophet of counter-culture. In some areas, notably the visual arts, this has resulted in a much wider appreciation of Blake's work. Anthony Gormley, for example, in a wide range of sculptures such as *Field* (1991), *Iron Man* (1993), and *Event Horizon* (2007), responded to a vision of the human figure that drew direct inspiration from, of all things, Blake's life mask as sculpted by James Deville in the early nineteenth century. A number of the so-called YBAs (Young British Artists) of the 1990s namechecked Blake, none more vividly than Chris Ofili, who painted huge canvases in response to the Romantic artist's biblical paintings, such as his *Satan* (1995) which responds to Blake's *Satan in His Original Glory* (*c*. 1805). Tracey Emin has more recently drawn comparisons between Blake's works and her installation 'My Bed' (1998).[16] In other instances, Eduardo Paolozzi's sculpture of Newton after Blake was unveiled outside the British Library in 1995, while Alastair Noble's *Illuminated Blake* (2001) uses light and the material of sculpture and its environment to 'challenge the spectator's perceptual experience' in a fashion that draws directly on the *Marriage*'s invocation to cleanse the doors of perception.[17] While the huge Tate Britain exhibition of Blake's works in 2000–1 would reveal him as a visual artist to a new audience, during this earlier decade the rise in his significance is perhaps as much due to the reorganisation of the Tate's collection to emphasise his position of one of the great three artists of British Romanticism, alongside Turner and Constable.

The notion of opposition as true friendship that began to emerge with writers such as Angela Carter as noted above was fundamental to Salman Rushdie's *The Satanic Verses* (1988), which draws greatly upon *The Marriage of Heaven and Hell* as well as on Blake's invocations of London, through whose chartered streets Gibreel wanders as a lost soul in the novel.[18] Rushdie was also influential in terms of demonstrating the widening scope of Blake on literatures in English, most notably as he was followed by writers such as Ben Okri, whose *The Famished Road* (1991) offers visionary experiences of the world similar to those of Blake, and who took the title for his 1999 poem, *Mental Fight*, from Blake's *Milton*. As well as these high literary sources, however, the 1990s also marked another high point in the popular reception of Blake, particularly two trilogies: Thomas Harris's Hannibal Lecter series and *His Dark Materials* by Philip Pullman. Harris actually wrote the first Lecter novel, *Red Dragon*, in 1981, but it was with the 1991 film *Manhunter* (remade as *Red Dragon* in 2002) that Francis Dolarhyde's transformation into Blake's painting of that name came to widespread attention. Similarly, the three novels *Northern Lights* (1995), *The Subtle Knife* (1997), and *The Amber Spyglass* (2000) adapted Blakean ideas, alongside Milton's conception of the war in heaven, for a new generation of youthful readers.

In many respects, Blake's emergence in the 1990s and early 2000s as a figure of inspiration for a wide variety of popular formats such as children's books, movies, and music represents some of the real vitality of his continuing influence into the twenty-first century. Jim Jarmusch's wonderfully idiosyncratic art house movie *Dead Man* (1995) may not have received much of an audience beyond its rapturous reception by critics, but it did no harm to the reputation of Blake to be portrayed by a bemused Johnny Depp. In the field of popular music, this period marked a renaissance of Blake that went far beyond the hippy rock of the 1960s, at least in terms of breadth if not always depth of responses. Some, such as Jah Wobble's *The Inspiration of William Blake* (1996), were profound reflections on the Romantic's poetry, while others, such as Bruce Dickinson's adaptations for *The Chemical Wedding* (1998), were more lighthearted. Further, as David Fallon points out, there was a whole subgenre of allusions to Blake's London in the work of Pete Doherty of the Libertines and for Billy Bragg. Nick Cave has frequently alluded to Blake, as in 'A Weeping Song' and 'The Hammer Song' on *The Good Son* (1990) and, more tongue in cheek, the death of Bill Blakey's boy in 'The Curse of Millhaven' from *Murder Ballads* (1999). It was also by the early 1990s, on 1992's *Jehovahkill*, that Julian Cope began to reference Blake; by 2008 on *Black Sheep*, he was exploring Blake extensively, becoming what Stuart Maconie calls 'Blake's natural heir'.[19] While a number of songwriters namecheck Blake from time to time, Cope is one of those musicians who does more than simply list a quotation or two, presenting on Blake at the 2008 exhibition, 'Blake's Shadow' at the Whitworth Art Gallery in 2008.[20]

As such, this brief survey of Blake's post-war reception demonstrates the peculiar vitality of his afterlife as a poet and artist. Very few historical figures are so widely referenced on the contemporary stage and in such a variety of forms and genres, including graphic novels (such as John Riordan's *William Blake, Taxi Driver*, 2008–9) and stage plays (notably Jez Butterworth's *Jerusalem*, 2009) as well as the poems, films, and artworks referenced here. While Blake's status as a writer in the academic canon may be subject to ever greater attenuation, in the sphere of popular culture his influence is more wide-ranging than ever before.

Notes

1. The key works are S. F. Damon, *William Blake, His Philosophy and Symbols* (1924); N. Frye, *Fearful Symmetry: A Study of William Blake* (1947); D. V. Erdman, *Blake: Prophet against Empire* (1954).
2. J. Faflak and J. M. Wright offer a good summary of this tendency in their introduction to *A Handbook of Romanticism Studies* (Chichester: John Wiley and Sons, 2012), p. 2.

3. Cited by M. Lussier, 'Blake beyond Postmodernity', in S. Clark and J. Whittaker (eds.), *Blake, Modernity and Popular Culture* (Houndmills: Palgrave Macmillan, 2007), pp. 151–62 (p. 152).
4. E. Larrissy, *Blake and Modern Literature* (Houndmills: Palgrave Macmillan, 2006), p. 85.
5. Cited in B. Miles, *Ginsberg: A Biography* (London: Virgin, 2000), p. 208.
6. W. Glausser, 'What Is It Like to Be a Blake? Psychiatry, Drugs and the Doors of Perception', in Clark and Whittaker (eds.), Blake, Modernity and Popular Culture, pp. 163–78 (p. 164).
7. E. H. Short, *William Blake* (New York: Haskell House, 1926), p. 39.
8. Larrissy, *Blake and Modern Literature*, p. 88.
9. S. Clark and J. Keery, '"Only the Wings on His Heels": Blake and Dylan', in S. Clark, T. Connolly, and J. Whittaker (eds.), *Blake 2.0: William Blake in Twentieth-Century Art, Music, Culture* (Houndmills: Palgrave Macmillan, 2012), pp. 209–29 (p. 210).
10. T. Connolly, '"He Took a Face from the Ancient Gallery": Blake and Jim Morrison', in ibid., pp. 230–47 (pp. 230–1).
11. J. Keery, 'Children of Albion: Blake and Contemporary British Poetry', in Clark and Whittaker (eds.), *Blake, Modernity and Popular Culture*, pp. 100–12 (p. 100).
12. Larrissy, *Blake and Modern Literature*, p. 95.
13. See C. Trodd on 'Anti-Aestheticist Discourse', in *Visions of Blake: William Blake in the Art World 1830–1930* (Liverpool: Liverpool University Press, 2012), p. 170.
14. Larrissy, *Blake and Modern Literature*, p. 137.
15. C. Ranger, 'Friendly Enemies: A Dialogical Encounter between William Blake and Angela Carter', in Clark and Whittaker (eds.), *Blake, Modernity and Popular Culture*, pp. 140–50 (pp. 140–1).
16. 'Tracey Emin and William Blake in Focus', Tate Liverpool, www.tate.org.uk/whats-on/tate-liverpool/exhibition/tracey-emin-and-william-blake-focus
17. M. Crosby, 'Blake and Contemporary Sculpture', in Clark, Connolly, and Whittaker (eds.), *Blake 2.0*, pp. 120–31 (p. 123).
18. Larrissy, *Blake and Modern Literature*, p. 154.
19. D. Fallon, '"Hear the Drunken Archangel Sing": Blakean Notes in 1990s Pop Music', in Clark, Connolly, and Whittaker (eds.), *Blake 2.0*, pp. 248–62 (p. 251).
20. See R. Young, *Electric Eden: Unearthing Britain's Visionary Music* (London: Faber & Faber), p. 592.

CHAPTER 10

Editing and Editions

Morris Eaves

> Time had the power to cancel all changes wrought by human artifice, overwriting all new revisions with further revisions, returning the flow to its original course.
> — Haruki Murakami, *1Q84* (2011)[1]

The first question must be: what *is* William Blake in the context of editing? If the answer is narrow – how Blake has been edited in relation to standard protocols – the account will interest few. But if editing is viewed as a complex, utterly human matter of perception, control, desire, and memory over shorter and longer stretches of time, then the case of Blake becomes both broadly interesting and telling – about Blake and about our own limitations, habits, and aspirations.

Though we often think of editing as a rule-bound, highly specialised craft anchored in physical objects, chiefly literary ones, editing occurs in dynamic, layered contexts that shape it. And viewed broadly, editing is an essential part of a host of essential processes and activities that make human life what it is. The narratives in which we attempt to capture such dynamic processes are necessarily static and highly reductive relative to the complex, elusive realities. Even at its most apparently neutral, editing is always on a mission governed by ideology in the broadest sense. Editing is the product of active thinking. An edition is action, cause, effect – and it expects actions, or effects, in return. Like memory, it is geared to the future, not the past. Regrettably, there is no space here to tell such a full and adequate story. We must put nuance and detail aside while keeping a few of the broader implications in view.[2]

In Blake's Prospectus of 1793, addressed 'To the Public', he announces his invention of a 'method of Printing which combines the Painter and the Poet' – relief etching using common tools, materials, and techniques – and the accomplishment of a double feat: reuniting word and picture while abolishing a stubborn barrier between 'the Artist, the Poet, and the

94

Musician' and their audiences: 'Even Milton and Shakespeare could not publish their own works.' If Blake hoped that other poets, artists, and musicians would adopt his method, of course he was wrong. But he seems never to have lost interest in using it to produce what became posthumously the central body of his work: his 'Illuminated Books' in 'Illuminated Printing' (E 692–3). Though he worked in several conventional media, his invention of a 'means to propagate' is one of his most salient, memorable features.[3] Attention-getting but also troublemaking: the force of his potential audience's prior investments in conventional habits are such that, even during his lifetime, the products of his method begin to dissolve into their culturally identifiable constituents, as individual poems and passages are separated from the word-image noise of his illuminated works and reprinted in conventional letterpress books.[4]

Convention and economic need forced Blake's own editorial hand in the opposite direction when commercial opportunities arose. Asked by a potential customer to produce a 'selection from the different Books of such [pictures] as could be Printed without the Writing' – Blake had already done this for Ozias Humphry – Blake defends his combinations as 'some of the best things For they when printed perfect [together, as on the copper] accompany [. . .] Poems [without which] they never could have been Executed' (Blake to Dawson Turner, 9 June 1818, E 771). As Haggarty and Mee point out, 'While drafting poems in [his] notebook, Blake himself acted as an editor.'[5] But subsequent self-editing incorporated the notebook drafts of *Songs* into composite works that were 'printed perfect' from the inked copperplates. Blake's self-editing for Humphrey and Turner reverses that work. He complies with their wish that he dismantle what Coleridge calls 'a strange publication – viz. Poems with very wild and interesting pictures, as the swathing' and behave like a visual artist – a category his customers recognise (*BR* 251). Here Blake self-edits to restore the cultural fault-line that conveniently separates poets from painters, reading from viewing. For such visually oriented customers – and, after all, Blake spent most of his life among them – the words get in the way; as, from the other side, the pictures distract readers such as Wordsworth and Coleridge (both appreciators of imagery in more conventional forms).

Frederick Tatham, Blake's younger friend and ultimately executor, clearly recognises the problem he would face in marketing such works as Blake's *Jerusalem*. He tries to solve it by editing rhetorically that 100-plate illuminated combination of text and design. His 'Life of Blake' (*c.* 1832) conjures a reader who would find the 'combinations' in *Jerusalem* 'chimerical' and 'the poem not only abstruse [. . .] but near ridiculous [and] heterogenous', alongside 'designs' that are as 'sublime', 'lofty', and 'noble' as any ever conceived. Reversing Coleridge's hierarchy, Tatham suggests that the 'poetry' might best be considered the 'mere Vehicle' for the more marketable designs (*BR* 674–5). Anticipating his potential buyer's bewilderment when faced with such strange and strident 'combinations', Tatham does not proceed to create a physical surrogate of the work as an editor would. Yet he does behave like an editor by anticipating the reader-viewer's needs and desires and offering a recipe for viewing and reading *Jerusalem*: an editorial rationale.

This push and pull between text and image, integration and division, which is well underway by the time of Blake's death, characterises the entire history of his editorial existence. His originality – call it what we will, his imagination, extravagance, strangeness – stands on an unstable assemblage of physical platforms that accommodate his fascinating array of pictures and words. His inscrutability is always a distraction but also a charisma that cannot be dispelled. 'He' depends on it and yet we, his posterity, must find ways simultaneously to dispel and maintain it as we like, when we like. Without it, he is too little; with it, too much. This is the editorial space that he bequeaths to us.

In the early decades after his death, Blake's visibility decreased and his original works scattered – lost, sold off in lots at auctions, stored here and there, no doubt with a waning sense of purpose, as former friends and admirers passed the bits and pieces along to their successors. Why did I inherit these, and why am I keeping them? they must have often asked, even as the posthumous editing got fitfully underway. Allan Cunningham's life of Blake in his *Lives of the Most Eminent Painters, Sculptors and Architects* (1830) may have had the most pervasive influence in keeping the memory of Blake as poet-artist alive, characterising the illuminated books *America* and *Europe*, for instance, as 'plentifully seasoned with verse' and *The Book of Urizen* as 'twenty-seven scenes' interspersed with 'wild verses, [...] scattered here and there' (*BR* 653, 638). Cunningham describes some of Blake's images – which is in fact one of the ways we preserve many otherwise lost images – and extracts and reprints some of the verses (consider a textual description of an image as an edition of that image severely remediated, that is, re-encoded).[6] J. J. Garth Wilkinson produced a printed edition of the *Songs* (1839) with an extensive Swedenborgian introduction: he 'strips away its illuminations and disciplines its hand-drawn lettering into type' – which is, by this time, a familiar editorial efficiency, almost unavoidable considering the meager options available for printing anything closer to a facsimile of the original, though

Wilkinson's objections to Blake's designs are more than merely practical.[7] The oddest product of these years is C. A. Tulk's remarkable edition of the *Songs* in only twelve copies (1843). Tulk converts the words to conventional typography but leaves blank the spaces for Blake's designs – 'spaced as in the Original, in order that any who chose, might copy in the paintings with which the original is adorned'.[8] Tulk's experimental edition was a kind of free-colouring book with spaces but no outlines.

Wilkinson's edition, though printed in a small run, travelled to the Swedenborgian and Transcendentalist communities in America for study and further extraction and reprinting, as other elements of Blake's work landed in Australia and New Zealand; some ricocheted back, such as Tulk's copy of the *Songs* – the copy Coleridge had read and Wilkinson had used as the basis for his edition before it went to Australia with one of Tulk's relatives and then returned to Britain, via bookdealer James Bain (*BB* 417). That is, once Blake was no longer present to focus the attentions of a small audience, filaments grew in several directions, ever more unconsolidated and accidentally recombined. It would take an epidemiologist to say whether Blake was spreading or simply fading away, a casualty of editorial entropy, or gathering strength for a revival. Only an alert and highly optimistic observer might have predicted what happened later, culminating in the publication of Alexander Gilchrist's *Life of William Blake, 'Pictor Ignotus'* in two hefty volumes in 1863. Gilchrist, his wife Anne, and devoted allies such as artist-poet Dante Rossetti, his writer-critic brother William Michael Rossetti, and the poet-critic Algernon Charles Swinburne worked mightily on several fronts to forge the reconvergence of those dwindling filaments. Their efforts would not so much restore their original form – which had proved insufficient – as organise and supplement them in re-energised structures sufficient to propel Blake forward to the next generation as a far more coherent and thus recognisable entity. In doing so, they produced a prototype of cultural resurrection, 'discovery', by editorial means.

Gilchrist and company did not transform Blake overnight from an engraver-painter whose traces were diminishing in time into the iconic British 'poet, painter, prophet' that Geoffrey Keynes celebrated in the 1960s. But if there is a single most important pivot point in Blake's editorial fate, it is signalled by W. M. Rossetti's remark in his review of a facsimile of the formidable 100-plate *Jerusalem*: 'Difficult under any circumstances, it would be a good deal *less* difficult to read these works in an edition of that [typographic] kind, with clear print, reasonable division of lines, and the like aids to business-like perusal.'[9] Rossetti is not merely advocating editorial principles. He is *wanting* something *for* Blake's work – wanting to do Blake a service in his best interest, something that he himself showed too little concern for. Thus the 'strange and beautiful integrity' that Swinburne found most particularly in illuminated printing was transformed – as, indeed, Swinburne agreed it should be – in response to the need for greater legibility and regular order.[10]

Such harsh but effective editorial measures soon became systematic and increasingly ambitious. Rossetti and Swinburne were hardly the first to segregate texts from pictures, but they were among the first to articulate the vital insight that appreciating Blake might require the sacrifice of his original forms to systematic, conventional treatment. The printed edition – by Rossetti himself, and then more ambitiously by E. J. Ellis and W. B. Yeats, whose three-volume edition aspired to sort out the words of even such obscure and lengthy manuscripts as *VALA/Four Zoas* – prepared the way for serious study and reflection on a scale previously unthinkable. This more disciplined editorial vehicle delivered a poet who, relieved of his pictorial burdens, could eventually rise into the ranks of major romantic poets alongside Wordsworth and Coleridge, while the pictures, their semiotic encumbrances shifted to print, could be liberated for the visual excitements afforded by a minor-major artist of special fascination for early adopters with an appetite for the unconventional. The ranking of writer versus visual artist was less significant than the editorial naturalisation of the split between the two, which provided more readily processed Blakes for each side of a divided cultural memory.

The editorial separation served Blake well, making possible levels of circulation, appreciation, and focused, structured understanding that would have been impossible otherwise. At the same time, crucially, the residual sense of Blake as a multimedia artist that survived the editorial separation provided him with a kind of brand identity. That sense fused with the difficulties and extravagances of both his words and pictures to generate a romantic aura that made him a singular survivor who beckons to and *needs* his adventurous audience and promises to reward it with gifts of a unique kind, even while resisting its most strenuous critical efforts. Blake's discomforts, which so often alienated his contemporaries, became, in the long run, the source of ineffable fascination.

More than a century of reading, viewing, and formal study were built on these printed foundations and their extensions. The scholarly editions of Keynes (1926, 1957), Erdman (1965), and Bentley (1978) and the many texts extracted from them for more popular editions provided the infrastructure of words that supports the indispensable Blake scholarship, translation (into many languages), and international readership that in turn generate such volumes as the present one. Editors were inspired to undertake ambitious secondary projects, such as Bentley's facsimile edition of *VALA/Four Zoas* and Erdman's monumental 'photographic and typographic facsimile' of Blake's notebook.[11] Meanwhile, in the channel of visual art – narrower and shallower but roughly parallel, the (broadly) editorial resources required under the conventions of art history, museum practice, and collecting were more slowly and irregularly supplied. As the two main channels began to merge, awkwardly, in the last quarter of the twentieth century, the sum was a formidably large but unshapely editorial aggregation. Dispersal, dismemberment, and translation seriously distorted the true picture of Blake's achievement. The lack of alignment with his original aims and accomplishments caught the attention of a new generation – I enter here – deeply invested in the role of Blake's neglected and misunderstood image- and word-making technologies. The corresponding editorial aims that materialised were clear if absurdly idealistic: build an artistically comprehensive Blake, who, however imaginatively original, nonetheless emerged from an environment for which we can account. And that is primarily why Robert Essick, Joseph Viscomi, and I undertook a new kind of edition.

There were, of course, many steps in this turn of events – which was in part an outgrowth of the rambunctious arguments of the 1990s over editorial theory and practice in anticipation of a new era of, as we called it, electronic editing. But the main editorial product was the William Blake Archive, designed to reflect the more inclusive scholarship made possible by – and inevitably limited by – the new World Wide Web with allied digital means and methods. X-editing, as I have labelled the everchanging, tentative, always compromised practices that working digital editors employ, has allowed a previously unattainable level of access to Blake's extant work.[12] This superconsolidation is new, but it incorporates, quite conservatively, the foundations laid in the twentieth century even as it has become a central editorial resource. It has aided, for instance, such complex scholarship – itself editorial – as Joseph Viscomi's meticulous account of the composition of Blake's *Song of Los*.[13]

'Posterity will know' (*Public Address*, E 572). The posterity in which Blake professed to put such faith extends indefinitely but uncertainly into the future. In 1982, just after the dawn of personal computing, Blake scholars still looked forward to 'filmstrips' of all the illuminated books even as they envisioned a time 'when the preservation and retrieval of critical commentary are wholly automated' via 'the Blake Variorium Computer Button'.[14]

The Blake Archive now sits where filmstrips, microfiche, slides, and laser discs once roamed.[15] Beyond that, the future is impossible to predict with any confidence, though we might timidly imagine that there will eventually appear, probably in the Archive, the first reasonably satisfactory edition of Blake's *VALA/Four Zoas* manuscript, which, ever since W. M. Rossetti mentioned it for the first time in the catalogue he compiled for Gilchrist's biography, has stubbornly defied all editorial assaults in print. It's probably safe to predict that editions in multiple media will continue to support a future for Blake study and scholarship in manifold domains of human life, aided eventually by artificial intelligence so powerful and so well integrated into human life on the planet that study, student, and subject may be utterly transformed in the process. I would not predict, however, that Blake, however eminently readable and viewable, can also become known and understood as Wordsworth and Jane Austen are known – capable of infinite varieties of interpretation but not, like Blake, essentially inscrutable. No edition, no future progress, can penetrate the core of the 'Blake' we bequeath, which is, no matter how preserved and represented, the opaque enticement that is his inviolable legacy. The grander question – will there be a legacy? – is entirely wrapped up in the future of the universe. But if I venture that editorial horizons are concomitant with the horizons of the universe, the only judicious response is 'Enough! Or Too much' (*Marriage* pl. 10, E 38).

Notes

1. H. Murakami, *1Q84*, trans. P. Gabriel and J. Rubin (New York: Knopf, 2011), p. 25.
2. Here I draw freely on several of my own earlier attempts to construct such narratives – some referenced below.
3. See M. Eaves, 'National Arts and Disruptive Technologies in Blake's Prospectus of 1793', in S. Clark and D. Worrall (eds.), *Blake, Nation and Empire* (London: Palgrave, 2006), pp. 119–35.
4. For early examples see Appendix V in *BR* 825–8.
5. S. Haggarty and J. Mee, *William Blake: Songs of Innocence and of Experience* (Basingstoke: Palgrave Macmillan, 2013), p. 14.
6. For description as a kind of edition, see M. Eaves, 'The Editorial Void: Notes toward a Study of Oblivion', *Huntington Library Quarterly*, 80.3 (2017), 517–38.
7. Haggarty and Mee, *Songs of Innocence and of Experience*, p. 53.
8. Inscription by Wilkinson in a copy of Tulk's edition, now in the British Museum; cited by S. Dent and J. Whittaker, *Radical Blake: Influence and Afterlife from 1827* (Basingstoke: Palgrave Macmillan, 2002), p. 23; see also their discussion, pp. 23–4.

9. W. M. Rossetti, 'Review of the Pearson Facsimile of Blake's Jerusalem and W. B. Scott's Reworked Blake etchings', The Academy (23 February 1878), 174–5 (p. 174). See also R. W. Peattie, 'William Michael Rossetti's Aldine Edition of Blake', *Blake / An Illustrated Quarterly* 12 (1978), 4–9, also available in the William Blake Archive; and M. Eaves, 'Graphicality: Multimedia Fables for "Textual" Critics', in E. B. Loizeaux and N. Fraistat (eds.), *Textual Studies in the Late Age of Print* (Madison: University of Wisconsin Press, 2002), pp. 99–122.
10. Swinburne to Rossetti, letter of 17 July 1874, in C. Y. Lang (ed.), *The Swinburne Letters*, 6 vols. (New Haven: Yale University Press, 1959–62), II, 311–12.
11. See G. E. Bentley, Jr, *Vala or the Four Zoas. A Facsimile of the Manuscript, a Transcript of the Poem and a Study of Its Growth and Significance* (Oxford: Clarendon, 1963); D. V. Erdman (with D. K. Moore) (ed.), *The Notebook of William Blake: A Photographic and Typographic Facsimile* (Oxford: Clarendon, 1973).
12. For 'x-editing', see M. Eaves, 'Crafting Editorial Settlements', *RoN: Romanticism on the Net* [now *RaVon*], www.ron.umontreal.ca/ University of Montreal, issues 41–2 (February–May 2006). www.erudit.org/revue/ron/20 06/v/n41–42/013150ar.html
13. See J. Viscomi, 'Blake's "Annus Mirabilis": The Productions of 1795', *Blake / An Illustrated Quarterly*, 41 (Fall 2007), 52–83. There is a substantial body of scholarship on the Blake Archive. See Articles about the Archive: www.blakearchive.org/staticpage/archiveataglance?p=articlesindex
14. J. E. Grant, 'Blake in the Future', in M. Eaves (ed.), *Studies in Romanticism*, special issue: Romantic Texts, Romantic Times: Homage to David V. Erdman, 21.3 (Fall 1982), 436–43 (p. 439).
15. M. Eaves, 'Picture Problems: X-editing Images 1992–2010', *Digital Humanities Quarterly*, 3.3 (Summer 2009), digitalhumanities.org/dhq/vol/3/3/000052/000052.html

PART II

Form, Genre, and Mode

CHAPTER II

Comedy

Fred Parker

> I hate scarce smiles: I love laughing.
> – Blake, Annotations to Lavater, E 585

Is comedy a surprising category to invoke in connection with Blake? Inveighing against caricature in art, he wrote: 'Fun I love, but too much Fun is of all things the most loathsome' (Blake to Trusler, 23 August 1799, E 702). Many of his most obvious and important models – Isaiah, Michelangelo, Milton, Ossian – are relentlessly serious, and many who admire Blake do so as an artist who is supremely in earnest, and who knows what it means to be in earnest. Yet he has one work of some length which can only be described as comic. *An Island in the Moon* is usually dated to 1784, and its early date and its peculiarities often cause it to be bracketed off from Blake's major achievement, as a trivial piece written before he became himself. This can be challenged. If you set aside the assumption that as an openly comical entertainment it must be unworthy of Blake, it becomes possible both to find it exhilarating in itself, and to feel resonances between its comic mode and the work that was to follow.

The *Island* is a prose narrative, though one which contains a large number of songs. Very little happens; most of the narrative is given up to highly inconsequential exchanges between the characters, whose names suggest the simplifications of farce or burlesque. We meet three philosophers – Suction the Epicurean, Quid the Cynic (a version of Blake), and Sipsop the Pythagorean (with his cat) – along with Etruscan Column the antiquarian, Inflammable Gass (an experimental scientist), Obtuse Angle the mathematician, Steelyard the lawgiver, Mrs Nannicantipot, and others. Topics that would be meat and drink to a serious conversational circle are tossed up and as rapidly flung aside: Voltaire, Chatterton, mathematics, pagan worship, church attendance, philosophy versus 'feelings', reading versus conversation, female eloquence, and so on. The piece is thus partly a skit on the salon ideal of cultured and improving conversation: the characters don't listen to one another, or they squabble or baldly disagree. Yet the main effect is not satirical: the narrative moves too fast and too absurdly for that, on the edge of nonsense writing, and no opinion or attitude is sustained coherently enough or for long enough to become a target. We are given just enough sense of intellectual substance and satirical possibility to feel the energy in their dispersal – as in Swift's *Tale of a Tub* (1704) or Gay's *Beggar's Opera* (1728), or in much good stand-up.

The *Island* may have been written as an entertainment for Blake's circle of friends, with in-jokes and local allusions which scholarship can only partly uncover. Yet even if our understanding of these were total, the sense of comical lunacy (the work is set on the moon), in the writing as much as in the characters, would remain. At one point the narrator simply undoes the narrative:

> Then Mr Inflammable Gass ran & shov'd his head into the fire & set his hair all in a flame, & ran about the room – No, no, he did not; I was only making a fool of you. (E 453)

Let me pause on this reprieve. The *Island*, like much comedy, offers for our amusement figures imprisoned in discourse, who live too narrowly through their minds. This will become a great Blakean theme: the wrongful dominion seized by reason in human life. Comedy's familiar corrective movement asserts the realities of the body and the physical world, bringing the overweening mind down to earth. Thus the blinkered scientist sets his hair on fire. But this kind of comedy is not Blake's way, since for him the constraining reality of the physical world is itself an illusion fostered by the overweening mind. Hence one great resource of comedy – the pratfall, the reassertion of gravity – is not an option. Instead, in rescuing his scientist, Blake makes the action insubstantial, inconsequential, *light* – somewhat as in his designs gravity operates only selectively, and some of his bodies stream upwards, as if rising were as plausible as falling.

The exuberant inconsequentiality of the *Island* undoes the time-bound constraint of causality, in a way that resonates with the prophetic works to come, where consequential narrative action increasingly disappears, either stalled or reduced to cyclicity, and regeneration arrives, if it arrives at all, from nowhere, like grace. With its cascade of nonsequiturs, the *Island* supplants causality with freedom. Freedom is felt also in the *Island*'s heterogeneity, its extreme hospitality to diversity. I have already touched on the range of characters and conversational topics, but even more striking is the range of songs that the characters sing to amuse each other, and as blessed relief from talking. Burlesques and nonsense-lyrics jostle against street-cries and love-songs, grotesque satires, and Handelian pastiche; in the midst of these, placed together but sung by different characters, are three lyrics that would appear (with tiny variants) in the *Songs of Innocence*. All his life Blake was passionately opposed to the notion of 'one law' regulating diversity, and the hybrid plurality of these songs enacts just such opposition.

We might gloss this as what Bakhtin called heteroglossia, or that 'double-voiced' quality of writing which undoes any single uniform intentionality.[1] But it can also be seen as a manifestation of eighteenth-century wit. Locke had defined wit as the faculty of finding resemblances in things that are really unlike, and subordinated it to judgement, the faculty of division, which distinguishes between things that seem similar.[2] But Blake, for whom division and separation are the mark of the Fall, reverses this evaluation, and in his later work makes connections everywhere. The psychological, the political, the metaphysical, the sexual, the theological, and the aesthetic – all these are, in Blake's writings, aspects of one another, not only metaphors for but also instantiations of one another.

It seems odd, perhaps, to speak of 'wit' in connection with Blake: the term suggests some surprising ingenuity in the connections made (look! you *can* see it like this!), whereas the prophetic or visionary Blake seems to be telling us that that is how things really are. But parody is one manifestation of wit, and Blake's delight in parody is nowhere clearer than in the *Island*. It has been persuasively suggested that its manner, as well as some of its content, owes much to the popular entertainments of the day, especially those put on at the Haymarket Theatre by Samuel Foote.[3] Foote was a comedian of genius, a cross between clown and satirist, who sent up contemporary figures and types with fantastical impersonations. Sometimes he would double the effect, playing one character playing another: Mother Cole the bawd would impersonate Squintum the Methodist (glancing at Whitefield), rather as Blake's Mrs Sistagatist evokes Parson Huffcap, or Sipsop vividly renders Jack Tearguts the surgeon. Foote's mimicry of his contemporaries spiralled into creative fantasy; his performances stood in relation to contemporary society as a parodist stands to a source text, with options of critical mockery and transformative re-creation both kept in play. This is very like Blake's way of sending up cultured conversation in the *Island*, where he was not only drawing on the parodic energy associated with Foote, but himself writing a parody of such performances.

Among Blake's subsequent writings, the most obvious inheritor of this comedic consciousness is the exuberantly hybrid and indecorous *Marriage of Heaven and Hell*. Here the mode of high visionary assertion goes hand in hand with a note of mischievous provocation. For Blake to title his visions 'memorable fancies' – playing off the 'memorable relations' in Swedenborg's later works – is simultaneously to stand outside them, teasing the reader with the recognition of their outrageousness. When he casually begins a section, 'As I was walking among the fires of hell' (pl. 6, E 35), or relates, deadpan, how Isaiah and Ezekiel came to dinner (pl. 12, E 38), or tells how the moralising Angel 'is now become a Devil' and his 'particular friend' (pl. 23–4, E 43–4), Blake's irreverence towards religious pieties doubles up with his flouting of readerly expectations of what is plausible. That Blake really had visions, which he believed corresponded to spiritual realities, took nothing away from his awareness of their 'fanciful' status in the eyes of the world which, at his best, he was addressing. The edgy mixture of open entertainment with antagonistic challenge in the *Marriage* is the hallmark of one kind of comedy, along with the projection of a knowing naivety, and the gleeful turning of things upside down. 'But the following Contraries to these are true' (pl. 4, E 34). Blake would later describe himself as 'a very contrary fellow' ('Blakes apology for his Catalogue' l. 16, E 505) – itself a kind of joke – and the *Marriage* works largely by counterstatement, invoking and then inverting the assumptions of conventional ethics. What qualifies this as comic, rather than simply polemical, is its *delight* in opposition, which signals the possibility that the oppositional stance is provisional, corrective, tending towards the final revelation that 'everything that lives is Holy' (pl. 27, E 45). As in many comedies, these disruptive energies hope to find their way to a marriage – even though Blake's saturnalia do not return to a purified status quo, but seek rather to establish a new world.

This pleasure in counterstatement and paradox, this contrariness, runs deep in Blake's work. It can be felt in the explosive comments (often very funny) he wrote in the margins of other works, or in the doggerel verses whose pointed crudeness and scurrility indict the so-fashionable pretensions of patrons and connoisseurs. Formally, it generates the parodic impulse which lives everywhere in his work. Despite his astonishing originality, Blake is continually rewriting or answering or playing off other writings: the Bible above all, *Paradise Lost*, Ossian, *King Lear*, Swedenborg's *Heaven and Hell*, eighteenth-century songs for children. 'The Sick Rose' sets out from Prior's 'A True Maid' ('Rose, were you not extremely sick?'); 'The Fly' revises the sentiments of Gray's 'Ode on the Spring'; and of course the *Songs of Experience* are juxtaposed to those of *Innocence*, with several directly recalling their companion poems.

Comedy

Parody is not necessarily comic. But the relation of Blake's poetry to its predecessors is generally ironic, with affiliations to the mode of wit as T. S. Eliot described it: 'a recognition, implicit in the expression of every experience, of other kinds of experience which are possible'.[4] This applies not only to parody – properly speaking, a relation between texts – but also to the way that Blakean Vision retains traces of the phenomenal/natural/empirical world which it transfigures. Writing to Thomas Butts, Blake explained how imaginative or spiritual perception involved him in 'twofold' or 'double' vision:

> For double the vision my Eyes do see,
> And a double vision is always with me.
> With my inward Eye 'tis an old Man grey
> With my outward a Thistle across my way.
> (Blake to Butts, 22 November 1802, ll. 27–30, E 721)

When the old Man is the salient image in the poetry, but a link back to the thistle is left live, so to speak, we have the conditions for wit as Eliot described it. The *Songs of Experience* are full of such moments. 'Crying weep, weep, in notes of woe!': the street-cry of the chimney-sweeper ('Sweep!') is still recognisable, though transfigured into the lament that, in Blake's imaginative perception, it more truly is (l. 2, E 22). 'My mother groaned! my father wept': in the opening line of 'Infant Sorrow' the parents' natural feelings as their child is born – the mother's labour-pains, the father's tears of relief and joy – are still visible, showing through their fierce re-imagination by Blake as alarm and dismay at the infant's fiendlike energy (E 28). The songs in *Experience* are highly diverse, but the originating attitude which they suggest, taken as a group, is something like that of Shakespeare's Feste (another contrary fellow) or behind him Erasmus's Folly:[5] where the satirist and the entertainer are continually exchanging masks, where nonchalance is a weapon against disenchantment, where the auditor is equally confided in and bamboozled, and where rationality is undone, as obliquity and truth-telling go hand in hand.

A comparable effect, as of double exposure, can also be found in the later prophetic writings. This is readily seen where Blake's mythic action has a recognisable location. As Orc's fires flame and Westminster howls, 'the Guardian of the secret codes' flees 'along Great George Street [. . .] to the wilderness' – the 'wilderness' being not only a desert of the spirit but also an area within St James's Park (*Europe* 12: 15, 19–20, E 64). Ololon, Milton's Emanation, conveniently descends to Blake's cottage garden in Felpham, a location sweetly illustrated on the same plate (pl. 36[40], E 137). More generally, the mythic action of these writings urgently asks to be grounded in reflection on institutional repression, or sexual power-struggles, or the self-alienated mind – realities of experience – even while it insists on the sublimation or transfiguration of those realities into mythic form. An analogy might be drawn with Pope's *Dunciad* (1728–43), where the re-imagination of contemporary culture as the eternal goddess Dulness manifests just that power of wit that the dunces know nothing of. The *Dunciad* is mock-heroic in its twofold vision, as Pope conjures sublimity from the oppressive mundanity of his culture, giving it (like Los hammering at his anvil) the very form it resists and denies; Blake's prophetic writings might be similarly described as mock-prophetic, in their sense of the distance travelled in seeing Jerusalem – or Babylon – in England.

Yet such wit becomes increasingly attenuated in Blake's later writings. We are less often reminded that the old Man is also a thistle. Blake also loses, or grows beyond, Pope's satiric anger. His increasing emphasis on forgiveness is facilitated by his sharp distinction of individuals from the states into which they fall, and in any case there are no oppressors in Blake's mythology who are not themselves equally suffering in dismal woe. Moreover, wit suggests a poised consciousness, comparing, mocking, and teasing, but the drive towards the annihilation of what Blake called 'self-hood' – pre-eminently in *Milton* – is ultimately incompatible with this.

The poetic preface to *Europe*, however, wonderfully illustrates how a comic consciousness can frame the prophetic mode. We enter the poem through an exchange between Blake and a 'mocking' fairy, who sings a Blakean doctrine of man's wilful refusal to be open to the joys of life. Blake:

> caught him in my hat as boys knock down a butterfly.
> How know you this, said I, small sir? Where did you learn this song?

'Laughing', the fairy promises that if Blake gets him 'tipsy' with 'a cup of sparkling poetic fancies', he will sing to him and show him how the world is not material but 'all alive'. So Blake carries him home, picking wild flowers along the way, which the fairy reveals as eternal, laughing when they whimper at being plucked. Then:

> When I came
> Into my parlour and sat down, and took my pen to write,
> My fairy sat upon the table, and dictated EUROPE.   (pl. iii, E 60)

Not only is the fairy an unmistakeably comic muse, but also Blake's engagement with this 'small sir' is equally full of humour. The easy co-presence of the familiar and the visionary – wild flowers and eternal flowers, the fairy sitting on the parlour table – gives the comedy its sanction: get a little drunk on poetry, and you *will* see the world as 'all alive'. And Blake's capture of the fairy captures also one of the great gifts of comedy: the sense, within the comic frame or form of art, of controlling or even making friends with forces which are known to be otherwise uncontrollable and potentially malign. The motif might seem merely rococo, were it not for the weight and darkness of the vision of Europe which it introduces. Yet to go from the fairy to the poem's terrific opening line – 'The nameless shadowy female rose from out of the breast of Orc' – is, for a moment, to hear *Europe* as mock-prophetic, as another 'memorable fancy'.

The poem about the fairy exists on a separate plate, and is included in only two printings out of twelve; there is thus some question about when Blake wrote it, and how consistently he intended to connect it with *Europe*. This suggests, perhaps, his ambivalence about the admission of the comic perspective. Yet that the latest printing is at least as late as 1818 shows that the comic lightness of the *Island in the Moon* never went entirely away. At the end of the *Island*, Quid is speaking anxiously to his wife about his plans to produce engraved and illustrated books: the envious will be against him. She replies supportively – 'do you outface them & then Strangers will see that you have an opinion' – and he takes heart:

> Now I think we should do as much good as we can when we are at Mr Femality's. Do you snap & take me up, and I will fall into such a passion. I'll hollow and stamp & frighten all the People there & show them what truth is. (E 465)

Some sense of an underlying comic consciousness, an element of staged performance in Blake's passionate contrariness and fearsome sublimity, might be one road towards the palace of wisdom.

Notes

1. For example, M. M. Bakhtin, *Dialogic Imagination: Four Essays*, ed. M. Holquist (Austin, TX: University of Texas Press, 1981), pp. 291–5, 301–2, 323–4.
2. J. Locke, *An Essay Concerning Human Understanding*, ed. P. Nidditch (Oxford: Clarendon Press, 1979), II, xi, 2, p. 156.
3. See the excellent discussion by M. England, 'The Satiric Blake: Apprenticeship at the Haymarket?', in W. K. Wimsatt (ed.), *Literary Criticism: Idea and Act. The English Institute 1939–1972. Selected Essays* (Berkeley, CA: University of California Press, 1974). Further arguments reinforcing the connection between

Foote and Blake are given in N. Rawlinson, *William Blake's Comic Vision* (Basingstoke: Palgrave Macmillan, 2003), pp. 245–7.
4. T. S. Eliot, *Selected Essays* (London: Faber, 1972), p. 303.
5. And behind Erasmus lies Lucian, whose 'Menippean satire' is sometimes seen as an indirect influence on, or analogue for, the *Marriage* in particular.

CHAPTER 12

Prophecy

Ian Balfour

The poetry and thinking of William Blake is substantially indebted to the variegated tradition of biblical prophecy and to a lesser extent to its literary afterlife in writers such as John Milton, his main precursor along these lines. It is clear that Blake thought of himself as something of a prophet, certainly as someone inspired from above: 'I am not ashamed, afraid or averse to tell you', he writes to Thomas Butts in 1803, 'what Ought to be Told. That I am every night under the direction of Messengers from Heaven Daily & Nightly' (E 724). The biblical prophet is traditionally understood to be a human vehicle for God's words, either directly, as is often explicitly announced as such, or indirectly via a sort of inspiration diffused and disseminated through the prophet's words and action. (Indeed, for several eighteenth-century thinkers, such as William Warburton in his *Divine Legation of Moses Demonstrated*, the prophets were adduced as models of action *as* speech.)[1] The prophets tend to be singular in their time and place, called by God to address certain configurations of his people and others. But Blake's fervent wish was for this singular figure of the prophet to be generalised absolutely. The motto closing the opening 'Preface' to Blake's epic *Milton* consists of this quotation of a desideratum from Moses: 'Would to God that all the Lords people were Prophets' (Num. 11:29 [pl. 1[i], E 96]), a passage itself strategically quoted by the historical Milton in his *Areopagitica*. For such a situation – all the Lord's people as prophets – to be thinkable, much less possible, the senses of prophet and prophecy need to be expanded beyond their typically reductive, received meanings. Blake was an intense and individualistic, even eccentric, reader of the Bible but his relation to the prophets, especially the so-called 'literary' prophets, was nonetheless primed by a then-recent set of analyses and 're-creations' of the Bible that laid some of the foundation for his extravagant mode of poetic prophecy.

The sense of biblical prophecy as poetry was rather impressionistic or sketchy before the middle of the eighteenth century. In the British tradition, it had emerged only sporadically, as in a text such as Sidney's *An Apology for Poetry* (c. 1595). The recognition of ancient Hebraic or Judaic prophecy as poetry was really only consolidated and bolstered by the precision and force of the efforts of Robert Lowth who, as professor of poetry at Oxford in the 1740s, delivered strikingly original lectures to be published as *De sacra poesi hebraeorum* (1753).[2] The Latin lectures impressed Gibbon and had a palpable effect on Christopher Smart but their widespread diffusion in English was delayed until their translation in 1787. Lowth's signature innovation was to show how Hebrew poetry depended in good measure on parallelism of clauses rather than on anything approximating the structures or strictures of Greek and Roman prosody.[3] This feature can be registered in the biblical-inspired verse of Smart as well as of Blake, as, say, in this passage from the opening speech of George Washington in *America*, one of the two poems Blake expressly designated as a 'prophecy':

> A bended bow is lifted in heaven, & a heavy iron chain
> Descends link by link from Albion's cliffs across the sea to bind
> Brothers & sons of America, till our faces pale and yellow;
> Heads deprest, voices weak, eyes downcast, hands work-bruis'd,
> Feet bleeding on the sultry sands, and the furrows of the whip
> Descend to generations that in future times forget.
>
> (3: 7–12, E 52)

Lowth's analysis moved briskly from the important technical account of parallelism to a more encompassing one emphasising the highly figured and sublime texture of biblical poetry (more than four lectures are devoted to the sublime), one that rendered or acknowledged as poetic much of what was formerly considered prosaic or quasi-poetic. The Lowthian strand of thinking, shared by numerous figures of his generation and even more in the following one, helped craft a new sense of the Bible as less historical (in its reference) and more (mytho-)poetic than ever before, with the earliest books of the Bible, such as Genesis and Job, thought to be the most mythical. In Germany, where Lowth's reception was early and intense, the newfound sense of the Bible as crucially dependent on this verbal aesthetic made it seem that Scripture was poetic, narrowly and broadly construed, and indeed not so remote from non-scriptural poetry, especially those modes written in a Christian or Judaic spirit. The Bible almost all of sudden emerged as eminently re-readable – subject to new interpretations – and newly re-writable. Blake could comment in the margins of Bishop

Watson's *An Apology for the Bible* (1797): 'It is strange that God should speak to man formerly & not now, because it is not true' (E 615).

The sense of the prophet as someone singled out by God to be a carrier of his message to the people co-exists in Blake with the levelling, democratic impulse that the prophet could be anyone and, in that respect, no one special after all. Both these impulses are present in *The Marriage of Heaven and Hell*, where the writer can say in the second 'Memorable Fancy':

> The Prophets Isaiah and Ezekiel dined with me, and I asked them how they dared so roundly to assert. that God spoke to them; and whether they did not think at the time, that they would be misunderstood, & so be the cause of imposition.
>
> Isaiah answer'd. I saw no God, nor heard any, in a finite organical perception; but my senses discover'd the infinite in every thing, and as I was then perswaded. & remain confirm'd; that the voice of honest indignation is the voice of God, I cared not for consequences but wrote.
>
> Then I asked: does a firm perswasion that a thing is so, make it so?
>
> He replied. All poets believe that it does, & in ages of imagination this firm perswasion removed mountains; but many are not capable of a firm perswasion of any thing. (pl. 12, E 38–9)

The Blakean persona brings Isaiah and Ezekiel back down to earth and renders them immediately present in his historical moment. The prophets speak with a distinctly Blakean vocabulary ('finite organical perception', discovering 'the infinite in every thing') and their message is a Protestant-friendly one of the authority of individual persuasion or conviction. The greatest prophet is, ideally, just one of us but at the same time Blake consistently identifies the prophet as an exemplary poet and one exercising extreme powers of imagination and vision.

If one looks at all the writings and sayings of those called prophets in the Hebrew Bible, it is not as if the profile of a single, well-defined genre emerges. The writings called prophetic feature histories, exhortations to assembled people (usually God's people, the prophet's own nation), oracles against foreign nations, denunciations of monarchs, visions (night-time or otherwise), and, less often than not, predictions of the future.[4] This last is the mode commonly thought, from the point of view of Christianity, to be most typical and even definitive of the prophet. Blake calls this 'the modern sense' of the prophet and, partly drawing on his great predecessor John Milton and an older Protestant sense of 'speaking forth' or 'speaking out', as in Jeremy Taylor's *The Liberty of Prophesying* (1647), he rails against it, proposing instead another model, arguably also somewhat reductive, but closer to the actual texture of prophetic discourse:

> Prophets in the modern sense of the word have never existed Jonah was no prophet in the modern sense for his prophecy of Nineveh failed Every honest man is a Prophet he utters his opinion both of private & public matters / Thus / If you go on So / the result is So / He never says such a thing shall happen let you do what you will. a Prophet is a Seer not an Arbitrary Dictator. ('Annotations to Watson', E 617)

This is emphatically not what Christian commentary later made of Hebraic prophecy, as the former was fixated on seeing the messianic and typological character of Hebrew scripture wherever it could more or less plausibly be found, as in the interpretation of Isaiah's notation of a certain Immanuel born to a young maiden, understood erroneously, with immense historical consequences, by Christian interpreters to mean 'virgin'.[5] Unlike apocalyptic literature, which is largely taken up with revealing *a* or *the* future, prophecy is more of a generically various mode that presents a posture of indignation and provocation concerned with the present and an immediate or near future, one just around the corner. That is certainly the ethos governing a good deal of *The Marriage of Heaven and Hell*, a bundle of different subgenres and generic impulses, which reads almost like an anthology of different biblical modes, reminding us that the Bible itself is an anthology. The books of the great literary prophets (Isaiah, Ezekiel, Jeremiah) have the texture of cobbled-together anthologies, as most palpably in the Book of Isaiah, within which scholars identify at least three different Isaiahs. There is, however, in the 'Argument' of *The Marriage of Heaven and Hell*, a clear sense that the present is a version of what has been seen before and to recognise this we are directed to consult some chapters of Isaiah which should be ready to hand:

> As a new heaven is begun, and it is now thirty-three years since its advent: the Eternal Hell revives. And lo! Swedenborg is The Angel sitting at the tomb; his writings are the linen clothes folded up. Now is the dominion of Edom, & the return of Adam into Paradise; see Isaiah XXXIV and XXXV Chap. (pl. 3, E 34)

This is not necessarily to say that Blake's (or our) situation has been predicted but that his – the advent of the new heaven coincides with the date of Blake's birth and the thirty-three years passed is an overdetermined Christological number – and maybe ours (it is 'now' again) is a repetition of something seen long ago by the prophets.

In political terms, it is congenial to Blake that the Hebrew prophet is so often set against the king. Though a common function of the prophet was to anoint the king, many of the former exhortations and oracles are delivered either for or against. The prophets tended not to offer timeless truths but directives and warnings. In this latter mode, their utterances were performative (in J. L. Austin's sense) and conditional ('if you go on So / the result is So'), geared far more to changing how the ancient Israelites acted rather than giving them a glimpse into an actual, fixed future seen by the prophet in advance. Their messages, explicitly or implicitly on behalf of God, were pointedly directed at certain groups. Something of this posture survives in the addressing of different sections of *Jerusalem* to distinctly different constituencies: 'To the Public', 'To the Jews', 'To the Deists', 'To the Christians'.

Consistent with this revisionary sense of prophecy, the two poems Blake expressly labelled 'Prophecy', *America* and *Europe*, were not so much concerned with predicting a future as with diagnosing recent and present historical moments as a kind of call to intellectual arms.[6] *America* schematically, but also in some detail, outlines the drama of the American Revolution, casting its action in a lexicon with a preponderance of figures derived from the Bible. In the passage quoted above with regard to Washington and America, the phrase 'sultry sands' seems more resonant of ancient Israel and Egypt than the shores of America. Yet the action of the revolutionary situations of these two poems, of revolution in both senses as disruption and return, prompts Blake to draw on biblical tropes of the harvest and the vintage, which, on the one hand, seem to indicate a finite, particular end (there is only one harvest or vintage per year), but, on the other hand, can be read as figures for *the* end. In biblical criticism, the modes of prophecy and apocalyptic are thought to be rather distinct, with the latter typified by the Book of Daniel and Revelation, and the former characterised by the likes of the books of Amos and Hosea and the trio of great literary prophets.[7] But the line is already a little blurry in the Bible itself, not least given that the book of Revelation is rife with quotations from the prophetic books, and given that both modes draw on a common stock of figures and schemes. This line is blurred further throughout Blake's work. The very fact that he can speak, paradoxically, of '*A* last Judgement' (E 563, emphasis mine) rather than use here the far more usual locution 'The Last Judgement' is an index of the relative non-distinction, at some points, between prophecy and apocalyptic in his thinking.

Whereas the early Lambeth books, as Christopher Bundock has recently argued, are teleological in their drive,[8] Blake's arguably most prophetic poem, his brief epic *Milton*, is in its texture discontinuous, recursive, and repetitive. Its outlines reveal that Blake is often rehearsing what is essentially one and the same moment: the moment in each day that Satan cannot find, the moment of inspiration, the moment when one prophet is folded or incorporated into another, the moment when Milton descends from Eternity to become one with the Blakean persona of the poem, entering through the 'tarsus' (think Saint Paul) of the latter's foot. All these (and more) moments of inspiration, quotation, incorporation, and descent are identified with each other. Together they assemble a picture of this paradigmatic moment as one of selflessness or loss of self as one voice gives way to another. The prophetic writings are citational from the start, quoting God's words and soon to be quoted by later prophets, writers of apocalyptic literature, and eventually by poets in the prophetic line. A prophet 'sacrifices' his or her words to a different higher or earlier source while affirming his or her status as a prophet. That *Milton* consists of various, more or less dilated sequences, all of which are a version of this moment when the self is no longer simply itself, speaking or acting as another, means that the poem, with various quasi-narratives all having a single referent, is an allegory. It means something other than what it, in the first instance, says. Blake sometimes had, like so many of his Romantic contemporaries, a dim view of allegory but he could also maintain that 'Allegory addressd to the Intellectual powers [...] is My Definition of the Most Sublime Poetry' (Blake to Butts, 6 July 1803, E 730).

As Blake's *Milton* approaches its close, we see one last descent cast in vertiginous oscillation of literal and figurative vision that recapitulates prophetic utterances (turned into writing) in an apocalyptic mode or something just short of apocalypse:

> Then as a Moony Ark Ololon descended to Felphams Vale
> In clouds of blood, in streams of gore, with dreadful thunderings
> Into the Fires of Intellect that rejoic'd in Felphams Vale
> Around the Starry Eight: with one accord the Starry Eight became
> One Man Jesus the Saviour. wonderful! round his limbs
> The Clouds of Ololon folded as a Garment dipped in blood
> Written within & without in woven letters: & the Writing
> Is the Divine Revelation in the Litteral expression:
> A Garment of War, I heard it namd the Woof of Six Thousand Years.
> (42[49]: 7–15, E 143)

What can it mean to have the revelation of the Book of Revelation as a text in the closing moments of *Milton*? Perhaps the most highly figurative text in the whole of the Bible appears in its sheer literality. Just as one might hope for some interpretative resolution to the enigmas of this brief epic, one is sent back to the riddling enigmas of Revelation. The phrase 'written within & without' recalls Revelation 5:1, a verse which in turn goes back to

Ezekiel 2:10. Blake often draws on Ezekiel, the most imagistic, diagrammatic, and schematic of the prophets. Prophecy in general may tend to the iconoclastic but Ezekiel himself can be emphatically iconic. Here, though, what surfaces is the word, the written, highly figured word. The action that Ezekiel–Milton–Blake urges in the end is something like the Augustinian injunction: 'tolle, lege'. Take up and read. That is, prior to the ethical imperative to act comes the requirement to figure out what, more or exactly, the prophetic message is calling for.

Notes

1. W. Warburton, *The Divine Legation of Moses Demonstrated*, 4 vols. (London, 1736). The 'essay on hieroglyphs' constitutes Book IV and is found in Vol. 2.
2. R. Lowth, *Lectures on the Sacred Poetry of the Hebrews*, trans. G. Gregory, 2 vols. (London, 1787). The text is a translation of *De sacra poesi hebraeorum*, 2 vols. (Göttingen: 1758 and 1761).
3. The major modern study of parallelism, which includes an account of Lowth, is that of J. Kugel, *The Idea of Biblical Poetry* (New Haven and London: Yale University Press, 1981).
4. Blake can call two poems of his 'A Prophecy' and scholars with some justification refer to other of his writings as 'prophetic', the latter of which draw on any number of subgenres or generic impulses characteristic of the biblical prophets without any one of those 'prophetic writings' being identifiable as 'a prophecy'. 'Prophecy' designates a genre, 'prophetic' a mode.
5. H. Marks points to the momentous, tendentious (mis)translation of the Hebrew *'almah* as 'virgin' when it more properly meant 'a young woman' of marriageable age, in the superb notes for his edition of *The English Bible: King James Version* (New York: Norton, 2012). The passage in question is Isaiah 7:14.
6. Though a good many Romantic poems are justifiably seen as prophetic in their mode, the designation of a poem as a prophecy is rare. Byron's 'A Prophecy of Dante' is one prominent exception.
7. On this not entirely stable distinction, see L. L. Grabbe and R. D. Haak (eds.), *Knowing the End from the Beginning: The Prophetic, Apocalyptic, and Their Relationship* (London and New York: Bloomsbury, 2003).
8. C. M. Bundock, *Romantic Prophecy and the Resistance to Historicism* (Toronto: University of Toronto Press, 2016), especially 141ff. Bundock's study is attentive to the complicated historical texture of prophecy, in its production, reception, and even its ontology. The historicity of actual biblical prophecy is elusive not least because of the ambiguity of Hebrew tenses, such that is often not even clear where a given passage in the prophets refers to the past or the future, a feature to which Robert Lowth is already attentive.

CHAPTER 13

Rhythm

Derek Attridge

No one, perhaps, has praised Blake's metrical achievements more highly than George Saintsbury, who, in his three-volume *History of English Prosody*, refers to the poet's 'extraordinary prosodic quality which, almost as much as his thought, his imagery, and his passions, distinguishes him as a poet'.[1] The importance to Blake of metrical technique is evident from his earliest publication, *Poetical Sketches*, which shows a young poet trying out a number of different metres and beginning to search for ways to refashion to his own purposes the models he found around him. These models were many.[2] The smooth blank verse of immediate predecessors such as Akenside or Thomson is reflected in the collection's opening blank verse poems, while the ballads in Percy's *Reliques of Ancient English Poetry* and the faux-medievalism of Chatterton's Rowley poems lie behind 'Gwin, King of Norway' and 'Fair Elenor' (the latter, however, is in iambic pentameter quatrains rather than the usual ballad stanza). Blake writes six (mostly) iambic pentameter stanzas in a rather inaccurate 'Imitation of Spencer', and mixes two-beat and three-beat lines in 'Mad Song', replicating the metrical freedom of several of the six 'Mad Songs' in Percy's collection. The most fruitful influence is Shakespeare's, not so much in the obviously imitative blank verse historical drama *King Edward the Third* but in the several short-lined 'Songs' that look back to the lyrics from the plays and forward to the *Songs of Innocence and of Experience*. 'My silks and fine array', to take one example, achieves impressive economy in its stanza form – a three-beat quatrain followed by a couplet made up, unusually, of a four-beat and a three-beat line. Here is the final stanza (the poem spoken, in another departure from tradition, by a woman):

    Bring me an axe and spade,
     B   B   B   [B]

      Bring me a winding sheet;
       B   B   B   [B]

When I my grave have made,
  B   B   B   [B]

Let winds and tempests beat:
  B   B   B   [B]

Then down I'll lie, as cold as clay.
  B   B   B   B

True love doth pass away!
  B   B   B   [B][3]

Other Shakespearean echoes abound: 'Love and harmony combine' has four-beat lines beginning and ending on the beat like Puck's 'Now the hungry lion roars' while the four-beat couplets of 'Blind-Man's Buff' begin with an explicit echo of the Winter Song from *Love's Labour's Lost*. In all these examples, apart from 'Mad Song', Blake very rarely departs from a duple metre with a strict syllable-count, but in another 'Song', 'I love the jocund dance', he introduces an occasional double offbeat to create a momentary triple movement.[4] This rhythmic flexibility is something that he will exploit to the full in many of his later lyrics.

One of the most striking departures from traditional forms comes in the blank verse poems. Here Blake's use of enjambment challenges the wholeness of the pentameter line in a manner unthinkable for the poets in whose footsteps he is following; 'To Summer', for instance, begins: 'O thou who passest thro' our vallies in / Thy strength'. This may be a beginner's awkwardness (Henry Crabb Robinson, in 1811, declares of the volume, 'The metre is usually so loose and careless as to betray a total ignorance of the art' (*BR* 600)), but it is noteworthy that in his later prophetic books Blake returned to just this type of extreme enjambment.[5] In general, however, *Poetical Sketches*, from a prosodic perspective, is a volume noteworthy more for the sense of an apprentice trying out various tools than for its originality.

Poetical Sketches was printed in 1783, though according to the 'Advertisement' the most recent poems in it date from six years earlier. It is impossible to say, therefore, when Blake made the significant breakthrough visible – and audible – in the best poems of *Songs of Innocence*. What we have is the evidence of three poems written in a copy of *Poetical Sketches* with the date 1784, and some lyrics included in a manuscript of the same year, the burlesque narrative *An Island in the Moon*. Among the former group is an early version of *Innocence*'s 'Laughing Song', in which Blake already appreciates the rhythmic liveliness to be achieved by moving between triple and duple rhythms (or anapaests and iambs). The poem opens as follows, with '1' and '2' indicating single and double offbeats:

When the trees do laugh with our merry wit,
  2   B   1 B   2   B 1 B

And the green hill laughs with the noise of it.[6]
  2   B   1 B   2   B   1 B

This four-beat metrical form is sometimes referred to as 'mixed metre', but it is a distinctive metrical form in its own right, sometimes called, after a similar Russian metre, 'dolnik'.[7] In making extensive use of this metre, Blake drew not on his illustrious poetic forebears but on popular, and especially children's, verse, in which the four-beat template is subjected to numerous variations while maintaining the infectious rhythm that renders it so memorable. Nor is it likely that he is thinking in terms of anapaestic and iambic 'feet'; these deeply ingrained rhythms are learned in childhood – or, more likely, babyhood – and not in the schoolroom.[8]

Also in *An Island in the Moon* are the prototypes of 'Holy Thursday' and 'Nurses Song', each showing an important development in Blake's metrical art. The former is in fourteeners, the seven-beat line much used by Renaissance translators that was to play a major part in Blake's later poetic career. The fourteener sets the ballad stanza's lines of four and three beats as a single sequence of seven beats, though with a tendency to pause after four beats as well as at the end of the line (where the rhyme and the unsounded beat fall). This break can be felt in many of Blake's lines:

O what a multitude they seemd, these flowers of London town
B   B B   B ‖ B   B   B   [B]

Seated in companies they sit with radiance all their own
B   B   B   B ‖ B   B   B   [B]

(E 462)

The early version of 'Nurse's Song' is a more effective use of dolnik verse than 'Laughing Song'; it moves easily between triple and duple rhythms, maintaining the lilt appropriate to the children's cheerfulness but darkening it with the Nurse's concerns. Compare the openings of the first two stanzas:

When the tongues of the children are heard on the green
     2   B   2   B   2   B   2   B

And laughing is heard on the hill
 1   B   2   B   2   B   [B]

```
Then come home my children the sun is gone down
  1    B        2    B    2   B    2       B

And the dews of night arise
  2     B   1  B   1 B  [B]
```

By the apparently simple device of shifting from a triple to a duple rhythm after 'dews', the language is invested with a sudden chill. In a fourth song that reappears in *Innocence* (as 'Little Boy Lost'), the same flexibility of movement is effectively used, though in this bleaker poem the duple rhythm is dominant.

In *Songs of Innocence and of Experience* (composed *c.* 1784–94), Blake developed the metrical resources he had started to exploit in *An Island in the Moon*, almost entirely eschewing the pentameter line (the exceptions are 'The Little Black Boy' and the lines that end the stanzas of *Experience*'s 'Little Girl Lost'). Instead, a host of variations on the four-beat, four-line stanza are put to brilliant use.[9] Many employ the full form of the stanza (the 'long measure' of hymnody), such as 'Introduction', 'The Chimney Sweeper', and 'Laughing Song' in *Innocence* and 'A Poison Tree', 'London', and 'The Tyger' in *Experience*. The ballad stanza or 'common measure' occurs, for instance, in 'Nurse's Song' in both sets of poems. Other varieties are two-beat lines ('The Sick Rose'), a mixture of two- and three-beat lines ('Infant Joy'), three-beat lines ('My Pretty Rose-Tree'), and several other combinations of two-, three-, and/or four-beat lines. We could add to this catalogue of four-beat variations most of the notebook poems.

Some of these poems observe a strict syllable count, a property more characteristic of the literary tradition than of popular verse. We can take the 'Introduction' to *Innocence* as an example:

```
Piping down the valleys wild
B 1   B    1 B 1    B

Piping songs of pleasant glee
B 1   B   1   B 1    B

On a cloud I saw a child.
B  1 B   1 B 1 B

And he laughing said to me.
B   1 B   1    B   1  B
```

These seven-syllable lines – the metre of 'Love and harmony combine' in *Poetical Sketches* – are the simplest realisation of the four-beat rhythm, with no offbeats before or after the line. (In traditional prosody the metre would be described as headless iambic or tailless trochaic.) This strictness imparts a slightly literary quality to the verse, implying an adult speaker – a quality shared by other poems that observe a strict metre, such as 'The Divine Image' and 'On Another's Sorrow' in *Innocence* and 'London' and 'Holy Thursday' in *Experience*. A possible source often mentioned for Blake's *Songs* is Isaac Watts's *Divine and Moral Songs for Children*, an immensely popular collection which appeared in hundreds of editions under various titles after its first publication in 1715. Watts's 'moral songs' are in a variety of four-beat stanzas, in both triple and duple metres, and metrically very regular. Though often in the voice of the child, they convey a sanctimoniousness that Blake challenged even as he (perhaps) borrowed their metrical forms.

The other large group are the dolnik poems, in which there is no consistent pattern of stressed and unstressed syllables, or if there is, it is one that involves both duple and triple rhythms. Between a third and a half of the *Innocence and Experience* poems are in dolnik verse, as are many of the notebook poems that did not make it into publication. (The figure is imprecise because there is no clear dividing line between 'regular' and 'dolnik' verse; for example, a number of Blake's otherwise regular poems have lines that open sometimes on the beat and sometimes on the offbeat.) We have seen in 'Laughing Song' and 'The Nurse's Song' from *Innocence* how effectively Blake can take advantage of the expressive potential of the dolnik's capacity for shifting rhythms, all the while remaining true to the popular origins of the form. It is in these poems, perhaps, that Saintsbury's superlatives are fully justified.

Around the same time as he was composing *Songs of Innocence*, Blake was embarking on the poetic (and metrical) journey that was to engage him for the rest of his life. The manuscript of *Tiriel* and the published *Book of Thel* both date from 1789, and both use a version of the fourteener (or septenary) to narrate episodes taking place in a world of Blake's own creation. Of the shorter poems, only the 'Holy Thursday' of *An Island in the Moon* and *Innocence* uses the fourteener, in the strongly rhythmical form inherited from Golding and Warner[10] which has an implied division into groups of four and three beats. Many lines in *Thel* follow a similar pattern:

Why fade these children of the spring? born but to smile & fall.
   B   B   B   B ¦¦ B   B   B

Ah! Thel is like a watry bow, and like a parting cloud.
  B   B   B   B ¦¦   B   B   B

Like a reflection in a glass. like shadows in the water.
B   B   B   B ¦¦   B   B   B

(1: 7–9, E 3)

Although this is a variety of dolnik verse, one factor that militates against the lines' falling into the familiar four-line, four-beat rhythm is the absence of rhyme, which prevents any larger rhythmic structures from emerging.[11] This feature remains constant through all Blake's prophetic books.

Many other lines of *Thel*, however, introduce variations that impair the regularity of the traditional fourteener. And when we turn to *Tiriel*, we find even more lines that break out of this stable rhythmic pattern and thus make it harder to talk of beats, which are perceived only when the disposition of stressed and unstressed syllables stays within certain limits. Instead, in such lines it is probably better to identify *stresses*, as follows:

Soon as the blind wanderer enterd the pleasant gardens of Har
 S   S   S   S   S   S   S

They ran weeping like frighted infants for refuge in Mnethas arms
  S   S   S   S   S   S   S

The blind man felt his way & cried peace to these open doors
  S   S   S   S   S   S   S   S

Let no one fear for poor blind Tiriel hurts none but himself.
 S   S   S   S   S   S   S   S

(E 277)

How should we read these lines? The answer to this question is important, because it bears upon the vast majority of the poetic lines Blake wrote. One option is to do whatever can be done to make the lines conform to a seven-beat paradigm; in the third line above, for example, we might suppress the stress on 'man' as we would in regular alternating verse, and similarly for 'blind' in the fourth line. We would also need to exaggerate the pauses between successive syllables carrying beats, and rush through sequences of several unstressed syllables. This seems to me a forced solution, and I would prefer to let the seven-beat rhythm emerge when the line positively invites it but otherwise to read with the stressing that makes most rhetorical sense. The verse retains a degree of rhythmicality, even though the strong alternations that produce the experience of beats disappear.[12] This rhythmic prose shows the clear influence of the Authorised Version of the Bible and of Macpherson's Ossian poems.

Blake himself justifies his choice of the long, irregular line in the preface 'To the Public' at the start of *Jerusalem*:

> When this Verse was first dictated to me I consider'd a Monotonous Cadence like that used by Milton & Shakspeare & all writers of English Blank Verse, derived from the modern bondage of Rhyming; to be a necessary and indispensible part of Verse. But I soon found that in the mouth of a true Orator such monotony was not only awkward, but as much a bondage as rhyme itself. I therefore have produced a variety in every line, both of cadences & number of syllables. (pl. 3, E 145–6)

This preface was probably written in 1803 or 1804, so was in part a justification for much of the verse he had written as well as for the major prophecies, *Milton* and *Jerusalem*, that he was just beginning. Much like Milton casting off rhyme, or like an early free verse poet casting off metre, Blake is claiming a new expressive freedom, an ability to choose his words not because they conform to a pre-existing scheme but because they best say and do what he wants them to say and do.

In the prophetic books of the 1790s that follow *Tiriel* and *Thel*, we find Blake experimenting with versions of his long line. *The French Revolution* lengthens the line still further, with many eight-stress lines and additional unstressed syllables, often producing a triple rhythm. *Visions of the Daughters of Albion* and *America* play freely around the seven-beat norm, starting most lines with the standard iambic opening and avoiding strong enjambments almost entirely. In *Europe* and *The Song of Los* Blake tries breaking up the line, with shorter units evincing the same irregularities of stressing of the longer ones. The *Books* of *Urizen*, *Ahania*, and *Los* test a consistent short line, usually of three or four stresses, that avoids the rhythmic swing of four-beat verse. However, for his most ambitious poems – *Milton*, *Jerusalem*, and the unpublished *Vala, or the Four Zoas* – Blake stuck to the most successful version of his invented form: the long line that settles from time to time into the seven-beat pattern but prefers to expand and contract, saving the rhythm from the monotony Blake disparaged by varying the number and disposition of unstressed syllables and by frequent enjambments. The resourcefulness of this metrical form can be fully appreciated only in a long passage, which space will not allow; a few lines from the first book of *Milton* will have to suffice. They describe the creations of Los, Blake's champion of inventiveness, and never stray far from the seven-beat unit with its tendency to pause after four beats:

> These are the Sons of Los, & these the Labourers of the Vintage
> Thou seest the gorgeous clothed Flies that dance & sport in summer

> Upon the sunny brooks & meadows: every one the dance
> Knows in its intricate mazes of delight artful to weave:
> Each one to sound his instruments of music in the dance,
> To touch each other & recede; to cross & change & return
> These are the Children of Los. (26[28]: 1–6, E 123)

Not all the verse of the prophetic books is as rhythmically controlled as this passage; much works more like efficient prose. As Blake admits in his preface to *Jerusalem*, 'prosaic numbers' suit the 'inferior parts', alongside the 'terrific' and the 'mild & gentle' (pl. 3, E 146). But, as he also says, 'all are necessary to each other'.

Notes

1. G. Saintsbury, *History of English Prosody*, 3 vols. (London: Macmillan, 1906), III, 9.
2. See M. R. Lowery, *Windows of the Morning: A Critical Study of William Blake's 'Poetical Sketches' 1783* (New Haven: Yale University Press, 1940).
3. 'B' indicates a beat, '[B]' the felt but unsounded beat at the end of the three-stress lines in the context of four-beat verse. This unsounded beat is realised in the musical settings of ballads, though when all but one of the stanza's lines have only three realised beats, as here, the effect of this 'virtual' beat is weak. See D. Attridge, *The Rhythms of English Poetry* (London: Longman, 1982) and *Poetic Rhythm: An Introduction* (Cambridge: Cambridge University Press, 1995).
4. In the terms of traditional foot-based prosody, he substitutes an anapaest for an iamb.
5. N. Frye highlights these early examples of strong enjambment in his valuable discussion of Blake's metres in *Fearful Symmetry: A Study of William Blake* (Princeton: Princeton University Press, 1947), p. 183.
6. Erdman does not print this poem, instead noting the changes in the final version (E 792). See W. H. Stevenson and D. Erdman (eds.), *The Poems of William Blake* (London: Longman, 1971), pp. 40–1.
7. Dolnik metre is one of the oldest in the English tradition, attested as early as the thirteenth century, and a staple for popular verse since then. Its strong rhythm and variation in syllable-count reflect its close association with song. See D. Attridge, *Moving Words: Forms of English Poetry* (Oxford: Oxford University Press, 2013), ch. 7.
8. If Blake had had an upbringing without nursery rhymes, he could have found a collection in the recently published *Mother Goose's Melody*; see A. Ostriker, *Vision and Verse in William Blake* (Madison: University of Wisconsin Press, 1965), p. 50.
9. On the variations of the four-beat rhythm, in both smaller and larger groupings of beats, see Attridge, *Rhythms*, pp. 84–96, and *Poetic Rhythm*, pp. 147–52.

10. Arthur Golding's translation of Ovid's *Metamorphoses* (1567) and William Warner's *Albion's England* (1586) were two notable long poems in fourteeners, both in rhyming couplets.
11. For this reason, I have not shown a virtual beat at the end of each line. Increasingly in the prophetic books, Blake uses enjambment that overrides any inclination to pause at line-end.
12. There has been a great deal of discussion of Blake's long line, often in the rather forced terms of classical foot-prosody; Ostriker's chapter in *Vision and Verse* (pp. 120–44) is representative. Frye recognises that the verse does not have a 'recurrent prosodic unit' (*Fearful Symmetry*, p. 185) and W. Kumbier, in 'Blake's Epic Verse' (*Studies in Romanticism*, 17 (1978), 163–92), challenges the idea that the varied rhythm is set against an abstract pattern, though his proposed musical notation is too detailed to be a useful alternative.

CHAPTER 14

Songs

Steve Newman

William Blake begins and ends in song. 'Song' is the first genre he names in his first published volume, *Poetical Sketches* (1783), and songs are plentiful in *An Island in the Moon*, the riotous and polymorphous satire composed about the same time. The last plate with text in the last of his prophetic books tell us that we have reached 'The End of The Song / of Jerusalem' (99: 7–8, E 259). The works he produces between *Poetical Sketches* and *Jerusalem* are filled with songs and singing, not only *Songs of Innocence and of Experience* but also *The Song of Los*, and 'the Song of Spring' in *Milton* (31[34]: 29, E 130). Blake's life, too, describes a song-filled arc. The recent discovery of his mother's Morvaian affiliations bolsters the conjecture that as a child he heard Moravian hymns, their rhythms and figures finding their way into *Songs of Innocence and of Experience.*[1] Then there are the songs he might have heard growing up in London, including the multifarious broadsides then sold on the streets and the songs performed at the pleasure gardens of Ranelagh and Vauxhall. Add to this the songs he may have read, such as those in Joseph Ritson's *A Select Collection of English Songs* (1783), for which he supplied nine engravings. Later in life, he is remembered to have been 'very fond of hearing Mrs. Linnell sing Scottish songs' and he 'sang, in a voice tremulous with age, sometimes old ballads, sometimes his own songs, to melodies of his own.' As he expired, he is reported to have 'burst out into singing of the things he saw in Heaven' (Gilchrist 294, 362).

If songs form a key context for Blake's life and work, his work also shows how songs can transform contexts; and in what follows I will sketch how he revises Street Cries, hymns, and songbooks, and how this bears on his representation of one specific context – the city where he spent almost all his life. In so doing, Blake poses trenchant questions about the emerging elite interest in collecting popular texts, about the role political hierarchy and cultural capital play in this attraction to 'the low', and, more broadly, about the transformative power of songs.

An Island in the Moon presents a farrago of songs as the Islanders travel from one parlour to another, ranging from a satire on the profession of surgery to a ribald piece in which Scipio Africanus tells Dr Johnson to 'kiss my Roman anus' to the precious pastoral of 'the song of Phebe and Jellicoe' (E 455, 458, 457). The city outside asserts itself when they are interrupted by the sounds of '1st Vo[ice]' asking if anyone 'Want[s] matches' and a '2d Vo[ice]', a fickle customer, replying 'Yes' and then 'No–'. What is the effect on the Islanders as this uninvited snatch of song moves from the street into their polite parlour?

> Here was Great confusion & disorder Aradobo said that the boys in the street sing something very pritty & funny about London O no about Matches Then Mrs Nannicantipot sung
>
> > I cry my matches as far as Guild hall
> > God bless the duke & his aldermen all.   (E 458)

As I have discussed elsewhere, this song mimics the Cries of London, which date from the fifteenth century and which remained much in vogue in the streets and on the stage of eighteenth-century London.[2] Representing the patter of those seeking custom in the city, they are re-packaged as a textualised and often-illustrated slice of urban sound by turns cacophonous and euphonious, reduced to quaint order for the reader. Similarly, the matchseller's song enters into the refined domestic space of the Islanders, travelling without respect to social boundaries as songs in the city are wont to do. As one song often evokes another, Aradobo remembers one 'about London'; that Blake washes out this phrase does not erase the sense that these Cries are indeed 'about London' in the sense of being both 'on the subject of' and 'in the vicinity of' the city. For the alternate Cry that Aradobo remembers and Mrs Nannicantipot then sings shows how the chaotic energy of the metropolis can be contained. Her Cry infantilises the singers – the initial Voices are not assigned an age, and not all matchsellers were children – and also places specific geographical and sociopolitical boundaries around the Cry, as it reaches only to an urban sign of great commercial power ('as far as Guild hall') and blesses the representatives of the ruling class. In this way, without apparent design, the unruly sounds of the city are contained.

For Blake, children are not so easily confined, and pat judgements about songs, the city, and political power cannot stand. This is born out in a song that appears a couple of scenes later in *An Island in the Moon*, what would in *Songs of Innocence* be titled 'Holy Thursday'. Against the disorder of the matchsellers we have neat rows of clean-faced children filing 'two & two' into London's grandest monument to Church and State, 'the high dome of [St] Pauls' on a particular day set by the liturgical calendar (ll. 2, 4, E 462). At first glance, this orderliness does not seem oppressive. 'Flow[ing]' like 'thames water', 'these flowers of London town' have an organic life that springs from the city, the 'of' in 'of London town' signifying as both of-as-from and of-as-metonym (ll. 4, 5). But if they are unlike the restricted, commercialised 'charterd Thames' of a darker 'London' that appears in *Songs of Experience*, they are also well ordered: 'Seated in companies' and marked out by clothing in particular colours, they resemble the livery companies that organise and rule the economic life of London.

Yet if the children have 'innocent faces clean' (l. 1), this only highlights that the forces responsible for arraying them so neatly are not innocent, whether or not the speaker is aware of this. In a deft re-contextualising of the poem within the history of charity schools more broadly and charity schoolchildren singing on Holy Thursday in particular, David Fairer homes in on the explosive implications of the term that the speaker uses to characterise them: 'The hum of multitudes were there but multitudes of lambs' (l. 7). Well before Burke's infamous stigmatising of 'the swinish multitude', the word 'multitude' had already emerged as a condensation point for anxiety about an unruly urban mass, and the reassuring qualification that these are 'multitudes of lambs' shows how easily 'on another occasion the "hum" might figure differently. How easily their voices could become those of a disorderly mob if left unregulated.'[3] Instead, they are arrayed to voice their thanks for the self-congratulatory benefit of those who rule over them.

This historicist account must be supplemented with one that acknowledges more clearly the power of song to transform context; the control of this 'multitude' is challenged when its ambient 'hum' comes into focus as song: 'Then like a mighty wind they raise to heavn the voice of song / Or like harmonious thunderings the seats of heavn among' (ll. 9–10, E 463). The phrasing of 'the voice of song' calls attention to the specific act of singing. Again, we have the subtle intensification that comes with 'of' – 'voice' might be read to be *from* song but also the epitome *of* song within a wider set of vocal possibilities. Here, the particular type of song is the hymn. Blake's era is particularly rich in hymnody, from Isaac Watts's *Divine and Moral Songs Attempted in Easy Language, for the Use of Children* (1715) to the Wesleys' Methodist hymns, to John Newton and William Cowper's *Olney Hymns*.[4] At this point, hymns were sung either in the older form of the metrical psalm, enshrined in Sternhold and

Hopkins's Psalter of the mid-sixteenth century, or the more recent form of Anglican chant. The metrical psalm, while often scorned by those higher in the status hierarchy, encouraged 'the congregation to take an active part in worship' while Anglican chant was limited mostly to the performer(s).[5] Blake, for his part, sets the poem that represents the hymn in the common meter of the metrical psalm, and this commonality is a sign of and source of their power. As the '[t]housands [...] rais[e] their innocent hands' (l. 8, E 462), they push against the physical and metaphorical bounds of the institution that would contain them and display them for the glory of the 'beadles' and other 'guardians of the poor' (ll. 3, 11). In the *Island* manuscript, Blake continues in this vein, the speaker likening the children *to* angels and also possibly eliciting a response *from* them: 'Let cherubim & seraphim now raise their voice high' (E 850). But he deletes these lines, coming back down to earth, as it were, and focusing instead on how the voices of the children, 'raise[d] to heavn', elevates them above 'the revrend men' who are supposedly their 'guardians' but who appropriately sit '[b]eneath them' (ll. 9, 11, E 463). The bringing of heaven into touch with earth carries over to the conclusion as the poem turns to the audience and concludes with the proverbial: 'Then cherish pity lest you drive an angel from your door' (ll. 11–12). Depending on how innocent we think this speaker is, we may or may not attribute him the consciousness that this line critiques 'the revrend men' whose charity is merely formal and thus cannot recognise angels when they see them, or, more radically, as an attack on the very idea of 'pity' as requiring a status difference predicated on an unjust economy ('Pity would be no more / If we did not make somebody poor', we are told in 'The Human Abstract' (ll. 1–2, E 27).) But however we read the last line, this song illustrates with particular clarity the power of song itself to alter and perhaps fundamentally critique the context that commands the singing.

In *Songs*, the social loci of singing present in *Island* are fainter. Largely absent, too, are the more extended experiments in *Poetical Sketches* with amatory song, 'mad song', and antiquarian stylings along the lines of Chatterton and Macpherson that are part of the elite collection of popular song in the era. What we do get is a profound exploration of the power of song in shaping the identity of singer and audience and the political effects of that power; and a key vehicle for that exploration is Blake's experiments in the visualisation of song. Elizabeth Helsinger has usefully observed that Blake's 'composite art' brings his songs closer to illustrated collections such as Ritson's; Blake 'seems to have shared Ritson's more generous attitude towards the varieties of print that might serve diverse audiences for song, more generous than Percy and other gentleman antiquarians.'[6] But then illustrations were still present in the ballads being sold on the streets of London and throughout the British Isles; although woodcuts had generally decreased in size and complexity in the move to slip songs in the eighteenth century, most ballads still carried some sort of illustration; and eighteenth-century ballads typically recycled older images, sometimes, it appears, to ironically juxtapose past and present.[7] Indeed, the elaborate illustrations in antiquarian collections themselves, such as *A Collection of Old Ballads*, might be recycled by enterprising low-end printers such as the Diceys.[8] So whether more directly from the streets or mediated through antiquarian collections, *Songs* is clearly affected by the visual and verbal elements of popular song.

Consider how 'Holy Thursday' is transmuted in its move from *Island* to *Songs*. The text is framed above and below by files of children (boys on top, girls below) led by adults, a visualisation of the order imagined and maintained by the authorities of school, church, and state. But the vibrancy of the colour and the turning of some of the children towards each other, rather than only facing front, pushes against the pious rigidities of officialdom, just as 'the interlinear vegetation, animals, birds, and human figures' are thicker here than in any other poem in *Songs*, a visual pun on the Living Word suggesting the vitality of the children's song echoing in St Paul's.[9]

Of course, what *Songs* also gives us that *Island* does not are Songs of Experience. For the speaker of this 'Holy Thursday', there is no joy to be taken in the sight of the children as he exposes the false kindness of charity: 'Babes reducd to misery, / Fed with cold and usurous hand' (33: 3–4, E 19). As for their song, he hears it as 'a trembling cry', since 'a song of joy' would be impossible in the 'land of poverty' in which they dwell (ll. 5–8); he elaborates on this geographical reading of their suffering:

> And their sun does never shine
> And their fields are bleak & bare
> And their ways are fill'd with thorns,
> It is eternal winter there.   (ll. 9–12)

Conversely, there can be no hunger or 'poverty' that 'appall[s] the mind' in a place where the sun shines and the rain falls (ll. 13–16, E 20). The Innocence of seeing the children as 'flowers of London town' is revealed to be the worst kind of naiveté. If we occupy this position uncritically, we are complicit in their suffering, conveniently obscured by the machinery of the ritual of their song in St Paul's.

But 'appall' – a pun on St Paul's? – is a tip-off that the speaker's eyes and ears are not the unerring guides he thinks they are, and this, in turn, brings us back to the power of songs to create, not just reflect, contexts. That the speaker of 'Holy Thursday' imagines the children's world as one where poverty 'appalls the mind' suggests that he may suffer from the same limitations in the way he hears and sees their song in his song. For him, their song becomes literalised, concretised as the sound of those trapped in an eternally wintry landscape. This literalism is then reiterated in the companion claim that where the sun shines, no appalling poverty can be found.

Like so many other speakers in *Songs*, this one is struggling to make sense of an intolerable situation, and one response Blake is aiming to elicit through his songs is what Helsinger, drawing on Bruce Smith's groundbreaking analysis of broadside ballads, resonantly calls 'empathetic mimesis'. Just as Blake's songs are 'full of the line and phrase repetitions and structural symmetries' typical of broadside ballads, they also 'offer the singer and the listener [...] the possibility of becoming many subjects, by internalising the sounds and rhythms of those subjects' voices'.[10] But the way that the speaker of 'Holy Thursday' (*Experience*) hears the charity-school children's song also reveals that 'empathetic mimesis' may itself mask a sort of mimetic violence. In the prophetic books that follow, Blake repeatedly stages scenes in which characters 'become what they behold', transformed usually for ill by the limited and limiting evidence of their senses, dominated by their context (see *Jerusalem* 39[44]: 32, E 187; 66: 36, E 218). Then there is the converse dynamic: we are prone to transform the objects of our vision or hearing to conform to our presuppositions and thus distort them to our ends. By assuming that the children's song could be nothing but the sign they dwell in a land of 'eternal winter', even if he can imagine some alternate sunny place, the speaker/hearer of 'Holy Thursday' overlooks that the children's song *right now* renovates the space they are in, a transformation audible to the ears of the Innocent speaker who has a more flexible stance towards the interaction of song and space, even if he, in turn, misses the oppression that places them where they are. *Songs*, through its composite art and its exploration of the dialectic of innocence and experience, uses song to enliven our eyes and perk up our ears to the way musical language enunciated by speakers not often afforded that privilege might reveal the relationship between 'the people' and the contexts that shape them and that they might shape.

However, if Blake's songs transform their contexts, they also must contend with the contexts of their own production and reception.

The labour-intensive methods Blake employed to elicit this response and his marginal place in the elite cultural economy of his time meant that his work circulated in his own time and for many decades thereafter much less widely than a broadside ballad of even limited popularity, pointing to the limits of song to transform material contexts. Though his work has the power to alter how we think of book and song, politics and vision, it cannot on its own rewrite the history of the media in which it is enmeshed.

Blake continues to rely on song both thematically and formally for the rest of his career, sometimes reminding us of the dangerous power of songs, especially when sung by women, to make listeners become what they behold/hear; for example, the lulling 'nightly song' that helps keep Enitharmon passive for '[e]ighteen hundred years' in *Europe* (9: 5, E 63). Songs echo in the city of Blake's senses and vision, especially in *Jerusalem*, where the narrator reports that 'The Shuttles of death sing in the sky to Islington & Pancrass / Round Marybone to Tyburns River, weaving black melancholy', a darkening vision countered by 'the Song that [Los] sings on his Watch' drawing on the calls of the watchmen who nightly patrol the streets of London (*Jerusalem* 37[41]: 7–8, E 183; 85: 21, E 244).

By far the best known of his later songs, and one that gives us a vision of a city renewed, is the hymn detached from the Preface to two of the four known copies of *Milton*, given the title 'Jerusalem' in the early twentieth century. Here, after Blake urges his audience in oratorical prose to resist 'the hirelings' in 'the Camp, the Court & the University', which all seek to 'depress Mental & prolong Corporeal War', he moves back into the rhythms and images of the metrical psalm (pl. 1[i], E 95). He begins with a question: is it possible that 'the Holy Lamb of God' and 'the Countenance Divine' graced the 'mountains green' and 'pleasant pastures', the same place dominated now by 'these dark Satanic Mills' (1[i]: 3–8)? The present thus seems to be a blighted urban landscape, though this is not an anachronistic reference to industrial mills but rather to a self-limiting restriction of one's sight to the 'same dull round' (*There Is No Natural Religion [b]* IV, E 2), the mill of a universe dominated by those who would deny holy vision to embrace the empiricism of Newton and Locke.

But the speaker's vision is not bound by or to 'the mill'. He launches into a series of imperatives that presuppose the agency to transform this state of affairs, beginning with 'Bring me my Bow of burning gold' (l. 9). This expanded present makes space for a future redemption that returns us to 'mountains green' and 'pleasant pastures', as the speaker declares:

> I will not cease from Mental Fight
> Nor shall my Sword sleep in my Hand
> Till we have built Jerusalem
> In Englands green & pleasant Land. (ll. 13–16, E 95–6)

Drawing on the collectivising power of the hymn, the 'I' of the speaker expands into a 'we' who will rebuild Jerusalem, telescoping place and time into a redeemed city envisioned in the singing itself.

Despite its transformative promise, the circumstances of its production means that 'Jerusalem' has even less of a chance to circulate its vision during Blake's lifetime than 'Holy Thursday', limited to two copies of a large and expensive work of consummate visual and verbal art, their early provenance unknown. Yet the longer history of 'Jerusalem' also confirms how songs are frequently not contained by their initial modes of production and circulation. Key to its popularity has been Hubert Parry's setting of it in 1916 at the request of Robert Bridges, which began its ascendance as an unofficial English national anthem. It has since been used by groups with a wide range of political orientations,[11] and the apex of this enshrinement, at least in terms of the sheer size of the audience, was its integration into the Opening Ceremonies of the 2012 London Olympics, directed by Danny Boyle. There, in the midst of the contemporary city, it begins Boyle's extravaganza of British history, as the pastoral English countryside is displaced by the emergence of smokestacks and bowler-hatted Victorian gentlemen – and then later by the National Health Service and the World Wide Web. Blake might recoil from his hymn being pressed into service for an event dominated by the hirelings of great nations who see sports as war by other means, saturated in corporate sponsorships that enrich the International Olympic Committee and the media conglomerates that broadcast it worldwide. But it is worth noting that Boyle, at least, hopes that a utopian message will survive the cacophony, that 'that through all the noise and excitement you'll glimpse a single golden thread of purpose – the idea of Jerusalem – of the better world, the world of real freedom and true equality [...]. And that it will be for everyone'.[12] Or, as Blake writes underneath the verse in *Milton*, quoting Numbers 11:29, 'Would to God that all the Lords people were Prophets' (pl. 1 [i], E 96). Boyle thus takes his place amidst the thousands who have made Blake's songs their own, ranging from the rich, dark art-songs of Benjamin Britten to the goofy ecstasies of Allen Ginsberg to the invigorating roots music of Martha Redbone.[13]

These diverse re-inscriptions of Blake lead us back to the attractions and complications of songs as context. Despite the work of musicologists, cultural historians, and those focusing on the history of the print trade, especially its lower reaches, we do not yet fully understand the processes behind the persistence or disappearance of songs, and the ways they are valued or not.[14] Songs may endure for centuries, such as 'Children in the Wood' or 'Auld Lang Syne'; or they may disappear quickly, such as topical ballads by Grub Street hacks or the seasonal songs at the pleasure gardens (though these, too, may have long lives). A broadside purchased for a penny not only costs less but also carries less cultural capital than that same song in an up-market song-book such as George Thomson's *A Select Collection of Scottish Airs* (1793–1818), or in an antiquarian collection such as Thomas Percy's *Reliques of Ancient English Poetry* (1765), which Blake owned (*Stranger* 26). The valuations themselves change over time – for instance, as folklorists began in the later nineteenth century to prize the authenticity of oral recitation over print and even manuscript. Similarly, the particulars of a song's performance – a dimension too-often forgotten in the focus of literary scholars on text – also mark differences in cultural profile. Hearing a ballad sung in the street is not the same as hearing a 'Border Melody' performed by Mrs Linnell, the wife of one of Blake's patrons, on that relatively new and genteel instrument, the pianoforte. Even when ambient rather than foregrounded, like a song heard faintly echoing down a street, even when silent, like the 'files of ballads dangl[ing] from dead walls' in *The Prelude*,[15] songs shape the texts that incorporate them in complex ways.

Notes

1. See K. Davies, 'William Blake's Mother: A New Identification', *Blake / An Illustrated Quarterly*, 33.2 (Fall 1999), 36–50.
2. On Street Cries in eighteenth-century England, see S. Shesgreen, *Images of the Outcast: The Urban Poor in the Cries of London* (New Brunswick: Rutgers University Press, 2002). See also S. Newman, *Ballad Collection, Lyric, and the Canon: The Call of the Popular from the Restoration to the New Criticism* (Philadelphia: University of Pennsylvania Press, 2007), pp. 141–54.
3. D. Fairer, 'Experience Reading Innocence: Contextualizing Blake's "Holy Thursday"', *Eighteenth-Century Studies*, 35.4 (Summer 2002), 535–62 (p. 555).
4. On Blake and hymns, see J. R. Watson, 'Romantic Poetry and the Wholly Spirit', in D. Barratt, et al. (eds.), *The Discerning Reader* (Grand Rapids, MI: Baker Books, 1995), pp. 195–217, and N. Hilton, 'What Has *Songs* to Do with Hymns', in S. Clark and D. Worrall (eds.), *Blake in the Nineties* (New York: St Martin's 1999), pp. 96–113.

5. W. H. Stevenson, 'The Sound of "Holy Thursday"', *Blake / An Illustrated Quarterly*, 82 (Spring 2003), 137–40 (p. 138).
6. E. Helsinger, 'Poem into Song', *New Literary History*, 46.4 (Autumn 2015), 669–90 (p. 680).
7. A. Franklin, 'Making Sense of Broadside Ballad Illustrations in the Seventeenth and Eighteenth Centuries', in K. Murphy and S. O'Driscoll (eds.), *Studies in Ephemera: Text and Image in Eighteenth-Century Print* (Lewisburg, PA: Bucknell University Press, 2013), pp. 169–94.
8. See D. Dugaw, 'Popular Marketing of "Old Ballads": 18th-Century Antiquarianism Reconsidered', *Eighteenth Century Studies*, 21 (1987), 71–90.
9. 'Illustration Description' to *Songs of Innocence and of Experience*, obj. 19, WBA.
10. Helsinger, 'Poem into Song', pp. 682, 681.
11. J. Whittaker, 'Mental Fight, Corporeal War, and Righteous Dub: The Struggle for "Jerusalem", 1979–2009', in S. Clark, T. Connolly, and J. Whittaker (eds.), *Blake 2.0: William Blake in Twentieth Century Art, Music and Culture* (Houndmills: Palgrave Macmillan, 2012), pp. 263–73.
12. For the text, see Riz Ahmed (@rizmc), tweet, 27 July 2012, #olympics2012, https://twitter.com/rizmc/status/228929779917807616
13. D. Fitch, *Blake Set to Music: A Bibliography of Musical Settings of the Poems and Prose of William Blake* (Berkeley, CA: University of California Press, 1990). Fitch issued a supplement in the Fall 2001 issue of *Blake / An Illustrated Quarterly*. For a useful survey, see K. Davies, 'Blake Set to Music', in Clark, Connolly, and Whittaker (eds.), *Blake 2.0*, pp. 189–208.
14. See C. M. Simpson, *The British Broadside Ballad and Its Music* (New Brunswick: Rutgers University Press, 1966), and R. S. Thomson, 'The Development of the Broadside Ballad Trade and Its Influence upon the Transmission of English Folksongs', Ph.D. diss., Queens' College, Cambridge, 1974. See also K. D. Murphy and S. O'Driscoll (eds.), *Studies in Ephemera: Text and Image in Eighteenth-Century Print* (Lewisburg, PA: Bucknell University Press, 2013).
15. J. Wordsworth, M. H. Abrams, and S. Gill (eds.), *William Wordsworth: The Prelude 1799, 1805, 1850* (New York: Norton, 1979), (1805) VII. 209.

CHAPTER 15

Sound

Michael D. Hurley

Blake is a poet of rich prosodical intensity, but also the author of recherché mystical riffs that many metrists categorise as prose, or at the very least, as 'belonging to a Debatable Land'.[1] The intricate, recursive euphony and strong ballad rhythm that mark his earlier verse give way to harsher and more diffuse dissonances in his later works, as he shifts from lyric to epic forms. But the man who started out writing 'songs' and ballads does not latterly forsake sound patterning as part of his expressive repertoire. On the contrary, it is in the later part of his career, when he comes to write his long, long-lined, unrhymed, and rhythmically equivocal 'prophecies', that he is most insistent on the oral origins and aural efficacy of his verse.

Jerusalem opens with the claim that the poem had been dictated to him from the divine voice which 'I hear, / Within the unfathomd caverns of my Ear' (pl. 3, E 145). As the last, lengthiest and broadest in scope of his prophetic books, that poem draws together and extends ideas scoped in his earlier 'prophesies': from his disavowal of 'paltry Rhymes; or paltry Harmonies' in *Milton* (41[48]: 10, E 142), to the extraordinary opening of *VALA / The Four Zoas*, which plays out the fate of man through sounds set against silence, secrets, and whispering. 'Hearing the march of long resounding strong heroic Verse / Marshalld in order for the day of Intellectual Battle' incites wrath in heaven, we are told (N1, p. 3, ll. 2–3, E 300). But divine truth cannot be won by intellectual battling alone: it requires the counter-marshalling of another kind of verse that can stir the imagination through 'the Auricular Nerves of Human Life' (N1, p. 4, l. 1, E 301). Blake arouses the reader by drawing on the warrant of divine dictation, and outwitting the limitations of propositional thinking through the non-semantic suggestiveness of sounds set to rhythms.

Blake's battle cry has mythic range, but he also commits himself in concrete terms. Rejecting the 'Monotonous Cadence like that used by Milton & Shakespeare & all writers of English Blank Verse, derived from the modern bondage of Rhyming', he offers readers of *Jerusalem* a poem of 'variety in every line, both of cadences & number of syllables', where 'Every word and letter is studied and put in its fit place', and 'all are necessary to each other' (pl. 3, E 145–6). Derek Attridge helpfully explains how this passage serves as Blake's justification for his choice of the long, irregular line, which tips away from what's recognisably verse to something more readily associated with prose (Chapter 13). But the 'necessity' to which Blake refers also alerts us to the extent to which his sounds work collectively and collaboratively, even (or especially) when he writes with his longer, metrically equivocal lines. Sounds realise 'variety' against each other, and 'fit place' is likewise determined by context. His rhymes are not merely 'sound effects', in other words (a descriptive phrase that is commonly used when discussing poetry in general and indeed Blake in particular);[2] they do not take effect, or affect us, as discrete sonic incidences. It is truer to say that his sounds 'convey' (as Susanne K. Langer understood it) 'the progress of an event through time'.[3] Rather than focus on the localised 'effect', then, it is 'necessary' to hear his sounds dynamically, synergistically, as evolving patterns that prime and recall each other.

Alexander Pope nicely captured this prosodic alchemy when he referred to poetry's 'Style of Sound'.[4] For Blake, however, there is something more at stake than mere style, and his poetics consciously reject the impeccably polished lines of eighteenth-century Augustine poetry that Pope exemplifies, attesting instead to a restless, Romantic spirit of revolution that valorises the poet as inspired *vates*. Blake looks backwards as well as forwards in this respect: he admires and in some ways seeks to emulate neoclassical linear design (and 'the hard and wirey line of rectitude' that he takes to be its ethical corollary (*Descriptive Catalogue*, E 550)); and his investment in the importance of man also allies him with a certain kind of eighteenth-century worldview. Yet his charged opposition to the conceit of scientific enquiry and his contradistinctive emphasis on the spiritual and imaginative makes him a radical firebrand for his time, seeking, through his disruptive energies, to recover the organic, spontaneous experience, by interplaying with sounds in ways ordinarily thought to be of debased style – from the tunes of the ballad and nursery rhyme, to broadsides, and the mythic resonances of Macpherson's *Ossian Poems*.[5]

In writing of the 'bondage' of rhyming, then, bondage is not an empty metaphor. Blake's concern touches the matter of having to write by numbers, to fulfil an abstract prosodical scheme, but his objection to this practice exceeds aesthetics. He believes the sonic qualities of his verse enable personal, social, and spiritual liberation, insofar as they excite the imagination, recalling the antinomian, revolutionary spirit of the Levellers and Ranters.[6] The equation Blake posits between poetic and society's health is stark, for being as baldy proportionate as it is boldly uncompromising: 'Poetry Fetter'd, Fetters the Human Race! Nations are Destroy'd, or Flourish, in proportion as Their Poetry Painting and Music, are Destroy'd or Flourish!' (*Jerusalem* pl. 3, E 146). Such claims are abstrusely abstract, but Blake grounds his understanding of poetry's power in its craft and execution; he consistently directs his readers to his poems' 'minute particulars'.[7]

End-rhyme is an instructive place to consider his prosodic particulars, marked as it is in Blake's verse not only by a sense of plenitude, but also by notable diversity and eccentricity. Although he 'consistently rhymes almost twice as much on long vowels as on shorts and dipthongs',[8] generally, his rhyme words are not especially rich or lush, in the manner of, say, Keats or even Coleridge. Nor are they especially strained or extravagant, when compared with those of, say, Hopkins or Swinburne, later in the century. Yet his rhymes nonetheless tease the ear, for the ways they are paired. Of the twenty poems collected in *Poetical Sketches*, eleven use end-rhyme, and each rhymes differently, and to different purposes. Some use alternating rhyme, others couplets, or mix between the two; one imitates Spenser's stanza ('An Imitation of Spen[s]er'), and another turns five four-line stanzas in quadruple end-rhyme ('Song' ['Love and harmony combine']).

Such delight and variety in sound is heightened in the lyric triumph of *The Songs of Innocence and of Experience*, all forty-five poems of which employ end-rhyme as a consistent feature. Many of the lines in these poems are short, and so their rhymes come thick and fast. 'The Ecchoing Green' exemplifies this pattern of plush sonic reprise, as may be heard from its first stanza:

> The sun does arise,
> And make happy the skies.
> The merry bells ring
> To welcome the Spring.
> The sky-lark and thrush,
> The birds of the bush,
> Sing louder around,
> To the bells' cheerful sound.
> While our sports shall be seen
> On the Ecchoing Green.   (ll. 1–10, E 8)

The poem performs the echoes its title describes – exciting a mood of titillated joy – and the end-rhymes especially ring out like 'merry bells', clear and pure, even though these rhymes are individually unremarkable.

What makes them plangent is not simply their proximity. Rhythm, rhetoric, grammar, and syntax sharpen their juxtaposition. The lines are structured by two main stresses, one of which falls on the rhyme words – partly because they rhyme, but also because the rhymes are the important words of the poem (rhetorically and grammatically), and because these words end their lines at a clear syntactical break (of ten lines, eight are indeed end-stopped by punctuation).[9] But it is perhaps only as we tip into the third and final stanza, as these 'merry' memories curdle into 'weary' words and sounds of the now 'darkening Green' (ll. 21, 30), that the bright and light loveliness of this earlier rhythmico-sonic gambol is fully felt, by contradistinction.

For the familiar ways in which Blake uses end-rhyme as a puissant feature of his verse, he also uses it in ways that are far less conventional than his contemporaries. This has been shown statistically,[10] but it is anyway already felt intuitively by the reader. Whereas many poems fold identical and cognate sets of sounds back into each other, often as a form of ultra-monorhyme risking 'semantic satiation', where the relentless repetition of identical sounds threatens to make the words meaningless, others are aurally arresting for the very reason that their rhymes refuse to snap shut. Of the poems from *Poetical Sketches* that use end-rhyme, a significant number repeat only their terminal consonants (e.g. 'grave' / 'have', and 'tomb' / 'come', in 'Song' ['My silks and fine array'], E 413). These rhymes are exceptions within their poetic contexts, and so take their identity and vigour for being unexpected; but in other poems near-miss rhymes play a dominant role (e.g. in 'Song' ['Fresh from the dewy hill'], E 416). Further unsettling the clinch of rhyme, Blake also plays our ears against our eyes. The second stanza of 'Song' ['How sweet I roam'd'] promises a rhyme that is perfect to look at ('brow' / 'grow'), but which semantic context tugs into imperfection:

> He shew'd me lilies for my hair,
> And blushing roses for my brow;
> He led me through his gardens fair,
> Where all his golden pleasures grow.   (ll. 5–8, E 413)

Pope was quoted above as providing a handy formulation for thinking about Blake's sounds, not as 'effects' but as 'style'; and Pope's pronouncements on the purpose of sound in verse are also heuristic. Not so much his prescription that 'sound must seem an echo to the sense' as his codicil that 'no harshness gives offence':[11] if we are to admire Blake's sound-symbolising, it is important to hear past the sweet trill of some of his earlier poems to appreciate also the combative urgency of his later works. To pick lines almost at random from *VALA / The Four Zoas*, 'His head shrill sounding in the sky' performs its thick sibilant shrillness; and a few lines on, the textured run of 'r' sounds in 'rugged wintry rocks' (clarified by the intervening 'g', 'd', 't', and 'ck' sounds) tips over its line ending to the sound-suggestive 'Justling together'. And a few lines after that:

> Bursting forth from the loins of Enitharmon, Thou fierce Terror
> Go howl in vain, Smite Smite his fetters Smite O wintry hammers
> Smite Spectre of Urthona, mock the fiend who drew us down
> From heavens of joy into this Deep. Now rage but rage in vain.
> (N1, p. 15, l. 14; p. 16, ll. 6–7, 9–12, E 309)

The drama of such lines – established through verbal and sonic parallelisms – makes a vividly sensual reading experience. Blake goes far beyond merely mimetic ambitions: he is aiming to do more than hammer home his sense of smiting, that is, by working that word for all its onomatopoeic worth. He surely does use sounds to 'echo' the prior verbal sense, but he also employs sounds to smite a new kind of sense. To take an example that cuts to the heart of his metaphysics as well as his poetics: he consistently uses sound to explore his preoccupation with opposing states – theological and ontological, circumstantial and theoretical, intellectual and emotional – and the idea that 'Without contraries is no progression' (*Marriage* pl. 3, E 34), by expressing these contrary states in words whose sounds recall and contrast with each other. Space does not permit an exhaustive survey, but even the briefest look at a poem such as *Milton* reveals how, through his destabilising use of the 'un'-prefix (from familiar terms such as 'unhappy' and 'unexampled' to ear-catching coinages such as 'unannihilated' or 'unpermanent'), Blake presses even harder than *The Marriage of Heaven and Hell* on the paradoxical, aporetic, and transrational claims of the mystic, in raising the notion that 'There is a place where Contrarieties are equally True' (30[33]: 1, E 129).[12]

While Blake sometimes seems, then, triumphantly to fulfil Pope's prescription that sound should 'echo' sense, at other times he appears to invert that relationship, such that the sense echoes, as it were, the sounds. This occurs at a local level in some of the 'un'-phrases quoted above, where sounds are linked to delineate contrasts and to challenge assumptions, rather than merely to imitate or illustrate. But taking his poems as a whole, we may hear that their overall tone is set by the pressure and texture of his sounds. The lyrical cycles of *Innocence* and *Experience* achieve their childlike immediacy at least as much from their nursery-rhyme prosodical structures as they do from their words. Without their keen sonic correspondences, which include play on sounds for their own ends beyond any obvious narrative purpose, the poems would read very differently. Take away the long-vowel end-rhymes and the alliterative patterns that render these verses so seductive to the voice, so incantatory and hypnotic, and the same words could seem sterile. At the other end of the scale, the grandly bombastic colour of his prophecies is defined by its seemingly unruly sounding. But these sounds are, we must appreciate, only seemingly unruly: Blake's interest in bardic poetry suggests that, far from wilfully abandoning the lyrical impulse in his later verses, he was in fact seeking sanction and purpose for an even more aurally arresting prosodical repertoire, through association with the prophets of the Old Testament. Robert Lowth and Thomas Howes had influentially shown how the Hebrew scriptures generate poetical order out of apparent disorder without obeisance to the strictures of classical literature, and Blake ardently took this cue. By exploring the aesthetic as well as discursive coherence of the oratorical styles evinced by these Christian prophets, which may – for the purposes of 'persuasive *argumentation*' – include abrupt transitions and juxtapositions, Blake fashioned a new sense of sound in his poetry. While Blake's later poems surely affront the fluent and mellifluous lyricism of the late eighteenth-century verse tradition, and stand also at odds with his own earlier writings, his later writings are in important respects more not less charged with sounding out his sense.[13]

However the relationship between 'sound' and 'sense' is conceived in Blake's verse, the hardening of these terms into separate categories that might merely 'echo' each other in the poem's 'argumentation' risks reducing his achievement. Sonic correspondences may be structural and local, demarcating stanzas; they may inflect individual words. Yet the music of Blake's verse also creates its own echo-chamber that includes the orbicular satisfactions of his full rhymes and fulsome contrasts as well as his oblique and often equivocal reprisals, within and between lines. His sounds concatenate through entire poems generating their own 'sense' that is not so much stable and paraphrasable as dialectical and even paradoxical: from his staged oppositions of innocence and experience and heaven and hell, to his rhymes and even his morphemic spins of the 'un-' prefix. Correspondingly, the sense of Blake's sound emerges also in a way that is not merely intellectual and lexical but also experiential and atmospheric, such as noted in 'The Ecchoing Green'. Blake does not offer us an efferent thesis, but 'a fragrance of sound, a melody of colour'. Swinburne, who caught this scent and sight in Blake, heard him as well as anyone, and so he also understood that, 'The sound of many verses of Blake's cleaves to the sense long after conscious thought of the meaning has passed from one.'[14] By playing on our 'Auricular Nerves', Blake outdoes 'conscious thought', as Swinburne suggests, by unsettling the usual, tidy relationship between 'sound', 'sense', and 'meaning' – and his verse style jags our ears for the very reason that it confounds the exegetical urge to tame it into paraphrase.

Notes

1. G. Saintsbury, *A History of English Prose Rhythm* (London: Macmillan, 1912), Appendix 1, p. 469.
2. 'Sound Effects' is frequently, and misleadingly, applied to poetry in general (see E. R. Weismiller, 'Sound Effects in Poetry', in Alex Preminger and T. V. F. Brogan (eds.), *The New Princeton Encyclopedia of Poetry and Poetics* (Princeton: Princeton University Press, 1993)), and to Blake's verse craft in particular (see A. Ostriker, 'Sound Effects', in *Vision and Verse in William Blake* (Madison, WI: University of Wisconsin Press, 1965)), ch. 6.
3. S. K. Langer, *Mind: An Essay on Human Feeling*, 3 vols. (Baltimore, MD: Johns Hopkins University Press, 1972), II, 134.
4. A. Pope, letter to W. Walsh, 22 October 1706, in *Letters of Mr. Alexander Pope: And Several of His Friends* (London, 1737), p. 37.
5. On Blake's echoing broadsides and other popular and sub-literary verse, see J. Hollander, 'Blake and the Metrical Contract', in H. Bloom and F. W. Hilles (eds.), *From Sensibility to Romanticism* (New York: Oxford University Press, 1970), pp. 293–310.
6. Ibid.
7. He refers to minute particulars no less than nine times in *Jerusalem* (E 185, 185, 194, 195, 205, 247, 248, 251), in ways that fold aesthetic, social, ethical, and indeed metaphysical concerns into a common commitment to particularity as such, as against abstraction.
8. Ostriker also notes a marked statistical proportion of long 'e' and 'i' sounds, seconded by 'a' sounds, as compared with samples from Watts, Gray, Collins, Coleridge, and Shelley (Ostriker, *Vision and Verse*, p. 82).
9. See R. Jakobson on how Blake's 'verbal art' not only shapes his poems' rhythmic sound, but also his sounds likewise shape the semiology of his poem's words: 'On the Verbal Art of William Blake and Other Poet-Painters', in K. Pomorska and S. Rudy (eds.), *Language in Literature* (Cambridge, MA: Harvard University Press, 1987), Ch. 29 pp. 479–89.
10. See Ostriker, *Vision and Verse*, Appendix B. Ostriker suggests Blake makes far more significant use of rhyming by like consonants between words (but where vowels differ, e.g. shade-bed) than Collins, Gray, or Coleridge (though he also uses off-rhymes less frequently in his later poems); and that he uses assonance

far more fully than any of them (Shelley is the only one of the four who uses any, and his use is extremely slight).

11. A. Pope, *An Essay on Criticism*, in *The Poems of Alexander Pope: A One-Volume Edition of the Twickenham Text with Selected Annotations*, ed. J. Butt (London: Routledge, 1965; repr. 1992), ll. 364–5.
12. For fuller analysis of Blake's destabilising prefixes, see M. D. Hurley, 'William Blake: Destabilized Particulars', in *Faith in Poetry: Verse Style as a Mode of Religious Belief* (London: Bloomsbury, 2017), ch. 1 (pp. 29–30).
13. L. Tannenbaum, *Biblical Tradition in Blake's Early Prophecies: The Great Code of Art* (Princeton: Princeton University Press, 1982), p. 30.
14. A. C. Swinburne, *William Blake: A Critical Essay* (London: John Hamden Cotton, 1868), pp. 9, 10.

CHAPTER 16

Sublimity

David Baulch

In the catalogue for his 1809 solo exhibition of paintings, William Blake refers to himself as a 'sublime Artist', yet he follows this claim by asserting that the 'Beauty proper for sublime art, is lineaments, or forms and features that are capable of being the receptacles of intellect' (E 544). While these comments convey the extent to which Blake identifies his aesthetic practice with the sublime, they also suggest that he overlooks the stark distinctions between the sublime and the beautiful upon which both Edmund Burke and Immanuel Kant insist. Thus, Thomas Weiskel concludes that 'Blake uses the word *sublime* as a general honorific.'[1] Whilst it is true that Blake's conception of sublimity is not congruent with Weiskel's largely Wordsworthian construction of 'the Romantic sublime', the sublime is neither a 'general honorific' in Blake's writings, nor a handy superlative. Rather, defining the sublime is a central concern in Blake's work as a painter and poet.[2]

To grasp what the sublime means in Blake's writings, it is necessary to recognise at least two distinct ways he uses the term. First, Blake uses the term 'sublime' to refer to a specific construction of the aesthetic within the period, when it was marshalled to describe a painterly style. In these instances, we can see both Blake's vociferous objection to Edmund Burke's aesthetic theory and the affinity of his own developing aesthetic with the Longinian sublime, especially as it was adapted to the discourse of painting in the eighteenth century. Second, Blake uses the term 'sublime' to refer specifically to a revolutionary poetic aesthetic he develops mainly in his post-1800 writings, and which he puts into practice in *VALA / The Four Zoas*, and *Jerusalem*.[3]

Blake's best-known engagement with the theory of the sublime is scribbled on the back of the title page of the eighth of Sir Joshua Reynolds's *Discourses* (1797):

> Burke's Treatise on the Sublime & Beautiful is founded on the Opinion of Newton & Locke on this Treatise Reynolds has grounded many of his

> assertions. in all his Discourses I read Burkes Treatise when very Young at the same time I read Locke on Human Understanding & Bacons Advancement of Learning on Every one of these Books I wrote my Opinions & on looking them over find that my Notes on Reynolds in this Book are exactly Similar. I felt the Same Contempt & Abhorrence then; that I do now. (E 660–1)

Here, Blake associates Reynolds's notion of the sublime with Edmund Burke's *A Philosophical Enquiry* (1757 and 1759), and displays his disdain for what he perceives as Burke's empirical approach to aesthetics. Blake links 'Burke's Treatise' with the writings of Francis Bacon, Isaac Newton, and John Locke – a trio pilloried in *Milton* and *Jerusalem*. Critics have come to see this marginal commentary as emblematic. Weiskel, for example, asserts that 'Blake's views on the sublime as an aesthetic category are perfectly clear in his annotations to Reynolds's *Discourses*.'[4] Similarly, for Vincent De Luca, Blake's comment on the back of the title page of 'Discourse VIII' is where 'Blake more or less identifies Burke as the baleful shadow behind Reynolds's own aberrations.'[5] Situating Reynolds within Burke's empirical construction of aesthetics, Blake apparently equates Reynolds with Burke in order to dismiss them both.

These scribbled lines do not tell the whole story, however.[6] In his marginalia to the *Discourses*, Blake – like Reynolds – draws on the theory of the sublime articulated in the fragmentary first century CE *Peri Hupsous*.[7] While Longinus's text enumerates the qualities of sublime writing and oratory, *On the Sublime*, as the text became known to the British, also influences conversations on the qualities of painting's 'greatest' or 'sublime' productions. Hence Reynolds makes his case for Michelangelo – also Blake's favourite painter – as *the* sublime painter, challenging the reigning neoclassical preference for Raphael. When Reynolds eschews Raphael's comprehensive mastery for the sudden, brilliant instants of the sublime in Michelangelo's work, he does so specifically through Longinus: '[I]f, as Longinus thinks, the sublime, being the highest excellence that human composition can attain to, abundantly compensates the absence of every other beauty, and atones for all other deficiencies, then Michael Angelo demands the preference.'[8] Both Reynolds and Blake reject Burke's sublime obscurity as a feature of paintings of the highest quality, advocating instead for the strongly outlined visual forms of the sublime style of history painting, which the *Discourses* derive from their adaptation of the Longinian tradition.[9] Concurring with Reynolds, Blake's marginal response flatly states, 'Obscurity is Neither the Source of the Sublime nor of any Thing Else' (E 658). Beyond the annotations to Reynolds's

Discourses, Blake relies on Reynolds's authority on the sublime in a letter dated 22 November 1802, where he attempts to correct the tastes of his patron, Thomas Butts, who asked for a painting in the popular picturesque style. Blake responds by loosely quoting Reynolds's letter to William Gilpin on the subject: '"You are certainly right in saying that Variety of Tints & Forms is Picturesque: but it must be remembered on the other hand. that the reverse of this – (*uniformity of Colour & a long continuation of lines*) produces Grandeur" – so says S^{ir} Joshua and So say I' (E 718–19). Blake clearly sees himself as part of the Longinian tradition informing Reynolds's notion of a sublime style.

Beyond the prescriptions for painting that were derived from Longinus's text, *On the Sublime* also provides Reynolds and Blake with a conception of the sublime as an aesthetic sensation. For Longinus, the particular aesthetic sensation of the sublime communicates an artist's 'boldness in thoughts' that allows an audience to feel that their 'soul is naturally elevated'. A reader feels an author's 'poetical image [...] palpably before the eyes', and he is thus elevated to the 'grandeur' of the subject.[10] Reynolds identifies this potential for 'elevation' through sensation with painting. Hence, for Reynolds, the sublime style of painting displays 'the most sublime ideas'. Sublime ideas foster a sensation incompatible with 'the lowest sensuality'.[11] To this assertion, Blake responds with unqualified approval: 'What can be better Said. on this Subject' (E 651). Yet while Blake and Reynolds agree that sublime paintings express sublime ideas, Blake's central point of disagreement with Reynolds's text concerns the origin of these ideas.

Blake's and Reynolds's opposing positions on the origin of sublime ideas are divergent possibilities native to Longinus's treatise. Both Reynolds's denial of innate ideas and neoclassical emphasis on imitation and Blake's romantic insistence on an artist's innate powers of originality find support in Longinus's text. In Section VIII, Longinus identifies 'five very copious sources of the sublime', and he divides them between two abilities that are innate, or 'immediate gifts of nature' as he puts it, and three that constitute a *techne* that one may acquire. Of the innate talents one must have to produce sublime work, 'boldness in thoughts' (Reynolds's 'sublime ideas') is first and next in line is the author's or orator's 'capacity of intense and enthusiastic passion'. For Longinus, the innate capacity for 'boldness in thoughts' is the 'most potent' ingredient of the sublime.[12] Nevertheless, when Longinus returns to the issue in Section XIII, he suddenly announces that there is 'also some other way, besides those already mentioned, which leads to things sublime [...] It is to imitate and emulate the great historians and poets of former days.'[13] Rather than a sixth source of the sublime, imitation and emulation effectively allow the capacity for innate ideas to be supplanted by previous works judged to be sublime. For the pedagogical purposes of the *Discourses*, Reynolds emphasises imitation, and it is on this point that Blake's views of the sublime diverge.

In *Discourse* VI, Reynolds offers his clearest statements that the greatest efforts in painting are products of imitation rather than the innate conceptions of genius. Reynolds's states, 'by imitation only, variety, and even originality of invention, is produced. I will go further; even genius, at least what generally is so called, is the child of imitation.'[14] Reynolds thus argues for a view of art in terms of a narrative of progress wherein criticism fixes rules and consolidates the achievements of the greatest artists. Blake's response reflects his contrary insistence on the individual's innate capacity for 'boldness of thought' as a crucial component of the sublime: 'If Art was Progressive We should have had Mich Angelo's & Rafaels to Succeed & to Improve upon each other But it is not so. Genius dies with its Possessor & comes not again till Another is Born with It' (E 656). For Blake, 'boldness of thought' cannot be imitated.

In conceiving of the sublime as a *techne* that can be learned by imitation, Reynolds freely ridicules *poiesis* as necessary for the sublime. If an artist must be divinely inspired to achieve the sublime, Reynold claims, the poet is 'himself but a mere machine, unconscious of the operations of his own mind'.[15] For an artist to believe that inspiration has a transcendent source, he renders himself a mere automaton of phantasmatic cherubs. While there are numerous anecdotes surrounding Blake's relations of just such visitations, and while Blake's work itself invokes such figures, the marginalia present a carefully qualified defence of 'boldness in thoughts' necessary for the sublime. In the marginalia, Blake does not assert that such winged figures are actual physical presences that visit poets and artists. Noting 'How very Anxious Reynolds is to Disprove & Contem Spiritual Perception', Blake suggests that what Reynolds mocks as inspiration and genius reveals his misunderstanding of the process of poetic and artistic creation (E 658). Blake's term 'Spiritual Perception' does not suggest classical *poiesis* as much as it asserts that the sublime is a mimesis of a distinct mental form. Blake makes clearer the distinction implicit in 'Spiritual Perception' elsewhere, when he writes that it is 'Manifest to all' that 'copiers of Nature are Incorrect while Copiers of Imagination are Correct' (E 575). In effect, Blake is making a distinction that points to neither Longinus's nor Reynolds's poles of *techne* and *poiesis*. While Blake is clearly drawing on the Longinian sublime as a central influence on the eighteenth-century discourse on painting, the Blakean sublime ultimately offers something new.

Following the assessments of De Luca, Peter Otto, Steve Vine, and others, it is clear that Blake uses the term 'sublime' to refer to a unique aesthetic sensation.[16] De Luca calls Blake's letter of 6 July 1803 to Thomas Butts 'the *locus classicus* for any extended consideration of Blake's idea of the sublime'.[17] Blake describes this poem as 'Sublime Allegory [...] addressd to the Intellectual powers while it is altogether hidden from Corporeal Understanding is My Definition of the Most Sublime Poetry' (E 730). As De Luca notes, Blake and Kant identify a similar division of faculties disclosed in the sublime.[18] However, their views of the implications of such an aesthetic diverge. Blake is no Kantian. For Kant, the aesthetic defines the transcendental conditions of human knowledge.[19] By contrast, Blake's 'Sublime Allegory' identifies the immanent potential for the production of that which is unprecedented. Rather than a transcendental sensation occasioned by the absolute ideas of Kantian reason that are unknowable in experience, the Blakean sublime is a sensation of that which is not yet an object of representation in the actual or material world; it 'is altogether hidden from Corporeal Understanding'. Here again, Blake's notion of the sublime relies neither on the natural nor the transcendent, but focuses instead upon the mental images produced by the 'Intellectual powers'. This is why Blake sees the sublime as revolutionary: through the aesthetic sensation of the sublime, that which is genuinely new has the potential to enter the world.

In *Milton*, for example, this potential of the sublime has distinctly political implications. The 'Preface' to *Milton* demands a revolutionary aesthetic, 'the Sublime of the Bible', that the poem associates with the sweeping social change it calls the 'New Age'.[20] The first sentence announces that 'The Stolen and Perverted Writings of Homer & Ovid: of Plato & Cicero. which all men ought to contemn: are set up by artifice against the Sublime of the Bible. But when the New Age is at leisure to Pronounce; [...] the Daughters of Memory shall become the Daughters of Inspiration' (E 95). In short, *Milton*'s 'Preface' objects to defining a *techne* of the sublime that produces art through imitation of 'Memory' as opposed to the 'Sublime of the Bible' that functions as a 'Spiritual Perception' or inspired mental image. There is also a politically revolutionary principle in Blake's notion of the sublime. Liberation from 'Memory' is the necessary precondition for the advent of a political 'New Age'. Thus the 'Preface' calls upon 'Painters! Sculptors! Architects' to resist 'Greek [and] Roman

Models' as a means of challenging the state's repressive and ideological apparatuses: 'The Camp, The Court, & the University' (E 95).

In *Jerusalem*, Blake's 'sublime Artist', Los, works to make 'Liberty' a political reality. Los's creations have the potential to be revolutionary for two reasons: first, they eschew the Enlightenment model of 'Reason', and second, they do not refer to any pre-existing tradition. At one point, the Blake narrator of the poem wonders aloud, 'What are those golden builders doing?' (12: 25, E 155). Los's 'sublime Labours' become the occasion for 'sublime Wonder' when the 'Spaces of Erin' emerge from the furnace of Los's strange creativity.[21] This 'sublime Wonder' suggests the unprecedented transformation of the English history of Irish subjection.[22] For Erin to be accorded her own spaces would certainly have occasioned 'sublime Wonder' as a British political policy in the eighteenth or nineteenth centuries. In *Jerusalem*'s finale, it is Los's 'sublime honour' in acting to dissolve the Enlightenment subject dominated by empirical Reason that makes possible Albion's 'Revolutions of Action & Passion' and the realisation of Jerusalem as a state of 'Liberty'.

In both *Milton* and *Jerusalem* there is no final sublime transcendence, political or religious, to a utopian world. The instant of liberty attained in the reunion of Jerusalem and Albion is just that – the instant of an aesthetic sensation that nonetheless is a literary or painterly image of the potential for that which is genuinely new, that is, revolutionary. By focusing on Blake's use of the term 'sublime', especially in post-1800 writings, we can begin to appreciate the extent of Blake's efforts to develop a revolutionary aesthetic, especially in the aftermath of the debacle of the French Revolution. While critics have long argued that Blake's engagement with all things political comes to end with the 1790s, a careful consideration of his protracted engagement with the sublime makes visible his continued and intensified efforts to put the aesthetic in the service of revolution.

Notes

1. T. Weiskel, *The Romantic Sublime* (Baltimore, MD: Johns Hopkins University Press, 1976), p. 67.
2. I omit the issue of the sublime style and engraving. See R. Essick, *William Blake Printmaker* (Princeton: Princeton University Press, 1980), pp. 63–76.
3. I omit any direct discussion of *The Four Zoas* and the sublime. See P. Otto, *Blake's Critique of Transcendence: Love, Jealousy, and the Sublime in* The Four Zoas (Oxford: Oxford University Press, 2000).
4. Weiskel, *Romantic Sublime*, p. 66.

5. See V. De Luca, *Words of Eternity: Blake and the Poetics of the Sublime* (Princeton: Princeton University Press, 1991), p. 52. De Luca does recognise that Blake's involvement with the Burkean sublime is both complex and profound in the illuminated books.
6. See J. Snart, *The Torn Book: UnReading William Blake's Marginala* (Selinsgrove, PA: Susquehanna University Press, 2006). Snart notes that, 'not all of his "Remarks" are indignant; some express outright agreement' (p. 136). Reynolds does not see himself as a Burkean. His treatment of the sublime is restricted to 'the language of painters' (p. 224).
7. Fragmentary and sometimes internally inconsistent, *Peri Hupsous* is a manuscript of uncertain date and authorship. Generally thought to have been written in the first century CE, the oldest copy of *On the Sublime* is from the tenth-century Dionysius Longinus, but the text did not become widely known until Francis Robortello's 1554 republication of it. *On the Sublime* reaches Britain through Nicholas Boileau Despréaux's French translation of 1674. For this chapter, I quote from the first English Language translation of the text by William Smith in 1739: *On the Sublime*, trans. W. Smith (London: S. Cornish and Co., 1739). For Longinus, the sublime and the beautiful are not opposites – rather the sublime indicates the highest degree of greatness written or rhetorical art can achieve: 'The sublime, when uttered in due season, with the lightening's force scatters all before it in an instant, and shows at once the might of genius in a single stroke' (p. 2).
8. J. Reynolds, *Discourses*, ed. P. Rogers (New York: Penguin, 1992), v, p. 86. In the first section of *On the Sublime*, Longinus states that 'sublimity flashing forth at the right moment scatters everything before it like a thunderbolt, and at once displays the power of the orator in all its plentitude' (*On the Sublime*, trans. Smith, p. 95).
9. Longinus considers the clarity of the 'image' produced by a text or orator to be a key element of the sublime: 'The design of a poetical image is to set the subject palpably before the eyes.' The sublime, for Longinus, places 'what you describe [. . .] before the eyes of your hearers' (ibid., p. 36). Thus, the literature and oratory Longinus calls sublime is inherently painterly and well adapted to subsequent treatises on the sublime in painting that emphasise the clarity of outline.
10. *On the Sublime*, trans. Smith, pp. 11, 10.
11. Reynolds, *Discourses*, IV, p. 63.
12. *On the Sublime*, trans. Smith, p. 11.
13. Ibid., p. 34.
14. Reynolds, *Discourses*, p. 101.
15. Ibid., p. 131.
16. The term 'sensation' – my preferred term to talk about what the sublime occasions in us – comes in part from Kant's use of the term to describe what is communicable in the aesthetic, and from Lyotard (in translation) (see the Further Reading list for details).
17. De Luca, *Words of Eternity*, p. 21.

18. Ibid., pp. 21, 24–7.
19. See S. Vine, 'Blake's Material Sublime', *Studies in Romanticism*, 41 (2002), 238–42.
20. M. D. Paley in *Energy and Imagination* (Oxford: Oxford University Press, 1970), and *The Continuing City* (Oxford: Oxford University Press, 1983) as well as L. Tannenbaum in *Biblical Tradition in Blake's Early Prophecies* (Princeton: Princeton University Press, 1982) point out the possible influence of Bishop Robert Lowth's *Lectures on the Sacred Poetry of the Hebrews* on the Blakean sublime.
21. For an analysis foregrounding the problem of labour in this passage, see D. Schierenbeck, '"Sublime Labours": Aesthetics and Political Economy in Blake's *Jerusalem*', *Studies in Romanticism*, 46 (2007), 21–42.
22. See R. N. Essick, 'Erin, Ireland, and the Emanation in Blake's *Jerusalem*', in *Blake, Nation and Empire*, ed. S. Clark and D. Worrall (Basingstoke: Palgrave, 2006), 201–13.

CHAPTER 17

System, Myth, and Symbol

Tilottama Rajan

Blake wrote: 'I must Create a System, or be enslav'd by another Mans' (*Jerusalem* 10: 20, E 153). Since then, starting with Yeats and Ellis in 1893, who were the first to publish *VALA / The Four Zoas* and emphasise its centrality, Frye, Damon, and others have drawn on self-summaries in *Milton* and *Jerusalem* that mask the inner turbulence of those poems, constructing Blake's system as a whole into which all the parts fit.[1] The 'system' is thus allied with the parallel fantasy of mythology, as organised by the logic of the symbol, which the Romantic philosopher Friedrich Schelling defines as realising the general in the particular or the whole in the part, whereas allegory and schematism disjoin them.[2] But the symbol is an epistemology rather than a reality: it posits an 'ideal of meaningfulness' that conditions our reading, the very need to theorise it being evidence of its ideality. Mythology was a particular projection of this epistemology, through which the Romantics hoped to renovate and unify modern life by uniting 'the dialectic of idealism' with realism.[3] Blake's system aims to be diagnostic, explaining the nightmare of history evoked in *Europe*, and prophetic, performatively moving us to outer revolution in the continental prophecies, salvaged as inner revolution in *Milton* and *Jerusalem*. And system is its QED. For without system, which Kant defines as the 'architectonic' totalisation of parts under 'one idea', we would have a 'mere aggregate':[4] myths rather than the desired new mythology.

Yet as Schelling says, the very search for a system 'presupposes' that originally knowledge 'does not exist in a system' and is an 'asystaton', something 'in inner conflict'.[5] This chapter focuses on the Lambeth Books (1793–5) as the dark interpreter of the apparently more assured later system. Blake's work of the 1790s is often read typologically through *Milton* and *Jerusalem*, which are seen as a consolidation that follows the deepening of the 1790s crisis in *VALA / The Four Zoas* (1797–1807). But when Blake began inventing his mythemes and ideologemes at Lambeth, they were 'giant forms' cast 'into the expanse', which were not yet 'arranged in libraries'.[6]

These books are bits and pieces of an encyclopedic work spanning history and pre-history: frontal views of episodes not yet composed into a narrative still under (de)construction. They fall into two groups, historical and metaphysical, or as arranged by the Princeton Illuminated Blake, Continental prophecies and psycho-cosmogonical Urizen books. Yet they introduce only a handful of Blake's later characters – Orc, Enitharmon, Los, Urthona, Urizen, Ahania, Fuzon, Palamabron: some false starts, others just named or not consistently present and identical across different texts. Rather than translating a concept into a character – as Damon's *Blake Dictionary* assumes – these names are acoustic forms whose content Blake is still discovering. Their strangeness figures the unreadability of events he struggles to grasp by naming them, while their uncouthness unleashes an anthropological primitivism of myth covered over by the more aestheticised pantheon of Greek mythology.

The Continental prophecies, *America* and *Europe*, are book-ended by the two parts of *The Song of Los*, 'Africa' and 'Asia'. Together they map revolution and reaction across world history and geography, as enacted by the firebrand Orc, son of Los (figuring imagination and later identified as a fallen form of the Zoa, Urthona). Thus 'Africa's' last line begins *America*, while Asia's kings hear their imminent demise in the howl from *Europe*, which ends on the verge of the French Revolution. Yet this Eurocyclic design is deeply compromised. *The Song* (1795), conceived as a retrospective frame for *America* (1793) and *Europe* (1794) even as the myth is falling apart in the Urizen books (1794–5), is merely schematic, consisting of two stubs. Whereas in mythology the particular realises 'the universal', in allegory it only 'means' or points to the universal, while in schematism the universal is a projection not grounded in the particular. The schematic or 'mechanical artist', whom Schelling compares to the geometer, creates according to a 'concept', producing a 'rough outline' in hopes of developing its parts into a 'fully concrete image'.[7] Though *America* is more detailed than *The Song*, particular persons (George V, Washington, the revolutionaries) are only gesturally aligned with universal, mythopoeic potencies, leaving the empirical and transcendental levels separate. *America* too falls short of what Coleridge calls symbol's 'translucence of the Eternal [. . .] in the Temporal', perhaps consciously disjoining sign and 'Reality' in allegory, which Coleridge describes as mere 'picture-language'.[8]

Moreover, in the Preludium the prophecy is inaugurated by Orc's rape of a nameless female, possibly Amerindian, while Orc himself taints America with 'darkness of Africa' (2: 8, E 52). Although Blake in the

1790s often naturalises violence as regeneration, these disturbing subtexts may be why the Bard breaks his harp in two copies, 'asham'd of his own song' (2: 18). In the more convoluted *Europe* Enitharmon, not yet identified as Los's emanation, is blamed for 1,800 years of botched history. But Enitharmon has been asleep, disconnecting cause and effect, a disjunction evident in the text's fracturing of the visual register into visionary and socially specific plates. Moreover, *Europe* too is self-critically divided between a misogynistic prophecy that ends with Los calling 'his sons to the strife of blood' (15: 11, E 66), and a Preludium spoken by a nameless shadowy female, perhaps Enitharmon herself before she is bound into Blake's myth and 'stamped with a signet' against her will (2: 10, E 52). Described surreally as a tree whose roots are 'brandish'd in the heavens' and whose 'fruits [are] in earth beneath' (1: 8), the female figures Blake's struggling, uprooted creativity whose unformed forms rebel against the form they are given. As Muse she fails to figure an inspiration that transcendentally precedes composition. 'Consumed and consuming', she produces Orc's fires but arises from his 'breast' (1: 1, 2: 4), and is herself brought 'into life' as she gives birth from her 'lab'ring head' (1: 11–12, E 51), at once the parent and (undelivered) embryo of gestation.

Through these origin-scenes and the opening of *Urizen*, which asks the Eternals to 'dictate [. . .] winged words' which it inconsistently describes as 'dark visions of torment' (2: 5–7, E 70), Blake sets his texts in the primal scene of their own uncertain conception. The Urizen books (*The [First] Book of Urizen, The Book of Ahania*, and *The Book of Los*) turn from history to pre-history, ostensibly to diagnose the causes of a malformed present in the archetypal drives that divide the world-soul after the separation of the faculties (later called Zoas). In his first sketch of this fall that is simultaneous with the creation, and thus unavoidable, Blake names only one 'Eternal', Urizen. To cure diagnosis through blame, commentators make Urizen the author of this trauma. They stamp Urizen as King and Priest, schematising him in a binary that opposes (U)reason to imagination so as to confine his disturbing metaphysical effects; and they project, beyond the ho(rizon) of these texts, a second birth of the Zoas or faculties from their fallen bodies. Yet Blake's unique fusion of cosmology and psychology opens his still embryonic system to a psychoanalysis of the paranoia and misogyny on which it depends to immunise itself against the doubts that arise from its increasingly disastrous unfolding. For Urizen can only be described by negatives, making it unclear who or what he is. As Blake writes, 'unknown, abstracted / [. . .] the dark power hid' which 'some' call Urizen (3: 5–7, E 70). Moreover, the poem's jammed syntax leaves us uncertain whether Urizen is cause or effect, agent or victim: when Urizen the 'winds merciless / Bound' (4: 19–20, E 72), the adjective could refer to Urizen or the winds. So has this 'obscure separation' (5: 40, E 73) withdrawn from the collective body or is it the Eternals, often mirror-images of Urizen, who 'confine' him in the North in an auto-immune response that reveals their plenum as already a void of avoidance? Is the 'primeval Priests assum'd power' (2: 1, E 70) a power Urizen seizes or one he is only assumed to have? Indeed, given that 'Priests' has no apostrophe, is it the other Eternals, figures for a recalcitrantly transcendental idealism, who assume power in banishing Urizen?

As Urizen 'lay[s] clos'd, unknown' in (or *as*) the 'petrific' landscape of primeval time, perhaps described as 'his' to personify something less tangible (3: 24–6, E 71), myth emerges as a compensation for science. For perhaps the 'horror' arisen in Eternity is some obscure geological or anthropocene mutation that the speaker can only explain by inventing the 'Demon' Urizen (3: 3, E 70). Moreover, the text's narrative grammar is also scrambled, as Chapter 3 attributes 'desarts' and 'armies' to Urizen (5: 14–16, E 73), before Los in two versions of Chapter 4 begins to form the part-subject Urizen, who could not have volitionally separated from the Eternals in Chapter 2 if he was not yet a complete subject. Thereafter Urizen is ejected and dejected over seven ages as a body in bits and pieces: spine first, brain and nerves, eyes and nostrils, then arms. The body is Kant's figure for the integrity of a system to which no contingent additions can be made that would alter its proportions, and as such can also be seen as an autoreferential figure for Blake's own corpus. But like contemporaneous biologists Blake is much concerned with what constitutes an 'organised' body, and the Lambeth books are closer to Deleuze's 'body without organs' than to Kant's architectonic body. The former does not lack organs; it simply lacks their 'organisation' in an order proceeding from head to foot. Unlike the organism, which has 'determinate organs', it is 'defined by an *indeterminate organ*', by 'provisional organ[s]' which are 'displaced' and 'posited elsewhere'. Its 'living reality' is 'hysteria'.[9]

Like Urizen's brain, the 'nervous' body of the Lambeth books 'branches' rhizomatically in different directions (11: 10–12, E 76), which cannot be unified in the service of a redemptive myth. It invents and discards or degenerates characters as provisional organs for a myth whose aporias Blake displaces but cannot resolve. Going behind the Continental prophecies' cast of Los, Enitharmon, and Orc, *Urizen* (1794) introduces a more transcendental (or primal) level of the system through the Eternals. Yet the Eternals are a failed draft and stand 'wide apart' from the poem (5: 41, E 73), since in Eternity there is no time and space, and hence there is everything but nothing. Contrary to Milton's *Paradise Lost*, distinctive life, 'bird, fish, serpent & element' (3: 16, E 70), emerges only with/as the Fall. That division is the very condition of possibility for life plunges Blake's myth into a spiralling self-division in which Urizen (though preceding Los in the text) is 'rent' from Los' side (6: 4, E 74), Los is divided by Pity and produces Enitharmon, she conceives Orc as a worm who issues from her, 'Howling ... with fierce flames' (19: 45), and the Eternals complete the 'tent' of their withdrawal, separating Los from Eternity (19: 37, 20: 2, E 79–80). In their growing absence, Blake develops the role of Los in ways that unravel its apocalyptic brevity in *Europe*, as Los struggles to shape 'Urizen', working on psychic rather than political matter. Yet since Los is now on a lower genealogical level than the Eternals, he lacks the agency he had in *Europe*. Enitharmon, as an object of pity, has also shed her villainness role. True, this function passes to Urizen, but the effect is to put these explanatory demons into a chain of substitutions. Insofar as Los replaces the Eternals as the site of Urizen's separation, he too seems a substitute marked by a prior narrative failure. Then Orc is crucified and replaced with Fuzon. But rather than being an agent of revolution, Fuzon follows the Eternals in leaving 'the pendulous earth', which he rationalises by calling it 'Egypt' (28: 21–2, E 83). Crucified in *Ahania* (1795), Fuzon too is discarded, his status as surplus limb marking Blake's system as one that grows by contingent additions, sometimes leading nowhere.

For Blake's contemporary Hegel, who resists the conventional Romantic symbol, 'symbolic' (as opposed to classical) art is still 'producing its content and making it clear to itself' and reflects 'the struggle of the spirit which continually invents without finding repose and peace'. The artist, caught in 'enigmas and problems', himself enters into 'the process of generation and parturition'.[10] Images of gestation are at the heart of the Lambeth books, especially the second group, where Urizen creates his 'world' by framing a 'roof' like a 'womb', even as he himself emerges as a 'globe of life blood' (*Urizen*, 5: 28–37, E 73; 15: 13, E 78). This womb that resizes itself as a globe, a world, a glob(ul)e of blood, and the orb of the sun recurs in the verbal and visual plates of *The Song* and *Urizen*, implicating Blake's own world-forming in its stalled gestation, and drawing masculine into female labour. Thus in the final plate of *The Song*, Los imposes spirit on matter by hammering a globe of fire in his furnace. But in *The Book of Los*, labouring to bind Urizen into a system, Los both works at a forge and on 'black marble', he himself also being this marble, which cracks into 'numberless fragments' (4: 3–25, E 92). The fragments include sporadic biblical references (to Adam, Christ, Moses), which function only as the negative of a systematic mythology that Blake cannot develop. Falling back in time, 'ages on ages' (*Book of Los*, 4: 31), Los then falls into the void and flails around like a 'babe / New born', producing a body whose organs emerge without any organisation (4: 38–45), like the texts themselves that lack any discernible architecture. Moreover, it is initially unclear if the body described is that of Urizen or Los. For the furnace, which is also an ocean and amniotic fluid, becomes Los's own body whose 'lungs heave incessant', as Los works from the outside on matter that works on him from within (4: 60, 54, E 93). As forge, anvil, and womb are confused, both male and female labour are dis-figured. In both *Urizen* and *Los* the sequence of birth is unsettled: characters who exist as whole subjects form again within the womb, so that birth comes in the middle of, rather than after, gestation as a process that continues endlessly.

The Book of Los is the reflexive coda to a series of texts that increasingly turn inwards to confront creativity at the level of its primary processes. Paranoia, hope, anger, and depression traverse these books as the 'unformed part' of an imagination that keeps inventing and 'crav[es] repose' (4: 59, E 93). But working on and in himself, Blake/Los is unable to separate himself from Urizen, as *Los* echoes lines, narrative sequences of birth and binding, and visual plates from *Urizen*, becoming *Urizen*'s conjoined twin.[11] Indeed, the problem is not that Urizen has separated from the Eternals but that Blake cannot neatly separate his characters into protagonists and antagonists to construct a system that would then fall into being 'Urizenic' or authoritarian. Eventually Los's furnaces, after 'endur[ing] / The chaind Orb in their infinite wombs' for 'Nine' (not seven) 'ages' do produce a separate Urizen, as Urizen's spine is 'bound down to the glowing illusion' of a 'Form' or system (5: 40–7, 55). Yet the 'immense Orb of fire' is thereby 'involved' in 'darkness and deep clouds', and there is 'no light' in this conclusion to an illuminated book that significantly contains no designs (5: 48–53, E 94).

The conventional view is that the Lambeth books are repeated and properly systematised in *Milton* and *Jerusalem*. But discussing the relation between the 'infantile' and 'adult series' in the context of repetition, Deleuze writes that embryology displays:

> systematic vital movements, torsions and drifts, that only the embryo can sustain: an adult would be torn apart by them. There are movements for which one can only be a patient, but the patient in turn can only be a larva. Evolution does not take place in the open air, and only the involuted evolves. [...] [T]hought is [...] one of those terrible movements which can be sustained only under the conditions of a larval subject.[12]

The adult Blake of the later prophecies, projected in embryo as the Eternals, cannot sustain the drifts, the terrible thought, which the larval, experimental subject of the Lambeth books is more willing to endure. But this does not mean that the Lambeth books are immature or minor. As Deleuze argues, 'every system' contains a 'dark precursor' that 'ensures the communication' of its different series, infant and adult.[13] As the infancy of the system, the Lambeth books unleash a torment that questions the philosophical bases of Blake's later redemptive system; introduce an art willing to be in uncertainties and doubts without reaching after fact and reason; and expose the adult system to a psychoanalysis of its defences solicited by the very combining of mythology, cosmology, history, anthropology, and psychology in a single system.

Notes

1. An exception is Ault, who sees the deep structure of Blake's myth as contingently generated by its surface happenings: a paradigm that extends beyond his analysis of *The Four Zoas*. See D. Ault, 'Re-Visioning the Four Zoas', in N. Hilton and T. Vogler (eds.), *Unnam'd Forms: Blake and Textuality* (Berkeley and Los Angeles: University of California Press, 1986), pp. 105–40.
2. F. Schelling, *The Philosophy of Art*, trans. F. Stott (Minneapolis, MN: University of Minnesota Press, 1989), pp. 46–8.
3. N. Halmi, *The Genealogy of the Romantic Symbol* (Oxford: Oxford University Press, 2007), pp. 1, 19, 133–48.
4. I. Kant, 'The Architectonic of Pure Reason', in *Critique of Pure Reason*, trans. and ed. P. Guyer and A. Wood (Cambridge: Cambridge University Press, 1998), pp. 691–701 (p. 691).
5. F. Schelling, 'On the Nature of Philosophy as Science' (1823), trans. M. Bullock, in R. Bübner (ed.), *German Idealist Philosophy* (Harmondsworth: Penguin, 1997), pp. 210–43 (p. 210).
6. Blake's description of the printing process in Plate 15 of *Marriage*.
7. Schelling, *Philosophy of Art*, pp. 46–8.
8. S. T. Coleridge, 'Definition of Symbol and Allegory', from *The Statesman's Manual*, in *Lay Sermons*, ed. R. J. White (Princeton: Princeton University Press, 1972), pp. 28–31 (p. 30). Vol. 6 of *The Collected Works of Samuel Taylor Coleridge*, 16 vols. (1969–2001).
9. G. Deleuze, 'Hysteria', in *Francis Bacon: The Logic of Sensation*, trans. D. Smith (New York: Continuum, 2002), pp. 44–55 (pp. 44–7). See also T. Rajan, 'Blake's Body without Organs: The Autogenesis of the System in the Lambeth Books', *European Romantic Review*, 26.3 (2015), 357–66 (pp. 358–63).
10. G. W. F. Hegel, *Aesthetics: Lectures in Fine Art*, trans. T. M. Knox, 2 vols. (Oxford: Clarendon, 1970), 1, 438–9.

11. For example, in *The Book of Los*, Los is described as a 'Solid / Without fluctuation (4: 4–5, E 91), like Urizen (*Urizen* 4: 12, E 71). *Los* 4: 54–63 (E 93) elaborates on the full-page Plate 11 in *Urizen*.
12. G. Deleuze, 'Repetition for Itself', in *Difference and Repetition*, trans. P. Patton (London: Continuum, 1997), pp. 70–128 (p. 118).
13. Ibid., pp. 119, 124–5.

PART III
Creative Cross-Currents

CHAPTER 18

The Bible

Stephen Prickett

Blake's uses of the Bible centre on one of the most curious paradoxes of his time.¹ On the one hand, formal religious practice in England at the end of the eighteenth century had declined to its lowest point before or since. In 1806 (the first year for which we have accurate statistics) two-thirds of the 10,000 or so parishes in England and Wales had no resident priest. On Easter Day 1800, in St Paul's Cathedral, London, the largest church in what was then the largest Christian city in the world, there were precisely six communicants. The rise of nonconformists and evangelicals – especially the Methodists and later the Clapham Sect – must be seen against the widespread institutional decay of the Established Church. Yet at the same time, the prestige of the Bible, as a *literary* model, had never been higher.

Nevertheless, powerful as Blake's own literary response to the Bible was, he was no less powerfully influenced by its moral teachings. That Blake was little understood in his own time does not mean that he was not influenced by current intellectual, spiritual, and aesthetic controversies. Most commentators on Blake's use of the Bible have stressed his unorthodoxy, his desire to create his own 'System' rather than 'be enslav'd by another Mans' (*Jerusalem* 10: 20, E 153). Readers of the oft-quoted 'Everlasting Gospel' (1818), for instance, might easily assume that he was a natural heretic, turning conventional assumptions upside down (see pl. e, ll. 13–14, E 524).

Yet whose were these conventional assumptions? Twenty years before this note-book outburst Blake had been caught up in a much more conventional biblical debate – and on an unexpected side. Bishop Watson, one of the few supposedly liberal bishops of the House of Lords, had undertaken a public refutation of Tom Paine's attack on the Bible in the second volume of *The Age of Reason* (1795). Blake's copy of Watson's *Apology for the Bible* (1798) is heavily annotated. Paine's attack had concentrated on the Hebrew atrocities of the Old Testament. Of Numbers 31, for example, Paine writes:

> Among the detestable villains that in any period of the world would have disgraced the name of man, it is impossible to find a greater than Moses, if this account be true. Here is an order to butcher the boys, to massacre the mothers, and debauch the daughters.

After a review of other, similar, atrocities, textual contradictions, and improbable events, Paine concludes:

> Of all the systems of religion that were ever invented, there is none more derogatory to the Almighty, more unedifying to man, more repugnant to reason, and more contradictory in itself than this thing called Christianity [...]. As an engine of power, it serves only the purpose of despotism; as a means of wealth, the avarice of priests; but so far as it respects the good of man in general, it leads to nothing here, or hereafter.[2]

Richard Watson, former Professor of Chemistry in Cambridge, now Bishop of Llandaff, had been chosen to lead the charge against Paine. His refutation is based upon then current arguments for 'natural religion'. Citing earthquakes, floods, famine, and pestilence as examples of the God-given natural order, he concludes that 'The Word of God is in perfect harmony with his work; crying or smiling infants are subjected to death in both.'[3] To his credit, Blake will have none of this. Though there was nothing new about this Deist premise that Nature reveals its Creator – it had been used by Morgan, Tyndale, and Bolingbroke earlier in the century – what is extraordinary is that Watson unquestioningly accepts it. Not for a moment does Watson suggest that New Testament teaching challenges the implications of the Old, or raise the Pauline doctrine of the Fall, that all Nature 'groaneth and travaileth' under the bondage of sin (Romans 8:22). For any other period, Blake's response would have been a paradigm of mainstream orthodoxy: 'To me [...] a defence of the wickedness of the Israelites in murdering so many thousands under a pretence of a command from God is altogether Abominable & Blasphemous.' To Watson's argument from the random violence of Nature, Blake writes:

> There is a vast difference between an accident brought on by a mans own carelessness & a destruction from the designs of another. The Earthquakes at Lisbon &c were the Natural result of Sin. but the destruction of Canaanites by Joshua was the Unnatural design of wicked men. (E 614–15)

On the back of the title page of his copy of Watson, Blake scribbled: 'To defend the Bible in this year 1798 would cost a man his life [...] Paine has not attacked Christianity. Watson has defended Antichrist' (E 611–12).

Blake's resistance to Natural Religion (also attacked in *There Is No Natural Religion*, 1788), and his stress on the theological significance of the Fall, was prophetic in ways he could not have foreseen. From what Thomas McFarland has called the 'Spinozistic crescendo' of the late eighteenth century, whereby all Nature (including humanity) becomes part of divinity, came a rejection of the Fall, and consequent closure of the traditional gap between God and his creation.[4] Implicit in this (as Hegel saw) is the idea of the perfectibility of man – a possibility which, taken up by Feuerbach and Marx, and suitably secularised and politicised, was to become one of the driving forces of twentieth-century Communist ideology. The trail is a long (and bloody) one, but clearly marked, and few Christians today would wish to argue with Blake's passionate and entirely orthodox resistance to contemporary apostasy.

At the same time, he was also caught up by what was increasingly seen as biblical aesthetics – a new word with a rapidly enlarged meaning at the end of the eighteenth century.[5] The new aesthetics begun by Robert Lowth's *Lectures on the Sacred Poetry of the Hebrews* (1753) had re-defined Hebrew poetry, proclaiming the sublimity of its rhetoric and diction. Together with his subsequent translation of Isaiah (1778), the *Lectures* were to strike a sympathetic chord all over Europe, and were widely translated and re-published. Translation of the *Lectures* was also necessary for much of the English-speaking world because they had been published, as they were delivered, in Latin. This meant that in a period when literacy was spreading rapidly – often well beyond the limits of the formal schooling – Lowth's work was initially only available to those with a thorough classical education, which did not, of course, include Blake. Though a full English translation, that of G. Gregory, did not appear until 1787, various sections had already appeared in a number of places – including the anti-Wesleyan *Christian's Magazine*, twenty years before, in 1767. Similarly, Hugh Blair had devoted a chapter to Lowth in his *Lectures on Rhetoric and Belles Lettres* (1783), as did Herder (for those who could read German) in his *Spirit of Hebrew Poetry* (1782–3).

The result was a slow aesthetic revolution across Europe. From Herder and the Jena Romantics in Germany to Chateaubriand in France, and Blake or Coleridge in England, the Bible was replacing the classics as the most potent literary model, and becoming, in Blake's words, 'the Great Code of Art' (*Laocoön*, E 274). Moreover, Blake's own multi-media prophetic works demonstrate how far this new biblical aesthetic could reach beyond words and rhetoric, potentially, at least, to incorporate all the arts.[6] A late piece, *Laocoön* (1820), shows the famous classical statue of the Trojan priest Laocoön and his sons Antiphantes and Thymbraeus being strangled by sea serpents – a sculpture now in the Vatican but which Blake believed to be a poor copy of a now-lost Hebrew statue representing 'Jehovah & his two Sons Satan & Adam as they were copied from the Cherubim Of Solomons Temple by three Rhodians & applied to Natural Fact or History of Ilium' (E 273). Around this Blake has scribbled a series of gnomic slogans on biblical themes:

> A Poet a Painter a Musician an Architect: the Man
> Or Woman who is not one of these is not a Christian
> You must leave Fathers & Mothers & Houses & Lands if
>   they stand in the way of
> Art [...]
> Prayer is the Study of Art
> Praise is the Practise of Art
> Fasting &c. all relate to Art [...]
> The Old & New Testaments are the Great Code of Art [...]
> Christianity is Art. (E 274–5)

The gnomic but authoritative tone is deliberately designed to echo that of Christ himself – but, unlike the parables, the call is now to aesthetics rather than moral behaviour. Or rather, Blake's aesthetics now seem to be the vehicle of religion in a quite new way. If this sounds extreme – and, of course, it is – there are enough parallels in other writings of the period for Blake's position to be understood more clearly in context. In the Prefaces to the *Lyrical Ballads* (1800, 1802), and later in *Biographia Literaria* (1817), Wordsworth and Coleridge had stressed the role of the imagination, both as the 'prime instrument of all human perception' and as the power by which we respond to poetry (and, by implication, other works of art).[7] We are not passive receivers of stimuli, but from the simplest of sense-data through to the most complex of responses to art, we are contributors, part-creators as Wordsworth has it, of all that we experience. We do not observe art; we both create it, and are possessed by it. We enter into it. In Blake's words:

> This World Is a World of Imagination & Vision [...] Why is the Bible more Entertaining & Instructive than any other book. Is it not because they are addressed to the Imagination which is Spiritual Sensation & but mediately to the Understanding or Reason. (Blake to Trusler, 23 August 1799, E 702–3)

What is true of art is also true of religion. Indeed, to discuss biblical hermeneutics in the light of poetic theory is not to apply an alien concept, but to restore a wholeness of approach that has been disastrously severed over the past two hundred years.[8] At the centre of this is the often-vexed question of the nature of religious language itself – not merely of the Bible, but of all theological language. For many evangelicals, the words of the Bible must be read literally and finally, with no possibility of further revision or development. Blake, like Coleridge, saw at once that almost all religious language is essentially figurative. 'Heaven', wherever it is, is not 'up'; Hell is not 'down'. Being 'at the right hand of the Father' is entirely metaphorical. Hence the Bible is not merely metaphor, but (in this sense) has no 'fixed' meaning. The most contentious example of this for the turn of the century was, of course, slavery. Led by the Quakers, more and more Christians saw the enslavement of other human beings as being incompatible with Christ's teaching. Though not concerned with slavery, the classic argument for such progressive change is Newman's *Development of Christian Doctrine* (1845), where, to the scandal of some, he argues that the Roman Catholic Church shows its authenticity not by its closeness to New Testament practice, but by its *distance* from it. Christianity does not consist of a set of static beliefs, but is a 'living', 'organic', and developing creed.[9] Whatever their differences, a belief in progressive revelation is a common thread running through Blake, Coleridge, and Newman. For such understanding, the artistic 'imagination' is the prime instrument of perception.

Contrariwise, for Blake's younger German contemporary, Friedrich Schleiermacher, art is unfulfilled if it is separated from its natural concomitant, religion.[10] Indeed, in an almost Blakean parallel he writes that:

> A human being should be like a work of art, which, though openly exhibited and freely accessible, can nevertheless be enjoyed and understood only by those who bring feeling and study to it.[11]

In this view, only the artist, the one who enters into the soul of things by actually creating (or, as Schleiermacher sometimes has it, 'self-creating'), is worthy of the title of Christian. Religious belief is a highly personal activity; it cannot be acquired second-hand. 'What one commonly calls belief, accepting what another person has done [...] is exactly what must be renounced by those who would penetrate into its sanctuary. To want to have and retain belief in this sense proves that one is incapable of religion.'[12]

So much for the idea of tradition! Nor was this view unique to Schleiermacher. His friend and collaborator Friedrich Schlegel was similarly unimpressed by the value of tradition: 'You should never appeal to the spirit of the ancients as if to an authority. It's a peculiar thing with spirits: they don't let themselves be grabbed by the hand and shown to others.'[13] But in 1799–1800 both Schlegels, like Schleiermacher and the other 'Jena' Romantics, Novalis or Schelling, not to mention Blake, Wordsworth, or Coleridge, considered art not just vital to religion, but actually indispensable to our sense of reality itself. Here is Schleiermacher again:

> No poetry, no reality. Just as there is, despite all the senses, no external world without imagination, so too there is no spiritual world without feeling, no matter how much sense there is.[14]

Blake would not have been aware of Jena Romanticism because much of his work actually precedes theirs. But they had in common a number of millenarian and pietistic sources – the most prominent of which were probably Jacob Boehme and the Moravians. Blake was heavily influenced by Boehme's mysticism. Goethe, Kant, Schleiermacher, and Schiller all had Moravian connections – as, more surprisingly, had the Wesleys from their time in Savannah.[15] Similarly he and the Jena Romantics had a common background in Lowth's ideas, which, though eminently orthodox and scholarly, had implications that in their own ways were much more radical than any millenarian tracts – as Herder and Blair had already recognised. Suffice it to say here that this Romantic idea that art is not merely the expression of religious experience, but is indispensible to it, is common across much of Europe by the turn of the century.[16] Blake's very limited conventional education, which had deprived him of the usual classical curriculum of the mid-eighteenth century, may well have proved to have been an advantage in that he became a lifelong autodidact. In the first years of the nineteenth century we find him studying much more orthodox material – by 1803 he was learning Greek, Hebrew, and Latin (Blake's letter to James Blake, 30 January 1803, E 727). As in the case of Lowth, his later reading turned him into an intellectual contemporary of figures such as Coleridge, even though he belonged to an earlier generation in age. The parallels between him and his contemporaries right across Europe imply a common *Zeitgeist* with many of his better-known peers. The similarities between a work like *The Marriage of Heaven and Hell* (1790–3) and certain passages in *The Athenaeum*, the journal of the Jena Romantics, written mostly by Friedrich Schlegel and Friedrich Schleiermacher seven years later, are remarkable. To consider Blake in isolation from his intellectual and historical context is to miss, and indeed, to distort, the significance of his work as a whole.

Notes

1. Trying to tease out which Bible Blake customarily used is almost impossible. The English translation most easily available in the eighteenth century would have been the King James version, but Blake's insistence that he understood the Bible 'in the Spiritual Sense' as opposed to the 'natural' makes his process of 'reading' more significant than any particular written text. In later life he claimed to have learned Hebrew to read the Old Testament, at least, in the original. However, the eighteenth-century English understanding of Hebrew was distinctly different from modern, which further muddies already opaque waters. See S. A. Spector, 'Blake as an Eighteenth Century Hebraist', in D. V. Erdman (ed.), *Blake and His Bibles* (West Cornwall, CT: Locust Hill Press, 1990), pp. 179–229.
2. T. Paine, *The Age of Reason: Part the Second* (London: 1795), pp. 12, 86.
3. R. Watson, *An Apology for the Bible: In a Series of Letters, Addressed to Thomas Paine* (London: 1796), pp. 14–15.
4. See T. McFarland, *Coleridge and the Pantheist Tradition* (Oxford: Clarendon Press, 1969).
5. The word 'aesthetic' was coined by Alexander Gottlieb Baumgarten in the middle of the eighteenth century, and became popular in German Romanticism with Kant's Third Critique. First recorded in English in 1798, with the rather limited meaning of 'received by the senses', the *Oxford English Dictionary* (*OED*) complained that the word was 'misapplied in German by Baumgarten, and so used in England since 1830'. In fact, even Baumgarten's use of the word to mean 'pertaining to the beautiful' was too narrow to catch the way in which by the end of the century it had come to stand for something much closer to 'pertaining to the theory – or theories – of art'.
6. For the 'multi-media' quality of Blake's work, see S. Sklar, *Blake's 'Jerusalem' as Visionary Theatre* (Oxford: Oxford University Press, 2012).
7. S. T. Coleridge, *Biographia Literaria* (1817), in J. Engell and W. J. Bate (eds.), *Collected Works*, Bollingen Series 75, Vol. VII (Princeton: Princeton University Press, 1983), Chapter XIII.
8. S. Prickett, *Words and the Word: Language, Poetics and Biblical Interpretation* (Cambridge: Cambridge University Press, 1976), p. 197ff.
9. J. H. Newman, *Essay on the Development of Christian Doctrine* (London and New York: Sheed and Ward, 1960).
10. F. Schleiermacher, *On Religion: Speeches to Its Cultured Despisers*, trans. Richard Crouter (Cambridge: Cambridge University Press, 1988), p. 158.
11. F. Schleiermacher, *Athenaeum Fragment* 336, in F. Schlegel, *Philosophical Fragments*, trans. P. Firchow (Minneapolis, MN: University of Minnesota Press, 1991), p. 67.
12. Schleiermacher, *On Religion*, p. 134.
13. F. Schlegel, *Critical Fragment* 44, in Schlegel, *Philosophical Fragments*, p. 6.

14. Schleiermacher, *Athenaeum Fragment* 350, in ibid., p. 70.
15. See R. Rix, *William Blake and the Cultures of Radical Christianity* (Farnham: Ashgate, 2007), p. 13ff.
16. See S. Prickett, *Origins of Narrative: The Romantic Appropriation of the Bible* (Cambridge: Cambridge University Press, 1996), pp. 184–203.

CHAPTER 19

Chaucer, Spenser, and Shakespeare

David Fuller

'The Nations still / Follow after the detestable Gods of Priam' (*Milton* 14: 14–15, E 108). Though *Paradise Lost* explicitly proclaims a new heroism, Christian and of the mind, greater than that modelled by the heroes of Homer and Virgil, implicitly, in its fundamental emotional and imaginative impact, it exalts the values of the classical poems on which it is modelled – or such was Blake's view. Like Shelley, Blake saw poets as unacknowledged legislators. Contra Auden, he believed that poetry makes something happen – not by sending people onto the streets, but by changing minds. The reader of poetry is therefore always potentially engaged in an intellectual and imaginative agon – like Los in *Jerusalem*, a struggle with the spectre; a struggle with conceptions derived from less than the poem's full imaginative implications. These conceptions may be, as in *Paradise Lost*, explicit; and they may be misinterpretations. They may be, as in Shakespeare, implicit. And they may be on a spectrum in between – between what Keats called the egotistical sublime (the mode of Wordsworth: the poet enters the poem and is his own expositor) and the poet with no ego centre (the mode of Keats himself: the invisible poet who leaves expository extrapolation to the reader). Chaucer is more Shakespearean: the poet in the poem is presented as less than fully aware; there is no surrogate spokesman; everything is fragmented and perspectival; the 'Retraction' of the *Canterbury Tales* speaks for the poet, but from outside the poem (and on almost any reading at odds with it).[1] Spenser is more Miltonic, but given the ways in which Christian and classical, the New Jerusalem (I, x) and the Garden of Adonis (III, vi) are welcomed equally, and how the Bower of Bliss seduces readers as it tempts the Knight of Temperance (II, xii), the poet prompts the reader's agon: the ethics of *The Faerie Queene* are firmly presented; they are also unravelled by the poem.[2]

How, then, did Blake – who read against the grain with Milton – read poets so various in their presentation of ideas as Chaucer, Spenser, and

Shakespeare; and what does his engagement with each poet suggest he derived from them? Since Blake's presentations of all three are largely through illustrations, fundamental to understanding his relation with them is the issue of how his approach to illustration is understood. There is a tradition of interpreting Blake's illustrations as critiques which require explication by reference to his mythology. There is no trace of this in early readers (William Michael Rossetti, Yeats). This mode of reading began with Joseph Wicksteed's commentary on the illustrations of Job. Though, therefore, the approach was developed with designs that are *sui generis* (combining image with text so as to prompt interpretive questioning), it has been applied widely to Blake's illustrations of other poets, including Chaucer and Spenser.[3] Readings of this type present Blake as working with visual codes keyed to a schematised mythology, a way of reading his visual art comparable to readings of his poetry that present him as in some sense an esoteric writer – whether covert political allegorist (David Erdman) or proselyte of secret wisdom traditions (Kathleen Raine). But in writing about his art Blake never refers to the symbolism of his writings, and his accounts of his designs for other poets make clear his literal faithfulness to their texts. Interpretation requires not reference to an esoteric code but detailed reading of the texts illustrated and reference to permanent issues of human experience – what Blake (in discussing Chaucer) called 'eternal principles [...] of human life' as these 'appear to poets, in all ages' (E 536).

Sir Jeffrey Chaucer and the Nine and Twenty Pilgrims on Their Journey to Canterbury is one of Blake's most important paintings (see Fig. 3.2). Begun perhaps as early as 1806, it was the centrepiece of his one solo exhibition (1809). His account of the painting occupies about one-third of the exhibition's catalogue-manifesto (*A Descriptive Catalogue*), and he continued to write about it in the 'Public Address' developed in his Notebook in the succeeding years. The engraving derived from the painting exists in five states, the last two of which date from the 1820s.[4] Blake's earlier work had not revealed much interest in Chaucer: Chaucer is among the (commissioned) Heads of the Poets painted for William Hayley's Library (1800–3; Manchester Art Gallery), and he is obliquely drawn into *For Children: The Gates of Paradise* (1793), where the inscription for emblem 6 recalls 'The Knight's Tale' (E 32, 801).[5] The Canterbury Pilgrims design, however, occupied Blake sporadically over a period of twenty years, years in which he engraved *Milton* and composed and engraved *Jerusalem*, where Chaucer appears as an aspect of the climactic awakening of the archetypal human being, Albion (98: 9, E 257). The final states of the engraving contain new text connecting the work with *On Homers Poetry* [and] *on Virgil* (c. 1822) and *Laocoön* (*c.* 1815, 1826–7), which imply not only continuing engagement with Chaucer but also a developing view of his poetry.

In the processional arrangement of its figures, the Canterbury Pilgrims may have been influenced by the Parthenon frieze as seen in the Elgin Marbles. Though these were not unpacked until 1807, and Blake may not have seen them himself, he would have heard about them from Flaxman, Fuseli, and Benjamin Haydon. This, with the architecture of the Tabard Inn and the background churches, and the costumes 'correct according to authentic monuments' (E 533) – that is, the tombs in Westminster Abbey which, as an apprentice engraver, Blake copied – gives a combination of classical symmetry and balance with the freedom and variety of Gothic that suggests qualities Blake might admire in Chaucer. The pilgrims themselves Blake saw as representing eternal types: 'the characters which compose all ages and nations [...] universal human life, beyond which Nature never steps' (E 532–3). It is a view Blake presented insistently in the accompanying catalogue essay: 'Every age is a Canterbury Pilgrimage'; each figure 'is an antique Statue, the image of a class [type], and not of an imperfect individual' (E 536). Chaucer's pilgrims can, therefore, be understood by analogy with figures of classical myth and legend – the opposite of that dominant strand in modern criticism which emphasises the historical locatedness of Chaucer's portraits. The Franklin is Bacchus, the doctor Esculapius, the Host Silenus, and so on. Understanding looks to archetypes, the 'eternal Principles that exist in all ages' (E 536). This focus prompts the reflection for which Blake's Milton blames himself, here as a view of Christian culture more generally: 'the Moderns have neglected to subdue the gods of Priam' (E 536). Without reading Chaucer through his own mythology, Blake finds in Chaucer something of his own view of the world.

Equally idiosyncratic is Blake's un-ironic reading, which presents most of Chaucer's pilgrims uncritically. The Knight is 'a true Hero, a good, great, and wise man' (E 533); the Shipman a 'genius of Ulyssean art' (E 537); the Pardoner, though 'the Age's Knave', is also 'suffered by Providence for wise ends' (E 535). This positive reading of 1809 is overturned by cryptic inscriptions added to the engraving in the 1820s. 'The Use of Money & its Wars' (E 687), applicable to the greed actuating the pilgrims in all walks of life – doctor, shipman, pardoner: Chaucer now shows the economic corruption underlying social conflict. 'An Allegory of Idolatry or Politics' (E 687), applicable to most of the religious figures in the cavalcade: Chaucer reveals the corruption of religion which makes it a tool of oppression. Blake's riddling engagement of the reader in sense-making means it is difficult to be other than tentative; but the inscriptions show that for Blake a reading may develop – even shift radically – as the views brought to reading change. They imply a practice of engaged, creative reading in which interpretation is an interaction with the reader's values and vision.

Like Chaucer, Spenser is not much present in Blake's work before the major illustration. 'An imitation of Spenser' (*Poetical Sketches*) invokes Spenser for help in transcending the tinkling elegancies of eighteenth-century convention. An inscription for the *Gates of Paradise* emblem 7 (E 32, 801) from a minor episode of *The Faerie Queene* (II, ii, 2) implies a good knowledge of the poem. 'Spenser creating his fairies' for the illustrations of Gray ('The Bard', p. 12, WBA obj. 64) shows two famous episodes – Despair (I, ix) and Mammon (II, vii). The head of Spenser for Hayley's Library (Manchester Art Gallery) has vignettes showing April from *The Shepherd's Calendar* (nymphs and the virgin goddess Cynthia) and Elizabeth I commanding Spenser to write *The Faerie Queene*.

The Characters in Spenser's 'Faerie Queene,' however, shows a quite different intensity of engagement. As with the Canterbury Pilgrims, the painting does not offer a wildly idiosyncratic reading of *The Faerie Queene*. Readings of this type – Una is 'a kind of Vala' and so on – lead not to imaginative interpretation but to indecisive puzzling. The 'seemingly endlessly shifting values' attributed to the painting arise not from the illustration but from the method of interpretation.[6] Blake does not illustrate with a paralysing complexity of which so much can be postulated that nothing is presented clearly. His advice is 'Enter into these Images in [...] Imagination approaching them on the Fiery Chariot of [...] Contemplative Thought'; 'make a Friend & Companion of [...] these images of wonder' (E 560). Contemplative thought, imaginative wonder: the living relation to art as to a friend or companion, giving as well as receiving. This is the basis on which the engaged spectator may hope to 'arise from his Grave [and] [...] meet the Lord in the Air' (E 560; echoing St Paul on apocalyptic transformation: 1 Thessalonians 4:17). Meaning depends in part – as Blake's additions to his Chaucer engraving show – on what the spectator brings. What appears without is (in part) within; meaning arises from the ways in which a work draws the whole person into responsive action.

The Characters in Spenser's 'Faerie Queene' was apparently intended as a complementary pair with the Canterbury Pilgrims, though the contention that there are detailed correspondences between the pictures is over-ingenious. Like Chaucer's pilgrims, the figures move in procession, but in the opposite direction. Like *The Faerie Queene*'s questing knights, they ride from a world of error which includes the Tower of Babel (II, ix) towards

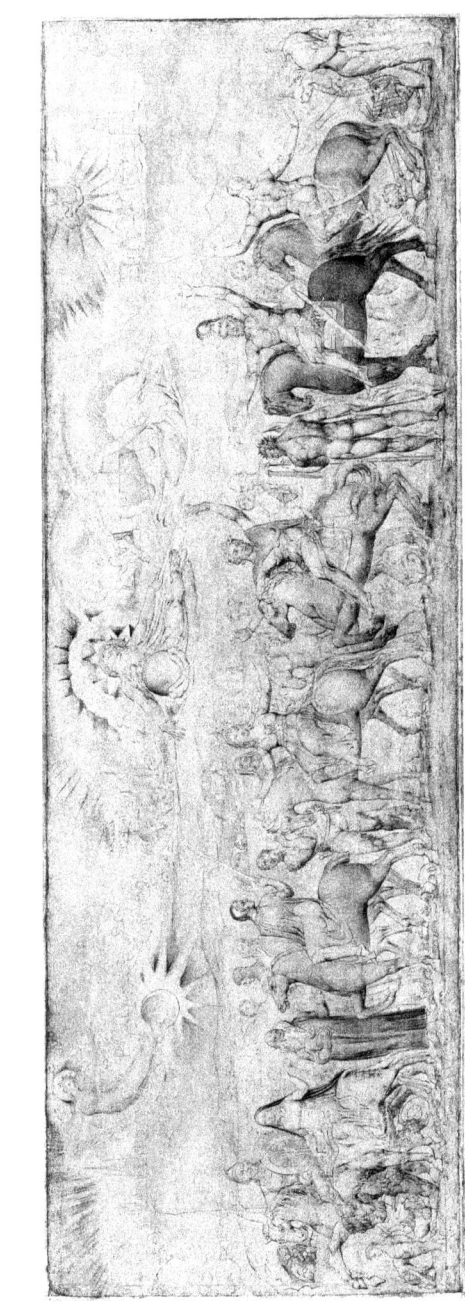

Fig. 19.1: W. Blake, *Characters from Spenser's Faery Queen*, c. 1825, watercolour, Petworth House and Park, West Sussex, © National Trust Images/John Hammond

the New Jerusalem (I, x; here a Gothic cathedral). The decayed state of the painting makes it difficult to identify all the detail of Blake's articulation,[7] but broadly he depicts the poem's central figures in Spenser's narrative order and in Spenser's terms (Fig. 19.1): Redcrosse on his rearing horse, Una on her ass, her dwarf, lion, and the defeated dragon; the Palmer, holding Amavia's baby, Ruddymaine, leading Guyon; Britomart, with her nurse, Glauce, and Satyrane; Artegal, Talus with his iron flail, and Prince Arthur (who appears in each book, but primarily in Book V) identified by his dragon helmet; Calidore, leading the Blatant Beast; at the end of the procession the defeated figures of Duessa and Archimago. In the background appear episodes and characters associated with each figure – behind Redcrosse, the cave of Despair, above Una the House of Holiness, above Guyon the Cave of Mammon, and so on. The upper level shows (right) an archer in the sun (Phoebus-Apollo, god of poetry), balanced (left) by a woman with the moon at her feet (Revelation 12; and Cynthia, virgin-patroness of the Fairy Queen). Between these a divine figure holds a world-globe, Justice balances her scales (rightly above Artegal), and the poet records his images of wonder.

'Allegory addressd to the Intellectual powers while it is altogether hidden from the Corporeal Understanding' is Blake's 'Definition of the Most Sublime Poetry' (Blake to Butts, 6 July 1803, E 730). In terms of this distinction, Blake may well have thought Spenser's allegory too often addressed to corporeal powers – in the Castle of Alma (II, ix), the body, the thirty-two warders are the teeth: not the suggestive power of symbol but the one-to-one correspondence of simple cryptogram. However, he would also have seen the poet's own translations in the poem (as he saw the extrapolations of Milton) as offering less than the full significance of its truly poetic visionary images. Like ancient writers he admired, Blake aims not to translate these into his terms but to rouse the reader-viewer's faculties to act (E 702), to make a companion of images of wonder – that is, to interpret Spenser's more resonant symbols in terms suggested by the interaction of their precise articulation with the reader's experiences and values. The painting prompts the reader to engage afresh with the poem through the medium of (largely literal) illustration.

Shakespeare has a more continuous presence in Blake's work than either Chaucer or Spenser. Though Blake wrote in 1800 that 'Shakespeare in riper years gave me his hand' ('To My Dearest Friend John Flaxman', l. 6, E 707), he was present from the beginning. Benjamin Heath Malkin reports that Shakespeare's narrative poems and sonnets were favourite studies of Blake's early years (*BR* 569). The lyrics of *Poetical Sketches* are broadly modelled on his songs.[8] Two groups of watercolours dating from *c.* 1780 and the early 1790s depict Shakespearean subjects (Butlin, 84.1–7, 245–50); and there are other isolated illustrations (Butlin, 154, 161, *c.* 1785). Another Shakespeare group, commissioned to illustrate a copy of the Second Folio (Butlin, 547. 1–6), includes two subjects Blake also painted in tempera, *As if an Angel Dropped Down from the Clouds* (from *1 Henry IV*, IV, i, 108–9; also Butlin, 658), and 'The Vision of Queen Katherine' (from *Henry VIII*, IV, ii; also Butlin, 247, 548, 549). Two sketches for *The Gates of Paradise* have captions from *Hamlet* (E 32, 801); another emblem has an epigraph from a Sonnet;[9] and a portrait of Shakespeare was included in Hayley's Library. With vignettes from *Macbeth*, this points to a repeated theme of Blake's Shakespeare illustrations, exploration of the supernatural – spirits, ghosts, fairies, visions, and prophecy. In *The Marriage of Heaven and Hell* Shakespeare is cited (with Dante) as an infinite resource (E 43); *The Song of Los* (pl. 5, Oberon and Titania) shows Blake drawing on Shakespeare in his most characteristic work, albeit in a way difficult to decipher; and in the 'Public Address' Shakespeare is invoked (with Milton) as exemplifying the true greatness of English art (E 576). To the Romantic generation this is how Shakespeare presented himself, as the epitome of native culture: not classical, not neoclassical. For an aesthetic in revolt against neoclassicism, Shakespeare was an international model – to Herder, Goethe, and Schiller in Germany, Hugo and de Staël in France, Pushkin in Russia, and Manzoni in Italy. But Blake is, as usual, also idiosyncratic: Shakespeare was (like Milton) 'curbd by the general malady & infection from the silly Greek & Latin slaves of the sword' (*Milton*, E 95) – a critique offered primarily as an example of the vulnerability of even the greatest spirits to the errors of classical culture. Counter to this, Shakespeare apparently contributed to Blake's exalted idea of the Poetic Imagination. While Blake is dismissive of any identification of Theseus with his author ('thus Fools quote Shakespeare', E 601), that did not prevent him taking seriously the view of imagination Theseus propounds in *A Midsummer Night's Dream*, Act V, Scene i. 'Sons of Los' (i.e. poets):

> surround the Passions with porches of iron & silver
> Creating form & beauty around the dark regions of sorrow,
> Giving to airy nothing a name and a habitation
> Delightful! with bounds to the Infinite putting off the Indefinite
> Into most holy forms of thought: (such is the power of inspiration).
> (Milton 28: 1–5, E 125)

'Giving to airy nothing a name and a habitation': it is the clearest Shakespeare allusion in Blake's poetic oeuvre.

Fig. 19.2: W. Blake, *As if an Angel Dropped Down from the Clouds*, 1809, Art Collection 2/Alamy Stock Photo

With some of Blake's Shakespeare illustrations, obliqueness and transformation are key. *As if an Angel Dropped Down from the Clouds* (also known as *To Turn and Wind a Fiery Pegasus*) depicts Shakespeare's image (from *1 Henry IV*, IV, i, 108–9) divorced from its dramatic context and subject (the chivalric charisma of Prince Hal) (Fig. 19.2; pen and grey ink, and watercolour, British Museum, London). It shows Blake as what Yeats called him, 'a too literal realist of Imagination'.[10] Others frame, comment, explain: Blake is the naked symbolist. His exhibition catalogue account explains ('the Horse of Intellect [. . .] leaping from the cliffs of Memory and Reasoning', E 546). The visual image presents. But what? The sun irradiates a horse, whose rearing posture suggests pure energy, greeting a leaping-flying angel-youth poised to unite with that energy; this spectacle of dynamic movement is viewed from above by a counter-image of inert passivity, a woman lying on a cloud reading. The meanings of this cannot be confined to Blake's doctrinal allegorisation. Fundamentally congruent with its source (exaltation of energetic charisma), the picture connects with it only obliquely.

Similarly with Blake's best-known image derived from Shakespeare, 'Pity'. This is one of the major series of Twelve Colour Prints of 1795. Though their subjects are from various sources (the Old and New Testaments, Milton, and Blake's prophetic books), their identical form and paired arrangement suggest that these form a related series – though no convincing exposition of unifying themes has been proposed. 'Pity' is based on lines from *Macbeth* (I, vii, 21–5):

> . . . Pity, like a naked new-born babe,
> Striding the blast, or heaven's cherubim, horsed
> Upon the sightless couriers of the air,
> Shall blow the horrid deed in every eye,
> That tears shall drown the wind.

As with *As if an Angel*, the poetry is divorced from its dramatic context: the design is a visualisation of Shakespeare's imagery, combining its alternatives of innocent and sacred outraged compassion (Fig. 19.3; colour print finished in ink and watercolour, Tate Gallery, London). A naked new-born baby leaps upwards from the womb, its mother stretched out below; above two angelic figures ride horses (literalised wind-couriers) whose closed eyes and outstretched posture indicate blindness and supernatural speed; the outward-facing angel protectively takes up the baby; streaks of pelting wind-blown rain suggest universal weeping. The image has been given opposite readings – negative, if viewed in relation to statements about pity in the prophetic books; positive if viewed in relation to visual values, especially the vigour of the striding baby, related to Blake's spirit of energy, Orc. The context in *Macbeth* is so ignored that the lines seem only a starting point;

Fig. 19.3: W. Blake, *Pity*, c. 1795, Art Collection 2/Alamy Stock Photo

and yet violated innocence, outraged compassion, supernatural presence, a natural world responsive to human suffering: the image is also an epitome of the play. In literalising the isolated image Blake epitomises the whole and creates an independent work powerful in itself without reference to its origin.

From Shakespeare, an idea of the imagination confirmed, an intense visualisation of poetic imagery; from Spenser, a reading of allegory in which symbolic values escape the poet's control to interact with the reader's imagination; from Chaucer, reading for archetypes, not distracted from fundamental meanings by historical contingency or an appearance of sophistication that degenerates into word-spinning. More generally, the construction of meaning as an interaction between poet and reader, and reading as a stimulus to the creation of independent new work. Blake's varied interactions with Chaucer, Spenser, and Shakespeare are an education in possibilities of serious reading.

Notes

1. L. S. Benson (ed.), *The Riverside Chaucer*, 3rd edn (Oxford: Oxford University Press, 1988), p. 328.
2. References in round brackets are to Book, Canto, and on occasion also Stanza numbers in Spenser's poem.
3. J. Wicksteed, *Blake's Vision of the Book of Job* (London: Dent, 1910); K. Kiralis, 'William Blake as Intellectual and Spiritual Guide to Chaucer's Canterbury Pilgrims', *Blake Studies*, I (1969), 139–90; R. S. Gleckner, *Blake and Spenser* (Baltimore: Johns Hopkins University Press, 1985). For a critique see D. Fuller, 'Blake and Dante', *Art History*, 11 (1988), 349–73.
4. R. N. Essick, *The Separate Plates of William Blake: A Catalogue* (Princeton: Princeton University Press, 1983), pp. 61–89.
5. See K. Raine, *Blake and Tradition*, 2 vols. (Princeton: Princeton University Press, 1968), 11. 312 n.28.
6. Gleckner, *Blake and Spenser*, pp. 206, 184.
7. See J. E. Grant and R. E. Brown, 'Blake's Vision of Spenser's *Faerie Queene*: A Report and an Anatomy', *Blake Newsletter*, 8 (1974–5), 56–85. The account in S. F. Damon, *A Blake Dictionary* (1965; rev. M. Eaves and repr., Hanover, NH: Dartmouth College Press / University Press of New England, 2013) contains major errors, particularly the misidentification of the central figure as Amoret.
8. Critical ingenuity may find in Blake echoes of Shakespeare, but almost nowhere are similarities striking: see J. Bate, *Shakespeare and the English Romantic Imagination* (Oxford: Clarendon, 1989, chapter 4), where words, images and narrative elements wrenched from their context are given an appearance of similarity which will not survive contextualised scrutiny.
9. D. V. Erdman (with D. K. Moore) (ed.), *The Notebook of William Blake: A Photographic and Typographic Facsimile* (Oxford: Clarendon, 1973), N21.
10. W. B. Yeats, *Essays and Introductions* (London: Macmillan, 1961), p. 119.

CHAPTER 20

Milton

G. A. Rosso

> Intelligent comment means that I am driven on [...] till I know the author so well that I allow him to speak in my name and am even able to speak in his name myself.
> – Karl Barth, 'Preface to the Second Edition', *The Epistle to the Romans* (1921)[1]

Milton's hold on Blake's imagination began early and evolved through each decade of his life, exerting an influence whose depth and range is matched only by the Bible. Blake read Milton as both of them read the Bible, which is dialectically, interpreting scriptural texts in both critical and creative ways.[2] While Milton engaged more publicly than Blake in political and religious activism, and while his learning – or certainly his training – in biblical and classical traditions exceeded Blake's, both men saw themselves as bardic visionaries even as they developed rational perspectives aimed at 'reforming the reformation' (as Milton puts it in *Areopagitica*), opposing both Anglican and Dissenting orthodoxy and any alliance of church and state. And despite differences in educational background (Milton was privately tutored and attended Cambridge; Blake was apprenticed to an engraver), their vocational paths also were similar: both cast themselves early as prophetic poets, both supported movements for revolutionary change, including regicide, and both experienced the defeat of revolutionary goals, compelling a shift towards non-violent, anti-war perspectives in later work. Both, nonetheless, retained an apocalyptic political theology rooted in millenarian tradition, with a belief in the potential of divine wrath to help achieve individual and social liberation.

Unlike Blake, however, who embraced the democratic ethos of his era, Milton oriented his thinking towards the political and spiritual elite. And later into his career than Blake, Milton's version of apocalyptic wrath, as evidenced in Samson's act of destruction in *Samson Agonistes* (1671), retained the option of revolutionary violence, although this position is countered by Jesus's pacifism in *Paradise Regained* (1671) and the narrator's critique of martial heroism in *Paradise Lost* (1667). These texts profoundly influenced Blake, especially in his major poems *VALA / The Four Zoas* (c. 1796–1807), *Milton* (c. 1804–11), and *Jerusalem* (1804–c. 1820) and in his contemporaneous illustrations to *Paradise Lost* (1807, 1808, 1822) and *Paradise Regained* (c. 1816–20).[3] But what has not been emphasised sufficiently is Blake's critique of Milton's Messianism, particularly his 'Arian' subordination of Jesus to God – his 'denial of the Saviours blood' as Blake writes in *Milton* (22 [24]: 54, E 118).[4] In this poem, Blake retains the 'contrary' approach to Milton he takes in *The Marriage of Heaven and Hell* (1790), contrasting Milton's obedient Son with his own law-breaking Jesus, though he incorporates Methodist and Evangelical Christology into his myth, a major shift that scholars are beginning to chart.[5] What this new scholarship underplays, though, is Blake's critique of Methodism's conservative politics, particularly its support of the British Empire and its reaction to the American and French revolutions, which for Blake sets up a return to (and the return of) the prophetic Milton – dramatised in Milton's 'unexampled' descent to Blake's garden at Felpham (2: 21, E 96).

While Blake's mature understanding of Milton dates from his Felpham experience under William Hayley's patronage (1800–3), Milton's influence extends across the spectrum of Blake's pre-1800 work. It appears in his first book, *Poetical Sketches* (1783), and one of his first major designs, *Albion Rose* (1780), and continues in the poetry and designs of the 1790s. Robert Gleckner and Michael Phillips have explored in detail Milton's presence in *Poetical Sketches*.[6] Joseph Wittreich and Steven Goldsmith have examined *Albion Rose* as a key to political readings of Blake, especially in terms of the design's print history and its relation to Milton's *Samson Agonistes*.[7] Blake issued it as a colour print in the mid-1790s, inviting comparisons between the central figure of the design and depictions of Orc in *America a Prophecy* (1793) and other works.[8] This Orc–Samson analogy, however, has been overshadowed by Orc's association with Satan in Blake's infamous reading of *Paradise Lost* in the *Marriage*.

It is important to situate Blake's provocative commentary within two contexts that he merges in this work: first, the critical history of Satan as the poem's hero, an idea initiated by John Dryden and that doubled as 'a Tory slur' against the republican Milton; and Edmund Burke's view that English supporters of the French Revolution were akin to Satan's rebel angels, 'at war with Heaven itself'.[9] Burke targets the Dissenting minister Richard Price and writers associated with the liberal bookseller Joseph Johnson, Blake's primary employer at the time. Burke is most alarmed by the prophetic idiom of Price's sermon, preached on the first anniversary of the French Revolution in a 'strain' not 'tolerated or encouraged' since 1648, the year that brought the execution of Charles I.[10]

Blake defends Price and the Johnson circle by transforming Milton's Satan into a figure of rebellion against tyranny and by reinterpreting hell as an emblem of insurgent creativity. This reading hinges on a critique of the orthodox morality Blake finds in Milton's epic:

> Those who restrain desire, do so because theirs is weak enough to be restrained; and the restrainer or reason usurps its place & governs the unwilling [...] The history of this is written in Paradise Lost. & the Governor or Reason is call'd Messiah. (pl. 5, E 34)

For Blake, the poem's chief theological error is that it demonises energy and deifies a conception of reason removed from its source in the body, a view he personifies in his figure of Urizen.[11] However, Blake does not simply invert the binaries of reason and desire or good and evil, proclaiming with Satan 'Evil be thou my Good'.[12] Rather, he rejects such logic and redefines desire as a longing for the infinite, for what transcends rational-empirical perception. Blake locates this epistemology in visionary experience and prophetic tradition: in a scene in which he dines with Ezekiel and Isaiah, Blake has the latter explain 'I saw no God. nor heard any, in a finite organical perception; but my senses discover'd the infinite in every thing' (pl. 12, E 38). By announcing that Milton unwittingly allies with the devil's party, Blake reclaims Milton's prophetic voice, opposing the moral rationalism of his Messiah with his own antinomian Jesus, who breaks the Mosaic laws because he 'act[s] from impulse: not from rules' (pl. 23–4, E 43). Blake's Messiah anticipates the impulsive acts of the rebel figure in the *Marriage*'s 'Song of Liberty', who 'stamps the stony law to dust' and proclaims 'Empire is no more!' (pl. 27, E 45), phrases that Orc repeats in *America* (8: 5, E 54; 6: 15, E 53). Blake thus announces the apocalyptic theology that underpins his poetry and designs of the 1790s, which engage a chief political issue at the core of Milton's prose after 1648.

That issue is the tension between Milton's defence of revolutionary violence and his claims for the superior value of spiritual and intellectual struggle. In *The Tenure of Kings and Magistrates* (1649), which justifies the execution of Charles I, Milton invokes the 'Heroick virtue' of the men who exercised 'the wrath of God' against a tyrant, citing key anti-monarchical texts from scripture (Deut. 17,1 Sam. 8) and appropriating Romans 13, the locus of conservative readings of Paul often cited by royalists. Paul urges Christians to submit to secular authority because 'There is no power but of God'; Milton counters that such a view applies only to 'lawfull and just power', not to the

Stuart regime, citing in turn Revelation 13, in which 'we read how the Dragon gave to the beast *his power, his seate, and great autority,* which beast [...] must be expounded to be the tyrannical powers and kingdoms of the earth'.¹³ This apocalyptic support of regicide continues in Milton's *Second Defense of the English People* (1654), where he again extols those 'heroes in battle' for expelling a tyrant and ties his own vocational concerns to national politics. Extending his self-portrait in *The Reason of Church-Government* (1642) in which he announced his epic ambition, Milton now contrasts himself with the revolutionaries: 'I exchanged the toils of war, in which any stout trooper might outdo me, for those labours' of the pen he considers 'much more useful and no less treacherous'.¹⁴ He argues that liberty is 'best achieved, not by the sword, but by a life rightly conducted', a mode of warfare 'far more noble than the gory victories of war'.¹⁵ Yet, in his *Treatise of Civil Power* (1659) written on the eve of the Restoration, Milton again articulates the basic tension of his work. He states that liberty is achieved only by 'the inward man' and that Christ can establish his spiritual kingdom 'without worldly force'; 'yet' the exemplary non-violence of Jesus, while the highest form of struggle, 'disproves not that a Christian commonwealth may defend itself against outward force',¹⁶ the very dynamic Milton reproduces in pairing *Samson Agonistes* and *Paradise Regained* in the 1671 volume.

These contraries in Milton's prose and major poems inform the Orc–Samson analogy in Blake's work of the 1790s, in which Blake is compelled by the Jacobin terror and execution of the French monarchs to engage directly with the issue of revolutionary violence. Printed in the year of the regicide (1793), *America* describes Orc as 'The terror' and depicts him 'staining the temple' with 'beams of blood' (5: 2, 6–7, E 53), an ambivalent image that refers both to Samson pulling down the pillars and to Christ on the 'beams' or cross. Blake reprises the Samson allusion in *Europe*, although he couples it with Milton's Satan in portraying the revolutionaries as 'immortal demons of futurity' who attack the 'council house; down rushing / On the heads of Albions Angels' (9: 10–13, E 63). In *America*, however, this act is followed on the next plate by a design of Orc rising from the ground (pl. 6; WBA obj. 8), an image of resurrection that recalls the figure in *Albion Rose*. The design appears above one of Blake's most powerful millenarian speeches: it begins with a proclamation of the millennial dawn ('The morning comes'), includes the liberation of African slaves, and ends with the declaration 'Empire is no more' (6: 1, 15, E 53). Significantly, though, Blake does not give voice to or depict regicide in his poems or prints of the 1790s, reserving that for his more rarified *Night Thoughts* illustrations.¹⁷

The complex dynamic at the heart of Milton's influence on Blake undergoes a profound shift during Blake's stay at Felpham, forming part of a major transformation in his myth and symbolism. Stemming from his vexed relationship with Hayley and his trial on charges of sedition, Blake experiences a vocational crisis of epic magnitude that results in a renewed commitment to the teachings and symbols of Christianity. Beginning with revisions to *Vala* or *The Four Zoas* and continuing in *Milton* and *Jerusalem*, Blake imports New Testament and Evangelical Christology into the centre of his myth, promoting the radical pacifism of Jesus as an alternative to the insurrectionary violence of Samson and Orc. If Samson's influence fades, however, Blake does not reject Orc but instead makes his suffering and liberation a central feature of Milton's task in *Milton*. In this work, the eponymous hero is inspired to return to earth by 'a Bard's prophetic Song' (2: 22, E 96), the cryptic section that opens the poem, and then is confronted with a series of trials modelled on Satan's temptations of Jesus in *Paradise Regained*, which force him to engage with his posthumous legacy in England.[18]

The main narrative of *Milton* centres on the poet's momentous return to earth to confront his divided legacy, particularly the distortion of his prophetic republicanism by the forces of Anglican orthodoxy and nationalism. As in earlier work, Blake personifies these forces in Satan and Urizen, but he foregrounds the role of female characters, presenting Milton's divided legacy through a concept of the double emanation, represented by Rahab and Ololon. Rahab signifies the enlistment of Milton into a nationalist narrative of sacrifice to the state; Ololon represents an alternative legacy in which Milton repudiates his own iconic status in British culture. Blake stages a dramatic confrontation between these symbolic figures in the great scene in his garden at Felpham in which Ololon exposes Rahab as the religious system that justifies imperial aggression and war (pl. 36[40]–42[49], E 136–44). Blake also identifies Ololon with Jesus, whose *self*-oblation defies the sacrificial logic of the state and whose second coming is portrayed as occurring on the 'Clouds of Ololon', an allusion to the biblical Son of Man returning 'in the clouds of heaven with power and great glory' (Matt. 24:30; Dan. 7:13). This bold identification enables Blake to re-envision Milton's view of gender from an apocalyptic perspective and to restore Jesus to the centre of his theology. It further allows Blake to recover the visionary and anti-war elements in Milton's epics, especially by associating Ololon with Milton's muse in *Paradise Lost*, the 'Celestial Patroness' who 'dictates' the poem to him nightly while 'slumb'ring' (IX, 21–3).[19] Ololon embodies this poetics of inspiration, which Blake regards as foundational to the prophetic tradition that connects him to Milton.

This poetics is operative visually in the illustrations to Milton's poetry that Blake produced between 1801 and 1820, the period in which he composed and printed the four extant copies of *Milton*.[20] One design in particular can serve to encapsulate Blake's relationship with Milton in this period. In the penultimate design of the *Paradise Lost* series, *Michael Foretells the Crucifixion*, Blake reveals the tight correlation between his poetic and pictorial understanding of Milton, paying homage to his precursor's vision while adding his own perspective (Fig. 20.1). The illustration captures the signal moment in Milton's theodicy when the archangel Michael reveals to Adam the meaning of the 'Woman's Seed' prophecy, from Genesis 3:15, that Eve's progeny will 'bruise the head of Satan' and bring redemption to humanity (*Paradise Lost* XII, 430). Michael foresees the fulfilment of the prophecy at Christ's crucifixion, an event Blake features in the design: Satan's serpent-form is coiled at the base of the cross, his head pierced by the nail that holds Jesus's feet to the cross, while his cohorts Sin and Death lie outstretched on either side. In a departure from the text, however, Blake depicts Eve at the scene with Michael and Adam, sleeping below the cross rather than alone in her bower. As does Milton, Blake portrays Eve asleep during the scene, but he incorporates into his design the later moment when Adam returns to the bower to relate the good news to Eve but finds her already awake, eager to inform him that she too has received the prophecy, for 'God is also in sleep' and has sent her a 'propitious' vision (*Paradise Lost* XII, 611–13). While Milton withholds the details of her vision, Blake implies that Eve imagines the redemptive scene he pictures above her while 'slumb'r-ing'. In this sense, Blake suggests that Eve's experience offers a mode of inspiration parallel to Milton's muse, which allows him to accentuate the female element within Milton's imagination.

The contours of Milton's influence on Blake stand revealed in this design, not least in the image of Death slain under the cross, his crown visible but powerless to save him. This image of apocalyptic regicide remains in tension with the messianic pacifism of the cross, a tension that animates the political theology of both poets.

Notes

1. K. Barth, 'Preface to the Second Edition', in *The Epistle to the Romans*, 6th edn, trans. E. C. Hoskyns (Oxford: Oxford University Press, 1968), pp. 2–15 (p. 8).
2. Blake probably read Milton's poetry in T. Newton's *The Poetical Works of John Milton* (1752–61) or W. Hayley's *Poetical Works of John Milton* (1794–97), and the prose works – including *Reason of Church-Government* (1641), *Areopagitica*

Fig. 20.1: W. Blake, *Michael Foretelling the Crucifixion to Adam*, 1808, pen and ink and watercolour, Museum of Fine Arts, Boston

(1644), *Tenure of Kings and Magistrates* (1649), *Second Defense of the English People* (1654), and *Treatise on Civil Power* (1659) among others – in J. Toland's oft-reprinted *Complete Collection of the Historical, Political and Miscellaneous Works* (1698).

3. In these years, Blake also illustrated sets of Milton's *Comus* (1801, 1815), *On the Morning of Christ's Nativity* (1809, c. 1815), and *L'Allegro* and *Il Penseroso* (c. 1816–20).
4. 'Arian' refers to the Christian priest Arius, who emphasised the Son's subordinate status to God the Father, a position deemed heretical at the Council of Nicea in 325 CE.
5. For an overview, see M. Farrell, *Blake and the Methodists* (Basingstoke: Palgrave Macmillan, 2014).
6. R. F. Gleckner, *Blake's Prelude: Poetical Sketches* (Baltimore, MD: Johns Hopkins University Press, 1982); M. Phillips, 'Blake's Early Poetry', in *William Blake: Essays in Honour of Geoffrey Keynes* (Oxford: Clarendon, 1972), pp. 1–28.
7. J. A. Wittreich, *Angel of Apocalypse: Blake's Idea of Milton* (Madison, WI: University of Wisconsin Press, 1975); S. Goldsmith, *Blake's Agitation* (Baltimore, MD: Johns Hopkins University Press, 2012).
8. See Goldsmith, *Blake's Agitation*, pp. 84–92.
9. See N. von Matzahn, 'Acts of Kind Service: Milton and the Patriot Literature of Empire', in B. Rajan and E. Sauer (eds.), *Milton and the Imperial Vision* (Pittsburgh, PN: Duquense University Press, 1999), pp. 233–54; E. Burke, *Reflections on the Revolution in France* (Harmondsworth: Pelican, 1968), p. 92.
10. Burke, *Reflections*, p. 94.
11. See G. Teskey, *The Poetry of John Milton* (Cambridge, MA: Harvard University Press, 2015), p. 294.
12. J. Milton, *Paradise Lost*, in M. Y. Hughes (ed.), *John Milton: The Complete Poetry and Major Prose* (New York: Odyssey, 1957), IV, 110. Further references to book and line numbers will come in the main text.
13. Cited in D. Loewenstein (ed.), *John Milton: Prose. Major Writings on Liberty, Politics, Religion, and Education* (Oxford: Wiley-Blackwell, 2013), p. 253.
14. Ibid., p. 323.
15. Ibid., pp. 379, 374.
16. Ibid., pp. 387–8.
17. In Night 1 on page 15 of the watercolour edition (WBA obj. 20), Blake draws an image of Death stamping on the necks of two kings, decapitating the one on the left.
18. See chapters 3–4 on *Milton* in G. A. Rosso, *The Religion of Empire: Political Theology in Blake's Prophetic Symbolism* (Columbus: Ohio State University Press, 2016).
19. Milton's muse, 'brooding on the vast Abyss', brings creation into being (*Paradise Lost* I. 21–2); Blake's Jesus tells Ololon to 'Obey / The Dictate' and with her 'brooding wings' to renew the world (*Milton* 21[23]: 54–7).
20. For an overview, see J. M. Q. Davies, *Blake's Milton Designs: The Dynamics of Meaning* (West Cornwall, CT: Locust Hill, 1993), pp. 3–12.

CHAPTER 21

The Eighteenth Century and Romanticism
David Duff

Blake's career spans the entirety of the British Romantic movement, from the antiquarian revivals of the 1760s to the 1820s, and he participates in each of its phases, responding to successive generations of writers and numerous literary trends. The intertextual character of his writing and his engagement with the shifting literary scene have been obscured by what Frye calls 'an overemphasis on his uniqueness' and by a critical tradition which has prioritised interpretation of his 'system' over study of the literary context in which he created it or the stages by which it evolved.[1] His isolation as a writer has also been overstated. Though his method of self-publication ensured that his literary work reached only a small readership, the readers included major writers such as Coleridge, Wordsworth, Lamb, Hazlitt, Southey, and Landor, who recognised his gifts and in some cases acknowledged affinities with their own work. Little of this comment was in the public domain but Blake was well-enough known to be included in the *Biographical Dictionary of Living Authors of Great Britain and Ireland* (1816; see *BR* 330), and his work was discussed in influential literary circles including those of his patron, William Hayley, the publisher Joseph Johnson, and other prominent men of letters such as Henry Crabb Robinson, Isaac D'Israeli, Thomas Frognall Dibdin, and Benjamin Heath Malkin. His illuminated books were considered collectors' pieces – D'Israeli owned at least eight of them (*BR* 328n.) – and Malkin and Robinson, who knew Blake personally, both published sympathetic accounts of his life and work – Robinson's in a Hamburg journal that was an important organ of German Romanticism.[2] Though Blake himself produced no formal criticism except a brief paper on Homer and Virgil (*c.* 1822) and an analysis of Chaucer in *A Descriptive Catalogue* (1809), his compositions frequently reference contemporary authors (e.g. *The Ghost of Abel* [1822], addressed 'To Lord Byron in the Wilderness') and his marginalia include penetrating comments on a range of modern writers including William Wordsworth. Negative criticism was another intertextual stimulus: when Robert and Leigh Hunt published hostile reviews of him, he exacted revenge by satirising them mythologically in his prophecies (the three-headed creature 'Hand' in *Milton* and *Jerusalem* is a composite character based on the three Hunt brothers, inspired by the typographical device of the pointing finger in *The Examiner* – a piece of coded intertextuality that typifies Blake's polemical wit).

Blake's eye for literary fashion is evident from his first collection, *Poetical Sketches* (1783), containing poems written from his twelfth to his twentieth year. The collection is often dismissed as immature and derivative because of references in the prefatory 'Advertisement' to the poems being 'the production of untutored youth', with 'irregularities and defects to be found in almost every page' (*BR* 29). However, this apparent apology was in reality an attempt to tap a contemporary fashion for juvenile composition that had begun with Chatterton and was later to produce such notable publications as Leigh Hunt's *Juvenilia* (1805), 'written between the ages of twelve and sixteen', Sydney Owenson's *Poems* (1801), 'written between the ages of twelve and fourteen', and Byron's *Hours of Idleness; By . . . a Minor* (1809).[3] In this long-running cult of juvenilia, part of a broader Romantic interest in precocious creativity, an author's youth and inexperience were considered selling points rather than drawbacks. The term 'sketch' in Blake's title taps a related publishing trend that linked the aesthetics of spontaneity and originality with unfinishedness.[4] As with Mary Heron's *Sketches of Poetry* (1786), Ann Batten Cristall's *Poetical Sketches* (1795) and the many other volumes – often by women poets – that deployed this inverted modesty trope, the professed roughness and 'irregularity' of Blake's verbal sketches were intended as paradoxical markers of their authenticity, the visual resonance of the term providing an additional point of interest (though this conventionally printed volume, unlike Blake's later, self-published works, contained no illustrations).

More important, though, than these paratextual signals was his imaginative engagement with other writers. *Poetical Sketches* is a virtual compendium of fashionable literary modes, from the Thomsonesque 'season' poems which open the volume to the 'Imitation of Spencer' and series of Shakespearean pastiches (*King Edward the Third*, two dramatic 'prologues' and a 'War Song to Englishmen') which occupy half of its seventy pages. Such eclecticism is typical of apprentice writers, but technical experimentation remains a hallmark of Blake's work, and the adjective he later applied to his paintings in *A Descriptive Catalogue*, 'experiment pictures', is equally applicable to his literary compositions (E 539). Three stylistic experiments in *Poetical Sketches* proved particularly important for his later development, each involving an engagement with the archaising trend that marked much of the literature of this period. The first is a sequence of songs and ballads modelled on Bishop Percy's *Reliques of Ancient English Poetry* (1765), an anthology Wordsworth credited with having 'absolutely redeemed' English poetry by restoring its connection with earlier, native traditions displaced by the French-inspired neoclassicism of Dryden and Pope.[5] One of Blake's poems builds directly on Percy by adopting the genre of 'mad song' of which the *Reliques* contained several examples, madness being a topic on which Percy claimed English poets had long specialised. Blake's 'Mad Song' reworks this popular seventeenth-century genre, his short, jerky lines and oscillating metre mirroring the mental derangement of the speaker. It is here that the image of the 'fiend in a cloud' makes its first appearance (E 407), a simile that Blake was to reuse in 'Infant Sorrow', where the 'howling woe' of the 'Mad Song' is replaced by the torment of a new-born infant confronted with the perils of 'the dangerous world': 'Helpless, naked, piping loud; / Like a fiend hid in a cloud' (E 28). That such a characteristic Blakean image, from one of the most imaginative and shocking of the *Songs of Experience*, should originate in his earlier experiment in generic revivalism underlines the formative role that Percy's *Reliques* played in Blake's poetic development.

Much of the psychological force of Blake's poetry can, indeed, be traced to Blake's grasp of the psychic complexities of early modern song, an example being his song 'How sweet I roam'd'. This anticipates his later songs in its ability to convey in a compressed, symbolic form the complications of emotional and sexual attachment ('He led me through his gardens fair' then 'caught me in his silken net, / And shut me in his golden cage' [E 404]), but, as Malkin noted (*BR* 568–9), he had learned both these skills from Elizabethan and Metaphysical lyric, as he had his command of paradox, hyperbole, unexpected metaphor ('conceit'), and other rhetorical devices. What identifies Percy and other eighteenth-century editors as his point of access to this earlier poetic archive is the co-presence in the *Poetical Sketches* of a more self-conscious revivalist register, illustrated by the trope of the 'ancient bard'. This trope features in several of the poems, most obviously 'To the Muses', a lament for the 'bards of old' whose 'antient melody' has ceased, leaving the modern poetic landscape deserted and silent except for the occasional 'forc'd' note (E 409). The motif of the ancient bard and the abandoned or broken harp is found in hundreds of poems from the 1760s to the 1830s,[6] the fashion reaching its zenith in Thomas Moore's *Irish Melodies* (1808–34), but Blake's knowledge of the Welsh and Irish bards probably came initially from the 'Essay on the Ancient English Minstrels' in Percy's *Reliques* – a piece of antiquarian scholarship as influential as any of the anthologised poems.[7] Blake's abiding fascination with the motif is demonstrated by his watercolour illustrations to Thomas Gray's Pindaric Ode 'The Bard' (1797–8) and his later 'fresco' painting of the same subject, exhibited in 1809. Further evidence is his adoption of a bardic persona in *Songs of Experience*, which opens and closes with 'the voice of the ancient bard' (the title of the last poem), and his reprise of this motif in *America* (1793), where the 'stern Bard' is so troubled by his own prophetic song that he takes his harp and 'dash'd its shining frame against / A ruin'd pillar in glittring fragments' (2: 18–20, E 51).

Another stylistic experiment with long-term consequences was Blake's adaptation of the pseudo-mediaevalism of Thomas Chatterton. In the 1780s the authenticity of Chatterton's 'Rowley' poems was still being vigorously debated and Blake had sufficient interest in the controversy to parody it in his philosophical satire *An Island in the Moon* (1784–5), where the issue of authorship gets comically transformed into the question of whether or not Chatterton was 'a Mathematician' (E 444). As late as 1826, Blake was still defending the authenticity of the Rowley poems (see E 664) but the evidence of his poetry suggests that what really interested Blake was not their ancientness but their expressive power. Rhythmic and verbal echoes of Chatterton haunt Blake's poetry, from the neo-Gothic ballad 'Gwin, King of Norway' in *Poetical Sketches*, the second stanza of which reworks lines from Chatterton's 'Bristowe Tragedie', to *The Marriage of Heaven and Hell*, which adapts a passage from the same poem in which Syr Charles Bawdin, awaiting execution, defiantly recalls previous brushes with death:

> Howe dydd I knowe thatt ev'ry darte
>   Thatt cutte the airie waie,
> Myghte notte fynde passage toe my harte,
>   And close myne eyes for aie?[8]

In *The Marriage*, Bawdin's poignant question becomes an inscription on a rock made by the Blakean Devil in the first of the 'Memorable Fancies':

> How do you know but ev'ry Bird that cuts the airy way,
>   Is an immense world of delight, clos'd by your senses five?   (E 35)

That the first of Blake's citations borders on plagiarism suggests that he shared the textual transgressiveness that was part of Chatterton's antiquarian poetic and one source of its iconoclastic appeal. That the second discards Chatterton's fake medieval diction and transforms Bawdin's words of defiance into a rhetorical question encapsulating the philosophical challenge of *The Marriage* shows how seminal Chatterton's historical inventions were in helping Blake to construct an imaginary world that transcended the perceptual limitations of a benighted present.

A similar claim might be made for Macpherson's Ossian poems, the third of the revivalist styles with which Blake experimented. Macpherson, like Chatterton, was the subject of ongoing controversy and Blake persisted throughout his life in maintaining of both writers that 'what they say is Ancient, Is so' (E 655). Yet, although the Ossian poems contribute to the archaic colouring of certain of the *Poetical Sketches*, their greatest technical influence is the form of prose-poetry they made available to Blake, and their demonstration of the evocative power of Celtic names and legends. The three Ossianic prose-poems with which *Poetical Sketches* concludes – 'The Couch of Death', 'Contemplation', and 'Samson' – directly foreshadow Blake's later prophecies, showing how Macpherson's loosening of the boundaries between verse and prose, and stylistic features such as repetition and parallelism, inversions, rhetorical questions, and tactical obscurity, helped to lay the foundations of Blake's prophetic style.[9] 'Samson' is of particular interest, since it is the first of many Blake works to use the Ossianic mode to treat biblical subject matter, Macpherson's influence combining with that of Milton and the King James Bible. When Blake, at a pivotal point in the narrative, writes of Samson that 'Dark thoughts rolled to and fro in his mind, like thunder clouds, troubling the sky; his visage was troubled; his soul was distressed' (E 435), he brings together these stylistic precursors to create a distinctively Blakean synthesis in which mental and physical landscapes merge and a new visionary cadence emerges. Later, in *Visions of the Daughters of Albion* (1793), Blake produces a metricalised version of this style, adopting the fourteener metre that became the standard verse form of his prophetic books, but retaining a recognisably Ossianic register not just in his choice of names ('Oothoon', modelled on Macpherson's 'Oithona') and stormy mountain setting, but also in his continuously modulating language of lamentation, and other stylistic features already noted.

The fact that the *Visions*, like the other Lambeth prophecies, blends these early influences with other formal and stylistic models, from Swedenborgian dream vision to contemporary political pamphlets, shows that Blake continued to experiment with old and new genres, his most characteristic – and most characteristically Romantic – form of experimentation being the mixing of genres. The most extreme example of this technique is *The Marriage of Heaven and Hell* (1790–3), where, as I have argued elsewhere, Blake employs a type of 'rough-mixing' which juxtaposes an extraordinary range of genres, forms, and styles in order to produce an aesthetic defamiliarisation effect inseparable from the ideological challenge he mounts.[10]

Critics have rightly seen parallels between Blake's *Songs of Innocence and of Experience* and Wordsworth and Coleridge's professedly experimental *Lyrical Ballads* (1798).[11] There is no evidence at this stage in his career of mutual influence, though Blake in the 1790s was clearly responding to other poets such as Erasmus Darwin and Joel Barlow, participating in the 'epomania' and the fashion for apocalyptic writing associated with the French Revolution.[12] There are possible connections, too, with contemporary female poets such as Mary Robinson and Charlotte Smith, though direct influence here is hard to trace.[13] At a later point, however, Blake closely read and commented on Wordsworth's work, and Wordsworth and Coleridge did the same with his. Coleridge's commentary, in two letters of 1818, included a poem-by-poem evaluation of the *Songs*, his greatest praise going to 'The Divine Image', 'The Little Black Boy', and 'Night'. Blake, he said, was a 'man of genius' and an 'apo- or rather ana-calyptic poet', compared with whom he himself was 'the very mire of common-place commonsense' (*BR* 336–8). Other members of Coleridge's circle also commented on individual songs, Crabb Robinson singling out 'The Tyger' as 'truly inspired and original' (*BR* 601), and Lamb, who heard it recited, calling it 'glorious' (*BR* 394). Hazlitt, too, was 'much struck' with the *Songs*, though he regarded them as 'too deep for the vulgar'; his favourite was 'The Chimney Sweeper' (*BR* 309). Southey, after visiting Blake in 1811 and being shown part of *Jerusalem*, said he 'admired both his designs & his poetical talents' (*BR* 310). Landor, who also met Blake around this time, later described him as 'the greatest of poets' and elsewhere made the highly astute observation that 'Blake had been Wordsworth's prototype' (*BR* 310n.). Lamb made a similar comparison, calling Blake simply a 'mad Wordsworth' (*BR* 313).

The most compelling evidence, though, of this affinity is Wordsworth's and Blake's own responses to one another. Though they never met, Wordsworth encountered Blake's work in Malkin's *A Father's Memoirs of His Child* (1806). He remarked, like others, on Blake's supposed madness (such comments should not be taken at face value since they reflect a fashionable discourse about 'mad' poets which colours much Romantic criticism) but added the telling comment that 'there is something in the madness of this man which interests me more than the Sanity of Lord

Byron & Walter Scott' (*BR* 693; cf. 312).[14] That interest was sufficiently strong for him and his sister to copy out from Malkin four of the *Songs of Innocence*. In 1826 Blake paid a similar tribute to Wordsworth by transcribing the 'Prospectus' to *The Recluse* from the Preface to *The Excursion* (1814), a copy of which Crabb Robinson had lent him. That Blake should give such keen attention to this key statement of Wordsworth's poetics is remarkable, but the engagement is complex and combative, as his comments to Robinson and his marginalia indicate. The 'Prospectus', he told Robinson, 'so troubled him as to bring on a fit of illness' (*BR* 701). He saw, in effect, two Wordsworths: a visionary, like himself, and an atheist, of the kind he despised. On a copy of Wordsworth's *Poems* (1815), he explained why: 'I see in Wordsworth the Natural Man rising up against the Spiritual Man Continually & then he is No Poet but a Heathen Philosopher at Enmity against all true Poetry or Inspirations' (E 654). Against the subtitle 'Influence of Natural Objects', he retorted: 'Natural Objects always did & now do Weaken deaden & obliterate Imagination in Me' (E 655). In conversation with Robinson he was even blunter, insisting some of Wordsworth's poems 'were from the Holy Ghost, others from the Devil' (*BR* 702). He saw too an irreconcilable gulf between the poet and the theorist in Wordsworth: over the 'Essay Supplementary to the Preface', he wrote: 'I do not know who wrote these Prefaces they are mischievous & direct contrary to Wordsworths own Practice' (E 655).

Much could be said about these brilliant antithetical observations, but the essential point is clear: Blake recognised in Wordsworth a kindred spirit, the one poet of his age with visionary powers to match his own, but a writer whose transcendentalism was contradicted and undermined by a deadening materialism. Blake's vehement resistance to that naturalising tendency in all its forms is the cornerstone of his radical Romanticism and of his vocation as the latter-day bard who 'kept the Divine Vision in time of trouble' (E 252).

Notes

1. N. Frye, *Fearful Symmetry: A Study of William Blake* (1947; Princeton: Princeton University Press, 1970), p. 6.
2. K. Junor, 'Crabb Robinson, Blake, and Perthes's *Vaterländisches Museum* (1810–1811)', *European Romantic Review*, 23.4 (2012), 435–51.
3. L. Langbauer, *The Juvenile Tradition: Young Writers and Prolepsis, 1750–1835* (Oxford: Oxford University Press, 2016).

4. R. C. Sha, *The Visual and Verbal Sketch in British Romanticism* (Philadelphia: University of Pennsylvania Press, 1998).
5. 'Essay, Supplementary to the Preface' (1815), in W. Wordsworth, *The Major Works*, ed. S. Gill (Oxford: Oxford University Press, 2004), p. 656.
6. For the ubiquity of this motif, see T. A. Hoagwood, *From Song to Print: Romantic Pseudo-Songs* (New York: Palgrave Macmillan, 2010).
7. M. McLane, *Balladeering, Minstrelsy, and the Making of British Romantic Poetry* (Cambridge: Cambridge University Press, 2008).
8. [T. Chatterton], *Poems, Supposed to Have Been Written at Bristol, by Thomas Rowley, and Others, in the Fifteenth Century* (London: 1777), p. 51 (ll. 133–6). For Blake's interest in Chatterton, see M. Butler, *Mapping Mythologies: Countercurrents in Eighteenth-Century British Poetry and Cultural History* (Cambridge: Cambridge University Press, 2015), pp. 184–92.
9. For an inventory of Ossianic allusions, see P. Miner, 'Unexplored Latitudes: Blake and Ossian', *Notes and Queries*, 58.4 (2011), 533–5.
10. D. Duff, *Romanticism and the Uses of Genre* (Oxford: Oxford University Press, 2009), pp. 181–4.
11. See especially H. Glen, *Vision and Disenchantment: Blake's Songs and Wordsworth's Lyrical Ballads* (Cambridge: Cambridge University Press, 1983).
12. S. Curran, *Poetic Form and British Romanticism* (Oxford: Oxford University Press, 1986), pp. 175–9; M. D. Paley, *Apocalypse and Millennium in English Romantic Poetry* (Oxford: Clarendon Press, 1999), pp. 32–90. See also D. King-Hele, *Erasmus Darwin and the Romantic Poets* (New York: St Martin's Press, 1986); and D. Erdman, 'William Blake's Debt to Joel Barlow', *American Literature*, 26.1 (1954), 94–8.
13. See the essays by T. Connolly, J. M. Labbe, and H. K. Linkin in H. Bruder (ed.), *Women Reading William Blake* (Basingstoke: Palgrave Macmillan, 2007).
14. J. Whitehead, *Madness and the Romantic Poet: A Critical History* (Oxford: Oxford University Press, 2017).

CHAPTER 22

Byron

Jerome McGann

Blake and Byron had no personal connection, and Byron was unaware of Blake. Blake did, however, know Byron's work and towards the end of his life he finally addressed it directly. When Byron published his play *Cain. A Mystery* in 1821, it provoked virtually universal public censure.[1] Blake too responded, but very differently. Addressed 'To Lord Byron in the Wilderness', *The Ghost of Abel* (1822) names Byron a cultural force as consequential as 'the Public', 'the Jews', 'the Deists', and 'the Christians' who are directly addressed in the four chapters of *Jerusalem* (1804–20). Byron appears to Blake's vision as the prophet Elijah *redivivus* in the age of the restoration of the thrones of Europe and the Congress of Verona. No other living contemporary was so singled out by Blake or hailed with that kind of exalted rhetoric. Yet *Cain* would not have been Blake's first acquaintance with the poet, given Byron's immense fame, and the form of Blake's address argues an affinity whose range and depth has not previously been considered. In certain respects, several of them crucial for both men and for our understanding of Romanticism in general, they were kindred spirits.

Scholars sometimes question whether Blake even read *Cain in toto*, much less the whole of the volume, which included *Sardanapalus* and *The Two Foscari*. The cost (15s) would have been prohibitive for Blake.[2] But consider that the only verbal echoes of Byron in *The Ghost of Abel* are not to *Cain* but to *Don Juan* (Canto I) and *The Two Foscari*.[3] The *Don Juan* echo is significant for what it implies about Blake's reading before the scandal of *Cain*, which I shall shortly take up. In addition, the quotation lifted from *The Two Foscari* shows that Blake probably read the whole of Byron's volume, which would have interested him as a critical reflection on cycles of historical violence. When Blake's Jehovah asks the Ghost of Abel 'What Vengeance dost thou require', the wraith replies 'Life for Life! Life for Life!' (E 271). His answer echoes Loredano's appeal to Leviticus 24: 17–21: 'life for life, the rule / Denounced for retribution from all time'

(*The Two Foscari* IV, 1, 22–3; *CPW* VI).⁴ Consider as well that Byron's three plays together schematise a universal history of violence – psychic, social, and imperial – that echoes the tormented history Blake imagined in similarly epochal terms in *VALA / The Four Zoas* and further codified in *Milton* and *Jerusalem*. With *Cain* and its unfinished sequel *Heaven and Earth* (1823), Byron would follow Blake in tracking the Western progress of that history to primitive biblical sources. Byron read those sources, again like Blake, against their orthodox interpretive grain.⁵ In the epoch of the French Revolution and its reactionary aftermath, Blake's antinomian religion and Byron's Enlightenment scepticism often spoke a common tongue.

Given the sharp things Blake wrote against 'unbelief' and the critical spirit of Enlightenment science and philosophy, we might wonder how he found common cause with the infidel Byron. But Blake would have recognised the special quality of Byron's scepticism, which called doubt itself to judgement.⁶ Byron's Enlightenment allegiances were for Blake, like the writings of Thomas Paine, the voice of one crying in a spiritual wilderness of ecclesiastical orthodoxy. Both Blake and Byron endorsed and practised Kant's Enlightenment injunction, *sapere aude*, each daring to think critically about knowledge and the pretensions of education, both secular and religious. Manfred begins his career as a chastened and desperate *philosophe*, confessing that 'The Tree of Knowledge is not that of Life' (*Manfred* I, 1, 12; *CPW* IV). Blake took the same point of biblical reference when he told Crabb Robinson that '"education [. . .] is the great Sin – It is eating of the tree of the Knowledge of Good and Evil"' (*BR* 696).

We can begin to understand the depth of Blake's interest in Byron by recalling certain foundational aspects of Blake's theology. These rested in his essentially Arianist understanding that Jesus was himself, in the eyes of the law, a 'Transgressor' (*Jerusalem* 13[14]: 27, E 107). '"What are called the Vices in the natural world, are the highest sublimities in the spiritual world["]', he said to Crabb Robinson in their conversations of 1825–6 (*BR* 700). His remarks about Jesus, the angels, and God Himself ('the Supreme Being') reveal the literality of his signature formula 'human form divine'. 'Jesus Christ', he told Robinson, '["]is the only God["] – but then he added – ["]And so am I and so are you["]'. He also 'spoke of error as being in heaven' and 'extend[ed] this liability to error to the Supreme Being', adding that 'he did not believe in the Omnipotence of God' nor in the purity of angels or men (*BR* 696, 700, 696). '"There is suffering in Heaven"', he told Robinson, '"for where there is the capacity of enjoyment, there is the capacity of pain["]' (*BR* 698). Though Jesus was the very model of divine humanity for Blake, he often spoke of 'the errors of Jesus': 'turning the money change[r]s out of the Temple', for example, which 'he had no right to do' (*BR* 421, 705). Most remarkable of all, he said that Jesus 'ought not to have suffered himself to be crucified' (*BR* 696). Indeed, that mistake might have been for Blake Jesus's 'worst' error since it entailed licensing the law of vicarious atonement, 'a horrible doctrine' in Blake's judgement (*BR* 705).

He could not have known that Byron dismissed the doctrine of vicarious atonement with similar contempt, though Byron spoke the idiom of Enlightenment rationalism.[7] Both saw that vicarious atonement shifted the responsibility for human error and guilt to a transpersonal order of normative Law. For Blake, the doctrine codified a system of unpayable indebtedness that opened a gulf, rather than a sympathetic relation, between Time and Eternity, God and Man. The structure of that cruel system, and in particular its affective character, is laid out in both *Milton* and *Jerusalem*. The Spectre of Los, plunged into 'torment [and] grief at worst', bears the burden of its curse, as we see when he cries out against the God of his condition: 'he is Righteous: he is not a Being of Pity & Compassion / He cannot feel Distress' (*Jerusalem* 10: 39, 44, 47–8, E 153). But Los explains that the 'furnaces / Of affliction' (*Milton* 38[43]: 20, E 139) and mortal death also turn a system of adverse wheels. It signifies the judgement of sin turning back on itself, 'as cogs are form'd in a wheel to turn the cogs of the adverse wheel' (*Milton* 27[29]: 9, E 124; *Jerusalem* 13: 14, E 156). This dynamic operates a system of redemptive affect, 'That whenever any Spectre began to devour the Dead, / He might feel the pain as if a man gnawd his own tender nerves' (*Jerusalem* 11: 6–7, E 154). Blake expressed the same view much earlier in the simpler and more direct idiom of 'On Anothers Sorrow'.

The Ghost of Abel, Blake's final exploration of these matters, is important because of the intervention of Byron into his field of vision. Blake's critical reading of Byron's play forces into the open vital tensions in Blake's work that are artistically important exactly because they go unresolved. Blake and Byron both argue that the works of human imagination are part of the lifeworld of human error and mistake. Formal instabilities and aesthetic irresolution are ineluctable features of what Blake called 'living form', 'Gothic' form ('On Virgil' E 270). That conviction led Blake to declare aesthetic method as the one field where education was imperative (see *BR* 700). Indeed, both men made a virtue out of exposing the limits of their own art.[8]

Keeping faith with Enlightenment reason chastened by reflection on the French Revolution and its reactionary aftermath, Byron undertook in his last eight years a broad critical analysis of Western political and social history. Those works run an uncanny parallel with Blake's similarly ambitious imaginative studies of Western history and culture. For Byron, *Cain* is the key text, even as *Childe Harold* Canto IV is perhaps the best point of reference for understanding the play's argument. Canto IV constructs itself as what amounts to a Cainite interpretation of history that Byron explicitly names 'man's worst – his second fall' (st. 97, *CPW* II).[9] For Byron (as for Blake), the expulsion from Eden is an existential condition, the murder of Abel is a horror. The first fall is not subject to redemption, it is rather the very condition of human life. The Second Fall is different, doubled, duplicitous and Canto IV of *Childe Harold* exposes the machinery of being 'doubly curst' (st. 124) in a sequence of lyric meditations that extend from Byron's entrance into Rome in stanza 78 to the end of the canto.

Byron's response to the Second Fall is a counter move of repeated resistance:

> Yet let us ponder boldly – 'tis a base
> Abandonment of reason to resign
> Our right of thought – our last and only place
> Of refuge.   (st. 127)

'The truth' that will dawn on the intrepid and errant mind, if it persists in its quest for truth, is that the 'faculty divine' is a human faculty (st. 127), according to the Blakean proverb 'Attempting to be more than Man We become less' (*VALA/Four Zoas* N9, p. 135, l. 21, E 403). This mind is 'chained and tortured – cabined, cribbed, confined / And bred in darkness' (st. 127). Imagining itself otherwise, the mind keeps slipping into various 'overweening phantasies' (st. 7) such as the fantasy of triumph that Lucifer offers Cain in his famous speech about intellectual freedom at the end of Act II.

Byron maps the action of 'man's worst, his Second Fall' as the psychomachia of *Cain*, where Cain's crime poses the crisis that is the climax of the play: how to *feel about* the Cainite world. Eve's curse is one way, Adah's is another, and while the play clearly endorses Adah's faithful if uncertain ethics, she does not carry the play's poetics. *Cain*'s most affecting poetic argument comes with and as Eve's curse, which is so overwhelmingly terrible that Eve herself emerges as the play's most piteous and ruined figure. *Cain* argues that Cain, judged and cast out, deserves mercy and forgiveness. But its deeper insight centres in Eve, whose need is plainly far more desperate and fearful because she has put on the armour of her pain and turned it to righteous judgement.

Cain thus diagrams the poetic argument about cursing and forgiving that Byron makes in *Childe Harold*. Putting on the armor of his accusers in the Forgiveness Curse stanzas (*Childe Harold* IV, 130–7), Byron creates himself in the image and likeness of Pauline forgiveness (Romans 12) and impersonal Justice (Nemesis).[10] That this image – this Byron – appears infuriated, like Eve in *Cain*, is the sacred heart of the poetic argument. Christian forgiveness '"does not forgive [...] at all"', as the fool Wamba points out in *Ivanhoe* (chapter 32), when it assumes the authority of the knowledge of good and evil. Such knowledge wears the covering of the law, and all law, even the law of love, is blind to the human cost. The 'dread Power' of Nemesis emerges from this scene to haunt the rest of the poem and to show that the Christian scale of Justice – Good and Evil – is fatally 'unbalanced' (*Childe Harold* IV, 139). To follow its law is to be 'doom'd to inflict or bear' it (III, 71).

That is why the poem makes a human individual – Byron here – the spokesman for the law, that he might feel and show the pain of a man gnawing his own tender nerves. His prayer for his accusers is clothed in cruelty and sorrow, for to put on the armour of the Lord is to wear a shirt of Nessus': 'my Clothing shall be Cruelty / And I will put on Holiness as a breast & as a helmet' (*Milton* 18[20]: 20–1, E 111). All the passages in Blake's work about secret holiness are mirrored in Byron's Forgiveness Curse, which bears a counter-secret in the remembered tones of the mute liar Byron (*Childe Harold* IV, 137). As the 'careful pilot of my proper woe', Byron confesses himself the perfect captain for a Ship of Fools ('[Epistle to Augusta]' st. 3; *CPW* IV).

The blow-up precipitated by *Cain* in 1822 has had a long cultural afterlife, not least the Mental Fight among scholars, still engaged, about Blake's representation of Byron. The controversy hangs on what Blake meant by identifying Byron with the prophet Elijah. Most scholars have read it as an endorsement of Byron's controversial life and work, and in particular of *Cain*.[11] But two prominent Blake scholars, Leslie Tannenbaum and W. H. Stevenson, have demurred.[12]

The action of *The Ghost of Abel* follows upon the question that introduces the action: 'Can a Poet doubt the Visions of Jehovah?' Tannenbaum/Stevenson assume that the answer to this rhetorical question has to be 'no' because *The Ghost of Abel* promotes a New Testament vision of absolute faith based on 'forgiveness and reconciliation'.[13] *The Ghost of Abel*'s climactic Chorus of Angels, Tannenbaum writes, map 'a progressive movement from the primitive concept of propitiatory atonement in *Genesis* 4 to the prophetic attack on false atonement – Elijah-Byron's iconoclastic reinterpretation of the Genesis story – to Blake's announcement of the true atonement represented by Christ'. In this view, Byron's *Cain* has not escaped the 'alien and inhospitable universe' of the Old Testament.[14] Raging in the Wilderness of the restored thrones of Europe, Byron wrote a play that 'doubt[ed] the Visions of Jehovah'.

Enlarging the context of the Blake/Byron nexus – my object to this point – delivers a fresh view of this controversy. Blake's theology of the adverse wheel also drives *The Ghost of Abel* (E 270–2), whose text consists of a play, a counter-play (within the play), and a choral finale. The initial action is utterly desolate, 'A rocky Country' cursed with a covenant founded in death and judgement (E 270). Eve correctly cries out against it as 'all a vain delusion / This Death & this Life & this Jehovah!' (1: 6–7). The 'Visionary Phantasm' of Abel – the 'Accuser & Avenger' – then comes to perfect the desolation, demanding a 'Vengeance' that 'this Jehovah' is expecting him to demand ('What Vengeance dost thou require') (1: 6–13).[15] When the ghost demands 'Life for Life', this Jehovah's reply is also a self-exposure of his own fear of death and judgment:

> He who shall take Cains life must also Die O Abel
> And who is he? Adam wilt thou, or Eve thou do this. (1: 14–16)

Although Adam initially recoils in fear at this Jehovah's question, his reaction produces a further, unexpected action of adverse 'Spiritual Vision', the presence of a 'Form Divine! Father of Mercies' in the machinery of death and vengeance that Abel's ghost and this Jehovah are enacting (1: 21–2):

> Eve come away & let us not believe these vain delusions
> Abel is dead & Cain slew him! We shall also Die a Death
> And then! what then? be as poor Abel a Thought: or as
> This! O what shall I call thee Form Divine! Father of Mercies
> That appearest to my Spiritual Vision. (1: 18–22)

Adam's vision moves Eve from her despair to a new vision of faith and hope. It is significant, however, that at this point we do not actually see what Adam and Eve are seeing. That comes as Blake's play within the play, which arises to *our* vision when Adam and Eve '*Kneel before Jehovah*' (E 271). From that point, 'This Death & this Life & this Jehovah' begin to be reimagined on an adverse and merciful wheel.

The central figure in *that* play is Jehovah, at whose transfiguration we, like the disciples of Jesus, are the watchers. This second action begins when Abel's ghost heaps scorn on the kneeling Adam and Eve, whom he correctly sees as figures of 'a Broken Spirit / And a Contrite Heart' (2: 4–5). Their abjection summons the ghost of Abel who is possessed by Cain's violent spirit and 'therefore My Soul in fumes of Blood / Cries for Vengeance'. The climactic event comes when Jehovah offers Abel 'a Lamb for an Atonement instead / Of the Transgres[s]or' (2: 8–11). This atonement is what *Milton* describes as 'a curse[d] offering' because its operation preserves Jehovah and his laws from judgement. But Satan arises to call Jehovah and his cursed system of sin and atonement to judgement: 'I will have Human Blood & not the blood of Bulls or Goats / And no Atonement O Jehovah' (2: 13–14).

Like Lucifer in Byron's *Cain*, Satan does not realise the deep import of his own words, which emerges when Jehovah's 'Will' echoes and reverses Satan's 'will [for] Human Blood'. When Satan declares that 'Thou [Jehovah] shalt Thyself be sacrificed to Me thy God on Calvary', Jehovah gives his startling assent: 'Such is My Will. *Thunders* / that Thou Thyself go to Eternal Death / In Self Annihilation even till Satan Self-subdued Put off Satan' (2: 18–20). Satanic law executes itself on Calvary. Satan: 'I will have Human Blood' / Jehovah: 'Such is my will'; Satan: 'Thou shalt thyself be sacrificed to Me Thy God' / Jehovah: 'thou thyself [shall] go to Eternal Death' (2: 13–19): those verbal repetitions are the poetic revelation of Jehovah as Satan, the brother and double of 'The Elohim of the Heathen [who] Swore Vengeance for Sin!' (2: 22). The argument repeats the one Blake had made thirty years earlier in *The Marriage of Heaven and Hell*.

The text of the play closes with the chorus celebrating the revelation of 'Elohim Jehovah', which is a kind of formulary for re-reading everything in the play as 'fixt in the Firmament by Peace Brotherhood and Love' (2: 26). The 'Covenant of the Forgiveness of Sins' is the universal brotherhood of mortal creatures. Crucial to see is that this 'Covenant' does not entail the extinction of 'The Elohim of the Heathen' (2: 22). Quite the contrary: *The Ghost of Abel* shows why Jehovah is enacting what Milton had spoken of in *Milton*: 'To claim the Hells, my Furnaces, I go to Eternal Death' (*Milton* 14 [15]: 32, E 108). The Jehovah of *The Ghost of Abel* is still the aspiring Devil of *The Marriage of Heaven and Hell*, 'he who dwells in flaming fire' (pl. 6, E 35). *The Ghost of Abel* thus resurrects (re-envisions) the Satanic Elohim twice, first as 'the Bottomless Abyss whose torment arises for ever & ever' (2: 21), second as the firmament of stars rolled into the starry heavens above the 'Mercy Seat' of the human world (2: 26). It is the Mercy Seat because 'Time is the mercy of Eternity' (*Milton* 24 [26]: 72, E 121).

The Tannenbaum/Stevenson reading of *The Ghost of Abel* – that Blake intended it as only a qualified endorsement of Byron – could be right in the sense that it could represent Blake's intention. Should we think so, we might also think that Blake had not quite grasped the force of Byron's intransigent vision of guilt and forgiveness. But I think he did. Because the paradisal imagination of 'Mutual Forgiveness of each Vice' will always be an act of human imagining, it is always subject to unsuspected limits. Error and vice are precisely an eternal condition of human life, which is why the agency of mutual forgiveness is both the proper and the never-to-be-achieved standard of judgement. The buildings of Los commit to a ceaseless 'Mental Fight' – 'ever consuming & ever building' because the greatest and undefeatable antagonist of artistic imagination is the artistic imagination itself (*Milton* 1: 13, E 95; *Jerusalem* 13: 61, E 158).

Blake gave a premonitory summary of the action of his play two years earlier in the 'Prologue' to the second version of *The Gates of Paradise*,[16] his most succinct commentary on the doctrine of 'Mutual Forgiveness for each Vice':

> Jehovahs Finger Wrote the Law
> Then Wept! then rose in Zeal & Awe
> And the Dead Corpse from Sinais heat
> Buried beneath his Mercy Seat. (ll. 5–8, E 259)

But those are not the last words of the 'Prologue' nor does *The Ghost of Abel* finish when 'The Curtain falls' on the choral hymn of 'Peace Brotherhood and Love'. Below the text Blake sets an illustration that recalls the wilderness 'Scene' (seen) at the opening of the play, but with a difference. This is a vision of 'The Voice of Abels Blood' swirling around three figures of death, lamentation, and howling affliction. Eve and Abel remain as they were at the start, but instead of 'Adam kneel[ing] by her' and 'Jehovah stand[ing] above', a tormented Cain sits to the right, marking the tableau as 'the Bottomless Abyss whose torment arises for ever & ever'. A fearful and piteous scene, it illustrates why a Revelation of 'Peace Brotherhood and Love' is the only response adequate to 'The Voice of Abels Blood'. 'I behold the finger of God in terrors!', Los declares in *Jerusalem*, and Blake echoes back the message: 'Even from the depths of Hell his voice I hear' (*Jerusalem* 12: 5, E 155; 3: 7, E 145). Because Los presides over a dreadful history of ruin and loss – human life being 'perfected in the furnaces of affliction' – Los has seen Loss as 'the finger of God going forth in terrors':

> Giving a body to Falshood that it may be cast off for ever.
> With Demonstrative Science piercing Apollyon with his own bow!
> God is within, & without! he is even in the depths of Hell!
>
> (*Jerusalem* 9: 34–5, E 152; 12: 5, 13–15, E 145)

The angelic hymn in *The Ghost of Abel* is far from the work's whole story. Being also the story of the hunted and fearful Elijah hearing 'the still small voice' in the wilderness, *The Ghost of Abel* ends with a vision of the finger of God writing *De profundis clamavi*. It is exactly the same voice that speaks the last couplet of *The Gates of Paradise* 'Prologue':

> O Christians Christians! tell me Why
> You rear it on your Altars high.   (ll. 9–10, E 259)

Byron's *Cain* and the outraged religious reaction it provoked reminded Blake why that was still an unquenchably burning question. *The Ghost of Abel* ends with its illustration of a world gripped in the tormenting Wastes of Moral Law. Not much has changed in England's social world since Blake wrote the portentous 'Argument' for *The Marriage of Heaven and Hell* some thirty years before. That is why Byron/Elijah is still in the wilderness and why a poet can doubt the visions of Jehovah even though the vision of mutual forgiveness might be judged a great, visionary truth: the knowledge of the Tree of Life, even a truth that could set you free (John 8:32). 'Imagination *is* Eternity' (*Ghost of Abel*, E 270). Without imagination's point of view one might actually believe – what Byron's detractors believed – that the wilderness cry of *Cain* was untruth, his accusers the Children of Light, and that Jerusalem was being built in 1820s England. Only 'the City of Golgonooza', the city of art, was being built 'by the Spectres' of the tormented Imagination: a creation that is the work of Los(s), 'ever consuming & ever building' (*Jerusalem* 13: 61, E 158).

Notes

1. For a good account of the hostility provoked by Byron's play, see R. Mortenson, *The Reception of Cain, A Mystery: Byron's Waterloo* (Seattle, WA: Iron Press, 2015).
2. See R. N. Essick and J. Viscomi (eds.), *William Blake: Milton a Poem and the Final Illuminated Works* (London: William Blake Trust; Princeton: Princeton University Press, 1993), p. 224, n. 5.
3. See ibid., p. 223, and A. Whitehead, 'A Quotation from Lord Byron's The Two Foscari in William Blake's The Ghost of Abel', *Notes and Queries* (September 2006), 325–6.

4. Byron's works are cited from J. McGann (ed.), *Lord Byron: The Complete Poetical Works*, 7 vols. (Oxford: Clarendon Press, 1980–93). References to *CPW* will appear in the main text.
5. Byron set out to extend *Cain*'s critical commentary on the foundational Old Testament texts with his drama *Heaven and Earth: A Mystery* (1823) but he lived to complete and publish only Part I. Both Byron and Blake seem to have read the recently discovered and translated *Book of Enoch*, which calls for the extermination of the line of Cain. See G. E. Bentley, Jr., 'A Jewel in an Ethiop's Ear', in R. N. Essick and D. Pearce (eds.), *Blake in His Time* (Bloomington, IN: University of Indiana Press, 1978), pp. 213–40, and Byron, *CPW* VI, pp. 682–3.
6. 'I deny nothing, but doubt everything.' (L. A. Marchand (ed.), *Byron's Letters and Journals*, 12 vols. (Cambridge, MA: Harvard University Press, 1973), II, 136.)
7. Blake told Crabb Robinson '"If another man pay your debt, I do not forgive it"' (*BR* 705), meaning that vicarious atonement prevented the key Blakean action of mutual forgiveness of sin. As for Byron, see the letter to Francis Hodgson of 13 September 1811: the sacrifice of Jesus 'no more does away with man's guilt than a schoolboy's volunteering to be flogged for another would exculpate the dunce from negligence, or preserve him from the rod' (Marchand, *Byron's Letters and Journals*, II, 97). See also *Manfred* III, I, 98–9, *CPW* IV.
8. The most notorious example in Blake is plate 3 of *Jerusalem*. Readers from Goethe forward, including Arnold and Swinburne, recognised that Byron's poetic strength was a function of the nakedness of his poetic address, where he made a virtue of his limitations. See, for example, *English Bards and Scotch Reviewers*, ll. 93–102, *CPW* I.
9. On Byron's concept of the Second Fall, see J. J. McGann, 'Tre Tipi di Ragione Romantica: Blake, Wordsworth, Byron', in P. Tortonese (ed.), *C'è del metodo in questa follia: l'irrazionale nella litteratura romantica*, trans. C. Gallo (Pisa: Pacini Editore, 2015), pp. 111–25.
10. The appeal to St Paul is explicit in the stanza Byron dropped after stanza 135 (see *CPW* II, p. 169).
11. For an illustrative overview, see Essick and Viscomi (ed.), *The Final Illuminated Works*, pp. 220–37, 254–63.
12. See W. H. Stevenson and D. V. Erdman (eds.), *The Poems of William Blake* (London: Longman, 1971), pp. 860–4, and L. Tannenbaum, 'Lord Byron in the Wilderness: Biblical Tradition in Byron's *Cain* and Blake's The Ghost of Abel', *Modern Philology*, 72.4 (1975), 350–64. See also S. F. Damon, *A Blake Dictionary: The Ideas and Symbols of William Blake* (Providence: Brown University Press, 1965), the entry for 'Elijah'. Damon says Blake 'hail[s] Byron as a true poet while correcting his ideas' (p. 118). Essick and Viscomi disagree with that reading (pp. 224–6).
13. Stevenson and Erdman, *Poems of William Blake*, p. 860.
14. Tannenbaum, 'Lord Byron', p. 364.

15. Jehovah expects it because, until he passes a Last Judgement on himself (the event of the adversative play within the play), he is himself caught up in cyclic violence and 'vengeance seven times over' (Genesis 4:15–16).
16. For useful commentary, see M. D. Paley, *The Traveller in the Evening* (New York: Oxford University Press, 2003), pp. 8–19.

CHAPTER 23

Pre-Raphaelites and Aesthetes
Elizabeth Helsinger

Dante Gabriel Rossetti may be best known to Blake students for the *Note-book* he purchased from William Palmer, brother of the artist Samuel Palmer (part of Blake's circle at his death), in April 1847, and for his contributions – beginning with the loan of the *Note-book* – to Alexander Gilchrist's 1863 *Life of William Blake*, '*Pictor Ignotus*,' the most important nineteenth-century biography. Publication of the *Life* marked the beginning of Blake's emergence from relative obscurity in Victorian Britain, a belated recognition of Blake's genius consolidated by two later publications from members of Rossetti's circle: Algernon Charles Swinburne's *William Blake, A Critical Essay* (1868) and William Michael Rossetti's edited volume of Blake's poetry for the Aldine Poets series in 1874.

Rossetti had first encountered Blake in the mid-1840s in Allan Cunningham's *Lives of the Most Eminent British Painters, Sculptors, and Architects* (1829–33), where he is presented as unduly obscure but undoubtedly mad. Torn between poetry and painting, the young Rossetti jumped at the chance to know more of a fellow poet-artist. He enthusiastically shared the *Note-book* (which contains drafts of many of the *Songs of Experience* together with drawings and other poetry and prose from c. 1787 to 1818) with family, friends, and fellow poets, including his brother William, his sister Christina, Swinburne, and Gilchrist. When Gilchrist died unexpectedly, just after completing his *Life* but before composing the comments on Blake's work that he had intended to include, Rossetti and his brother William helped Gilchrist's widow Anne complete the *Life* and see it through publication. William compiled a bibliography of Blake's visual designs while Dante Gabriel wrote on Blake's art and provided descriptions accompanying the *Life*'s reproduction of Blake's illustrations to the Book of Job. Rossetti also chose, edited (sometimes rather freely), and wrote introductions to *Songs of Innocence and of Experience* (included in its entirety), *The Book of Thel*, generous selections from *Poetical Sketches*, and unpublished poems from the *Note-book*, all printed as the second volume of the published *Life*. Gilchrist portrayed Blake as a gentle, childlike poet-artist, almost a saint removed from his world, but sane; he passed lightly over the later prophetic books. Swinburne's 1868 *Essay on William Blake* sought to redress Gilchrist's omissions with an account of the prophetic books. He insisted on the coherence of Blake's ideas and provided a passionate defence of the poet as a rebel against political, artistic, and sexual repressions. William Rossetti's 1874 edition of Blake's poetry largely retained his brother's choices and emendations but achieved a wider circulation, making Blake's lyric poetry, at least, much more widely available.

This story of Blake's debt to Gilchrist, the Rossettis, and Swinburne has been examined many times.[1] But what of the Pre-Raphaelite and Aesthetic poets' debts to Blake? How was Blake's work absorbed and reinterpreted in their poetry and visual art?

Dante Gabriel Rossetti responded to Blake's work in two important ways. First, Blake was for Rossetti a poet-artist of a particularly visualising imagination such as he felt himself to be – like Dante, whose *Vita Nuova* Rossetti was translating in the late 1840s, and with whom Rossetti felt a strong personal identification.[2] Blake was a model much closer in time and country for Rossetti's efforts to visualise, in painting and poetry, the world of his own imagination (and of Dante's) in the drawings and paintings he produced as a member of the Pre-Raphaelite Brotherhood (1849–c. 1854), a group of young artists devoted to re-energising British arts by following the example of painters before Raphael. Rossetti applied a Pre-Raphaelite passion for simplicity and precise detail – truth to nature – to partly immaterial, visionary subjects: as in his *Ecce Ancilla Domini! (The Annunciation)* (1850; Tate), or *Dante Drawing an Angel on the First Anniversary of Beatrice's Death* (1849, 1853; Ashmolean). It was the latter in its watercolour version that brought Rossetti to the attention of the influential art critic John Ruskin in 1854. (Of *Dante Drawing an Angel*, Ruskin wrote to Rossetti, 'I think it is a thoroughly glorious work – the most perfect piece of Italy, in the accessory parts, I have ever seen in my life.')[3] But Blake was also responsible for their meeting: Ruskin's introduction to Blake's drawings in the 1840s by the artist George Richmond (another of the circle around Blake at the time he died) prepared him to appreciate the visionary realism of Rossetti's *Dante Drawing an Angel*. Ruskin's praise and patronage gave Rossetti a confidence in his visual art that he had not received from his fellow Pre-Raphaelites, encouraging him to produce the fine watercolours of the later 1850s that formed an important part of a second generation of Pre-Raphaelite work by Rossetti, William Morris, and Edward Burne-Jones.[4]

Blake's materialised visions were realised as a composite art of the page, bringing poetry and vision together in the almost total control Blake was able to exercise over the physical look of his illuminated printing. Rossetti too turned to the arts of the book in the 1860s, designing covers and illustrations for his own and his friends' books. He stopped short of Blake's inventive mastery of a truly composite form, but his disciple and friend, that other poet-artist Morris, went much further, finally founding his own press in the 1890s to bring together the material and poetic arts – what Morris called the 'ornamental' and the 'epical' forms of the book – in the volumes he designed and printed at Kelmscott Press.[5]

Blake was also for Rossetti an influential example of a great lyric poet. Rossetti understood that term in a special sense. Blake was the poet whose most perfect poems were songs: the six songs, so titled, of *Poetical Sketches* and the *Songs of Innocence and of Experience*. These are at the centre of Rossetti's case, in Gilchrist's *Life*, for 'the simplicity and purity of his style as a lyrical poet' (Gilchrist 381). Rossetti noted how Blake's songs broke with dominant eighteenth-century metrical practices to recall the songs in Elizabethan plays; they also recalled to Rossetti some of the old songs to which Thomas Percy's *Reliques of English Poetry* (1765) and Walter Scott's *Minstrelsy of the Scottish Border* (1802–3) had called attention. These were ballads and songs that Rossetti and his siblings greatly admired. Blake mattered to the young Rossetti's emerging practice as an example of a poet who mastered the arts of the simple song: his verses invoked a simplicity of metrical form and verbal address that not only deliberately recalled older forms from a putatively simpler age but also owed part of their lyrical 'beauty and power of expression' to their cryptic but suggestive style, whose apparent simplicities could nonetheless say so much (Gilchrist 383). 'Simplicity and purity of style' – these were qualities at the heart of the original Pre-Raphaelite enterprise in both visual and poetic arts, as their short-lived publication, *The Germ* (1850), insisted. They are evident in the poems Rossetti published in that journal, particularly 'The Blessed Damozel' and 'My Sister's Sleep', and they can also be seen in Rossetti's *Dante Drawing an Angel*: his portrait of another poet-artist in a cluttered medieval studio inscribing his visions in visual form as he was also to do in the *Vita Nuova*. Interrupted by his friends, Dante's explanation is (in Rossetti's translation, inscribed on the drawing), 'Another was with me' – a visitor from the spiritual world. Rossetti aimed for a similar resonance between the spiritual and the material worlds in both his paintings and his watercolours and in much of his early verse. This was exactly the characteristic of Blake's work – as in his illustrations to Edward Young's *Night Thoughts* and Robert Blair's *The Grave* – that his contemporaries, citing Samuel Johnson on Milton, deplored: giving material form to matters of the spirit.[6]

Rossetti did not abandon his attachment to the lyric simplicities of songs, ballads, and their visual counterparts when the first Pre-Raphaelite Brotherhood dissolved in the mid-1850s. Both were central to the medievalising interests of the second Pre-Raphaelite generation (including Morris, Burne-Jones, and more distantly, Swinburne) that formed around Rossetti in the late 1850s and early 1860s. When Rossetti turned to the serious study of Blake in 1862–3, working on Gilchrist's *Life*, he continued to compose verses (as he had done for his earlier paintings of the Virgin Mary) for the paintings of beautiful women in mythological guise at which he was then at work, making those works, like his earlier ones, into a form of double art – if not quite Blake's composite art. Nor did Rossetti forget the examples of Blake and Dante when he finally published a volume of original verse in 1870. Though the sonnet is at the centre of his most intellectually ambitious poetry, a set of songs – with their reminiscences, for Rossetti, of Blake as well as earlier poets – were originally intended to form part of his sonnet sequence, *The House of Life*, the major work of his later career. The Blake-like resonance and prosodic freedom of 'Sudden Light' (1854) and 'The Sea-Limits' (1849), two of the earliest of the songs collected in his 1870 *Poems*, both composed in the years shortly after his first strong involvement with Blake and Dante, is especially marked. His verses at once imitate and reflect upon the mind's uneven engagements with the real, its imaginative excursions into past and future. The sounds of verse, like the sounds of the tide, become 'Time's self [...] made audible'; the returning rhythms of rhymed verse of alternating tetrameter and trimeter, like the sea, tell 'the lapse of time' ('The Sea-Limits'), and imitate in their repetitions and returns the unpredictable returns of memory ('Sudden Light'):

> I have been here before,
> But when or how I cannot tell:
> I know the grass beyond the door,
> The sweet keen smell,
> The sighing sound, the lights around the shore.[7]

Dante Gabriel and William Rossetti were not the only members of that family for whom Blake was important, however. A line of lyric affinity runs from Blake to the poet Christina Rossetti's *Sing-Song* (1872) by way of Blake's subversive rewritings of Isaac Watts's *Divine Songs Attempted in Easy Language, for the Use of Children* (1715, many times reprinted) which Christina also knew; another runs from Blake through the songs and ballads collected by Percy and Scott, which Christina adapted for several lyrics in her first two volumes, *Goblin Market and Other Poems* (1862) and *The Prince's Progress* (1866). Alicia Ostriker remarks, in her study of Blake's prosody, that he wrote 'serious poetry with the basic rhythmical and linguistic tools of a prattling child'.[8] Like Blake, Christina exploited that verse's apparent simplicities for her own ironical purposes, deliberately cultivating the link (especially acceptable, indeed expected, for a woman poet) with popular nursery verse, itself part of an originally oral tradition, for her own subtly critical purposes. She adapted the melodies of children and the unlettered poor to break with metrical conventions and conventional gendered expectations, very much in a Blakean spirit, not only in the nursery poems of *Sing-Song* but in poems such as 'Wife to Husband' (1861), 'Cousin Kate' (1859), and her best-known longer lyric, 'Goblin Market' (1859).

Swinburne's Blake was a rebel, the poet-prophet who acknowledged only the laws of his own poetic vision and who had to be studied whole, including his prophetic books. 'He was born and baptized into the church of rebels', Swinburne begins his essay; 'in a time of critical reason and definite division, he was possessed by a fervour and fury of belief [. . .] He lived and worked out of all rule, and yet by law.'[9] Swinburne discovered in Blake what Colin Trodd calls 'a kind of incandescent realism, a luminescent art of great physical intensity'; 'an art at once incarnational and transcendental'.[10] But for Swinburne, the possibilities of such visionary realism were not just optical. Swinburne's Blake, one might say, is a visionary realist of the auditory imagination. That is, Blake seemed one whose ideas, taking titanic mythopoetic form, demanded a poetic music of their own. Swinburne's Blake was always the poet-craftsman who went against what counted as poetry in his time to give physical intensity to the mythical forms of coherent belief. Thus, as Anna Barton suggests, for Swinburne Blake's perversity, his swerve from the straight and narrow of accepted beliefs, especially political and sexual, was also 'perversification'.[11] Swinburne was exhilarated not only by the ideas and vast Titanic forms but also by the sounds of their 'incredible names': by the windy music of the prophetic books that Cunningham, Gilchrist, and even Rossetti found frightening, and which many simply be dismissed as mad.[12] Swinburne, on the contrary, insisted on Blake's sanity and on the coherence of his beliefs;

it did not matter that they were not susceptible to neat systematising, or that they gave sensory form to the immaterial spirit. He compared the vastness of Blake's conceptions and the sound of the 'semi-metrical' or 'prose poems' of the prophecies with the force and sound of the sea, Swinburne's highest compliment – an element, whether linguistic or natural, in which Swinburne was never so joyful as when deeply immersed, however troubled the waters or the verse from the point of view of regular metrical versification or of familiar or comfortable structures of belief.[13] Swinburne's great contribution was to take Blake's mythopoetics seriously.

His spirited defence of Blake as one who followed art's laws, not society's (what became known as the Aesthetic doctrine of art for art's sake), is properly understood within the context of the early 1860s, as Swinburne experienced them: Anne Gilchrist had warned him of Mac's (Alexander Macmillan, Gilchrist's publisher) puritanical sensibilities; the British and American press were highly critical of the new sensation fiction; Swinburne was well aware of the legal prosecution (for obscenity) of Charles Baudelaire's poetry in France; and he himself experienced a storm of criticism (leading to the withdrawal by his publisher of a whole printing) on the publication of his first volume of lyric poetry, *Poems and Ballads*, in 1866.[14] Blake's resistant perversity, his absolute faith in the rightness of his visions and his verse, was for Swinburne a welcome example at the right time, just as he had been for Rossetti at a moment when his confidence in his visual art was shaky. Around Blake, envisioned as an Orc- or Los-like figure, Swinburne could rally in defence of Baudelaire, of Walt Whitman, of himself – and after the attacks on Rossetti's *Poems* as distastefully 'fleshly' in 1871, of Rossetti, counting Blake along with his other heroes, Percy Shelley, the Italian patriot Giuseppe Mazzini, and Victor Hugo.[15]

While he acknowledged the power of the long-lined 'semi-metrical' experiments of Blake's prophetic books, Swinburne did not follow him there; he could not bring himself to imitate those ventures beyond the borders of metre. He did appreciate Blake's *Songs*, coming to them just after his immersion in old ballads and songs of the North for a projected edition of Border balladry and song, in the same years that he composed similar supposedly traditional Border songs for his unfinished novel of modern life, *Lesbia Brandon*. In keeping with his preference for unbowdlerised versions of old songs of rape, incest, and adultery and their rougher music, Swinburne praised the mastery of Blake's often irregular shorter lyrics, but preferred the *Songs of Experience* because he found them deeper in thought, more awake to the possibilities of evil produced by rigid moral laws.[16]

Blake's powerful attachment to liberty probably strengthened Swinburne's own republican sympathies; he could claim Blake with Shelley, Hugo, and Whitman as support for his forays into political song in the next decade (*Songs Before Sunrise*, 1871, and *Songs of Two Nations*, 1875). Blake was probably still more a stimulus to Swinburne's own mythmaking. The most immediate links are with 'Hertha' (1869), Swinburne's great pantheistic defiance of a rigid monotheism. But Blake's influence is also to be suspected in Swinburne's literary mythmaking, centred on the figure of a rebellious Sappho, from 'Anactoria' (1866) to the more fully developed personal myths of poetic origins in 'On the Cliffs' and 'Thalassius' (1880). In Swinburne's later work, especially 'By the North Sea' (1880), the wind- and sea-music of Blake's prophetic books again sounds as both a poetic and a mythic force.

The poetry and visual art of the Rossettis, the book arts of Morris, and the poems of Swinburne do not, of course, sound or look like Blake's. Yet Blake's example was empowering to these Pre-Raphaelite and Aesthetic poets, who intervened to help rescue Blake from obscurity. In their own practices, Blake pointed a way forward in their individual desires to push beyond the limits of the conventional. They were following Blake's example when they used old songs and nursery verses for lyric and ironical purposes, combined truth to material things with a visionary simplicity of visual and poetic style, and put the sonorous possibilities of prosody in the service of political song and a mythopoetic imagination. Discovering Blake, they gained the confidence to conceive the tasks and the possibilities of poetry and art anew.

Notes

1. D. Dorfman's *Blake in the Nineteenth Century: His Reputation as a Poet from Gilchrist to Yeats* (New Haven and London: Yale University Press, 1969) is still the indispensable account, supplemented by the work of many later scholars – most recently, S. Haggarty and J. Mee in *William Blake: Songs of Innocence and Experience, A Reader's Guide to Essential Criticism* (Basingstoke: Palgrave Macmillan, 2013).
2. See E. Helsinger, '"How They Met Themselves": Dante, Rossetti, and the Visualizing Imagination', in S. Schütze and M. A. Terzoli (eds.), *Dante und die Bildenden Künste: Dialoge – Spiegelungen – Transformationen* (Berlin and Boston: De Gruyter, 2016), pp. 243–60.
3. Ruskin's letter to Rossetti, 10 April 1854, in W. E. Fredeman, *The Correspondence of Dante Gabriel Rossetti: The Formative Years, 1835–62*, 2 vols. (Bury St Edmunds: D. S. Brewer, 2002), I, 335.

4. See T. Hilton, *John Ruskin: The Early Years* (New Haven: Yale University Press, 2000), pp. 209–10.
5. W. Morris, 'The Early Illustration of Printed Books', in W. S. Peterson (ed.), *The Ideal Book: Essays and Lectures on the Arts of the Book* (Berkeley, CA: University of California Press, 1982), p. 22.
6. See Dorfman, *Blake in the Nineteenth Century*, p. 13 and note 8.
7. D. G. Rossetti, *Collected Poetry and Prose*, ed. J. J. McGann (New Haven, CT: Yale University Press, 2003), pp. 178–9 ('The Sea-Limits'), ll. 2, 7; p. 174 ('Sudden Light'), ll. 1–5.
8. A. Ostriker, *Vision and Verse in William Blake* (Madison, WI: University of Wisconsin Press, 1965), p. 77.
9. A. C. Swinburne, *William Blake, A Critical Essay*, in *The Complete Works of Algernon Charles Swinburne: Prose Works*, ed. E. Gosse and T. J. Wise, 7 vols. (London: William Heinemann, 1926), VI, 55–6.
10. C. Trodd, *Visions of Blake: William Blake in the Art World 1830–1930* (Liverpool: Liverpool University Press, 2012), pp. 17, 18.
11. A. Barton, 'Perverse Forms: Reading Blake's Decadence', in K. Boyiopoulos and M. Sandy (eds.), *Decadent Romanticism: 1780–1914* (London: Routledge, 2015), pp. 15–26 (p. 20).
12. See Swinburne, *Blake*, pp. 233–4.
13. 'This poetry has the huge various monotonies, the fervent and fluent colours, the vast limits, the fresh sonorous strength, the certain confusion and tumultuous law, the sense of windy and weltering space, the intense refraction of shadow or light, the crowded life and inanimate intricacy, the patience and the passion of the sea' (ibid., p. 230).
14. See H. Seagroatt, 'Swinburne Separates the Men from the Girls: Sensationalism in *Poems and Ballads*', *Victorian Literature and Culture*, 30.1 (2002), 41–59.
15. Robert Buchanan's attack on Rossetti, Morris, and Swinburne as 'The Fleshly School of Poetry' first appeared in volume 18 of *The Contemporary Review* (August–November 1871).
16. Swinburne, *Blake*, p. 161.

CHAPTER 24

Yeats, Eliot, and Auden

Edward Larrissy

The lives of Yeats, Eliot, and Auden span a period in which Blake's reputation grew to the extent that he was recognised as a major poet and thinker. All three inherit a movement towards direct presentation of feelings or states of mind as the true sources of pleasure in poetry, an emphasis encouraged, for instance, in the criticism of John Stuart Mill and Arthur Hallam. It is a tendency which leads up to Modernism, but it is important to remember that it remoulds Romanticism in its own image: the lyrical poetry of Keats and Shelley, the mood poems of the early Tennyson, are promoted; while once-dominant figures such as Samuel Rogers or Thomas Campbell are relegated. Blake is a beneficiary because of the intensity and symbolic compression of much of his lyric poetry.

Yet the poet may still aspire to offer a grand narrative, and this is certainly the case with Yeats, Eliot, and Auden. Constrained by the imperative to avoid prosaic ramblings, how better to offer a comprehensive view than by the use of an explanatory myth in which sensuous imagery conveys wide symbolic implications without descending to dreary discursiveness? In this light, Blake's mythology, seen as original, can offer hints as to how the modern poet should proceed.

Blake's graphic art was of less significance to these three writers than were his literary methods and philosophy, though the three-volume edition Yeats brought out with Edwin Ellis, *The Works of William Blake, Poetic, Symbolic and Critical* (1893), included a serious attempt to convey the visual qualities of Blake's illuminated books. Indeed, Yeats was a pioneer in the promotion of Blake's excellence. Eliot's debt to Blake, far greater than has been acknowledged, is coloured by his suspicion of too personal and idiosyncratic a vision, which he associated with a flawed legacy of Romanticism. Auden is interested more in Blake's social and psychological thought than in his poetic techniques or esoteric sources. Blake assists him in his early Marxist and Freudian social critique. Such was the esteem in which Auden held him that he also enlists Blake as a guide to the thinking which led him back to Christianity at the end of the 1930s. The return to Christianity in Eliot and Auden includes the acceptance that it can still operate as a living mythology in poetry, but it is a return to something that has been transformed and renewed by acquaintance with elements in Blake's Christian thought.

The true crucible of the young Yeats's interest in Blake lay in the London circle of his painter father, John B. Yeats, who joined a group of artists, called 'The Brotherhood' in conscious imitation of the Pre-Raphaelites. But here, there was more talk of Blake than practice of painting.[1] Edwin Ellis was also part of this circle, and it was with him that W. B. Yeats took the message beyond the group in a way that was influenced by their shared esoteric interests. The notes in their edition are usually seen as forming 'one of the most idiosyncratic and poorly put-together among literary critiques', as Deborah Dorfman puts it. Nevertheless, she concedes that their edition is also 'brilliant and revolutionary'.[2] Incidentally, there is no evidence for Yeats's bizarre claim that Blake had Irish ancestry.[3]

The chief debt Yeats owes to Blake is the idea of the fundamental significance of contrary states and their use as an enabler for poetic thought and composition. The idea is, of course, a staple of many esoteric traditions with which Yeats would have been familiar. It is the employment of the idea as a device of poetic composition, as in *Songs of Innocence and of Experience*, which cements the importance of an influence to which Yeats's critical writings also bear witness. An obvious example is the juxtaposition of 'The Song of the Happy Shepherd' and 'The Sad Shepherd' at the beginning of the 'Crossways' group of lyrics which Yeats put together in 1895. Just as significant is the larger juxtaposition of that whole section with the succeeding one, 'The Rose' (1895).[4] Both of these sections allude to the Kabbalistic Tree of Life, but offer contrasting perspectives upon it: 'Crossways' refers to the various pathways through the spheres of the Tree, and to the fact that these pathways could represent conflicting energies, not least because the Tree itself possessed two contrasting aspects, of Mercy and Rigour.[5] 'The Rose', on the other hand, represents the flowering of the Tree in its fundamental unity. Yeats also exploited contraries beyond their use as an engine of composition. The fundamental principle of *A Vision* (1925 and 1937), his great esoteric synthesis, is that the world of human thought and history consists of a complex, dynamic structure of interacting contrary principles in perpetual motion, reminiscent of the complicated opposed and reciprocal movement to be found in Blake's poem 'The Mental Traveller'.

More broadly, Yeats sees Blake as an aesthetic pioneer from whom he could learn. His advocacy of Blake in the 1890s was connected with the development of his concept of Symbolism – a conception which, though idiosyncratic in his own handling, he seems to have felt was aligned with French *symbolisme*. When Yeats speaks, in 'The Symbolism of Poetry', of 'organic rhythms and words as subtle, as complex, as full of mysterious life, as the body of a flower or of a woman', he is thinking, in large measure, of Blake's work, for he concedes that such poetry may sometimes be 'obscure or ungrammatical as in some of the best of the Songs of Innocence and Experience'.[6] This essay comes from the very Blakean-sounding *Ideas of Good and Evil* (1903), which collected a number of important critical essays from the 1890s, including two which are explicitly about Blake: 'William Blake and the Imagination' and 'William Blake and His Illustrations to *The Divine Comedy*'.

Yeats was also impressed by Blake's mythopoeic powers, for he discerns in them a solution to a predicament of the modern poet, namely the difficulty of finding an authoritative symbolic system: '[Blake] was a symbolist who had to invent his symbols [. . .] Had he been a Catholic of Dante's time he would have been well content with Mary and the angels.' Had he lived in the same period as Yeats, he might 'have gone to Ireland and chosen for his symbols the sacred mountains, along whose sides the peasant still sees enchanted fires, and the deities which have not faded from the belief, if they have faded from the prayers, of simple hearts.'[7] The challenge for poets is to find a living mythology. Blake constructed his own (Yeats thinks), and it was successful. But Yeats, he himself implies, was able to improve on this by making use of a system still alive in the hearts of the Irish people, and thus able to connect with a living society, and even with its cultural politics.

Yeats turned against his own early style, with consequences that all can see in his middle period and later: the adoption of a bold and carefully crafted rhetorical manner, which bears little sign of the pallid suggestiveness of some of his early work. If in 'The Autumn of the Body' (1898) he had spoken approvingly of 'faint lights and faint colours and faint outlines and faint energies', by May 1903, in a letter to George Russell ('AE'), he criticises such qualities and says that he feels within himself 'an impulse to create form'.[8] But the continued references to Blake merely confirm that the latter is recognised as the poet of assertive, rather than 'faint' energies.

Eliot's most developed response to Blake is the essay on him in *The Sacred Wood* (1920), the collection which also contained such groundbreaking works as 'Tradition and the Individual Talent' and 'Hamlet and his Problems'. Eliot wishes to sift the good in Blake (impersonal technical accomplishment) from the bad (personal and idiosyncratic mythology). This is precisely because he recognises that Blake has become 'a wild pet for the supercultivated' – a description which sounds uncannily like Eliot himself in those days.[9] Hence, one might suggest, the need to ensure that he can mould such readers in the right way. *The Sacred Wood* outlines Eliot's poetic and critical project, and apart from expounding the theory of impersonality, he needs to discourage the perpetuation of Romantic 'personality'.

Blake possessed 'peculiar honesty' which was 'peculiarly terrifying'. Yet the honesty Eliot means is not the same as sincerity or discursive statement: it is a 'peculiarity of all great poetry', and it never exists 'without great technical accomplishment'. In other words, the honesty emerges from the craft of poetry, and not from sincere emotions. Blake learnt his technical accomplishment through his 'immense powers of assimilation'.[10] This also, as Christopher Ricks astutely observes, sounds a trifle like Eliot himself.[11] It is important that 'the artist should be highly educated in his own art', but it is not necessary that he be educated in ideas by 'the ordinary processes of education', for these 'consist largely in the acquisition of impersonal ideas which obscure what we really want'. This piece of the argument may seem surprising, since Eliot promoted 'impersonality' in art. But he is attempting to distinguish between artistic impersonality (good) and 'impersonal ideas' (bad). Further confusion may be sown by the fact that Eliot proceeds to recommend a certain type of those very 'impersonal ideas', for Blake's philosophy was too personal: 'Blake did not have that more Mediterranean gift of form which knows how to borrow as Dante borrowed his theory of the soul.'[12] David Goldie offers useful clarification: 'Eliot distrusted the "impersonal ideas" of public opinion that caused Tennyson to squander his talents or Swinburne's raucous "impersonality", yet he celebrated Dante's ability to absorb a whole impersonal belief system.'[13] This is connected to the problem of Blake's mythology. Eliot observes that Blake is like a 'resourceful' Robinson Crusoe who assembled his philosophy from 'odds and ends about the house'. His mythology illustrates 'the crankiness, the eccentricity, which frequently affects writers outside of the Latin tradition'.[14]

Eliot's 'tradition' may have been more impersonal than Blake's. Yet he does some Blakean things with it. There are examples in *The Waste Land*: a staging of the anonymous city encounter; the suggestion of a mythological figure whose parts are spread out across named districts of London.[15] There are also striking examples to be found in *Gerontion*, in the lines: 'in the juvescence of the year / Came Christ the tiger', and 'These tears are shaken from the wrath-bearing tree' (ll. 19–20, 47).[16] Hugh Kenner noticed that the latter phrase recalls 'The Poison Tree', which was 'water'd' with 'tears' (49: 5–6, E 28).[17] The former reference is to Blake's 'The Tyger', from *Songs of Experience*, and is by no means superficial. Blake's *The Marriage of Heaven and Hell* equates Christ with a justly fiery and wrathful principle, and includes the famous 'Proverb of Hell' which states that 'The tygers of wrath are wiser than the horses of instruction' (pl. 9, E 37). Blake's Christ is antithetical to cowardly conceptions of humility, and certainly to those who posture as humble, as the speaker of *Gerontion* does. Thus, when Eliot's speaker states that 'The tiger springs in the new year. Us he devours' (l. 48) he admits that he is suffering the consequences of inhabiting a state typical of Blake's *Experience*: he lacks 'Energy'. In the new year, time of hope and also, as in *The Waste Land*, of regret, this tired and cowardly soul, who never fought at 'the hot gates' (l. 3), contemplates the bitter fruits of experience – 'tears' – falling from the poison tree.

Eliot's concern with tradition develops, as the 1920s progress, towards his return to Christian orthodoxy. The weightiest fruits of this return, *Four Quartets*, also bear the imprint of Blake. While this may not seem immediately obvious, Eliot himself avowed that, while writing *East Coker*, Blake kept 'getting into it'.[18] Perhaps the most obvious influence is the idea of the timeless moment, 'the still point of the turning world', as Eliot terms it in *Burnt Norton*.[19] This is reminiscent of the 'Moment in each Day that Satan cannot find' in Blake's *Milton*, which, while it does not belong to the linear time of Satan's 'Watch Fiends', can, once found, '[renovate] every Moment of the Day if rightly placed' (*Milton* 35: 42–5; E 136). Eliot, then, owes more to Blake than is generally recognised.

Blake elicits Auden's admiration early and late. Indeed, James Fenton refers to one aspect of Auden as 'Blake Auden'.[20] Contemporaries recognised the stylistic influence. Michael Roberts, editor of *The Faber Book of Modern Verse*, reviewing *Another Time* in *The Spectator* (1940), noted that it opened with 'a very effective dedicatory poem in Mr. Auden's most characteristic Blake-ish manner'.[21] Fenton's summary is apposite: 'Blake sat at Auden's left when he wrote, urging concision, definite views, plain language. He was not the Blake of the long line, of the interminable prophetic books, but the fiery Blake of *The Marriage of Heaven and Hell*, the Blake of the notebooks.'[22] *The Marriage* is a major influence on the early Auden, especially in *The Orators*. When this first appeared, William Plomer noted the influence of Blake in a review.[23] In a very perceptive discussion, Richard Hoggart explains its debt to Blake's idea of 'the tension of contraries' in *The Marriage*.²⁴ The figure most reminiscent of Blake in *The Orators* is 'the Enemy', who represents one side of a fundamental social conflict. Like Blake's Urizen, the Enemy operates on both social and psychological levels. While he is perfectly capable of direct attack, he also spreads doctrines intended to undermine individual mental health: '*Unless you do well you will not be loved*' and can cause mental illness and psychosomatic symptoms.²⁵ The Enemy is an agent of repression, and it is in this light that one can deduce Auden's interpretation of a Proverb of Hell such as 'He who desires but acts not breeds pestilence' (pl. 7, E 35). The imprint of 'Proverbs of Hell' is felt everywhere in the aphoristic style of *The Orators*: 'Men miserable without diversion. But diversion is human activity. A man doing nothing is not a man.' The Enemy's likeness to Urizen comprises a similarity to a sinister idea of God, as purveyed, for instance, by the mock hymn, 'Not, Father, further do prolong / Our necessary defeat.'²⁶ A parody of a hymn is reminiscent of Blake's *Songs*, and an unhealthy atmosphere of humiliation and submission pervades the speaker's tone: the 'Father' is supplicated not to prolong 'Our necessary defeat'. There is no defence against his 'accusations', in which respect he is like Blake's 'Accuser'. The strange word order of the first line insinuates a relevant ambiguity, since 'Not, Father', while it is patently the beginning of a negative injunction, could also represent a kind of 'Nobodaddy' (E 471).

An identifiable Blakean element can be found in the way Auden frames his revulsion from the ego: he seems to have discerned a likeness to Blake's 'Selfhood'. Thus, in uncollected lines to Chester Kallman, written around 1939, he asserts: 'Every I must weep alone / Till I Will be overthrown.'²⁷ Compare this with Blake's annotation to Swedenborg's *Divine Love*: 'There can be no Good-Will. Will is always Evil' (E 602). Auden makes a connected point about T. E. Lawrence: 'Only the continuous annihilation of the self by the Identity, to use Blake's terminology, will bring us the freedom we wish for, or in Lawrence's own phrase, "Happiness comes in absorption".'²⁸

Towards the end of the 1930s, Auden became disillusioned with the political ends he had envisaged for art in a 'low dishonest decade', and began to move back towards Christianity. In the unpublished prose work, 'The Prolific and the Devourer' (1939), the title of which is taken from *The Marriage of Heaven and Hell*, 'the Politician' is the enemy of art: 'The Prolific and the Devourer: the Artist and the Politician. Let them realise that they are enemies.' In this account, the politician is a devouring parasite, ultimately dependent on the artist's vision. The artist must not harness art to political ends: 'The artist qua artist is no reformer. Slums, war, disease are part of his material, and as such he loves them'; or, 'The voice of the Tempter: "Unless you take part in the class struggle, you cannot become a major writer".' The Church identifies the Tempter of the Gospels with Satan.[29] Thus the use of *The Marriage of Heaven and Hell* goes deeper than the borrowing of a suggestive opposition. Yet this Tempter carries a message which is itself opposed to the one Auden had espoused in *The Orators*. Blake had assisted Auden in the development of a sophisticated form of politically motivated writing in the 1930s. Now he is enlisted in the service of an idea of art's transcendence of the political. Thus Auden's case is similar in one respect, at least, to those of Yeats and Eliot: while their ideas and poetic practice may have evolved, Blake must continue to accompany them on their journey.

Notes

1. W. M. Murphy, *Prodigal Father: The Life of John Butler Yeats 1839–1922* (Ithaca, NY: Cornell University Press, 1978), pp. 61, 67.
2. D. Dorfman, *Blake in the Nineteenth Century* (New Haven, CT: Yale University Press, 1969), p. 192.
3. E. J. Ellis and W. B. Yeats (eds.), *The Works of William Blake, Poetic, Symbolic and Critical*, 3 vols. (London: Bernard Quaritch, 1893), I, 2–4.
4. R. J. Finneran (ed.), *The Collected Works of W. B. Yeats*, Vol. I: *The Poems*, 2nd edn (New York: Scribner, 1997), pp. 5–7, 25–47.
5. On 'paths', see G. Scholem, *Major Trends in Jewish Mysticism* (New York: Schocken Books, 2011), pp. 143–6; on 'rigour' and 'mercy', see D. Hirst, *Hidden Riches: Traditional Symbolism from the Renaissance to Blake* (London: Eyre and Spottiswoode, 1964), pp. 36–7.
6. G. Bornstein and R. J. Finneran (eds.), *The Collected Works of W. B. Yeats*, Vol. IV: *Early Essays* (New York: Scribner, 2007), p. 120.
7. Ibid., p. 86.
8. Ibid., p. 140; J. Kelly and R. Schuchard (eds.), *The Collected Letters of W.B. Yeats*, Vol. III: *1901–1904* (Oxford: Clarendon Press, 1994), p. 369.
9. T. S. Eliot, *The Sacred Wood*, 2nd edn, repr. (London: Methuen, 1960), p. 151.
10. Ibid., pp. 151–2.
11. In T. S. Eliot, *Inventions of the March Hare*, ed. C. Ricks (London: Faber, 1996), p. xxvi.
12. Eliot, *Sacred Wood*, pp. 154, 156.
13. D. Goldie, *A Critical Difference: T.S. Eliot and John Middleton Murry in English Literary Criticism, 1919–1928* (Oxford: Oxford University Press, 1998), p. 81.
14. Eliot, *Sacred Wood*, p. 157.

15. On city encounter, see B. Bergonzi, 'Eliot's Cities', in M. Thormählen (ed.), *T. S. Eliot at the Turn of the Century* (Lund: Lund University Press, 1994), pp. 59–76 (p. 61). On named districts, compare *Milton*, 6: 4–5, E 99, and *The Waste Land*, in C. Ricks and J. McCue (eds.), *The Poems of T. S. Eliot*, Vol. I: *Collected and Uncollected Poems* (Baltimore, MD: Johns Hopkins University Press, 2015), pp. 65–6.
16. In-text line references are to T. S. Eliot, *Gerontian*, in Ricks and McCue, *Collected and Uncollected Poems*.
17. H. Kenner, *The Invisible Poet: T.S. Eliot*, 2nd edn (London: Methuen, 1965), p. 110.
18. H. Gardner, *The Composition of Four Quartets* (London: Faber, 1978), p. 85.
19. T. S. Eliot, 'Burnt Norton', in Ricks and McCue, *Collected and Uncollected Poems*, l. 62.
20. J. Fenton, 'Blake Auden and James Auden', *The Strength of Poetry* (Oxford: Oxford University Press, 2001), pp. 209–27.
21. M. Roberts, 'Not This Time?', *The Spectator*, 100 (26 July 1940), 301–2 (p. 301).
22. Fenton, 'Blake Auden', p. 213.
23. W. Plomer, 'Review of W.H. Auden The Orators', *Sunday Referee* (22 May 1932), 6.
24. R. Hoggart, *Auden: An Introductory Essay* (London: Chatto and Windus, 1965), p. 36.
25. Auden, *The Orators*, in Mendelson, *The English Auden*, pp. 91, 90; 82.
26. Ibid., pp. 78, 109–10.
27. See Mendelson, *The English Auden*, p. 456.
28. Quoted in H. Greenberg, *Quest for the Necessary: W.H. Auden and the Dilemma of Divided Consciousness* (Cambridge, MA: Harvard University Press, 1968), p. 56.
29. Auden, 'The Prolific and the Devourer', in Mendelson, *The English Auden*, pp. 404, 403.

CHAPTER 25

Whitman, Crane, and the Beats

Linda Freedman

In 1868, Algernon Charles Swinburne drew a comparison between William Blake and Walt Whitman which had a lasting effect on Blake's literary reception in America. The most persistent theme among twentieth-century American counter-cultural critiques of democracy laments the loss of a Whitmanesque ideal. Blake frequently appears as a source of hope for its renewal. Yoked together with Whitman, Blake became relevant to the kind of literary anxiety which finds in spiritual restoration a source of democratic progress. This chapter gives a selective overview of Blake's reception as a Whitmanesque prophet-artist from Swinburne's 1868 essay to Ginsberg's drug-induced vision of his own prophetic calling.

According to Swinburne:

> The points of contact and sides of likeness between William Blake and Walt Whitman are so many and so grave, as to afford some ground of reason to those who preach the transition of souls or transfusion of spirits.[1]

The force of Swinburne's comparison was mystical; Whitman appeared not just as Blake's kindred spirit but also as his reincarnation. It was political too. In 1868, Swinburne was one of a group of avant-garde international radicals determined to use poetry for social and political advancement. Swinburne aligned Blake with Whitman in order to make his poetry seem fresh and relevant to modern republicanism. In 1866 Swinburne had written to Moncure Conway that Blake was a 'republican under the very shadow of the gibbet [...] a lover of America, of freedom, and of France from the first and to the last'. He identified Blake and Whitman on grounds of transcendence and prophetic vision, arguing that they 'preached almost exactly the same gospel' of sexual and political liberation.[2] The link between sexual and political liberation, for which Whitman had become both famous and infamous by this point, was rather common in radical writing of Blake's day – the ending of Blake's *America* has a parallel in Thomas Spence's belief that 'it is supposed the chains of hymen would be among the first that would be broken, in case of revolution'.³ But Swinburne looked to Whitman and modern America to make his case for Blake's social usefulness. Blake was championed as a republican poet in the American grain.

Whitman's response became rather acidic when one friend, John Swinton, suggested that his poetry may indeed be indistinguishable from Blake's. In a letter to mutual friends, William and Ellen O'Connor, dated 27 September 1868, Whitman wrote:

> He, Swinton, gives me rather new information in one respect – says that the formal resemblance between several pieces of Blake and my pieces, is so marked that he, Swinton, has, with persons that partially know me, passed them off temporarily as mine, and read them aloud as such. He asked me pointedly whether I had not met with Blake's productions in my youth, etc. – said that Swinburne's idea of resemblance was not so wild, after all. Quite funny isn't it?

O'Connor obviously knew his friend better than Swinton because he replied with exactly the right words to pacify him:

> Swinton's discovery of the resemblance in form between *Leaves of Grass* and Blake's poetry is, in my humble opinion, a mare's nest of the first water. The resemblance is extremely superficial – about as much between the Gregorian chant, bellowed by bull-necked priests with donkey lips, and a first-class, infinitely varied, complex-melodied Italian opera, sung by voices half-human, half-divine.⁴

It was all very well for Swinburne to pay tribute to Whitman as the emergent and prophetic voice of a new American-led democratic poetic. But to suggest, as Swinton did, that Whitman's poetry was not only foreshadowed by that of someone old, English and dead, but worse, also indistinguishable from it, was guaranteed to raise the hackles of the self-proclaimed American bard. To add insult to injury, Swinton had dared to imply that Whitman was copying Blake.

Whitman's response to Swinburne's idea of resemblance was motivated consciously, or unconsciously, by the anxiety he was suffering about his own capabilities as the literatus who would lead America into futurity. After the civil war, Whitman's vision became increasingly shadowed by worry and uncertainty. In 1868 he was engaged in writing *Democratic Vistas* which, unlike the 1855 *Leaves of Grass*, is a rather desperate sounding of its own empty prospects. He was also increasingly agonised by America's relationship to her parent country. He could claim with strange nostalgia, 'We do not blame thee, elder World, nor really separate ourselves from thee' ('Song of the Exposition', 1871), and also insist that 'Shakespeare [...] belongs essentially to the buried past [...] [and his works] belong in America about as much as the persons and institutes they depict ('A Backward Glance', 1888).[5]

In the late 1860s, Whitman felt his poetic control over American national identity slipping. Swinton clearly hit a nerve. In an unpublished note, contemporary with the publication of Swinburne's *Essay*, Whitman wrote the following third-person review:

> Of William Blake and Walt Whitman. Both are mystics, extatics but the difference between them is this – and a vast difference it is: Blake's visions grow to be the rule, displace the normal condition, fill the field, spurn the visible, objective life, and seat the subjective spirit on an absolute throne, wilful and uncontrolled. But Whitman, though he occasionally prances off, takes flight with an abandon and capriciousness of step or wing, and a rapidity and whirling power, which quite dizzy the reader in his first attempts to follow, always holds the mastery over himself, and, even in his most intoxicated lunges or pirouettes, never once loses control, or even equilibrium. To the pe[rfect] sense, it is evident that he goes off because he permits himself to do so, while ever the director, or direct'd principle sits coolly at hand, at any a moment. In Walt Whitman, escapades of this sort are the exceptions. The main character of his poetry is the normal, the universal, the simple, the eternal platform of the best manly and womanly qualities.[6]

It was not new for Whitman to want to control his poetic reputation by writing reviews of his own work. One of the interesting things about this piece is that it was never published, indeed we do not know whether it was ever intended for publication. But it is a fair assumption that if Whitman had wanted to publish it, he could have succeeded. The review feels more like a vent for his irritation rather than a piece of self-promotion, yet it is also indicative of his need for self-assurance. The distinction that Whitman draws between himself and Blake confirms his own position as the innocently prophetic voice of American democracy, which is deliberately opposed to the rapturous absolutism of the English bard whose uncontrolled visions seat him on a kingly – and undemocratic – 'throne'.

Whitman's discomfort never registered in Blake's subsequent reception in America. When Hart Crane turned to Blake as a source of hope for his vision of America, he saw him as a Whitmanesque prophet-artist who might redeem the fallen state of democracy.[7] Crane's major long poem, *The Bridge*, was written partly in response to Eliot's major poem, *The Waste Land*. It was a poem in the same vein as Eliot's, depicting modernity as a mass of human history, but it openly sought to rebut Eliot's nihilism. In a letter to Gorham Munson in 1923, Crane wrote: 'I feel that Eliot ignores certain spiritual events and possibilities as real and powerful now as, say, in the time of Blake.'[8] In *The Bridge*, Blake, filtered through Whitman, redeems the hollow tedium of modern living. In the *Proem* to *The Bridge*, Crane suggested the corruption of Whitman's 'multitudes' now 'bent towards some flashing scene' (l. 10).[9] Crane's hopes for American democracy rested on his ability to produce a kind of 'Blakean' verse, a transtemporal vision that penetrates into the heart of modernity by focusing on the prophetic moment that holds all time within it. The section in *The Bridge* that most directly alluded to Blake's poetry was 'The Tunnel'. The epigraph, 'To find the Western path / Right thro' the Gates of Wrath' was taken from Blake's 'Morning' in the *Notebook* (p. 95; E 478). 'The Tunnel' re-enacted the quest of Blake's poem through darkness to regeneration, unity, and fulfilment. Set in contemporary New York, the first stanza included another reference to Blake: 'Someday by heart you'll learn each famous sight / And watch the curtains lift in hell's despite' (ll. 6–7). Turning Manhattan into a tormented theatre of the absurd, Crane played on Blake's portrayal of selfish love in 'The Clod and the Pebble'. Blake had written:

> Love seeketh only Self to please,
> To bind another to Its delight:
> Joys in anothers loss of ease,
> And builds a Hell in Heavens despite.   (ll. 9–12, E 19)

Crane's deliberate misquotation created a sense of discordancy as well giving a feeling of history. Like Eliot's *Waste Land*, Crane's text was formed from fragmented voices. But where Eliot saw the barbarians at the gates, Crane's quest through darkness was ultimately hopeful.

'The Tunnel' ends with a world fighting to be born anew amidst the boredom and stagnation of contemporary life:

> Kiss of our agony thou gatherest;
> Condensed, thou takest all – shrill ganglia
> Impassioned with some song we fail to keep.   (ll. 116–18)

Whitman's 'multitudes' are present in the 'shrill ganglia / Impassioned with some song we fail to keep', in the 'waters' that break through the crust of the modern world and the 'Word that will not die' (ll. 121–2). It is in this vision of hope that Crane finds the way out of darkness, counting the echoes of past greatness that assemble to invest the present moment with eternal meaning. In the third section of the *Waste Land*, entitled 'The Fire Sermon', Eliot had written:

> Burning burning burning burning
> O Lord Thou pluckest me out
> O lord Thou pluckest
>
> Burning[10]

In a direct response, Crane turns plucking into gathering:

> Kiss of our agony Thou gatherest,
>   O Hand of Fire
>   gatherest –   (ll. 136–8)

With Blake and Whitman as his guides, Crane showed his reader that the way to salvation was through embrace. The sensual 'Kiss of our agony' is foregrounded in the 'shrill ganglia', a mass of fraught nerve endings animated by feeling. It is no accident that the movement, 'Thou gatherest', is incomplete and that the section ends with a dash that is simultaneously a moment of arrest and an indication of possibility and continuity. In order to remain alive, Crane suggested, America must always be renewing and enlarging itself. Blake gave him hope for such renewal.

This vision of Blake as a Whitmanesque prophet-artist found its moment in the explosion of literary Blakeanism that occurred in mid-twentieth-century American counter-culture. In the mid-1940s, shortly after the end of the Second World War, Allen Ginsberg met William Burroughs, Jack Kerouac, Herbert Huncke, and Neal Cassady on the campus of Columbia University. They would become the best known of all the Beats. In these early years of friendship, they romantically and idealistically spoke of a 'New Vision' of American literature, a phrase they adapted from Arthur Rimbaud. Ginsberg later recalled, 'About 1945 I got interested in Supreme Reality with a capital S and R, and I wrote big long poems about a last voyage looking for Supreme Reality.'[11]

Blake was a formative influence on this group of friends, who devoured his poetry alongside other works of British and American Romanticism, French existentialism, tragedy and poetry, particularly that of Rimbaud, Goethe, Dostoyevsky and the Russian Socialist poet Vladimir Mayakovsky.[12] Ginsberg recalled that when he and Kerouac visited Burroughs at home in 1945, 'he physically gave us his library'.[13] The books included a copy of Blake's *Songs*. In 1959, Kerouac sent Donald Allen a biography for his anthology of *New American Poetry* in which he referred to this period as 'a romantic phase with Rimbaud and Blake which I called my "self-ultimacy" period, burning what I wrote in order to be more "self-ultimate"'.[14]

Ginsberg, the most prominent Blakean of this generation of Americans, also identified strongly with Whitman, describing the driving force behind his poetry as one which combined his vision of Blake's prophetic calling with his understanding of Whitman's democratic personality: '[t]he presumption was of prophecy, part Blakean inspiration, part ordinary mind from Whitman [...] that is to say, the poet who speaks from his frank heart in public speaks for all hearts'.[15] From hearing Blake, Ginsberg thought he felt closer to understanding a fundamental connectedness and human commonality in all things. He explained:

> The thing that I understood from Blake is that it is possible to transmit a message through time which could reach the enlightened, that poetry had a definite effect, it wasn't just pretty or just beautiful, as I had understood pretty beauty before – it was something basic to human existence, or it reached something, it reached the bottom of human existence. But anyway the impression I got was that it was like a kind of time machine through which [Blake] could transmit [...] his basic consciousness and communicate it to somebody else after he was dead – in other words, build a time machine.[16]

Ginsberg's description of prophecy as a 'time machine' updated Swinburne's Romantic sensibility for a mid-twentieth-century audience. He thought that reading Blake enabled him to access an underlying godhead, at once integral to, and fundamentally at odds with, the linear movement of history. When he discovered Whitman's choice of Blake's engraving, 'Death's Door', for his tombstone, Ginsberg said that it was an example of 'old bards taking their lineage from each other'.[17] He clearly saw himself as continuing that lineage, at once historical and connected across time.

Ginsberg found Blake's prophetic 'time machine' liberating in the first instance. But by 1963 he felt tied to the identity he had forged in Harlem and it no longer felt authentic. Worrying that he had become 'hung up on a memory of an experience', his sense of Blake's usefulness became increasingly political. Ginsberg perceived America to be Urizenic in its foreign and domestic policies but also saw the hope of redemption in the counter-cultural protests of left-wing Beats, hippies, and yippies. Like Swinburne and Crane, he saw a mystical connection with Whitman, which could potentially revive the fallen state of democracy and society.

Whitman's own frustrations with the parallel simply fell away from the American reception of Blake as writers such as Crane and Ginsberg continued to look to the prophet-artist to restore the spiritual life of democracy. In *America* we can clearly see an example of the late Romantic discordance which shadowed the vision of a new world. A few copies of the 'Preludium' ended:

> The stern Bard ceas'd, asham'd of his own song; enrag'd he swung
> His harp aloft sounding, then dash'd its shining frame against
> A ruin'd pillar in glittring fragments; silent he turn'd away,
> And wander'd down the vales of Kent in sick & drear lamentings.
> (2: 18–21, E 52; copies M, A, E, F, I, B, and O)

As prophecy tips into lament, Blake's prophet-artist, Los, expresses his own sense of frustrated purpose. Blake was characterised by Swinburne as one who, like Whitman, was able to democratise the voice of prophecy and use the role of prophet-artist to advance social change. Yet it may well be that Whitman and Blake have a truer affinity in the difficulty they foresaw in making the democratised prophetic voice more than a harp dashed against 'A ruin'd pillar in glitt'ring fragments'. Both poets knew, and poetically registered, the difficulty of their social and artistic enterprise. This affinity got a little lost in the subsequent American reception of Blake as an artist who, like Whitman, might redeem the society that American writers of the twentieth-century repeatedly saw as fallen. But it was never very far away as writers such as Crane and Ginsberg examined the limits, as well as the reach, of their own prophetic voices and the lineage that connected them with Blake.

Notes

1. A. C. Swinburne, *William Blake: A Critical Essay* (1868; repr. London: Heinemann, 1925), p. 300. The first English edition of Whitman's poetry appeared the same year as Swinburne's *Essay on Blake* and was edited by W. M. Rossetti, who was friends with Swinburne and also part of the circle that was responsible for Blake's mid-century revival in England. Whitman had read Gilchrist's *Life of Blake* (1863), which included excerpts from the major prophecies and it was there that he saw the engraving for his tombstone. He was also friends with Gilchrist's widow, Anne, and may well have discussed Blake with her, though there is nothing about him in their correspondence.
2. D. Dorfman, *Blake in the Nineteenth Century: His Reputation as a Poet from Gilchrist to Yeats* (London: Yale University Press, 1969), p. 159.
3. T. Spence, 'The Restorer of Society to Its Natural State' (c. 1805), in *The Political Works of Thomas Spence*, ed. H. T. Dickinson (Newcastle Upon Tyne: Avero, 1982), p. 76.

4. W. Whitman, *The Correspondence*, ed. E. H. Miller, 6 vols. (New York: New York University Press, 1961), II, 48–9, 49n.
5. W. Whitman, *Leaves of Grass*, ed. H. W. Blodgett and S. Bradley (New York: New York University Press, 1965), 'Song of the Exposition', pp. 195–205 (l. 69); 'A Backward Glance O'er Travel'd Roads', pp. 561–74 (p. 567).
6. C. Gohdes and R. G. Silver (eds.), *Faint Clews and Indirections: Manuscripts of Walt Whitman and His Family* (Durham, NC: Duke University Press, 1949), p. 53.
7. Crane presumably read Blake's works in the 1893 edition by W. B. Yeats and E. J. Ellis, to which he had access. The edition was complete with lithograph reproductions of many plates, albeit subject to various barbarisms.
8. Cited in C. Fisher, *Hart Crane: A Life* (London: Yale University Press, 2002), pp. 162–3.
9. All citations of Crane refer to H. Crane, *Complete Poems of Hart Crane*, ed. M. Simon (New York: Liveright, 2000), p. 97. Line or page references appear in the main text.
10. T. S. Eliot, *The Waste Land and Other Poems* (London: Faber, 1972; repr. 1999), p. 39.
11. 'Allen Ginsberg' (1966), in G. Plimpton (ed.), *The Paris Review Interviews: Beat Writers at Work* (London: Harvill, 1999), pp. 33–73 (p. 54).
12. Ginsberg was very well versed in Blake's poetry and designs. He read him as a student in Columbia in the 1940s and continued to read and teach him throughout his life.
13. A. Ginsberg, 'Kerouac's Ethic in the Light of His Buddhism', in *Deliberate Prose* (New York: Harper Collins, 2001), pp. 361–78 (p. 368).
14. J. Kerouac, *The Selected Letters 1957–1969*, ed. A. Charters (London: Penguin, 2000), p. 248.
15. A. Ginsberg, 'Foreword', in M. Kraus, *Allen Ginsberg: An Annotated Bibliography* (Metuchen, NJ: Scarecrow Press, 1980).
16. Plimpton, *Paris Review Interviews*, p. 291.
17. A. Ginsberg, *Your Reason and Blake's System* (Madras and New York: Hanuman Books, 1988), p. 12.

PART IV

History, Society, and Culture

CHAPTER 26

Animals

Kurt Fosso

No other poet or painter of the Romantic era depicts a wider range of animal life, 'wild & tame', than does William Blake (*Jerusalem* 61: 31, E 212). He does so from his early illuminated work *There Is No Natural Religion*, with its sketched dog and several birds, to his late *Illustrations to the Book of Job*, featuring not just dogs, birds, lions, horses, oxen, sheep, serpents, spiders, and a frog and a grasshopper, but also God's colossal creations Behemoth and Leviathan. In addition, several poems from *Songs of Innocence and of Experience* consider from their ironic vantages the being and in some measure the dignity and worth of various non-human creatures, most notably 'The Lamb', 'The Fly', and 'The Tyger'. Then there are the twenty animal-related proverbs of *The Marriage of Heaven and Hell*, and, closing its 'Song of Liberty' coda, Blake's fiery proclamation, 'every thing that lives is Holy' (pl. 27, E 45). Likely culled from 'Spinosism' and pantheistic notions in the mystical tradition (*BR* 437, 696),[1] this universal declaration on behalf of all 'that lives' was for Blake so radical and so contrary to anthropocentric reason as to be thrice repeated verbatim: in *Visions of the Daughters of Albion*, *America*, and *VALA / The Four Zoas*. The liberative statement looms as well elsewhere within the poet's oeuvre, particularly in *The Book of Thel* and at the harvest finale of *Milton a Poem*.

The terrain of animals 'in' Blake is indeed vast and richly meaningful, extending from the poet's far-ranging representations of non-human creatures, including amid Britain's colonial worlds, to his acquaintance with and material uses of animals, all making possible his visionary art and life of vision. That vision expansively encompasses humans' own essential animality, beckoning empiricist Reason to open itself to the miraculous in Nature (see 'You don't believe', E 501) and marvel at the animal otherness within (even impenetrably within) and around human beings themselves.[2] By so doing, Blake challenges the Newtonian ratio of the human subject and its self-enclosing science. For as one of the *Marriage*'s devils scrawls, as an epigraph to the species-rich Proverbs, 'How do you know but ev'ry Bird that cuts the airy way, / Is an immense world of delight, clos'd by your senses five?' (pl. 7, E 35). The proverb calls upon readers to wonder but more specifically to consider and imagine that such animal worlds necessarily and richly vary between species, with each creature's unique eye and anatomy altering all. 'With what sense does the tame pigeon measure out the expanse?', Oothoon inquires in *Visions* (3: 2, E 47), while the *Marriage* similarly hails the 'roaring of lions' and 'howling of wolves' as 'portions of eternity too great for the eye of man' (8: 27–28, E 36). In fact, for all Blake's seeming disparagement of external 'nature' as 'barren' without 'man' (*Marriage* 10: 68, E 38), his art's insistent focus upon animals suggests their vital importance for opening the 'doors of perception' to access 'the infinite which was hid' (pl. 14, E 39) – and hidden in and as the immensity, diversity, and alterity of animal being.

Blake's poems, designs, engravings, and other works represent almost a menagerie of different species[3] and their envisioned perspectives, both wild and tame: fearsome lions, tigers, and wolves as well as domesticated dogs and cats, baboons and monkeys, towering elephants, and free-ranging zebras – along with the zebra's bred-and-trained cousins, the ass (donkey) and horse. Blake also depicts or mentions foxes, badgers, bears, deer, rabbits, bats, moles, and rodents; such farm animals as sheep, goats, pigs, oxen, and cattle; passerine birds (larks, wrens, robins, ravens) as well as doves, swans, geese, chickens, eagles, and owls. In addition he draws or describes the sea's whales, dolphins, fish, and medusae; plus amphibians and reptiles – especially snakes – gastropods, and what may seem a surprising number of insects, arachnids, and worms. *Milton* alone provides nearly an entomological catalogue:

> the Earth-worm, the gold Beetle; the wise Emmet;
> Dance round the Wine-presses of Luvah: the Centipede is there:
> The ground Spider with many eyes [. . .]
> The ambitious Spider in his sullen web; the lucky golden Spinner;
> The Earwig armd: the tender Maggot emblem of immortality:
> The Flea: Louse: Bug: the Tape-Worm [. . .]
> The slow slug: the Grasshopper that sings & laughs & drinks [. . .]
> The cruel Scorpion is there: the Gnat: Wasp: Hornet & the Honey Bee.
>
> (27: 12–21, E 124)

What other poet of this era or any era describes and portrays so many of the natural world's smallest and even parasitic creatures?[4] Indeed, within this list the 'tender' flesh-eating maggot becomes the celebrated 'emblem of immortality' for its place in the lifecycle of death, decay, and regeneration. Other of *Milton*'s descriptions similarly bestow dignity and wisdom –

surely for the 'wise Emmet' – upon the lowliest of all that lives, composing an inclusive Nature explicitly containing even 'conventionally objectionable creatures'.[5]

Blake's interest in animals and his appreciation of their worthiness both in themselves and as sources of wonderment was, for all his visionary eccentricity, also in step with the times, as with George Stubbs's admiring horse portraits, the animal-inhabited landscape paintings by John Constable, and Ralph Beilby and Thomas Bewick's richly illustrated *General History of Quadrupeds* (1790) and widely popular *History of British Birds* (1797, 1804). As these works suggest, and as a number of contemporary poems by the likes of Anna Seward, Anna Barbauld, and Samuel Taylor Coleridge further evince, turn-of-the-century Britain was becoming more interested in and 'collectively emotional about animals',[6] hence the rules instituted in some grammar schools forbidding animals' mistreatment, the licensing of London's slaughterhouses, and the formation of the RSPCA. It was an age, moreover, in which John Oswald and Joseph Ritson both made impassioned appeals for non-violence towards animals and for a 'vegetable diet', when Sarah Trimmer's *Fabulous Histories* (1786) instructed children to respect other creatures, and Francis Hutcheson argued that animals have 'a *right* that no useless pain or misery should be inflicted on them'.[7] Such revisionist notions beckoned satire, as in *A Vindication of the Rights of Brutes* (1792) by Thomas Taylor, whom Blake knew (*Stranger* 83).

At the time, particularly in natural history and comparative anatomy, humankind was itself being re-categorised, most markedly in Carl Linnaeus's revolutionary taxonomy, *Systema Naturae* (1735), which placed humanity among the rest of *Animalia*, the revised tenth edition situating *Homo sapiens* in the order of primates with the monkeys and apes.[8] Blake probably never perused Linnaeus, but he provided engravings for the poet-scientist and evolutionist Erasmus Darwin's *Botanic Garden* (1791), which employs Linnaeus's 'system' and similarly locates humans within an 'economy of nature' among all other 'animal bodies'.[9] Along these lines, Blake's biblical parody *The (First) Book of Urizen* represents the god of reason's own evolutionary phylogeny and repressive displacement of his body's animal forms,[10] and *Jerusalem* similarly contends that, as Judaic tradition tells, 'Man contained in his Limbs, all Animals [. . .] & they were separated from him by cruel Sacrifices' (pl. 27; E 174). As Keith Thomas observes, the long-standing view of 'the world as made for man and all other species [being] subordinate to his wishes' was in this era indeed being 'gradually eroded'.[11] And Blake in his way contributes to this undermining of humanity's privileged genesis and ordained place above the animals. Taking ambivalent stock perhaps of just such erosion, Blake's nature-goddess Vala opines, 'The Human is but a Worm' (*Jerusalem* 64: 12, E 215).

As for the period's related, emerging concern for animal rights, Blake appears to have shared certain of his contemporaries' sentiments, to judge especially from the 'Auguries of Innocence', espousing the moral and spiritual detriments of abuse:[12]

> A dog starved at his Masters Gate
> Predicts the ruin of the State
> A horse misusd upon the Road
> Calls to Heaven for Human blood
> Each outcry of the hunted Hare
> A fibre from the Brain does tear [...]
> The Game Cock clipd & armd for fight
> Does the Rising Sun affright.   (ll. 9–14, 17–18, E 490)

The prophesied consequences of cruelty are dire, including not only social ruin but also, on an individual scale, the 'tear[ing]' of a 'fibre' from the hunter's brain when he hears but ignores his prey's 'outcry'. Whatever Blake's neurological understanding, the outcome is plain enough: the human is harmed by abusing animals, and not just psychologically or morally, as Locke and others had argued, but physically, resulting in a diminished *capacity* to sympathise with other creatures' feelings, sufferings, and desires to live. Even if we read this rending as more spiritual than physiological, the augured damage seems irrevocable, and occurs whether the abused beast is the hunted, such as a fox or stag, or some animal spectacle, as in cock fighting and, the Augury implies, in such other condemned entertainments as bear baiting.

Still, excepting his description in *VALA / The Four Zoas* of a lamb pleading to its shepherd, 'Take thou my wool / But spare my life' (N1, p. 18, ll. 2–3, E 310), Blake nowhere contends that farm or other animals should not be eaten and otherwise used so long as such usage is not cruel. 'The Lamb misusd breeds Public Strife / And yet forgives the Butchers Knife', the 'Auguries' assures (ll. 23–4, E 490). *Mis*treatment is what harms human sentiment and contributes to discord; hence, it follows, 'All wholsom food' should be 'caught without a net or a trap' (*Marriage* 7: 13, E 36). But although Albion, Blake's mythical god of England, may lament that, trapped or no, 'not one sparrow can suffer, & the whole Universe not suffer also' (*Jerusalem* 25: 8, E 170), and despite Blake writing elsewhere that 'The Ox in the slaughter house moans' (*Urizen* 25: 1, E 82), the poet of course ate beef, mutton, and other meat (E 461, 711, 775), as did most Englishmen. For that matter, to fashion his art, Blake required not only paper, ink, copper plating, and other supplies produced from plant and mineral sources but also an arsenal of animal-based materials: goose-feather and other bird quills, camel's (chiefly squirrel) hair paintbrushes, leather ink-daubers, 'Virgins wax' from honeybees (E 700), ox gall, animal-glues, and watercolour pigments derived from bone, shells, blood, and insects.[13] Tallow candles served to smoke the etching grounds and illuminate his work at night. The drawn image of an animal thereby required the material *of* animals, and even Blake's printing press was in a real sense a product of animal labour, having been transported, like most all his art's supplies, by the horsepower of equines, living engines of his 'Chariot of fire' (*Milton* 1: 12, E 95).

Those horses quite surrounded Blake in London, where he'd have heard their hooves clopping along the streets and past his door, at times accompanied by the shouts of horsemen, coach drivers, and wagoners. Strolling the rural suburbs, he'd have witnessed horses pulling field plows, drawing drays, and grazing. But Blake also had a personal acquaintance among that large, ubiquitous species. For during his sojourn in Felpham, Sussex (1800–3), he came to closely know an equine he praised and prized as 'belovd': a pony or pony-sized horse named Bruno (E 748). The poet almost certainly learned to horseback ride upon Bruno, and in time became a fairly competent horseman, it seems, with the unique perspective gained from travelling with his patron, William Hayley, at times daily, on 'Horseback [. . .] over the fields of corn' (E 504; cf. *BR* 137). Especially after making this equine companion, Blake frequently depicts horses as guiding or conveying humans not just across fields but also towards the infinite, as powerful animal portions and vehicles of Eternity. It is scarcely an exaggeration to say that horses and horsepower made Blake's visionary art possible and influenced his vision of all 'that lives', as of course did various other non-human animals.

Of these creatures there is only one other we can confidently say the poet knew well: a pet cat given to him by friends (*BR* 127). Blake's marvellously drawn cats in several watercolour designs (*c.* 1797–8) demonstrate his familiarity with felines prior to receiving that kitten, and the Blakes may well have had other cats as pets or mousers and, to judge from his poetry, at least been familiar with some hapless 'Dog at the wintry door' (*Urizen* 25: 2, E 82). According to one of his circle, Blake in fact claimed he preferred cats to dogs as 'so much more quiet in [their] expression of attachment' (*BR* 127), which suggests he knew both animals well enough to form an opinion. But Blake's art focuses much more on these animals' wild cousins: the tiger, lion, leopard, and ounce (lynx), and in lesser numbers the wolf and the fox. It is owing to such untamed creatures' instincts and untrammelled genius, versus what domestication, breeding, and training forge, that the Proverbs proclaim, 'The tygers of wrath are wiser than the horses of instruction' (*Marriage* 9: 44, E 37). That is not to say that for the infernal proverbist horses are not wise, or for that matter that domestic animals such as felines are unwise; only that unadulterated instinct and related emotion convey more alterity and less of humanity's reflective subordinating stamp. 'Ask the wild ass [zebra] why he refuses burdens', Oothoon bids (*Visions* 3: 7, E 47). For his domesticated cousin has been bred precisely *for* human 'burdens', and therefore, by this logic, possesses less of its specific natural wisdom and *world* ('of delight') – which again is not to say that the 'attachments' formed with feline, canine, or other creatures did not provide Blake with opportunities for wonder and wilder imagining.

But how still to know the worlds of animals both wild and tame? In *Songs of Innocence*, for instance, 'The Lamb' mainly tells the tale of its innocent child-narrator's inculcated views: of all life as a gift from God, of wool as 'clothing', and of the lamb's name as a participatory sign for Christ (l. 5, E 8). Lost on this innocent is why Christ is so named, save because 'He is meek & he is mild' and 'became a little child' (ll. 15–16, E 9), echoing Charles Wesley's popular Methodist hymn with its 'Loving Jesus, gentle Lamb!'[14] What the child cannot conceive is a pastoral economy of lambs slaughtered and only thereby 'made' paschal symbols for a saviour crucified as a sacrificial lamb. Yet by the same token it is only because of thousands of years of pastoral husbandry that any lamb exists to be so read. What the creature is in itself becomes, in this ironic song, uncertain and a provocation. Within the poem's pastoral system, the child's benediction, 'Little Lamb God bless thee' (l. 19, E 9), doubly resounds, and all the more for the term *bless*'s etymology as a symbolic or actual marking with animal blood.

In the Song of Experience 'The Tyger', Blake's naïve adult similarly perceives the tiger in figurative terms that leave the animal's own being in question. The beast remains for him an inconceivable enigma, created by an 'immortal' alone able to 'grasp' the creature's 'deadly terrors' (ll. 3, 15–16, E 24–5). 'Did he who made the Lamb make thee?' he asks and almost objects (l. 20, E 25). And yet his ironic queries suggest that there is some trace at least of that animal maker's 'dread feet' in the tiger (l. 12, E 24), and some corporeal part, too, of the created tiger in its creator. Their shared animality is thus akin to, and a complement to, the mingling of lamb, divine Jesus, and child, and arguably as problematical, too, in the blurring of identities, save in the terms 'The Fly' proffers for its speaker's identification with a swatted insect: of a common and shared yet also distinctive, non-reducible animality. In this way, miniscule or large, mild or terrifying, these and other of Blake's animals prompt readers to marvel at and then to question precisely the order and division of things and, wondering more at 'every thing that lives', to strive amid the miraculous 'to make all Nature out' (E 501).

'So Man looks out in tree & herb & fish & bird & beast / Collecting up the scatterd portions of his immortal body' (*VALA/Four Zoas* N8, p. 114[110], ll. 6–7, E 385). Just as truly for Blake, a 'fool sees not the same tree that a wise man sees' (*Marriage* 7: 8, E 35) or quite the same tiger, lamb, fly, horse, bird, emmet, or kitten. And in that difference Blake's expansive art offers both wonderment and motivation. Hence, at the apocalyptic finale of *Milton*, 'Immediately the Lark', a beckoning source of avian genius, 'mount[s] with a loud trill from Felphams Vale', while:

> The Waggons ready: terrific Lions & Tygers sport & play
> All Animals upon the Earth, are prepard in their strength
> To go forth to the Great Harvest & Vintage of the Nations.
> (42[49]: 29, 38–9, 43[50]: 1, E 143–4)

Milton's conclusion portrays an intensely wished-for 'liberation of an unrealised potential, an alternative nature, within'[15] as well as outside humankind's historically bound finitude and servitude, as a dynamic pan-animality of the eternal unbounded 'Human Form Divine' (32[35]: 13, E 131). Blake's humanism becomes in this way markedly decentred, marvelling from its own animality, and through its art's animal materials, at 'world[s] of delight' for all that lives, 'wild & tame'.

Notes

1. See S. Makdisi, *William Blake and the Impossible History of the 1790s* (Chicago: University of Chicago Press, 2007), pp. 243–51, 275.
2. 'animality, n.': 'the state or fact of being an animal', and 'animal nature or life' (*OED Online*, Oxford University Press, January 2018). Cf. E. Darwin, *Zoönomia; or, The Laws of Organic Life*, 2 vols. (1794–96; New York: AMS Press, 1974): 'all warm-blood animals have arisen from one living filament [...] endued with animality' (II, 505).
3. See, for example, Blake's frontispiece (*c.* 1802) for *Designs to a Series of Ballads* by William Hayley.

4. Robert Burns famously addressed a louse, and several hymns and songs by Isaac Watts and by Charles and John Wesley similarly take up 'creeping creatures' like the emmet and worm – as, too, does Anna Laetitita Barbauld, notably in her children's primer *History of Insects*.
5. K. Hutchings, *Imagining Nature: Blake's Environmental Poetics* (Montreal and Kingston: McGill-Queen's University Press, 2002), p. 203.
6. P. Johnson, *The Birth of the Modern: World Society, 1815–1830* (New York: HarperCollins, 1991), p. 718.
7. F. Hutcheson, *A System of Moral Philosophy* (1755), cited by K. Thomas, *Man and the Natural World: Changing Attitudes in England 1500–1800* (1983; New York: Oxford University Press, 1996), p. 179.
8. C. Linnaeus, *Systema Naturae Per Regna Tria Naturae*, 10th edn, 2 vols. (Stockholm: Laurentius Salvius, 1758), I.
9. E. Darwin, *The Botanic Garden; A Poem, in Two Parts*, 2nd edn (London: J. Johnson, 1791), pp. 3, 28 n. 1.
10. See C. Kreiter, 'Evolution and William Blake', *Studies in Romanticism*, 4 (1965), 110–18; and T. J. Connolly, *William Blake and the Body* (Basingstoke: Palgrave, 2002), esp. pp. 78–83. Blake's term for Urizen and the other Eternals, *Zoa*, draws upon the ancient Greek for 'animal' and 'animal life'.
11. Thomas, *Man and the Natural World*, p. 51.
12. Cf. D. Perkins, 'Animal Rights and Auguries of Innocence', *Blake / An Illustrated Quarterly*, 33.1 (1999), 4–11.
13. On paint ingredients in Blake's era, see R. Dossie, *The Handmaid to the Arts*, 2nd edn, 2 vols. (London, 1764), I, 57–141; cf. *BR* 46, 384. Regarding animal-glues, see J. Clennell, *Monthly Magazine*, 14 (1802), cited by R. N. Essick, *William Blake, Printmaker* (Princeton: Princeton University Press, 1980), p. 122. Cf. Viscomi 121.
14. 'Gentle Jesus' (1742), in G. Osborn (ed.), *The Poetical Works of John and Charles Wesley*, 13 vols. (London: R. Needham, 1870), VI, 442.
15. E. P. Thompson, *Witness against the Beast: William Blake and the Moral Law* (New York: New Press, 1993), p. 229.

CHAPTER 27

Antiquarianism

Noah Heringman

In the *Descriptive Catalogue* that he wrote to accompany an exhibition of his work in 1809, Blake identifies the source of his large painting *The Ancient Britons* by announcing that 'the British Antiquities are now in the Artist's hands' (E 542). Although several other works in the exhibition address national concerns, including Horatio Nelson's naval triumphs of 1801 to 1805, syncretism rather than nationalism is the main driver of Blake's antiquarian pursuits. As he explains in the same passage, 'the antiquities of every Nation under Heaven, is no less sacred than that of the Jews. They are the same thing as Jacob Bryant, and all antiquaries have proved' (E 543). Antiquaries or antiquarians (Blake uses both words in this passage) approached the study of the past in a way that was understood to be different from the practice of history. With the benefit of hindsight, we can now see antiquarianism as the ancestor discipline of art history and archaeology; its most famous practitioners, including Johann Joachim Winckelmann and Heinrich Schliemann, have been claimed as pioneers by those modern disciplines, which came into being after Blake's death. In this passage, which also announces the publication of Blake's *Jerusalem* – a 'voluminous' poem on 'the ancient history of Britain' – Blake refers both to Bryant and (implicitly) to William Stukeley, another British antiquary whose work Blake encountered during his seven-year apprenticeship to the engraver James Basire, a specialist in antiquarian and scientific illustration.

Blake's strong commitment to syncretism – the endeavour to recreate a unified body of knowledge by correlating diverse ancient mythologies and monuments from around the world – led him to posit a consensus among 'all antiquaries' in the *Descriptive Catalogue* and in ambitious mythological poems such as *Jerusalem*. In other works, however, he shows a keen awareness of the controversial nature of antiquarianism and participates in some of its controversies with characteristic vigour. Beginning the *Catalogue* with an account of his paintings of Nelson and William Pitt (see Figs. 7.1, 7.2), Blake locates these 'mythological' heroic portraits provocatively in a non-Western tradition, calling them 'similar to those Apotheoses of Persian, Hindoo, and Egyptian Antiquity, which are still preserved on rude monuments' (E 530). One of Blake's controversial predecessors in the field of antiquarian syncretism was 'Baron' Pierre Hugues d'Hancarville, one of the first antiquaries to publish images of 'Hindoo Antiquity' in England.

A contrast between Blake and Horace Walpole (1717–97), another writer inspired by antiquarianism, will help to illustrate the controversial nature of Blake's position as well as the social and institutional framework of antiquarian practice in eighteenth-century London. Writing in 1785, Walpole condemned antiquarian syncretism as a pernicious practice, placing much of the blame on d'Hancarville and casting the arguments that Blake employed in a negative light. Walpole chastises d'Hancarville's *Researches on the Origin, Spirit, and Progress of Greek Art* (3 vols., 1785) for 'ascrib[ing] universal knowledge and invention to the Scythians, as Bryant did to the Lord knows whom', and declares that he himself has 'no [...] regard for the Phoenicians, Pelasgians, Vics, Egyptians, Edomites, Scythians, and Gentoos'. Many antiquaries traced ancient Greek art to various more ancient sources in the East, but Walpole, convinced that Greece is 'the one nation worth studying', was disgusted by the notion that 'the Grecians borrowed from the Egyptians, Tartars, Indians, etc.'. Whereas Blake looks to 'rude monuments' for traces of the 'stupendous originals' (E 530) that he associates with the sacred art of antiquity, Walpole condemns d'Hancarville, Bryant, and others for 'discovering arts and sciences among rude nations'. In the same letter, Walpole applies this criticism to another antiquarian publication, the learned journal *Archaeologia*, published from 1770 to the present by the Society of Antiquaries of London. Although Walpole himself had belonged to this society, he invokes the long tradition of satire against antiquaries by translating this title jokingly as 'old women's logic'.[1]

The Society of Antiquaries employed dozens of artists in the late eighteenth and early nineteenth centuries, including Basire and his apprentice Blake, the anti-classical polemicist John Carter, and Charles Stothard, the son of Blake's rival Thomas Stothard. Membership was expensive, and most artists had neither the money nor the prestige needed to join the society. Sociologically and intellectually, Blake resembles the antiquarian 'outsiders' who pursued research and publication projects without institutional support, a group including artist-antiquaries such as Carter as well as 'popular' antiquaries such as Joseph Strutt and Joseph Ritson.[2] The Society of Antiquaries' membership was diverse enough, however, to foster intense controversy between medievalising partisans of 'Gothic' and partisans of neoclassical values (Walpole aligns himself with the latter group in this late letter) and between advocates of historic preservation and advocates of renovation, among other issues.³ Its institutional publication projects also had the merit of employing numerous draftsmen and engravers and promoting what might now be described as collaborative research. The antiquarian network surrounding the Society of Antiquaries of London, their engraver Basire, and their printer and publisher John Nichols encompassed corresponding antiquaries and antiquarian societies from other parts of Britain and the wider world (the *Gentleman's Magazine*, published by Nichols, was an important venue for this correspondence) as well as artists, patrons, and collectors, thus extending far beyond the elite group of fellows elected to the society. Carter and Jacob Schnebbelie were among the affiliated artists who launched independent illustrated publication series on British antiquity, and Blake himself advertised 'The History of England, a small book of engravings' in 1793 (E 693), a project that seems to have originated not long after his apprenticeship with Basire. D'Hancarville, one of Blake's likely sources on Asian antiquities, was an illustrator himself and Walpole's disdain for d'Hancarville's comparative mythology is linked to his contempt for this menial occupation.⁴

Unlike history, antiquarian scholarship depended essentially on images. Alain Schnapp has argued that 'illustration was the technique par excellence of the antiquary', summing up in visual terms the key role of European antiquarianism – which flourished from the sixteenth through the nineteenth centuries – in the intellectual process that he terms the 'discovery of the past'.⁵ The socially fraught and unequal collaboration between scholars and artists, between book-learned and self-taught practitioners, was therefore vital. Although the antiquaries were dismissed as amateurs by their self-consciously objective successors in the modern disciplines of history, art history, and archaeology, a revaluation of their achievement has been underway ever since Arnaldo Momigliano published his seminal essay, 'Ancient History and the Antiquarian', in 1950. The complex antiquarian networks brought to light by more recent scholarship offer new perspectives both on Blake's career and on some of the overarching concerns of several generations of Blake criticism.⁶ These networks also provide a larger European context for the British authors and debates most often considered by Blake scholars.

Because of the broad purchase of antiquarianism, however, and because of Blake's characteristically thoughtful and controversial participation in it, it must be regarded as more than just a context for approaching his work. The study of Blake also contributes directly to the recovery of antiquarianism as an essential field in the history of ideas. Although much work has been done since Momigliano reopened the subject for consideration, the prejudice against antiquarianism consolidated within the newly professionalised disciplines of history and archaeology in the mid-nineteenth century still thrives in many intellectual circles. Even though the Society of Antiquaries continues to function as an institutional network for professionals in various historical and archaeological fields and continues to publish *Archaeologia* among other series (*Vetusta Monumenta*, which featured Blake's apprentice work, ceased in 1906), 'antiquarianism' in some contexts still retains the pejorative connotation of 'mere antiquarianism', mere hobby-horsical dabbling, a caricature captured vividly in Sir Walter Scott's *The Antiquary* (1816).[7] Literary scholarship has played an essential role in showing that some of antiquarianism's most biting critics (including Scott and Walpole, among others) were nevertheless antiquaries themselves, and in tracing the satirical tradition established around antiquaries and other amateur scholars as far back as the seventeenth century. Blake himself was far from immune to the charge of credulity traditionally levelled by these satires.

There were real grounds for ridicule in several notorious cases of antiquarian credulity and/or imposture, such as the spirited and erudite defence of the authenticity of Thomas Chatterton's 'Rowley' poems by Jeremiah Milles, published when he was president of the Society of Antiquaries in 1782. Blake, too, believed in the authenticity of these eighteenth-century forgeries of fifteenth-century verse, along with James Macpherson's 'translations' of third-century Celtic epics, as he noted in the margins of his copy of Wordsworth's 1815 *Poems*: 'I Believe both Macpherson & Chatterton, that what they say is Ancient Is so' (E 665). It stands to reason that their works were among the 'British Antiquities [...] now in the artist's hands' in 1809. Blake's riposte to Wordsworth's dismissal of these 'pretended treasures of antiquity' makes especially clear that accurate representation of the past was not all that was at stake in antiquarianism. It also provided a forum in which practitioners who gained their knowledge not from formal study but in the field – as Blake did over years of making drawings of medieval monuments for the Society of Antiquaries – could have an influence on what counted as antiquity, on the location of cultural prestige in time and place. Although Blake was certainly an idiosyncratic antiquary and at odds with the elitism and the empiricism associated with antiquarianism in some of its dominant forms, he would have been the first to recognise that dismissing antiquarianism as a scholarly practice is both unhistorical and smugly presentist.

Blake's involvement with antiquarianism illuminates many aspects of his philosophy of art, including his advocacy of an 'English school' of painting and his criticisms of the Royal Academy. Antiquarianism was also essential for the construction of his mythology. As Blake alerts us in the *Descriptive Catalogue*, Albion emerges as the central character in that mythology under the influence of syncretic accounts of British antiquity by Stukeley and others. Stukeley's insistence on an Old Testament setting for British antiquity also helps to explain Scriptural elements in Blake's myth, while influences from classical antiquity, especially Neoplatonism, are valuable for understanding Blakean characters such as Thel and processes such as the Fall into Generation. Blake's learned synthesis of these diverse strands of antiquity can seem at odds with his occasionally pugnacious advocacy of a popular British antiquarianism, but both positions are among the many avenues that antiquarianism offered for the construction of an artistic identity within a larger social field.[8]

The *Descriptive Catalogue*, by situating the 'acts of Albion' within the whirl of numerous ancient mythologies, helps to contextualise Blake's many local polemics both against classical authority and on behalf of Christian and/or British antiquity. When he reveals in this text that 'the antiquities of every Nation [...] are the same thing' because 'Antiquity preaches the Gospel of Jesus' (E 543) – which is not exactly what Bryant argued or 'proved' – Blake sounds a bit like an evangelical colonialist. When he subordinates the patriotic rhetoric surrounding Nelson to a 'Hindoo' typology, however, or 'plead[s] the authority of the ancients' to defend his representation of Indian manners in his drawing 'The Bramins' (E 548), he sounds more like d'Hancarville, Richard Payne Knight, Charles-François Dupuis, and other radical freethinkers who relativised Christian European values through the study of comparative religion. The more orthodox Bryant, whose *New System or Analysis of Ancient Mythology* Blake helped to illustrate during his apprenticeship (1774–6), argued that all mythologies arose in the course of the global diffusion of population that followed the biblical Flood, and hence could be traced to Genesis. At times, Blake wields the thesis of Hebrew originality as a weapon against the neoclassicism that he found so dominant as a student at the Royal Academy after his apprenticeship, and in the professional context of fine art. So, for example, he returns decisively to the Laocoön, a Hellenistic sculpture central to the canon of neoclassicism, in a late engraving entitled 'Jehovah & his two Sons Satan & Adam as they were copied from the Cherubim of Solomons Temple'. This caption, with other added text, retools his commercial illustration of the Laocoön into a polemic against Greco-Roman originality. Blake's memorable dismissal of 'silly Greek & Latin slaves of the Sword' in *Milton* (pl. 1[i], E 95) may also be traced to his early professional connection with the Society of Antiquaries, where the most radical members of the Gothic faction asserted the merits of non-classical antiquity with similar intensity. John Carter, for example, ridiculed the 'armless Venuses' adored by connoisseurs in his column in the *Gentleman's Magazine*.[9]

A concern with the history of religion follows necessarily from the empirical study of ancient monuments and texts that was the main focus of antiquarianism, but in addition to art history and archaeology this concern also anticipates another modern discipline emerging in the nineteenth century: anthropology. Histories of humankind, or 'conjectural histories', by Jean-Jacques Rousseau and Adam Smith, among many other Enlightenment philosophers, did much to promote broad interest in customs and manners in eighteenth-century Europe. Their characteristic method of using narratives about modern non-European peoples considered 'primitive' to illustrate the cultural practices of ancient peoples infused both antiquarianism and natural history with a strong interest in 'stages' of cultural development. To borrow a suggestive phrase from Maureen McLane, popular antiquaries who promoted the English ballad revival understood traditional ballads as 'savage cultural production', analogous to Greek oral tradition before Homer as well as to song forms encountered by explorers outside Europe.[10] Blake himself engraved several illustrations for *A Select Collection of English Songs* by Joseph Ritson (1783), one of the main proponents of the ballad revival. This kind of antiquarianism helped to provide the impetus for Blake's *Songs of Innocence and of Experience*, as suggested by the passage of music from the pipe to the voice to the page in the 'Introduction' to *Innocence* and underscored by Blake's remark in 1798 that if Native Americans were 'savages' then Homer was too, '& yet he was no fool' (E 615). In Blake's lifetime it was the Pacific rather than North America that provided the scene of first contact between European explorers and non-European peoples, and Blake first gained exposure to the more scientifically inflected discourse about these encounters through Basire's relationship to the Royal Society, which (along with the Admiralty) sponsored Captain Cook's voyages. During his apprenticeship, he engraved a drawing by William Hodges of a woman from the Pacific island of Tanna (Vanuatu), one of the scenes of first contact on Cook's second voyage. Blake visually echoes this engraving from Cook's published narrative (1777) in his frontispiece to *Songs of Experience*.[11]

This ethnographic aspect of antiquarianism also helps to explain Blake's positive use of the word 'primitive' in later works such as *Jerusalem* (E 171). From this literature and from his artisanal practice Blake derived his more empirical sense of the ancient or primitive arts, specifically useful arts, which he fused in his myth-making with a more esoteric sense of spiritual science derived from ancient wisdom. Together with the myth of Albion's fall, Blake develops his paradigm of primitive arts and sciences throughout *VALA / The Four Zoas, Milton,* and *Jerusalem,* themselves 'poems of the highest antiquity', as he assured visitors to the 1809 exhibition (E 542). In all these works he seeks to establish that 'the Primeval State of Man, was Wisdom, Art, and Science' (*Jerusalem* 3: 48, E 146), as against a fallen state in which we are 'abstracted from the roots of science' (*VALA/Four Zoas* N9, p. 133, l. 15, E 401) – a word that Blake insisted on using in its encyclopedic sense.

Blake's antiquity is a performance of antiquarian syncretism on the levels of content (his myth) and of method. Albion, in his various guises as the Eternal Man, Adam Kadmon, the world's body, the Patriarch of the Atlantic, or a tattooed Ancient Briton, recapitulates Blake's own antiquarian method, inspired by comparative studies of myth and by his own fieldwork among the 'Gothic monuments' of London. The Giant Albion's vast body in *Jerusalem* not only suggests an animated earth but also recalls the divine wisdom still directly experienced by the giants who precede humans on the earth in various mythologies. Giambattista Vico, for example, credits these aboriginal giants with 'robust sense and vigorous imagination'.[12] Addressing the Jews in *Jerusalem*, Blake writes, 'You have a tradition, that Man anciently contain in his mighty limbs all things'. Taking his cue from Stukeley and his antiquarian successors, Blake deduces that Adam and Noah were Druids and that Britain was 'the Primitive Seat of the Patriarchal Religion' (pl. 27, E 171).[13] One the one hand, then, Albion's body, itself synthesised from various myths, incorporates the arts and sciences that Blake sees as deriving from the native organisation of human faculties. On the other hand, Blake pursues this synthesis on a methodological level by collating what he finds in Bryant on the ancient Hebrews with verbal and visual material on the Ancient Britons and with classical material including the legend of Atlantis (*Jerusalem* 48: 30–50: 7, E 197–8). Blake's response to the doctrine of ancient myth as scientific allegory (as in the story of Atlantis) also finds visual expression in one of his engravings for Erasmus Darwin's *Botanic Garden*, 'The Fertilization of Egypt', in which he adds the figure of a bearded sky god to Henry Fuseli's original design, cementing the association between myth and religion.

Some of the earliest biographical sources on Blake confirm the importance of his early exposure to antiquarianism for his later career. Benjamin Heath Malkin, who knew Blake, reported in 1806 that in copying 'those neglected works of art, called Gothic monuments' for the antiquaries, Blake 'saw the simple and plain road to the style of art at which he aimed, unentangled in the windings of modern practice' (*BR* 563). Echoing Malkin, G. E. Bentley wrote in 2001 that the 'echoes' of these 'monuments in the Abbey and in Gothic churches around London [...] stayed with him throughout his life, determining his style and his subjects and his sympathies' (*Stranger* 41). Bentley cites the example of Blake's first surviving print, a figure copied from Michelangelo's *Crucifixion of St Peter* that he engraved as an apprentice in 1773 (see Fig. 3.1) and revisited throughout his career, adding visual details and finally a caption that renamed the subject of the print in 1810: *Joseph of Arimathea among the Rocks of Albion*. As Richard Gough, one of Blake's employers at the Society of Antiquaries, said of another draftsman on his team, Blake became 'a true practical Antiquary' during his apprenticeship.[14] At the same time, he began a course of reading in antiquarian scholarship and theory that allowed him to situate his study of ancient monuments and his own artistic production in a world-historical framework. His efforts to establish and restore the primitive or original human arts and sciences respond to the controversies and share the ambitions of antiquarianism and the other 'human sciences' of his time. When Blake identifies Poetry, Painting, Music, and Architecture as the Four Arts of Eternity in *Milton* (pl. 27 [29], E 125), his analysis resonates with numerous eighteenth-century accounts of what we would now call prehistoric cultures, ranging from Bernard Mandeville's *Fable of the Bees* (1724) to d'Hancarville's *Collection of Etruscan, Greek and Roman Antiquities* (1766–76). These philosophical accounts hold to a more or less progressive narrative of human knowledge; but for Blake, resurrecting the ancient body of knowledge enables the perennial process of making art.

Notes

1. Walpole to Lady Ossory, 9 July 1785, in *The Yale Edition of Horace Walpole's Correspondence*, ed. W. S. Lewis, 48 vols. (New Haven, CN: Yale University Press, 1937–83), XXXIII, 478–9.
2. See further M. Butler, 'Antiquarianism (Popular)', in *The Oxford Companion to the Romantic Age*, ed. I. McCalman (Oxford: Oxford University Press, 1999), pp. 328–37, and R. Sweet, *Antiquaries: The Discovery of the Past in Eighteenth-Century Britain* (London: Hambledon and London, 2004), esp. pp. 309–44.

3. Blake recalls these controversies, overlaying his own concerns over many years of art-making, in his last engraved work, 'On Virgil': 'Grecian is Mathematic Form. Gothic is living Form' (E 270).
4. Lewis, *Walpole's Correspondence*, XXXIII, 479.
5. A. Schnapp, *The Discovery of the Past* (New York: Harry N. Abrams, 1997), p. 237.
6. On antiquarian networks, see A. Schnapp (ed.), *World Antiquarianism: Comparative Perspectives* (Los Angeles: Getty Research Institute, 2013); on Blake's social and intellectual milieu, see E. Hungerford, *Shores of Darkness* (New York: Columbia University Press, 1941); K. Raine, *Blake and Tradition*, 2 vols. (Princeton: Princeton University Press, 1968); J. Mee, *Dangerous Enthusiasm: William Blake and the Culture of Radicalism in the 1790s* (Oxford: Clarendon Press, 1992); S. Makdisi, *William Blake and the Impossible History of the 1790s* (Chicago and London: University of Chicago Press, 2003).
7. www.rc.umd.edu/praxis/antiquarianism/praxis.antiquarianism.2014.siegel.html
8. On Blake and Neoplatonism, see Raine, who pithily describes the frontispiece to *Songs of Experience* as 'Gothic in style, [...] Platonic in content' (*Blake and Antiquity* (Princeton: Princeton University Press, 1977; repr. 1979), p. 22). T. Brylowe argues that Blake deliberately sharpened the distinction between classical and 'popular' antiquarianism; she defines the latter as the study of 'British artifacts and architecture, old ballads, and vernacular languages' ('Of Gothic Architects and Grecian Rods: William Blake, Antiquarianism, and the History of Art', *Romanticism*, 18.1 (2012), 89–104 (p. 89)).
9. J. Carter, 'Durham Cathedral', *Gentleman's Magazine*, 72 (1802), 231.
10. M. McLane, *Balladeering, Minstrelsy, and the Making of British Romantic Poetry* (Cambridge: Cambridge University Press, 2008), p. 172.
11. See R. Joppien and B. Smith, *The Art of Captain Cook's Voyages*, 3 vols. (New Haven, CT: Yale University Press, 1985–8), II, III.
12. G. Vico, *The New Science of Giambattista Vico, Unabridged Translation of the Third Edition* (1744), trans. T. G. Bergin and M. H. Fisch (Ithaca, NY: Cornell University Press, 1948), section 375, p. 104.
13. De Luca points out that other antiquaries after Stukeley, such as Rowland Jones and James Parsons, also make the case that the British Druids predate Abraham and hence both Babel and the Fall. See his *Words of Eternity: Blake and the Poetics of the Sublime* (Princeton: Princeton University Press, 1991), p. 188.
14. R. Gough, *Sepulchral Monuments in Great Britain*, 2 vols. in 5 (London: Printed by J. Nichols, 1786–96), II, 7. Blake made a dozen drawings for the first volume of this work during his apprenticeship; Jacob Schnebbelie, of whom Gough writes here, made about 150 for the second volume.

CHAPTER 28

Education and Childhood

Louise Joy

Blake occupies a central position in the history of literature for young people, his reputation as a children's poet resting almost exclusively on the *Songs of Innocence and of Experience*. In fact, this work is not unique among Blake's corpus in its apparent inclusion of children within its implied audience. In 1791 Blake illustrated the second edition of Mary Wollstonecraft's work for children, *Original Stories from Real Life*, etching onto the faces of Wollstonecraft's generic child characters startlingly individualised expressions. In so doing, as Dennis Welch has observed, Blake foregrounds not Wollstonecraft's moral but 'his interpretation of the children's reaction to it and of the adults' reaction to them'.[1] By interpolating new lines of sight, Blake's illustrations to *Original Stories* prompt us to reflect on the perspectives in play when adults seek to address children through artistic media. Does the peculiar convolution of the relations between art and pedagogy in the case of children's literature necessarily result in adults speaking *for* children, or might art, particularly composite art, even if or when it functions as a site of instruction, open up possibilities for speaking with, or listening to, children?[2]

Blake wrestled throughout his career with the complexities inherent in the attempt to speak with children via art. His juvenile *Poetical Sketches*, written between 1769 and 1777, registers in the very *sturm und drang* of its vacillations between hope and disappointment the instability of an adolescent voice. Such frustrations associated with the difficulty of breaching the epistemological gap between child and adult perspectives are also a preoccupation of *The Book of Thel*, in which Thel's youth – primarily identified by way of her virginity – is depicted as a state of semi-consciousness, one which the later poem, 'The Land of Dreams', suggests is no longer available in adulthood: 'O when shall I again return' (l. 12, E 486). The thematic affinity between childhood and insight which this nostalgia implies is a recurrent presence in Blake's work, one which often resonates with distinctively Rousseauvian vibrations, albeit sounded in

254

a modulated key. For instance, the description of Orc as a 'hairy youth' functions as a counter-intuitive oxymoron (*America* 1: 11, E 51) – one which calls attention to the strangeness of the kinship it posits between childhood and pre-civilisation even as it sets it up – since in the wake of Rousseauvian thought, both characteristics (rusticity and inexperience) separately betoken liberation from custom. But while the destructiveness of socialisation is bemoaned in poems such as 'The Mental Traveller', wherein the primal scene comprises a mother binding 'iron thorns' around the head of 'the Babe [...] born a Boy', Blake nowhere sentimentalises childhood (ll. 13, 9, E 484). 'The Lamb' may remind us that Christ was incarnate in the figure of a child; but for all that Blake's children, like the Christ child, are faithful, they are also 'wanton' ('Auguries of Innocence' l. 33, E 490). The child's caprices are redundant, though, fundamentally impotent, since the child is doomed, from the start, to be bent according to the adult's will. William Godwin saw the child as a 'raw material put into our hands, a ductile and yielding substance, which, if we do not ultimately mould in conformity to our wishes, it is because we throw away the power committed to us, by the folly with which we are accustomed to exert it'.[3] But Blake repeatedly represents birth as a tragedy, and the adult's attempts to 'mould' the child as an infliction of suffering where joy might have been possible: 'howling, the Child with fierce flames / Issu'd from Enitharmon', his voice heard only by the dead (*Urizen* 19: 45–6, E 79).

Just as Blake's works lay bare the struggles of children to be heard, so too they register the difficulties entailed in speaking to children. If Blake's *For Children: The Gates of Paradise* (1793) sought to appeal to the young, as its title implies, then its success is questionable. Only one copy is known to have been owned by a real child, Harriet Jane Moore, who was given the book by Henry Fuseli in 1806 when she was five (*BB* 187, 193).[4] Indeed, Joseph Byrne has claimed that *For Children* is 'not really a book for children – at least not bourgeois children', since it is 'seemingly designed to give children nightmares'.[5] Blake's own qualms can be inferred from his subsequent decision to reconceive the work as *For the Sexes: The Gates of Paradise*, a change which seemingly retracts the hand originally proffered to young readers. Other works by Blake formally resemble the kinds of poems which Ann and Jane Taylor were so effectively to popularise for children in *Rhymes for the Nursery* (1806), but tonally, they disrupt this family resemblance. 'A Cradle Song', from Blake's notebook, complicates the ostensibly soothing nature of its pretext – a baby sleeping – by plaiting together the acoustically cognate 'wiles' and 'smiles', the internal rhyme hinting at a semantic correspondence that fosters scepticism towards, not sympathy with, the child (ll. 7, 8, E 468). In similarly mutated fashion, the title of the manuscript, 'Mr Blake's Nursery Rhyme', may suggest an indebtedness to the *Mother Goose* rhymes newly circulating in published form in the 1780s, but the coherence of its putative social critique disavows the usual delinquency of such verse.

Even *Songs of Innocence and of Experience* thwarts easy categorisation as a work for children, the very pre-eminence of this issue as a critical concern reflecting its significance as a preoccupation within the work itself. From early on, anthologists for children were prepared to embrace certain poems from *Innocence*: 'Holy Thursday' featured in the Taylors' *City Scenes; or, a Peep into London* (1818), and 'The Chimney Sweeper' was included in James Montgomery's *The Chimney-Sweeper's Friend* (1824). But critics have not always been ready to accept at face value that quality of ingenuousness in his work which Northrop Frye identified as Blake's 'namby-pamby'.[6] Some, such as Martha Winburn England, have insisted that Blake 'meant every namby-pamby word', and therefore that *Songs* straightforwardly addresses a child audience.[7] Others, such as Harold Bloom, have proposed that we allow the poems to resist 'namby pamby' by presuming the presence of an incredulous adult reader, invoking Blake's remark that what 'can be made Explicit to the Idiot' was 'not worth his care' (E 702).[8] Blake himself, though, never mistook immaturity for stupidity, as he made clear in a letter to the Revered Dr Trusler of 23 August 1799: 'Some Children are Fools & so are some Old Men' (E 703). Indeed, he reported proudly that 'Particularly [My Visions] have been Elucidated by Children who have taken a greater delight in contemplating my Pictures than I even hoped', confirming both his aspiration to reach a child audience and his surprise at appearing so to do (E 703).[9] This serves as a reminder that even if, as Heather Glen and Donelle Ruwe have argued, most of the poems in *Songs* lie beyond the child's grasp, Blake's visual art offers what Nicholas Williams has identified as 'an alternative route to literacy', one which enables the illiterate child to circumnavigate the mediating figure of the literate adult.[10]

The apparent contradiction that *Songs* both addresses and fails to address children can be reconciled if, as Alan Richardson suggests, we adopt the 'role' of 'the child reader', or as Zachary Leader puts it, we 'take seriously lines which sound sentimental or "childish"', and, 'like children at their books', 'live out the themes of *Innocence* through the very act of reading.'[11] But what does it mean to read *like children at their books*? The success of one of the eighteenth century's most frequently republished and imitated children's books, Isaac Watts's *Divine Songs*,

Attempted in the Easy Language of Children (1715), indicates the wide acceptance in the period of a view that reading like a child entailed assuming the role of a pupil. Numerous critics, including Mary V. Jackson and Patricia Demers, have shown that children's literature in the eighteenth century was valued primarily on account of its perceived educational rather than aesthetic merits.[12] Watts's Preface to *Divine Songs*, addressed 'To all that are concerned in the Education of Children', stresses the 'awful and important charge that is committed' to those adults responsible for the oversight of children's reading, making clear his overtly pedagogical agenda. The precariousness of the balance he attempts to achieve – 'to sink the language to the level of a child's understanding' while striving 'yet to keep it (if possible) above contempt' – indicates the fragility of the exercise: at stake is not merely the enlightenment of the child but also the poem's aesthetic credibility.[13] It was precisely this fear that to pare down poetic language was to degrade it which motivated Anna Laetitia Barbauld in 1781 to doubt 'whether poetry ought to be lowered to the capacities of children, or whether they should not rather be kept from reading verse, till they are able to relish good verse.'[14] In her own *Hymns in Prose for Children*, Barbauld eschews rhyme, metrical patterning, and traditional stanzaic forms, opting instead for a kind of poetical prose comprising highly figurative, elevated diction shaped into short stanza-like paragraphs. While Blake made innovative use of poetical prose elsewhere in his works, the form that he adopts for his own most decisive foray into children's literature indicates that he shared Watts's faith in the child's ear for poetry.

But for all that Blake, like Watts, has confidence that the incorporation of the child reader need not be at the poem's aesthetic cost, his critics have not always been able to dispel the anxiety that is whisperingly present in Watts's parenthetical aside, an anxiety that stylistic plainness signifies intellectual deficiency. The persistent recourse among Blake critics to the term 'namby-pamby', a term which Henry Carey coined in his 1725 poem of that name to denigrate the intellectual bankruptcy of mere 'Jingles', contains residues of Carey's scorn.[15] Even as he seeks to promote Blake in his Advertisement to *Poetical Sketches*, the Reverend Anthony Stephen Mathew felt the need to apologise for the poet's 'untutored youth' (*BR* 29). This characterisation of Blake's work as *childlike* lingered even as the defence of the poet's youth could no longer plausibly be invoked. The way that Blake's admirers have therefore often sought to explain the apparent formal guilelessness of *Songs* is by reading it not as an attempt to speak *to* the child (like *Divine Songs*) or to speak *as* the child (as the term 'namby-pamby' implies), but instead to speak *for* the child. Hence Benjamin Heath Malkin saw in the songs' 'simplicity' and 'unfinished' nature signs of Blake's 'genius' (*BR* 565), while Alexander Gilchrist claimed that Blake's metrical and grammatical 'irregularities' exhibited his 'sympathy' – his capacity imaginatively to assume the perspective of children (Gilchrist 73–4). If we accept Gilchrist's view, then Blake opens up the possibility that to read *like children at their books* is an exercise not *just* in listening, in fact perhaps not *even* in listening at all, but an exercise in speaking out.

The nature of the departure that this entails can be seen in relief through a comparison of Blake's frontispiece with the frontispiece of another highly popular eighteenth-century children's book, John Newbery's *A Little Pretty Pocket-Book* (1744), to which the title page of Blake's *Songs of Innocence* plate implicitly refers. Newbery's pioneering work had hit upon a formula – the pairing of short verses on secular, everyday subjects with woodcut illustrations – which had proven commercially profitable and ripe for imitation in the second half of the eighteenth century. Its opening image, entitled 'Instruction with Delight', features a comfortable interior in which two children stand close to their seated nurse. They listen as the nurse reads aloud, their eyes fixed on the nurse's own. The closed window behind seals off the outdoors; like the lapdog at their heels, domestication is the children's lot. In Blake's twist on the tableau, the nurse holds out the book and the two children lean in close. Their heads bend over it; their eyes are absorbed by it; their hands touch it. As commentators have frequently noted, Blake's is an alfresco scene, the branches providing a secluded bower for this educational encounter, anticipating the second plate of 'The Little Black Boy' in which the curvature of Christ's back as he tends to the children at his lap is congruent with the bend of the branch overhead.[16] It is tempting to perceive in this a nod to Rousseau, who had championed informal outdoors learning, though we might pause to remember that the trope is present too in Sarah Fielding's *The Governess* (1749) and Ellenor Fenn's *School Occurrences* (1782–3).[17] Certainly, whereas Newbery channels an enlightenment cliché in which the light mediated by the window parallels the light mediated by the book, Blake's children bask directly in the sunlight. But we might also see in Blake's organic classroom an implicit rejection of the belief later codified by Joseph Lancaster that the layout of the schoolroom be meticulously organised to ensure efficiency and participation.[18] The intimacy of Blake's scene runs directly counter to the move towards mass education advocated by Lancaster and Andrew Bell at the turn of the nineteenth century.[19] Indeed, the relaxed atmosphere of Blake's children at their books is indistinguishable from the atmosphere of children at play; the only difference, as in 'Spring', is that it is the lamb, and not the book, which exerts its pull.

For Blake, then, education emphatically did not take place in institutions. 'Thank God I never was sent to school', he boasted ('You say their pictures', E 510), and where he represents educational establishments in his work, as in the 'Holy Thursday' poems, it is to condemn the 'eternal winter' that their regimental, mandatory regimes inflict ([*Songs of Experience*], l. 12, E 19). By contrast, Blake's frontispiece represents children *yearning* to see, hear, and touch the book. In *Some Thoughts Concerning Education* (1693), John Locke had emphasised the importance of engaging the child's senses in order to keep his attention.[20] A century later, Maria and Richard Lovell Edgeworth placed the notion of 'play' at the heart of their philosophy of education, advocating the importance of voluntary participation to secure the child's pleasure in the educational activity at hand. They coined the term 'practical education' to encapsulate a manner of learning that involves learning first-hand from one's own active experimentation.[21] The child's 'joy' in Blake's 'Introduction' to *Innocence* – at once sensory, affective, an eruption of play, an emblem of pleasure – is precisely what eighteenth-century progressive educationalists in this Lockean tradition sought to harness in and through education. Just as in the Edgeworths' model, Blake invites the child reader to choose to participate. As Alan Richardson has shown, Blake categorically rejected catechistic response, a staple of mainstream eighteenth-century pedagogy, as a meaningful way of learning.[22] *Songs* offers instead a way of imagining that the child might speak and think, and not merely listen and learn.

Hope and scepticism about the possibility that art might educate vie throughout Blake's work. *The Marriage of Heaven and Hell* animates, but ultimately wreaks violence on, the prospect of didacticism. The prophetic works drive towards, though ultimately resist, an alignment between poetry and wisdom. But in attempting to speak not just for but also to and with children, Blake's composite works open up the possibility that education might comprise an event to lean in to, to touch – to desire. They not merely enact the possibility of mutual instruction – a belief codified by Andrew Bell in his *Analysis of the Experiment in Education* (1797), that the teacher learns through teaching, just as the pupil teaches through being taught – they altogether dissolve the distinction between teacher and pupil. By encouraging us to read like children at their books, they summon us to carry out a practical experiment in which we, the child reader, are both subject and object of enquiry, the book at once our lesson and our play.

Notes

1. D. M. Welch, *Blake / An Illustrated Quarterly*, 13.1 (1979), 4–15 (p. 10).
2. These problems continue to vex children's literature studies. See M. Gubar, 'On Not Defining Children's Literature', *PMLA*, 126.1 (2011), 209–16.
3. W. Godwin, *The Enquirer* (London: 1797), p. 112.
4. Thanks from the editor to Keri Davies for confirming this detail.
5. J. Byrne, 'Blake, Joseph Johnson, and "The Gates of Paradise"', *The Wordsworth Circle*, 44.2/3 (2013), 131–6 (pp. 134, 132).
6. N. Frye, *Fearful Symmetry: A Study of William Blake* (Princeton: Princeton University Press, 1947), p. 233.
7. M. W. England, 'Wesley's Hymns for Children and Blake's *Songs*', in M. W. England and J. Sparrow (eds.), *Hymns Unbidden: Donne, Herbert, Blake, Emily Dickinson and the Hymnographers* (New York: New York Public Library, 1966), pp. 44–63 (p. 54).
8. H. Bloom, *The Visionary Company: A Reading of English Romantic Poetry*, rev. edn (Ithaca, NY: Cornell University Press, 1971), pp. 35, 43.
9. For a fascinating discussion of the perils of marketing Blake's poems to children, see M. Ferber, 'Not for the Kiddies', *Academe*, 87.4 (2001), 50–2.
10. H. Glen, *Vision and Disenchantment: Blake's Songs and Wordsworth's Lyrical Ballads* (Cambridge: Cambridge University Press, 1983), pp. 8–32; D. Ruwe, *British Children's Poetry in the Romantic Era: Verse, Riddle, and Rhyme* (Basingstoke: Palgrave Macmillan, 2014), pp. 10–12; N. M. Williams, *Ideology and Utopia in the Poetry of William Blake* (Cambridge: Cambridge University Press, 1998), pp. 54–5.
11. A. Richardson, *Literature, Education, and Romanticism: Reading as Social Practice 1780–1832* (Cambridge: Cambridge University Press, 1994), pp. 146; 153–66; Z. Leader, *Reading Blake's* Songs (Boston, London, and Henley: Routledge and Kegan Paul, 1981), p. 91.
12. M. V. Jackson, *Engines of Instruction, Mischief, and Magic: Children's Literature in England From its Beginnings to 1839* (Lincoln: University of Nebraska Press, 1989); P. Demers, *From Instruction to Delight: An Anthology of Children's Literature to 1850*, 3rd edn (Ontario: Oxford University Press, 2008).
13. I. Watts, *Divine Songs, Attempted in the Easy Language of Children* (London: 1715), p. 6.
14. A. L. Barbauld, *Hymns in Prose for Children* (London: 1781), p. iv.
15. H. Carey, *Namby Pamby: or, a Panegyrick on the New Versification Address'd to A— P—* (Dublin: 1725), l. 3.
16. For example, S. Gardner, *Blake's* Innocence *and* Experience *Retraced* (1986; London: Bloomsbury Academic, 2013), pp. 15–16.
17. J.-J. Rousseau, *Emile, or, On Education*, trans. A. Bloom (Harmondsworth: Penguin, 1991); S. Fielding, *The Governess, or, the Female Academy* (London: 1749); Mrs Teachwell, *School Occurrences* (London: J. Marshall, 1782).

18. J. Lancaster, *Improvements in Education, as It Relates to the Industrious Classes of the Community*, 3rd edn (1803; New York: Collins and Perkins, 1807) and *The British System of Education* (1810; Georgetown: Joseph Milligan and William Cooper, 1812).
19. A. Bell, *An Analysis of the Experiment in Education, Made at Egmore, Near Madras*, 3rd edn (London: Cadell and Davies, 1807).
20. J. Locke, *Some Thoughts Concerning Education*, ed. J. W. Adamson (Cambridge: Cambridge University Press, 2011).
21. M. and R. L. Edgeworth, *Practical Education*, 3 vols. (London: J. Johnson, 1801), I, v–x.
22. Richardson, *Literature, Education, and Romanticism*, pp. 64–77.

CHAPTER 29

Empiricism

Nicholas M. Williams

Empiricism is a term which carries both a general and a specific meaning. Generally, it refers to the idea that all knowledge is derived from sensory experience and thus names a key foundation for scientific inquiry and experimentation. Specifically, in reference to a branch of philosophy, it describes John Locke's theoretical account of the mind's development from sensory experience (in *An Essay Concerning Human Understanding* (1690)), as well as contributions by later philosophers, including George Berkeley, David Hume, Thomas Reid, and others. Empiricist philosophy opposes itself to Rationalist philosophy, which grounds ideas in the activity of reason alone, without recourse to the senses. The power and ongoing influence of empiricism, in both its general and specific manifestations, almost cannot be overstated. As the basis of scientific inquiry, empiricism plays a central role in the development of the modern worldview, from Francis Bacon's early account of the scientific ethos to the establishment of the Royal Society of London for the Advancement of Science in 1662, the revolutionary insights of Isaac Newton in the late seventeenth century and, throughout the eighteenth century, the gradual professionalisation and spread of science and technology. Empiricist philosophy, even though the main texts themselves might not have found a large readership, contributes to the model of human psychology that will become dominant in the century following Locke (in, for instance, the emergent literary form of the novel): a secular, even materialist, notion of human psychology and personality as the accretion of sensory experiences of a social and physical world. In what follows, I will consider William Blake's antagonistic relationship to Locke's empiricist philosophy and to Newton's scientific theories of motion, before suggesting his more nuanced relationship with the later empiricist thought of Berkeley.

According to Blake, Locke's *Essay* is a book he had read and commented upon in his youth (the annotated copy is unfortunately lost to posterity), and one which stirred 'the Same Contempt & Abhorrence' in both youth and adulthood ('Annotations to Reynolds', E 660). Since the time of Northrop Frye's foundational *Fearful Symmetry: A Study of William Blake*, and its opening chapter laying out 'The Case against Locke', a broad consensus has emerged regarding Blake's objections to Locke, which indeed begin with what might be called Locke's primal scene of the simple experiencing mind. For Locke, that mental experience, consciousness, the contents of which constitute all the concepts which will be developed from them, has two distinct sources: sensation (perception of the physical world) and reflection (the mental 'notice which the Mind takes of its own Operations').[1] Although reflection does involve a type of inward perception (a point Frye overlooks), Locke's distinction of sensation and reflection, and his attribution of knowledge solely to the latter, risks unmooring the faculties of knowing, thinking, creating, and so on from the sensory particularity which, in Blake's opinion, gives their products value and life. Another Lockean distinction, within sensation itself, between primary and secondary sensory qualities, causes Blake even stronger fits of disgust. Primary sensory qualities, according to Locke, are those which are 'utterly inseparable from the Body' of the object, such as '*Solidity, Extension, Figure*, and *Mobility*', which remain no matter how the object is manipulated by its viewer (II, viii, 9). Secondary qualities are 'in truth [...] nothing in the Objects themselves, but Powers to produce various Sensations in us by their *primary Qualities*', and include 'Colours, Sounds, Tastes, etc.' (II, viii, 10). This distinction, clearly, attempts to import some reliable non-phenomenological substrate (matter) liberated from the tricks and freaks of perception, but, in the context of the 'Annotations to Lavater', Blake utterly rejects the notion of an object distinct from its particularities of colour, form, feel, and so on: 'Deduct from a rose its redness. from a lilly its whiteness from a diamond its hardness from a sponge its softness from an oak its heighth from a daisy its lowness & [...] rectify every thing in Nature as the Philosophers do. & then we shall return to Chaos' (E 595). Rather than representing a headlong flight from sensation, then, Blake's objections to Locke involve a fidelity to the domain of perception, a refusal to substitute the abstract of matter for the particularity of the perceptible.

If that is the case, though, what is one to do with the repeated laments at the limitations of the five senses, showing up throughout Blake's texts? To sample only a few instances of this strain in Blake's work, one might turn to *The Marriage of Heaven and Hell*, where the critique of Milton includes the charge that his version of 'the Son' is only 'a Ratio of the five senses' (pl. 6, E 35) or to Oothoon's initial complaint in *Visions of the Daughters of Albion*, that '[t]hey told me that I had five senses to inclose me up' (2: 31, E 47). Instances that make the direct connection to Blake's constant empiricist targets, the trio of Bacon, Newton, and Locke, include the description of the 'serpent-form'd' temple of the 'fiery King' in *Europe*, called 'Verulam' in allusion to Bacon's title as Baron Verulam, and decorated with lucent stones '[p]lac'd in the order of the stars, when the five senses whelm'd / In deluge o'er the earth-born man' (10: 2, 5, 10–11, E 63). And the retelling of the shrinking and binding of humanity in *The Song of Los* includes a process of 'closing and restraining: / Till a Philosophy of Five Senses was complete / Urizen wept & gave it into the hands of Newton & Locke' (4:15–17, E 68). These formulations seem to equate sensory experience with sexual oppression, or Urizenic logocentrism, or even the earth-destroying flood of Genesis, but the emphasis falls as much on the misplaced certainty of there being five and only five experiential portals, as on that sensory experience itself. Beyond the explicit matter of number, Blake targets Locke's constant recourse to *the* senses, as if human experiences of environment could be sorted and determined, disentangled into separate and knowable channels. Among the excitements of Oothoon's imaginative survey of animal sensory experience in *Visions of the Daughters of Albion* is her liberation of the term 'sense' from its Lockean determination as 'the senses' and her insistence that the sensory experiences of others be approached through means of the question:

> With what sense is it that the chicken shuns the ravenous hawk?
> With what sense does the tame pigeon measure out the expanse?
> With what sense does the bee form cells? have not the mouse & frog
> Eyes and ears and sense of touch? Yet are their habitations.
> And their pursuits, as different as their forms and as their joys
> Ask the wild ass why he refuses burdens: and the meek camel
> Why he loves man: is it because of eye ear mouth or skin
> Or breathing nostrils? No. for these the wolf and tiger have. (3: 2–9, E 47)

The question form refuses to define Oothoon's intentions: does she mean that these animal capacities are not well described as 'sense' and that therefore the answer is that no sense operates here? Or is the question more open-ended, probing for a sense other than those of 'eye ear mouth or skin / Or breathing nostrils'? In the absence of a Lockean determination of 'the senses', what is left is a respect for different experiences, different bodies, and an environment transformed by the multiplicity of perceptual affordances at play.

Such fundamental questions of the nature of sensory experience and its role in knowledge production might seem remote from the concerns of

Isaac Newton, since his practical and theoretical scientific researches are turned outward to the physical universe rather than inward to the essential capacities of human experience. Newton is yoked with Locke and Bacon in Blake's texts more for the conclusions he draws about physical reality from his empirical studies than for his reliance on sensory observation. Working out Blake's relationship to Newton's model of the physical world – to the theory of gravitational forces, the resultant account of planetary motion, the mechanical account of motion generally, or the prediction of dynamic processes made possible by the calculus – can be challenging, due both to the mythological terms in which Blake deals with him and to the undoubted power he attributes to Newton's system. Additionally, Blake has left us no testimony of his direct knowledge of Newton's texts, but the frequency of references to the scientist suggest that he, along with his age, saw Newton as the model for materialist scientific thought and the explanatory system known as 'mechanism'. Newton's world-historical significance in Blake's texts is indicated, for instance, in Los's address to Satan in *Milton* – 'Art thou not Newton's Pantocrator?' (4: 11, E 98), borrowing a Pauline term for God – as well as Blake's assigning the scientist the role of blowing the trumpet of the Last Judgment in *Europe* (13: 4–5, E 65). Leading critical expositors of this connection also suggest that Blake acknowledges the force of Newtonian explanation, while seeking to displace it. For Donald Ault, whose *Visionary Physics: Blake's Response to Newton* remains the foundational text on this question, 'in [Blake's] final vision he construes the intellectual structure of Newton's system as a consolidation of the elements of normal perception which attempt to substitute for and fulfill the true drives of the imagination'.[2] Stuart Peterfreund, in *William Blake in a Newtonian World*, also recognises the explanatory power of Newton's formulations for Blake, reminding readers that Blake's notion of the pivotal 'moment of time' is derived from Newton's temporal unit, the fluxion (a connection first suggested by F. B. Curtis).[3] The difference, for Peterfreund, between Blakean and Newtonian worldviews is that what Newton reifies through the figurative logic of metonymy, Blake expands and revitalises by means of metaphor. Thus, for Peterfreund, the Newtonian speaker of 'The Tyger' limits and determines the being of God by his metonymic equation of 'fearful' creature and 'immortal' Creator, a mechanistic mode of thought which unsurprisingly produces a mechanistic God.[4] Both critics persuasively suggest that for Blake's intellectual warfare with Newtonian concepts, the domain of 'normal perception' (what Blake called 'Single vision' (E 722)) remains one fully accounted for by Newtonian premises.

Despite the coherence of these critical accounts, however, and able as they are to describe both Blake's serious engagement with Newton and his ultimate rejection of the Newtonian model, they risk suggesting that Blake's path beyond Newtonian 'normal perception' abandons the empiricist concern for perception altogether, having recourse to either the 'true drives of the imagination' (Ault) or the poetic resources of metaphor (Peterfreund). An alternative account of Blake's critique of Newton, one that remains engaged with sensory experience, can be drawn from a provocative distinction the poet makes in the short late work, 'On Virgil', between 'Mathematic Form' and 'Living Form': 'Mathematic Form is Eternal in the Reasoning Memory. Living Form is Eternal Existence. / Grecian is Mathematic Form / Gothic is Living Form' (E 270). Given Newton's mathematical depictions of motion, of planetary and other objects, in the *Principia Mathematica* and other works, the scientist would seem an apt representative of Mathematic Form,[5] but, as is often the case in Blake, Living Form remains thinly described here. The nature of Living Form might be suggested, however, by reference to the work of another empiricist philosopher, George Berkeley, whom Blake read and annotated,[6] and who proposes a refutation of Newton's gravitational force and its mathematical calculation of motion in a 1721 Latin work *De Motu* (On Motion). While Berkeley's most famous appearance in later literature – Samuel Johnson's 'refutation' of him by kicking a stone – parodies the philosopher as a dreamy idealist, his constant resource in questioning Newton's gravitational force is the standard of experience. For him, a force in matter and an attractive power drawing bodies towards each other are 'occult qualities', artefacts of explanatory regimes not deducible from the perceptible qualities of extension, solidity, and figure. They are improper borrowings from the world of animate beings, beings for whom concepts such as 'force' are given meaning by their own psychological experiences of self-motion, but who err in animating the object world around them. Berkeley does not deny the extraordinary predictive power of the mechanical apparatus of material forces, but suggests that mechanics oversteps its conceptual boundaries when it leaps from mathematical repeatability to a statement about the essential nature of matter: 'For all forces attributed to bodies are mathematical hypotheses just as are attractive forces in planets and sun. But mathematical entities have no stable essence in the nature of things; and they depend on the notion of the definer'.[7] This scepticism about mathematical descriptions of reality seems not so far removed from Blake's demotion of 'Mathematic Form' in favour of 'Living Form'.

What remains when the mathematic calculation of gravitational forces is counted out of court in describing movement is the sheer fact of motion itself, and Berkeley claims that Newtonian mechanical accounts accrete around and ultimately hide the fundamental experience of motion:

> The force of gravitation is not to be separated from momentum; but there is no momentum without velocity, since it is mass multiplied by velocity; again, velocity cannot be understood without motion, and the same holds therefore for the force of gravitation [. . .] In brief, those terms *dead force* and *gravitation* by the aid of metaphysical speculation are supposed to mean something different from moving, moved, motion and rest, but, in point of fact, the supposed difference in meaning amounts to nothing at all. (§11, p. 213)

Berkeley's impatience with 'metaphysical speculation' and his wholesale dispersion of the problems of motion (e.g. Zeno's Paradox), by which 'philosophers have rendered easy things very difficult' (§45, p. 220), places him in a line of thinkers who avoid the Cartesian despair which comes with alienation from one's own senses, a line which must include meditators on motion such as Henri Bergson and Giles Deleuze. Berkeley's insistence on the irreducibility of the perception of movement, his claim that the perception of movement registers the irreducibility of movement itself, point to a cosmology founded on the unalienated access of a perceiving subject to the moving universe it occupies, a cosmology of 'Living Form'. As an explanation of the nature of things, this account of the complementarity of perception and motion seems related to one of the more famous passages in *Milton*, where we are told that '[t]he nature of infinity is this':

> That every thing has its
> Own Vortex; and when once a traveller thro Eternity
> Has passd that Vortex, he perceives it roll backward behind
> His path, into a globe itself infolding; like a sun:
> Or like a moon, or like a universe of starry majesty,
> While he keeps onwards in his wondrous journey on the earth [. . .]
> Thus is the earth one infinite plane, and not as apparent
> To the weak traveller confin'd beneath the moony shade.
> Thus is the heaven a vortex passd already, and the earth
> A vortex not yet pass'd by the traveler thro' Eternity. (15: 21–6, 32–5, E 109)

As if to confront Newton on his own ground of planetary motion, this vagrant astronomical doctrine refuses to submit motion to the ontological priority of objects; rather, objects, including planetary objects, are the epiphenomena of movement, emerging in the perceptual experience of the traveller's passage. The weak Newtonian traveller who calculates the predictable workings of the 'universe of starry majesty' and takes those calculations as a definitive account of things fails to acknowledge his own status as living and moving traveller and fails to see the given world's implication in his own movement. Characterising earth as plane rather than globe (or plane before globe) is not to ally Blake with the Flat Earth Society, but to posit earth as the scene of perceived motion rather than an object of perception, a 'vortex not yet pass'd' but nevertheless an ideal setting for passage.

There are limits to the analogy between Blake's Living Form and Berkeley's irreducible motion, and limits to Blake's sympathies with the philosopher, as Hazard Adams has persuasively suggested in his probing of Blake's annotations to *Siris*. In particular, by locating all the power of animation in the living and perceiving mind, Berkeley effectively de-animates moving objects and thus the moving body:

> [M]any suspect that motion is not mere passivity in bodies. But if we understand by it that which in the movement of a body is an object to the senses, no one can doubt that it is entirely passive. For what is there in the successive existence of body in different places which could relate to action, or be other than bare, lifeless effect? (§49, p. 221)

Where Berkeley's creative mind can ultimately dispense with phenomenal experience, Blake's Spiritual Body never dispenses with the senses, calling them in the annotations to *Siris*, 'the Four Rivers of the Water of Life' (E 663). As Adams notes, next to Berkeley's description of Aristotle's theology being concerned with things 'abstracted and immoveable', Blake marginally objects that 'God is not a Mathematical Diagram' (E 664).[8] The monist Blake extends the power of living form to the bodies of his mythological gods, to the body of the man who is god, Albion, rising to his feet to walk, to the bodies of every 'human form divine' which lives and moves, and to the non-human bodies of 'every thing that lives [and] is Holy' (*Marriage* pl. 27, E 45).

Notes

1. J. Locke, *An Essay Concerning Human Understanding*, ed. P. H. Nidditch (Oxford: Clarendon Press, 1975), II, i, 4. Further references appear in the main text.
2. D. D. Ault, *Visionary Physics: Blake's Response to Newton* (Chicago: University of Chicago Press, 1974), p. 163.

3. See F. B. Curtis, 'Blake and the "Moment of Time": An Eighteenth-Century Controversy in Mathematics', *Philological Quarterly*, 51 (1972), 460–70.
4. S. Peterfreund, *William Blake in a Newtonian World: Essays on Literature as Art and Science* (Norman, OK: University of Oklahoma Press, 1998), pp. 126–38.
5. As Sarah Haggarty kindly reminded me, Northrop Frye suggests another likely source for Mathematical Form in Plato's *Timaeus* (see *Fearful Symmetry: A Study of William Blake* (Princeton: Princeton University Press, 1947; repr. 1990), p. 286).
6. Blake annotated an eccentric work of Berkeley's entitled *Siris: A Chain of Philosophical Reflexions and Inquiries Concerning the Virtues of Tar-Water and Divers Other Subjects Connected Together and Arising One from Another* (1744). Among the 'other subjects' is a critique of Newton's theory of gravitational forces that returns Berkeley to the material of the earlier work *De Motu*, suggesting that Blake at least had access to Berkeley's thoughts on Newton.
7. G. Berkeley, *De Motu*, in *Philosophical Works Including the Works on Vision* (London: J. M. Dent, 1980), §67, p. 226. Further references appear in the main text.
8. H. Adams, *Blake's Margins: An Interpretive Study of the Annotations* (Jefferson, NC: McFarland, 2009), p. 158.

CHAPTER 30

Life Sciences

Denise Gigante

William Blake was actively engaged with the Romantic problematic of life through the developing fields of biological study – anatomy, neurology, physiology, evolutionary morphology, botany, teratology, pathology, medicine, embryology, and embryogenesis among them. He inhabited a historical moment, somewhere between God and cellular biology, when life was still viewed holistically as a power or principle connected to the emergent organism. Only with the development of cell theory, initiated by the publication of Theodor Schwann's *Microscopical Researches* (1839) over a decade after Blake's death, would the study of life shrink from the totality of living form to a smaller independent unit of life, the self-enclosed cell. 'Each cell is', Schwann announced, 'within certain limits, an Individual, an independent Whole.'[1] The cell defined a new whole that was suddenly explicable through the laws of biochemistry. As science moved further into subcellular space, with the discovery of chromosomes and genetics, that unified episteme – the wide-ranging inquiry into the philosophical enigma of life – would break down into separate fields of specialised science. In the meantime, Blake's work formed part of an interdisciplinary inquiry into the meaning of life.

There were various names for the vital power emanating from leading European research centres at this time. In 1757 when Albrecht von Haller demonstrated the powers of sensibility and irritability in muscular and nervous tissues, marking out a path for life study beyond mechanism, the idea of life force (*vis viva*) came into vogue. Two years later, Caspar Friedrich Wolff published *Theoria Generationis*, which named an essential force (*vis essentialis*) responsible for self-organisation that was translated into German in 1764 as an essential power (*Kraft*). Friedrich Casimir Medicus named this life-power *Lebenskraft* in 1774, and in 1789 Johann Friedrich Blumenbach added purpose (*Zweck*) to that power, turning it into a teleological, formative force or drive (*nisus formativus, Bildungstrieb*). Blumenbach's *Über den Bildungstrieb* was translated into English in 1792 by the Scottish physician Alexander Crichton as *An Essay on Generation*, and in 1799 Samuel Taylor Coleridge left England for Göttingen to study with the author.

However Blake may have scorned the French for a type of philosophical materialism that could result, for example, in Julien Offray de La Mettrie's *L'homme machine* (1747), they too had their *forces produtrices*. Georg-Louis Leclerc Comte de Buffon posited the notion of shelf-shaping 'organic particles' in his magisterial, thirty-six volume work of natural history (*Histoire Naturelle*), published in the 1750s. These particles he imagined to be guided by an interior mould (*moule intérieur*), which the Germans interpreted as *Kraft*. Pierre Louis Moreau de Maupertuis, a physicist influenced by Buffon, came up with the idea of a physical force modelled on Newtonian attraction, but equipped with memory that would explain genetic similarities. And Paul-Joseph Barthez, in his *Nouveaux élémens de la science de l'homme* (1778), spoke of a *principe de vie*.

Across the Channel, in London, Blake was active in the intellectual ferment comprising the culture of life science and vitalism. His main connections to this world were his varied and eclectic reading, his attendance at public lectures, his work as an engraver for James Basire, his affiliation with the publisher Joseph Johnson, his studies at the Royal Academy with the anatomist William Hunter, and his dealings with major figures such as John Hunter (William's brother) and Erasmus Darwin, whom he encountered through mutual acquaintances.[2]

As these ties were themselves tangled, let us begin with the pre-eminent British physiologist of the era – the British counterpart to Blumenbach – whom Blake satirised as 'Jack Tearguts', namely John Hunter. From 1782 to 1784, Blake lived with his wife Catherine Sophia (née Boucher) on the corner of Leicester Square, at 23 Green Street, around the corner from Hunter. Both men visited the soirées in the drawing-room of Harriet Mathew and her husband Reverend Anthony S. Mathew. The Mathews' son studied as a medical student with Hunter, and Mathew himself helped to finance Blake's first book, *Poetical Sketches* (1783), which appeared the same year Hunter moved to Leicester Square.

Hunter's wife, Anne Home Hunter, the sister of the physician Sir Everard Home, was herself a poet and songwriter. Blake designed an image for the cover leaf of the musical setting, by Thomas Commins, of Anne's 'Elegy' in 1786.[3] He may have sung with her at the Mathews', or visited the Hunters' garden at Earl Court, where Hunter performed his experiments on the vitality of plants. This work came to fruition in his 1778 lecture, *Of the Heat, &c. of Animals and Vegetables*. Anne refers to it in

'The Mulberry Tree: An Elegy', which describes 'bright ey'd Science' measuring the tree's shade.[4] Hunter did business with Blake's first employer, James Basire, and Blake engraved anatomical specimens in the Hunterian collection, which can be seen today in the Hunterian Museum in London. In *An Island on the Moon*, he satirised Hunter's work as a surgeon:

> I only wish Jack [*Hunter*] Tearguts had the cutting of Plutarch he understands anatomy better than any of the Ancients hell plunge his knife up to the hilt in a single drive and thrust his fist in, and all in the space of a Quarter of an hour. he does not mind their crying – tho they cry ever so hell Swear at them & keep them down with his fist & tell that hell scrape their bones if they dont lay still & be quiet. (E 454)

Blake might not have liked the practice, but he would have respected Hunter's theory of the 'living principle'.

Hunter's first approach to vitalism came in a 1772 essay on posthumous digestion, in which he remarks: 'The diseases which the living body undergoes (mortification excepted) are always connected with the *living principle*, and are not in the least similar to what may be called diseases or changes in the dead body.'[5] By the time of his death in 1793, Hunter had decided that the living principle was superadded to organisation and circulated in the blood. His posthumous *Treatise on the Blood, Inflammation and Gunshot Wounds* (1794) contains a plate with three figures that might seem out of place in a medical work on flesh wounds. Figure 1 of that work contains three sketches of embryological development in eggs, no doubt from the geese he raised, as Amanda Jo Goldstein observes with reference to Blake, 'in order to keep himself flush with mundane eggs for experimental vivisection'.[6]

Writing to request a copy of Hunter's *Treatise*, Samuel Taylor Coleridge registers its impact on the vitalism debate by quoting his own poem written one year after its publication, 'The Eolian Harp' (1795). The lines he quotes are from the poem's climactic epiphany: 'And what if all of animated Nature / Be but organic harps diversely fram'd / That tremble into thought as o'er them sweeps / Plastic & vast &c.'[7] The quotation stops just short of the 'one Life' the poet refers to as responsible for animating nature. In his own *Theory of Life* (1816), Coleridge imagines himself to be standing on the shoulders of John Hunter as the empirical mass of life study from which he drew in his German-influenced theory. Coleridge's friend, the surgeon Joseph Henry Green of Guy's Hospital (also one of John Keats's teachers in medical school) used Coleridge's vitalist *Theory of Life* as the basis for his Hunterian Oration to the Royal College of Surgeons in 1840.

But by the time Hunter died, his idea that the circulatory system contained the principle of life was out of date. Taking the temperature of the times in *An Essay toward a Definition of Animal Vitality* (1793), John Thelwall wrote that, 'from what we are now acquainted with concerning the nervous system, there would be much better reason to suppose, with some later philosophers, that the life of the animal is in the *brain*, rather than in the blood'.[8] Blake had access to theories from emergent fields of life science that were probing the brain for its mysteries. The first was the physiognomy of Johann Kaspar Lavater. He annotated Lavater's *Aphorisms on Man* the same year (1788) that he engraved Lavater's portrait for the frontispiece of Lavater's *Essays on Physiognomy*, translated into French by Henry Hunter and published by Joseph Johnson. Blake engraved four plates for the volume, including a portrait of Democritus (opposite p. 159) by Peter Paul Rubens.[9] Related to physiognomy was the science of phrenology, developed by Johann Gaspar Spurzheim. Phrenologists read the shape of the skull for character, looking for bulging areas of the brain connected to personality characteristics, as physiognomy read the lines of the face. In Spurzheim's *Observations on Insanity* (London 1817), Blake records a vision of a spiritual visitation from the poet William Cowper, who might as well be speaking for Blake to the author: 'O that I were insane always I will never rest. Can you not make me truly insane [. . .] You retain health & yet are as mad as any of us all – over us all – made as a refuge from unbelief – from Bacon Newton & Locke' (E 663). Any reader of Blake will recognise his unholy trinity, empiricist science. Annalise Volpone also argues for the influence of Alexander Crichton's 1798 *An Inquiry into the Nature and Origin of Mental Derangement: Comprehending a Concise System of the Physiology and Pathology of the Human Mind and a History of the Passions and Their Effects*, to which Blake had access through William Hayley's Turret Library in Felpham, on Blake's work and thought.[10] When Blake and his wife, Catherine, returned to London from Felpham, after their residence near Hayley from 1800 to 1803, Catherine was suffering the pains of a rheumatism she had contracted there in their damp, cold cottage. Blake sent her to St Thomas's Hospital for three months of electrical shock treatment by the physician John Birch. Her swollen legs seem to have found some relief from this experimental therapy, for Blake called it 'Electrical Magic' (E 759).

It was the Swiss physiologist Albrecht von Haller who laid the ground for the medical use of electricity in his work on sensibility and irritability in the 1740s. Haller's thesis, *De partibus corporis humani sensibilibus et irritabilibus*, presented to the University of Göttingen in 1752, was promptly translated into German, English, French, Italian, and Swedish, prompting a flood of controversy about the nature of the vital power responsible for nervous reaction and muscle contraction in living or recently deceased organisms.[11] Blake produced a portrait of Haller for Thomas Henry's *Memoir of Albert de Haller* (1783), published by Johnson. He also engraved a portrait of the author for the frontispiece of John Brown's *The Elements of Medicine* (1795), which used Haller's work on sensibility and irritability as the basis for a theory of excitability. Brown gauged health according to the body's capacity to respond to stimula. Overstimulation or understimulation were equally pathological conditions to be treated by the Brunonian system of medicine, first explained in *Elementa Medicinae* (1780). In his dedication to the volume, the editor Thomas Beddoes – Coleridge's friend, English physician, and father of the poet Thomas Love Beddoes – called Brown an 'Unfortunate Genius'.[12] In this, he fared better than Blake, who was dubbed an 'unfortunate lunatic' by Robert Hunt, and a 'quack' by his brother Leigh Hunt, in *The Examiner* (see *BR* 283, 263). The fact that Brown's excitability theory was more influential in Germany than in Britain suggests that the influence of vitalist thinking at the time worked both ways.

Another shady area of Romantic life science was David Hartley's doctrine of vibrations. Blake produced the frontispiece portrait of Hartley for Johnson's 1791 reprint of Hartley's *Observations on Man, His Frame, His Duty and His Expectations* (1749). In it, Hartley had claimed that the medullary substance of the nerves consisted of particles whose agitation produced a vibration in a subtle and elastic ether surrounding them. These caused fainter vibrations in the brain, which produced 'ideas' of sensation, as in John Locke's model of human understanding. Hartley applied Locke's theory of association to the nervous system, arguing that vibrations created by external stimuli, or internally by the heat and flow of the blood, link together, through the physiology of the brain, to produce mind: memory, consciousness, ultimately identity. Blake thought little of Locke's empiricist sensation psychology, but Coleridge thought enough of Hartley to name his first son after him.

In general, Blake rails against 'Demonstration', the method for obtaining the empirical proof required by the inductive method of post-Baconian science. He particularly hated the 'vacuums' produced in the atmosphere through Joseph Priestley's public demonstrations with the air pump, a mechanism that withdrew air from the interior of a glass bell jar by means of a pump. His experiments had unfortunate results on small animals, such as birds and mice, trapped in the bell jar. *An Island in the Moon* is a satire of the Lunar Society to which Priestly belonged, and in it Blake caricatures Priestly as 'Inflammable Gass the wind finder' (E 449).

He is just one of several loony scientists on the lunar island, who descend directly from Jonathan Swift's satire, in the third book of *Gulliver's Travels*, of the Royal Society virtuosi as crack-brained inhabitants of a floating island. Blake's Inflammable Gass 'gases on' like a windbag for half an hour about 'a bottle of air' in his possession containing a plague (E 451). Blake calls the plague 'Flogiston', a reference to Priestley's 'dephlogistated air' or oxygen. Given the fact that Priestley and his wife Mary Wilkinson emigrated from Europe to America in 1794, one may think of the engraved plates in *America: A Prophecy* and *Europe: A Prophecy*, both produced also in 1794, that depict a man pouring out a black plague that spreads through sheaves of grain. When the lunar experimenters in *An Island on the Moon* break the jar of the air pump, Gass panics: 'He saw the Pesilence fly out of the bottle & cried out we are putrified, we are corrupted. our lungs are destroyd with the Flogiston' (E 462).

The last major figure that fills out the picture of Blake's relation to contemporary life science was another member of the Lunar Society: the polymath Erasmus Darwin. Darwin spoke of a 'spirit of animation' in *Zoonomia, or, The Laws of Organic Life* (1794–6). He speculated about certain life-creating and preserving powers (*vis fabricatrix* and *vis conservaatrix*) that might provide evidence for the possibility that 'the world itself might have been generated, rather than created', which is a possibility that Blake explores artistically in *The First Book of Urizen*.[13] Blake engraved plates for Darwin's *The Botanic Garden; with Philosophic Notes*, published by Johnson in 1791. The work is a poem in two parts, *The Loves of the Plants* (1789) and *The Economy of Vegetation* (1791), which contains extensive footnotes explaining Darwin's theories of vegetation and generation – two of the most important concepts in Blake's longest illuminated prophecies, *Milton* and *Jerusalem: The Emanation of the Giant Albion*. The former, begun one year after Darwin's *The Temple of Nature* (1803), opens with the figure of Albion 'slain upon his Mountains / And in his Tent, thro envy of Living Form' (E 96). The latter is obsessed not only with 'Vegetation' and 'Generation', but also with 'Regeneration', the capacity of a plant or animal to reproduce parts that have been destroyed: the aim is to restore Albion from a lifeless mechanism to living form. Blake's own artistic experiments with organicism and living form began with the production of his illuminated books, starting with the *Songs of Innocence* (1789), in which letters sprout organically into vegetable and human forms. Close study reveals that biological conceptions of life and its origins provide *the* context for understanding Blake's concept of organic, or living, form.

Notes

1. T. Schwann, *Microscopical Researches into the Accordance in the Structure and Growth of Animals and Plants*, trans. H. Smith (1847; New York: Kraus, 1969), p. 2.
2. On Blake's relationship to the former, see J. M. Oppenheimer, *New Aspects of John and William Hunter* (London: Heinemann Medical Books, 1946); to the latter, D. King-Hele, *Erasmus Darwin and the Romantic Poets* (Houndsmills: Macmillan, 1986).
3. See the intaglio copperplate engraving for *An Elegy Set to Music* by Thomas Commins, pub. 1 July 1786 by J. Fentum (The Morgan Library and Museum).
4. For a helpful discussion, see S. A. Rispoli, 'Anatomy Vitality, and the Romantic Body: Blake, Coleridge, and the Hunter Circle, 1750–1840', Ph.D. diss., University of North Carolina at Chapel Hill, 2014.
5. J. Hunter, 'On the Digestion of the Stomach after Death', *Philosophical Transactions of the Royal Society*, 62 (1772), 447–54 (p. 447); my emphasis.
6. A. J. Goldstein, *Sweet Science: Romantic Materialism and the New Logics of Life* (Chicago: University of Chicago Press, 2017), p. 241.
7. J. Engell and W. J. Bate (eds.), *The Collected Works of Samuel Taylor Coleridge*, vol. 1 (Princeton: Princeton University Press, 1969), pp. 294–5.
8. J. Thelwall, *An Essay toward a Definition of Animal Vitality; Read at the Theatre, Guy's Hospital, January 26, 1793* (London: 1793), p. 15.
9. S. Erle, *Blake, Lavater and Physiognomy*, Studies in Comparative Literature 21 (Cambridge: Legenda, 2010).
10. A. Volpone, 'William Blake's Last Prophetic Books and Contemporary Brain Science', in I. Natali and A. Volpone (eds.), *Symptoms of Disorder: Reading Madness in British Literature, 1744–1845* (Amherst: Cambria, 2016), pp. 67–94.
11. H. Steinke, *Irritating Experiments: Haller's Concept and the European Controversy on Irritability and Sensibility, 1750–90* (New York: Rodopi, 2005), p. 364.
12. J. Brown, *The Elements of Medicine*, ed. T. Beddoes, 2 vols. (London: Joseph Johnson 1795), I, v.
13. E. Darwin, *Zoonomia; or, The Laws of Organic Life*, 4th edn, 2 vols. (Philadelphia: Edward Earle, 1818), I, 393, 401.

CHAPTER 31

London

Saree Makdisi

'I write in South Molton Street, what I both see and hear / In regions of Humanity, in Londons opening streets', Blake writes in *Jerusalem* (pl. 34, E 180). In fact, London appears throughout the work of its greatest poet, from the 'charter'd Thames' and 'flowers of London town' of *Songs of Innocence and of Experience* to the often darker and more complex lines of *Milton* and *Jerusalem* ('London', E 26; 'Holy Thursday', E 13). We see Los traverse the metropolis, for example, from 'Highgate thro Hackney & Holloway towards London', then on eastward to 'Stratford & thence Stepney & the Isle of Leuthas Dogs', before circling back to 'the winding places of deep contemplation intricate' where 'the Tower of London frownd dreadful over Jerusalem' (*Jerusalem* pl. 45, E 194). Certain urban or then suburban districts come up repeatedly in *Jerusalem* (e.g. Westminster, Battersea, Chelsea, Marylebone, Lambeth), and the text assigns great significance to particular sites, such as Tyburn or the Tower or London Stone – later, and largely because of Blake himself, a point of obsession for post-modern London writers including Iain Sinclair, Peter Ackroyd, and China Miéville.

Blake's London was a city of enormous transformation. This sense of change is referred to not only in Blake's poetry but also in his private letters. Sometimes this is positive, as for instance in an 1803 letter to Hayley where Blake notes, following his return from his sojourn on the south coast, that 'the shops in London improve; everything is elegant, clean, and neat; the streets are widened where they were narrow; even Snow Hill is become almost level, and is a very handsome street, and the narrow part of the Strand near St. Clement's is widened and become very elegant' (26 October 1803, E 738). And sometimes it is less so: 'In London every calumny and falsehood utter'd against another of the same trade is thought fair play', Blake complains in another letter to Hayley just a few months later; 'Engravers, Painters, Statuaries, Printers, Poets, we are not in a field of battle, but in a City of Assassinations' (28 May 1804, E 751). Indeed,

Blake's London was at once a city of dramatic improvements (albeit only a foretaste of the great transformations that the second half of the nineteenth century would bring) and a city of great, and increasing, difficulty for many – possibly even most – of its inhabitants: something Blake would have been acutely aware of as he moved around the metropolis either on his regular walks or, more gradually and over a span of years, as he and Catherine shifted their place of residence from one area to another (though generally, as we shall see, in keeping with a consistent geographical logic).

For one thing, London's population was beginning its vast expansion during Blake's lifetime, a phenomenon he and his fellow-citizens would have felt in the most intimate and personal ways. At the dawn of the nineteenth century, London had a million inhabitants and was already by far the largest city in Europe; despite high mortality rates, especially among children, its overall population would increase by 100,000 or so every year, jumping past five million by the last third of the nineteenth century, and on to seven million by the turn of the twentieth.[1] This expansion and its consequent pressure on Blake's city was not just a matter of sheer numbers, however. Many of those walking, riding, or stumbling into London through his lifetime were country people wholly unprepared for life in a great city and overwhelmed by what they discovered there.[2] Moreover, the city's physical and above all its infrastructural development lagged far behind the needs and pressures of its exponentially growing population: people found themselves living in altogether inhuman circumstances, packed together sometimes two or three to a bed – never mind a room – in densely populated slums entirely incapable of sustaining life in a healthy manner: not without reason did Cobbett refer to the city as 'the great wen'.[3] Water supplies, especially in the roughest districts, were contaminated with filth, and sewage systems in the modern sense were unheard of (both would be developed much later); the combination led to outbreaks of disease. Jobs, money, and food were all – for tens if not hundreds of thousands of people – haphazard, catch as catch can.[4]

We tend to think of eighteenth- and nineteenth-century London as somehow always already modern, but in fact Blake's London was a city of contradiction as well as of change: on the one hand, a city of intensive and active modernisation (including the sorts of improvement Blake sometimes refers to in his letters) and, on the other hand, a city of intense difficulty and privation and brutalisation, if not outright assassination.

Thus although we often think of the growing cities of the Midlands and beyond as the hubs of industrial modernisation in England, London was – and would remain through Blake's lifetime – the centre of modern manufacturing in the entire country, if not the world. It was the industrial city par excellence and employed hundreds of thousands of manufacturing workers. London had, and until much later in the nineteenth century it would retain, more steam engines than any other city, and its manufacturing production would remain unrivalled until at least the 1850s. Its port was – and until the twentieth century it too would remain – by far the most important in Britain: the centre of commercial and industrial activity not only for the nation but also for an expanding empire gradually spanning the entire planet. London's docks also experienced a vast expansion through Blake's lifetime, which left its indelible mark on the cityscape with the construction of the West India Docks on the Isle of Dogs in 1799, the London Docks at Wapping in 1805, the East India Docks a little downriver at Blackwall in 1806, the massive walled Tobacco Dock in 1811, and, close to 'the winding places of deep contemplation intricate' in the shadow of the Tower, St Katherine's Docks, which were being constructed in the final years of Blake's life and would open the year after he died (*Jerusalem* 45: 22, E 194).[5]

For all its modern industrial and commercial prowess, however, London was also in Blake's lifetime a city of scavengers and beggars, a city of those living precariously on (or over) the margins of civilised life. Some might consider this to be a sign of London's lingering resistance to modernisation, but actually this widespread precariousness, as our own time demonstrates, is one of the hallmarks of modernity, however much it might be overshadowed by the glimmering towers and spectacles to which we devote such attention. In fact the number of Londoners living in such circumstances grew exponentially through Blake's lifetime and on into the nineteenth century as the city's population continued to increase while, like the infrastructure itself, the number and availability of decent jobs lagged far behind what was needed.

The greatest authority on this side of London life, Henry Mayhew, would publish his minutely detailed documentation of the London poor a couple of decades after Blake died, but, especially given that Mayhew notes how many forms of scavenging had already gone extinct by the 1850s, we may safely assume that London streetlife in Blake's time was not dramatically different from that of his own. 'Those who obtain their living in the streets of the metropolis are a very large and varied class', Mayhew notes, 'indeed, the means resorted to in order "to pick up a crust", as the people call it, in the public thoroughfares (and such in many instances it *literally* is) are so multifarious that the mind is long baffled in its attempts to reduce them to scientific order or classification.' He recounts a bewildering number of finely graded forms of occupation in London's streets, including highly specialised costermongers (ranging from those, like Hannah More's Betty Brown, who sell fruits and vegetables, to those selling everything from clothes pegs and bonnet boxes to stationary and last dying speeches). In addition to these, he documents a staggering number and variety of street wanderers, including street performers, street artisans, chimney sweepers, working pedlars, crossing-sweepers, lamp-lighters, tinkers, dustmen, street musicians, ballad singers, prostitutes, and the many classes of street scavengers and finders – numbering in their thousands – who literally picked up their sources of subsistence in the public thoroughfares, including 'the "pure" pickers, or those who live by gathering dogs' dung; the cigar-end finders, or "hard-ups", as they are called, who collect the refuse pieces of smoked cigars from the gutters, and having dried them, sell them as tobacco to the very poor; the dredgermen or coal-finders; the mud-larks, the bone-grubbers; and the sewer-hunters'.[6]

The 'blank confusion' Wordsworth found in this (London's 'Parliament of Monsters', as he called it in Book VII of the *Prelude*) appears in a different form in Blake's work, much more quietly and subtly. Wordsworth found the noise and sheer variety of London – 'the same perpetual whirl / Of trivial objects, melted and reduced / To one identity, by differences / That have no law, no meaning, and no end' – bewildering and overwhelming.[7] But Wordsworth was a dullard and a country boy, whereas Blake was a sharp-eyed Londoner born and bred. The sights and sounds of London, which he took for granted, operate generally in the background of his work, though they do come to the surface, for instance, in the cries of the chimney sweeper, the harlot and the soldier in 'London' in *Songs of Experience*, and, of course, in the 'marks of weakness, marks of woe' the narrator of that poem sees and hears 'In every cry of every Man, / In every Infants cry of fear, / In every voice: in every ban' (ll. 4–7, E 26–7).

For Blake's work consistently returns to the logic of London, even if that logic was not always visible. In fact it has to be admitted that it sometimes seemed altogether absent, especially in those tumultuous years of the late eighteenth and early nineteenth centuries. Blake's London was, after all, not a single city with a single governing authority, but a sprawling mess of urban and suburban conglomeration spanning literally dozens of different local authorities with widely varying, greater or (usually) lesser, degrees of actual governance. The City of London and, to its west, the city of Westminster had the greatest degrees of political and administrative development, particularly the former. But in between and all around them there were districts and parishes with the barest minimum of coordination and regulation, and it was in these areas that much of the overall growth both of population and of construction took place. As London grew and started absorbing what had once been outlying villages (Kensington, Chelsea, Hampstead, etc.), there was no attempt at any kind of central coordination or planning. There was no authority in charge of street names or house numbers, and these developed without any kind of coherence, so that people had to rely on informal methods of asking directions or finding their way with reference to well-known landmarks. There was no authority in charge of paving, lighting, street maintenance, water, sewerage, or even police (Robert Peel would not lead the charge to form the Metropolitan Police until two years after Blake's death, and the Metropolitan Board of Works would not be formed until the 1850s, and the London County Council not until the 1880s). There were not even accurate maps of the metropolis, and the existing ones (including Horwood's great 1799 map) included streets that did not exist while eliding some that did, especially in the poorer districts, where maps quite simply gave up and broke down into an incoherent jumble.[8]

As a result, urban growth and development took place haphazardly as this or that developer randomly convinced this or that great landowner to develop part or all of their estate in what would become the sprawling expanse of London. The greatest such development in Blake's time was John Nash's Regent Street project, which tore a great gash right through Blake's beloved Soho and yielded not only Regent Street itself but also Piccadilly Circus and Oxford Circus and a number of other developments from Waterloo Place at its southern end to Regent's Park at its northern limit (which also marked at the time the northern edge of London, beyond which there were still open fields). Other developments would come later and would completely transform the topography and layout of the city to the one we are familiar with today, which Blake would have found baffling, but those later projects all have their roots in the kinds of development that were already taking place in Blake's London, as people in impoverished districts were unhoused and narrow streets demolished to make way for wider boulevards.

At the same time, the Thames came to be spanned by new bridges. Until shortly before Blake was born, only London Bridge crossed the river, and watermen used to ferry people back and forth at other crossings with no great efficiency. Blackfriars and Westminster bridges were added later in the eighteenth century, and, in Blake's time, new bridges went across at Battersea, Southwark, Vauxhall, and Hammersmith, as well as Waterloo Bridge in 1817. All these bridges facilitated what was and would remain through Blake's life the primary mode of transport in the city: walking (the omnibus, horse-drawn tram and eventually the train would all come later). These new developments of course facilitated the development of the city on a wide scale and in particular enabled growth south of the Thames, including in Lambeth, where Blake lived for several of his most productive years.

The growth, development, and government of London may have been haphazard in Blake's life, but that does not mean there was not a certain kind of logic at work in the metropolis, into which Blake's work taps at various levels. This logic is first spelled out in 'London', which traces the networks of surveillance and power shaping the city's distribution of space, and Blake returns to it at much greater length in *Jerusalem*, where we can see the tensions between London, Golgonooza, and Jerusalem, all of which are versions or expressions of different aspects of the same gritty urban reality that Blake lived and knew so well.

Think of the 'charter'd streets' Blake traces in 'London'. What he is getting at here is the distribution of commercial activity through the city: the way in which capital and labour, space and time, are distributed across the metropolis. There was a certain consistency to this that endures, albeit in altered form, up to our own time. Certain kinds of work were concentrated in particular districts across London. Tanneries and leather factories were clustered around Southwark; jewellery, watches, and fine instruments were produced in Clerkenwell; Spitalfields had its silk-weavers and associated industries; furniture makers were concentrated around Shoreditch and shoemakers around Bethnal Green; West Ham and the nearby Lea Valley had various noxious industries including rubber, glue, paint, and matches (made famous by the great strike at Bryant and May's factory later in the nineteenth century). Publishers were concentrated in various areas including the district of St Paul's Churchyard, where Blake would have often visited Joseph Johnson, and Fleet Street would remain, at least until the advent of Rupert Murdoch, synonymous with printing and journalism in particular.[9]

Nor, as Blake reminds us, was the Thames itself any less chartered than the city's streets. We have already seen how ports and docks spread up and down the river through Blake's lifetime, and there were countless associated trades and industries, most obviously shipbuilding and maintenance, which also grew extensively through this period. But the river was also a site of many other kinds of industry, as were its tributaries and the various canals connecting waterways together, including coal warehousing, gasworks, and corn and flour mills. The Albion Flour Mills near Blackfriars were the first in England to use steam engines. They were torched by rioters in 1791,[10] and Blake would have passed their burned-out ruins every time he crossed the Thames to and from Lambeth through the tumultuous decade that he lived there. Lambeth itself may have once been the site of open fields and quaint churches, but in the nineteenth century it became home to noisome candle and soap factories, printing presses, laundries, breweries, mills, and factories producing sauces and meat extracts.

Part of the same logic that dispersed the most noxious and unhealthy forms of production to the city's margins was the concentration of fine houses and high-class shops in the City, along the Strand, and in particular on both sides of Piccadilly in St James's (where Blake was baptised) and Mayfair (along the northern fringe of which he lived in South Molton Street for several years later in his life). In fact no account of Blake's London would be complete without some account of the various neighbourhoods Blake and Catherine lived in through their relatively long life together. Blake was born and grew up in Soho, on Broad Street, at the corner of today's Broadwick and Marshall streets. For the seven years of his apprenticeship to James Basire, he was based at Great Queen Street, at the northeastern edge of the area around Covent Garden, near what is today the Kingsway (which then did not exist). He then moved back for a couple of years to his parents' house in Soho, and then, after marrying Catherine, moved to Green Street (today's Irving Street), on the southeast edge of Leicester Square, which now seems separate from Soho because of Shaftesbury Avenue, which splits today's Soho from Chinatown – but in Blake's day there was no Shaftesbury Avenue, Chinatown (such as it was then) was closer to the docks, and the area around Leicester Square would have been sociogeographically continuous with Soho. From there, the Blakes moved back to the heart of Soho, first back to Broad Street and then to nearby Poland Street. They then moved across the river to Hercules Buildings in Lambeth, and then on to Felpham for three years (the only time Blake did not live in London), then back to London, first to South Molton Street, for seventeen years – the longest time Blake and Catherine lived in any one place, and their last surviving London residence – and then, finally, to Fountain Court, off the Strand (see *BR* Appendix 2: 'Blake Residences', 733–56).

There is a discernable pattern to Blake's London residences. Soho always remained the centre of gravity of his life: almost all of the places he and Catherine lived for the rest of their lives were within half a mile of where he was born. The only exceptions were Felpham (which anyway was an unusual departure from the pattern) and Lambeth –

but that was not much more than a mile from Soho, an insignificant distance for a prodigious walker like Blake. Life in and around Soho offered Blake a privileged location from which to assess the changes taking place across the entire city. For one thing, it was (and remains) at the geographical centre of the metropolis, with Whitechapel about two miles to the east and Kensington about two miles to the west. And Soho immediately abutted districts of both unspeakable squalor (St Giles's) and nearly unimaginable wealth and privilege (St James's and Mayfair), so the socioeconomic spectrum of the metropolis could also be assessed from its vantage point.

The meaning of Soho became even clearer in the final decade of Blake's life with the opening of Regent Street, which was explicitly intended to demarcate a line of separation spatially distinguishing London's different social strata from one another. All through the period of the Regent Street construction, Blake lived just to the west on South Molton Street, so he would have seen this line of social and class demarcation solidifying and hardening in parallel with the social and political attitudes rising to hegemony at the time – to which he was intensely sensitive – as he came and went between Mayfair and Soho (which would eventually find itself on the wrong side of the line of demarcation). By the time Regent Street was complete, he and Catherine would move for the last time to Fountain Court, off the Strand, from which he could catch a view across the Thames to Lambeth, where he would have seen many dark Satanic mills gradually encroaching on the area where he had spent his most productive and prosperous years.

Thus although Blake is sometimes configured by scholars as one of those stereotypical Romantic poets about whose commitment to Nature one hears so much, he was one of the most profoundly urban writers of his or any other generation. He bore witness to the beginning of the great transformation of London as the metropolis was reborn into the dynamic global city it is today – with all the ineradicable political, racial, class, and social tensions that development and globalisation have always involved, all of which find forms of expression in his work.

Notes

1. See R. Porter, *London: A Social History* (London: Penguin, 1994), pp. 226–7.
2. See F. Sheppard, *London 1800–1870: The Infernal Wen* (Berkeley, CA: University of California Press, 1971), pp. 1–45.
3. W. Cobbett, *Rural Rides* (London: 1853), p. 42.

4. See G. Stedman Jones, *Outcast London: A Study in the Relationship between Classes in Victorian Society* (New York: Pantheon, 1984), pp. 52–66.
5. On London's docks, see J. Marriott, *Beyond the Tower: A History of East London* (New Haven, CT: Yale University Press, 2011), esp. pp. 94–122.
6. H. Mayhew, *London Labour and the London Poor* (London: 1861), pp. 3–6.
7. W. Wordsworth, *The Prelude* (1850), in J. Wordsworth, M. H. Abrams, and S. Gill (eds.), *The Prelude 1799, 1805, 1850* (New York and London: Norton, 1979), VII, 718, 722–8.
8. For more on maps and mapping, see S. Makdisi, 'William Blake, Charles Lamb, and Urban Anti-Modernity', *SEL: Studies in English Literature*, 56.4 (2016), 737–56.
9. See Marriott, *Beyond the Tower*.
10. Porter, *London*, p. 233.

CHAPTER 32

Money

Matthew Rowlinson

In his early satire *An Island in the Moon* (*c.* 1784–5), Blake represents himself in caricature as a Cynic philosopher, whose name is also a slang term for money: Quid.[1] Quid's rants send up his creator's ambitions as a poet – 'I think that Homer is bombast & Shakespeare is too wild & Milton has no feelings they might be easily outdone' (E 455) – and as an engraver and publisher: 'then said he I would have all the writing Engraved instead of Printed & at every other leaf a high finished print all in three Volumes folio, & sell them at a hundred pounds a piece. they would Print off two thousand' (E 465). This passage anticipates the replacement of letterpress with relief engraving in Blake's illuminated books, and to that extent must be taken seriously as a clue to his plans. But in the size of the edition it describes, and especially in the envisioned price of a hundred pounds, it adopts the same mode of hyperbole as the earlier references to Homer, Shakespeare, and Milton. Later, Blake would speak and write with embarrassment of selling his works for money, and in his mature work he mounts a sustained critique of exchange and abstraction. *An Island in the Moon*'s portrait of the artist as a young entrepreneur does not necessarily contradict the later work; hyperbole and embarrassment both register Blake's ambivalent relation to money and to the new technologies and business models he saw transforming the production and sale of printed images.

Britain in Blake's time did not possess a single homogenous monetary system; the medium of exchange differed for large and small payments, and different trades, classes, and regions had different circulations. The monetary question became a political flashpoint in 1797 with the passage of the Bank Restriction Act, which responded to the outflow of gold from Britain during the war with revolutionary France by suspending the legal requirement that Bank of England notes be redeemable on demand in gold or silver coin. But throughout the eighteenth century, the inhomogeneity of the monetary system had led Britons to strongly held identifications with particular forms of currency: of this period, one could almost say, tell me what money you use and I will tell you who you are. One of J. C. Lavater's *Aphorisms*, published in England in 1789, was interpreted by Blake very much in this way. Lavater wrote that 'Men convey their character not seldom in their pockets'; Blake's marginal note reads, 'I seldom carry money in my pockets they are generally full of paper' (E 599). For Blake at this date 'money' meant the mix of precious metal and token coin that was the ordinary medium of exchange for retail trade and for the payment of wages. Banknotes were prohibited in England for sums under £10, so for the bulk of the population most everyday transactions were carried out in coin, including a badly dilapidated circulation of silver and, for larger amounts, smaller but more frequent issues of guineas, the gold coin first issued in 1663, whose value had been pegged by law at 21s. since 1717. The 'paper' that filled Blake's pockets in 1789 would not have included banknotes, and seems likely to refer to notes of hand and bills of exchange, forms of negotiable debt that in the cash-poor environment of eighteenth-century trade frequently served as money-substitutes.[2]

After the Restriction Act, the gold and silver circulation was in significant part replaced by banknotes. The gold guinea effectively disappeared from circulation to be hoarded or exported. After 1803, it was no longer minted; when in 1807 a special issue of guineas was produced for export to pay Wellington's troops in the Iberian Peninsula, their value had increased to 27s. The divergence of the nominal value of the currency from its actual value in precious metal was the subject of intense political controversy throughout the first two decades of the nineteenth century, occasioning the Report of the Parliamentary Bullion Committee in 1810, David Ricardo's response 'The High Price of Bullion, a Proof of the Depreciation of Bank Notes' (1810), and William Cobbett's bestselling *Paper Against Gold* (1810–11; coll. edn 1815), among many other titles.

The transition to a paper circulation accelerated the financial revolution that drove early capitalism in eighteenth-century England and was a crucial step in the emergence of a homogenous British currency, in which the pound as an abstraction, distinct from any specific material embodiment, became the uniform medium of exchange. The Restriction Act established that this system was in the last instance regulated by the Bank of England, even though in Blake's lifetime most paper currency was issued by privately owned banks with a regional base of operations. During the Restriction era (1797–1821), these acquired a new economic importance as the main issuers of currency, which they used to expand their loan portfolios. The banking industry as a whole expanded; in 1810 Cobbett complained that while in 1797 there had been 230 provincial banks in

England, as he wrote the number had grown to 721.³ Transfers of funds between regions during this period were carried out by bills of exchange; a national market for bills was made by the quasi-banking firm of Overend and Guerney, founded in 1800, which quickly became England's most important financial institution beside the Bank of England.

Like other artists working in commodity cultures in his time and since, Blake condemned money in works that he nonetheless made for sale. By setting his work in the context of monetary history, we see a registration of this contradiction in his descriptions of the antithesis between money and imagination in terms that are themselves imaginative. Even as the coin disappeared from circulation, the guinea remained Blake's typical figure for money, always described with attention to its material properties: brilliance, tactility, size. In a 1799 letter to the Rev. Dr John Trusler, who refused Blake's designs because he found too much 'Fancy' in them (*Stranger* 181), Blake wrote: 'I see Every thing I paint in This World, but Every body does not see alike. To the Eyes of a Miser a Guinea is more beautiful than the Sun & a bag worn with the use of Money has more beautiful proportions than a Vine filled with Grapes' (E 702). Again, in 1808, Blake wrote: 'I assert that for My self I do not behold the Outward Creation & that to me it is hindrance & [. . .] as the Dirt upon my feet [. . .] What it will be Questiond When the Sun rises do you not see a round Disk of fire somewhat like a Guinea O no no I see an Innumerable company of the Heavenly host crying Holy Holy Holy is the Lord God Almighty' (E 565–6). In both of these passages, Blake disclaims seeing guineas, while giving an intensely visualised representation of them.

Guineas were not only important to Blake as a figure for 'Outward Creation'. He reckoned the value of his work in guineas and fractions of a guinea throughout his life, even when they were no longer in circulation.⁴ In a list of work Blake completed as an apprentice engraver, for instance, his biographer includes two quarto engravings completed in 1796 at £2.2.0 apiece – that is, two pounds and two shillings, or two guineas (*Stranger* 66). The prices Blake charged for his early illuminated books in 1793 were listed in his Prospectus in shillings (E 693), with the highest being half a guinea (10s. 6d.), reflecting his belief that printing from relief etchings would enable him to sell his books at a lower cost than letterpress editions with separately printed intaglio plates. After the turn of the century, Blake's prices increased, as the demand for his work proved to come from a small circle of predominantly professional-class patrons, for whom he typically printed individual copies of the work, often with unique hand-colouring. Prices listed in a letter of 1818 ranged from £3.3s. (3 guineas) each for *Innocence* and *Experience* to £10.10s. for *Milton* (Blake to Dawson Turner, 9 June 1818, E 771). When Blake is setting a price on his work, then, he reckons in guineas; that this practice accompanies and perhaps reflects embarrassment about selling it at all appears in an anecdote from 1826, when Blake was living in near-poverty. The diarist Henry Crabb Robinson records how 'He told me my copy of his Songs [*of Innocence and of Experience*] wo^d be 5 Guas [guineas] And was pleased by my man^r of reciev^g this inform^n[.] he spoke of his horror of Money. Of his turning pale when money had been offerd him &c &c &c' (*BR* 435).

By reckoning in guineas when pricing his work, Blake identifies it not with a numerical abstraction, but with a determinate number of a specific gold coin – a coin that, for most of the period under discussion, was no longer in circulation. Blake's gold guineas substitute the idea of a material thing for an abstract unit of account, or for its representation on a paper note or bill. That Blake's concern is to imagine the exchange value of his art in terms of material particulars, rather than abstractions, emerges from the fact that he reckons differently when not directly setting prices on his works. In 1804 he asks William Hayley for a loan: 'I must now [. . .] beg the favor of some more of the needful the favor of ten Pounds more will carry me through this Plate & the Head of Romney for which I am already paid' (E 755). The transactions relating to Blake recorded in surviving account books also show some loans, as well as many payments on account, reckoned in pounds (see, e.g. *BR* 790). It would be good to know the medium in which these transactions were carried out; it would almost certainly have been paper, and on at least one occasion there is evidence of Blake's being paid with a promissory note (*BR* 771).

The nearer Blake is to writing about his work as an object of purchase and sale, however, the more he tends to reckon its value in guineas. In this respect, Blake's accounts and price lists are of a piece with his art, where money is always materialised as gold coin. We saw an example from his writing in the letter to Trusler; the few images of money he produced follow the same rule, as in the heap of coins in the watercolour illustrations of Gray's 'The Bard' he made in 1797–8 (p. 12; WBA obj. 64), or the 1805–6 illustration of Job 42:11 ('every man also gave him a piece of money, and every one an earring of gold'), where money is represented by coins in a sack, forming together with a gold earring and an urn an image materialising the concept of money as a store of value (see *Illustrations to the Book of Job*, The Butts Set (*c.* 1805–6, 1821–7; WBA obj. 19)).

In representing pieces of money as things, and things as pieces of money, Blake denies the growing abstraction of money from any specific material embodiment that characterised the English monetary system in the late eighteenth and early nineteenth centuries. In this respect, his representation of money is of a piece with his entire *oeuvre*, in which he throughout rejects abstraction and asserts, as Saree Makdisi puts it, that 'all being exists in "minute particulars"'.[5] Makdisi connects this motif in Blake's thought to his use of relief etching in making his illuminated books. Unlike letterpress editions, Blake's books do not aspire to uniformity between copies: changes in the colour and quantity of ink between impression, changes in the plates over time, and Blake's hand colouring ensure that no two impressions of any of his etched plates are identical. The contrast with the intaglio engraving techniques that were perfected in the late eighteenth century and used to produce paper money has been noted by Robert Essick: 'In these prints, both craftsmen and publisher wanted complete uniformity among all impressions – a mechanical uniformity that found its ultimate and most artistically deadening expression in banknote engraving'.[6] In contrast, Makdisi writes, 'the illuminated books constitute a body made up of minute particulars, each of which flourishes in and through its relationship to all the others; they constitute a body of differentiated and infinitely proliferating "identities" that share a common essence', rather than referring to a single ontologically prior abstraction.[7]

The critique of abstraction embodied in Blake's works does not of course only refer to monetary history. It also marks a general rejection of major tendencies in the print culture of his day. In the field of textual production, these were the divorce between publishing and the direct production and sale of printed books, and the emergence of text in the abstract as a form of value independent of any specific material embodiment.[8] In the field of the image, the period was characterised by the high technical development of intaglio engraving, and the emergence of print workshops, like those of Rudolph Ackerman and John Boydell, where large editions of identical images were produced and often coloured by teams of anonymous craftsmen, whose individual labour was subsumed into a corporate product.[9]

The thingly and particular character of Blake's work joins it by unusually thick ties to the material and social context of his life. We know that Blake's relations with the purchasers of his works, with employers who hired him as an engraver, and with his patrons, were typically mediated by money – though on at least two occasions patrons made part-payments to him in coal (*Stranger* 398). But the works themselves, in their materiality, do not resolve into the interchangeability that characterises money in the abstract, such that a pound is a pound.[10] Differing from each other, the different copies of Blake's works embody different relations with the people around him who became their owners, resisting the homogenisation of human relations mediated by money alone.

Even money, however, is never purely abstract. It can, for instance, turn into a collectible. And, of course, collectibles can turn into money. The materiality and non-interchangeabilty of Blake's works are the very traits that have since the nineteenth century made Blake scholarship inseparable from institutions of collecting and connoisseurship in which money plays a central role. The journal *Blake / An Illustrated Quarterly* annually publishes Robert Essick's survey of important recent sales and acquisitions under the title 'Blake in the Marketplace'. Today, were such a thing to come on the market, any of the illuminated books printed by Blake would probably be worth over a million US dollars,[11] more than fulfilling the youthful Blake's self-satirical rant on his plans to sell books for £100 a piece. Wealthy collectors including J. Paul Getty, Paul Mellon, and Pierpont Morgan have over the last century and a half assembled the great Blake archives which make modern scholarship on his work possible, and which provide the basis for its remediation in digital form, most notably in the Blake Archive <www.blakearchive.org>. This extraordinary scholarly resource makes high-quality scans of Blake's works available to anyone with access to the World Wide Web. Copyright in artefacts reproduced in the Archive, however, remains the property of their owners, as an abstract form of value legally joined to but distinct from the material object on which it based. Like Blake in his own time, scholars and collectors today can find the money values that shadow his work embarrassing.[12] The unstable and politically charged relation of technological reproduction to materiality, abstraction, and monetary value remains intrinsic to the historically unfolding meanings of Blake's works, as it has been since they were made.

Note

1. J. Viscomi notes the monetary meaning of 'Quid': 'Blake's Invention of Illuminated Printing, 1788', *BRANCH: Britain, Representation and Nineteenth-Century History*, ed. D. Franco Felluga. www.branchcollective.org/?ps_articles=joseph-viscomi-blakes-invention-of-illuminated-printing-1788. He is incorrect, though, in assuming that the term has always referred to a pound, as it does today. In the eighteenth century it could refer to a guinea or other coin; see 'quid, n.', *OED Online*, Oxford University Press, June 2017, www.oed.com/view/Entry/156468.

2. On the connection between the idea of 'character' and circulating paper currency in eighteenth-century England, see M. C. Finn, *The Character of Credit: Personal Debt in English Culture, 1740–1914* (Cambridge: Cambridge University Press, 2003).
3. W. Cobbett, *Paper against Gold and Glory against Prosperity*, 2 vols. (London: J. M'Creery, 1815), 1, 460.
4. Blake's pricing in guineas was not unusual. Fine art and other high-end retail prices in the UK were often given in guineas right up until decimalisation in 1971.
5. S. Makdisi, *William Blake and the Impossible History of the 1790s* (Chicago: University of Chicago Press, 2003), p. 319.
6. R. Essick, *William Blake, Printmaker* (Princeton: Princeton University Press, 1980), p. 120.
7. Makdisi, *Impossible History*, p. 321.
8. On the emergence of intellectual property as an abstraction in late eighteenth-century English law, see M. Rose, *Authors and Owners: The Invention of Copyright* (Cambridge, MA: Harvard University Press, 1993); on the emergence of the 'commodity text' as an abstract form of value during the early nineteenth-century takeoff of publishing into full capitalism, see N. N. Feltes, *Modes of Production of Victorian Novels* (Chicago: University of Chicago Press, 1986). For a discussion of these developments in relation to monetary history, see M. Rowlinson, *Real Money and Romanticism* (Cambridge: Cambridge University Press, 2010).
9. Makdisi, *Impossible History*, pp. 147–8.
10. 'The essence of all *money* [...] is its unconditional interchangeability.' G. Simmel, *The Philosophy of Money*, ed. D. Frisby, trans. D. Frisby and T. Bottomore, 2nd edn (London: Routledge, 1998), p. 427.
11. In the recently concluded (2016) suit filed by the Rosenbach Library in Philadelphia against the executors of Maurice Sendak's estate, Sendak's copy J of the *Songs of Innocence* and Copy H of the *Songs of Innocence and of Experience* were described by the plaintiffs as 'expected to sell for several million dollars'. P. Dobrin, 'Rosenbach sues Sendak Foundation over rare books', *Philadelphia Inquirer*, 10 November 2014, www.philly.com/philly/columnists/peter_dobrin/20141110_Rosenbach_sues_Sendak_Foundation_over_rare_books.html. For more on this lawsuit, see R. N. Essick's 'Blake in the Marketplace, 2014', *Blake / An Illustrated Quarterly*, 48.4 (Spring 2015), and 'Blake in the Marketplace, 2016', *Blake / An Illustrated Quarterly*, 50.4 (Spring 2017).
12. The 'Frequently Asked Questions' section of the Blake Archive, for instance, includes the following: 'You've got some nerve trying to dictate what I can and can't put on my own pages. Do you think Blake would have wanted to see his work smothered by copyright laws? Why can't you just look the other way?' *The Blake Archive*. 'Frequently Asked Questions', www.blakearchive.org/staticpage/archiveataglance?p=faqs

CHAPTER 33

Moravianism

Alexander Regier

During her first marriage, William Blake's mother, Catherine, was an active member of the Moravian congregation in London. The role in literary history of this strange and unorthodox religious congregation has been drawing increasing attention in literary studies, especially among Blake scholars.[1] Even though it was relatively small, the Moravian church was a notorious presence in the eighteenth century, originating in Central Europe (Moravia). This small, idiosyncratic Protestant group might have been quashed by the Counter-Reformation had it not been for the Saxon count Nikolaus Ludwig von Zinzendorf (1700–60) whose Pietist leanings led him to protect them in 1722. Eventually, Zinzendorf became its spiritual leader and bishop of the Moravians, and oversaw the travel of their missionaries, and their characteristic hymnody, to all corners of the globe, including Greenland, the West Indies, Suriname, Australia, and the American colonies. Yet their radical, often polyglot history has been forgotten by most literary criticism, even though it would certainly have been known to Blake's mother and also to Blake himself.

The Moravians first arrived in London in 1728, using the British capital as a gateway to their missionary travels. Many historical figures who are relevant to Blake's work, such as Charles and John Wesley, or Emanuel Swedenborg, were either members of, or tried to be part of, the congregation. Moravians actively intersected and overlapped, as Michael Farrell and Robert Rix have shown, with other congregations, such as Methodists (Blake's mother, for instance, was married according to a Church of England service).[2] The complex history of the Moravian church in Britain and London is very much part of the wider historical and religious context in which Blake wrote, thought, and composed.

Four of the most important and distinctive historical aspects of the Moravian congregation were, first, its unusual eschatology, including an erotic Christianity that emphasised the saviour's blood, his wounds, and especially his side-wound (*pleura*). Second was the multilingual character of their congregations in which German and English functioned alongside one another as languages of devotion, religious service, and instruction. Third, the Moravians had a prolific role in British literary history. They translated many hymns from German into English, making them an integral part of British hymnody. Many of the hymns we consider traditionally British or Anglican in fact are translations from the German or have their origin in the Moravian church.[3] The congregational practice of the Moravians emphasised the importance of song especially. Finally, the Moravians paid more attention than was common to the role of children, both in relation to instruction, especially singing and in understanding the child as a literal symbol for the human condition. The child becomes the most powerful symbol for a Christianity whose pillars are innocence, faith, and intuition.

Catherine Blake's engagement in the London Moravian church means that she was an active member of an unusual, well-known, and polyglot congregation. She would have come across some of the more radical Moravians hymns, such as the German 'Mein aller liebstes Lammelein' that would have been sung in translation by the London congregation:

> My dearest, most beloved Lamb!
> I, who in tend'rest union am
> To all thy Cross's air-doves bound,
> Smell to and kiss each Corpse's wound;
> Yet at the *Pleura* smart,
> There pants and throbs my Heart.
> I see still, how the soldier fierce
> Did thy most lovely *Pleura* pierce,
> That dearest Side-hole!
> Be prais'd, O God, for this Spear's blow!
> O thank thee soldier, for it too.
> I've lick'd this Rock's salt round and round;
> Where can such relish else be found!
> In this Point, at this season,
> His Smart o'erwhelms my reason.[4]

Three of the pillars of Moravian thought and practice previously mentioned are easily discerned in this hymn. It is a poem that comes into the Anglophone sphere through translation. Its celebration of the erotic dimension of Christianity is arresting: the speaker smells and kisses Jesus's corpse while the suggestive panting and throbbing of his heart is linked to Christ's side wound. The suggestion of its vaginal quality, made explicit by various Moravian bishops, is reinforced in the hymn through the description of the piercing spear that penetrates Christ's body. Not surprisingly, this kind of hymn contributed to the notoriety of the Moravians.[5] But such hymns were certainly a part of Moravianism in the first part of the eighteenth century, the time immediately before Catherine was a member of the congregation.

It is worth considering the concrete situation in which this poem may have been sung in London. Catherine would not only have performed Moravian hymns like these during services; she also may have memorised some of them and might well have sung them while she weaned her son or carried him through Soho. Even though we have no evidence that by the time Blake was born she continued to go to Moravian services, she never openly rejected her strong connection with the congregation.[6] What is certain is that the songs we learn by heart stay with us long after we have left the schools, churches, or other institutions in which we learned and memorised them.

What does all of that tell us about William Blake? I do not argue that Blake himself was a Moravian. However, I do suggest that there are meaningful links between his work and Moravianism, its religious beliefs, and its aesthetic practice. The link between the Moravian hymns and Blake's early work, such as *Songs of Innocence and of Experience* (1789), for instance, is particularly powerful. Consider that Blake uses a lot of symbolism and imagery that is associated with Moravianism, such as this very physical, almost erotic description of the lamb in 'Spring':

> Little Lamb
> Here I am,
> Come and lick
> My white neck.
> Let me pull
> Your soft Wool.
> Let me kiss
> Your soft face.
> Merrily Merrily we welcome in the Year.   (ll. 19–27, E 15)

The poem combines two central aspects of Blake's thinking that appear anew if we consider their relation to Moravianism. First, the erotic dimension in Blake's portrayal of the lamb. The affection for this 'Little Lamb' goes beyond standard Christian practice and has a lot in common with the creature celebrated in 'My dearest, most beloved Lamb'. Second, Blake puts the child at the centre of this artistic vision, presenting her as a privileged figure in her ability to connect to the spiritual and artistic world. Both examples showcase the important connections between Blake's language and the artistic vision and practice of the Moravians.

The Moravians and Blake go beyond standard invocations of the lamb in Christian iconography. In much Moravian thought, the lamb becomes the site through which Christ's relation to mankind is understood. It was, and still is, the symbol, which defines the Moravian motto: 'Our Lamb has conquered'. The animal becomes both Christ and a member of the flock, both a sacrificial non-human and, through resolving that tension within itself, the symbol of spiritual continuity. As Blake puts it, 'He is called by thy name, / For he calls himself a Lamb' ('The Lamb', ll. 13–14, E 9). The linguistic performance of calling and naming, and the ontological force that this calling implies, suggests that the matter of language and such sacrifice are connected in both texts.

In understanding these difficult relations, sexuality and physicality play an important role for Blake and the Moravians. 'My dearest, most beloved lamb' is a good example for the Moravian focus on the sexual nature of Christ's body and his wounds. The hymn zeroes in on the side-wound as an ultimate pinnacle of the blood-and-wounds imagery that was typical of Moravian language. In 1750, Catherine applied to be part of the Congregation of the Lamb, an elite circle within the London church, and wrote to the church Elders that 'Our Savour [sic] was pleased to make me Suck his wounds and hug the Cross more then Ever.'[7] Her son's 'Spring' reverses the role of human and animal. In the poem, the lamb is encouraged orally to approach the human: the child presents him/herself ('Here I am') and suggestively asks the lamb to 'Come and lick / My white neck'. The sexual connotations are hard to miss in both cases. In Catherine's application as well as in 'Spring', the lamb becomes the speaker's lover. In Blake's poem, we can picture the animal licking the neck from above, putting the child's head underneath the lamb's: a sign of subservience or devotion in the animal kingdom, including the human animal. Although it is not as immediately and obviously unusual as the Moravian hymn, Blake's stanza is certainly more disconcerting than many readings suggest. The Moravian context alerts us to this quality of religious eroticism in Blake's verse, including its articulation via a child, in a new way.

The eventual chiastic reversal of lamb and child in Blake's poem comes as no surprise to readers of the *Songs* to which dual structures are, of course, key. Rather than Christ-as-lamb or Christ-as-shepherd it is the child that takes the initiative: 'Let me pull / Your soft Wool'. The physical, sensuous reality of this lamb is described with precision. Its surface provides resistance, as when we pull wool, albeit a 'soft Wool'. The tone does not become too confrontational and the child asks for permission to engage in this intimacy: 'Let me kiss / Your soft face'. The licking of the Neck is paired with a kissing of the face; once more the actors are reversed. Such mutually entwining, chiastic love is how we can welcome the new year of fecundity – it is a new year of spring, not a calendar year – twice over: 'Merrily, Merrily we welcome in the year'. 'Spring' starts a new cycle, once more, with physical intimacy and musical celebration.

Who, then, sings this song? A child. As in many of Blake's works, the child is a privileged figure who vocalises what others cannot see or speak. (It is as common as it is inaccurate to understand Blake's singling out of the figure of the child as an attitude that begins with Romanticism.) Blake figures the child as an immensely sensitive creature who can access the spiritual world in ways that are closed to most 'experienced' adults. The Moravians have, more so than other Christian groups, a similar understanding of adolescents. In fact, at one point during the eighteenth century they took quite literally the idea that we should all be children of God. They encouraged childish games and child-like use of language, as Paul Peucker relates: 'Playing and childlike behavior became the appropriate expression for the joy Moravians experienced in their hearts, a joy to be shared with everyone. For Zinzendorf this joy was directly related to eschatology, as he compared a playing congregation with a group of children playing around the throne of the Lamb.'[8] Although he had no eschatology, Blake certainly believed that the behaviour of a child was spiritually significant, even revelatory. Manifestly in *Songs* and beyond, he understands the child's special epistemological and ontological insights as spiritual aspects of our existence.

Blake and the Moravians both argue that we need to take seriously the idea of the child as an important guide in and for the production of art and the world. In the 'Introduction' to *Songs*, the poet encounters a child who 'laughing said to me. / Pipe a song about a Lamb' (ll. 4–5, E 7). This encounter supposedly leads to the collection we encounter as readers. One of the aims of the *Songs* is to produce songs that every child may 'joy to hear' and repeat (l. 12), not a set of songs that will instruct or regiment. The joy will lead us to want to relive it, just like we want to read these often repetitive poems over and over again, to memorise them like Catherine memorised the Moravian hymns. Crucially the memorisation of these *Songs*, just like the hymns, is generative and creative. It is quite different from a mechanical mnemonic exercise. Rather, it produces a different kind of knowledge, the kind of insight that allows the lambs to 'know that their

Shepherd is nigh' ('The Shepherd', l. 8, E 7). It is a form of knowledge that is intuitive and not as much concerned with epistemology as it is to understand the relation between poetry and existence. In the production of that knowledge, the attempt to understand this complex relation, the aesthetics of song has a special place for Blake, just as it occupied a special position for the Moravians.

Might this musical dimension lead us beyond the formal relations between Blake's poetry and the Moravian hymnals? The Moravians were known more than other religious groups for their musical tradition and their celebration of God through the sung (even more so than the spoken) word. In contrast with, for example, Pietist movements, they encouraged the performance of poetry as part of a musical setting.[9] One crucial part of how the congregations, including the London one, were organised was through choirs: there were choirs for men, women, and children all of whom practised and sang on a regular basis as part of church life. The role of children was considered particularly important, illustrated by publications such as the common *Hymn-Book for the Children belonging to the Brethren's Congregation, Taken chiefly out of the GERMAN little Book* (1756). Texts such as this ask us to imagine how one might tap into the experience of a child and its song as a way to grasp something about what Blake terms 'the Two Contrary States of the Human Soul' (*Songs* title-page, E 7). Given these parallels, it is difficult to imagine that Blake was unaware of the Moravians' attitude to music. He certainly appears to have known one of its hymnals, John Gambold's *A Collection of Hymns of the Children of God* (1754).[10]

Eventually the (often multilingual) Moravian influence on English-speaking hymnody was mostly forgotten, yet it remains one of the most important factors in the formation of British religious song in the eighteenth century.[11] Many hundreds of the Moravian compositions, including the example of 'My dearest most beloved lamb' discussed above, were translations from the German. The Moravians had brought their hymns with them from their German headquarters in Herrnhut, Saxony and continued to import them when they had settled in London. Plenty of them were translated and, eventually, published together with their emerging Anglophone efforts. Among the earliest translators is John Wesley who, with his brother Charles, was an early member of the Moravian congregation in London before they turned to Methodism (adopting many of the Moravian hymns).[12] Even in the diaspora, Moravian choirs all had a German singing hour (the so-called 'Singstunde'), and kept much of the congregational life bilingual. During the period that Catherine visited the

Moravian church in Fetter Lane, it was common for members of the congregation to participate in some of these German or bilingual singing hours.

The multilingual background of British hymnody is one of the most important yet neglected dimensions of scholarship on the Enlightenment and Romanticism, including work on Blake. Discovering it means that we need to pay attention to the multilingual origins of Blake's immediate context, and what that means for reading his poetry. Blake himself, of course, had a fraught relationship to the German Royal Family and indicated on various occasions that their national background was unpleasant to him.[13] However, he also was good friends with the Swiss-German Fuseli, a reader of German literature, and occasionally sought the company of the strong Anglo-German presence in London at the time to which people such as Joseph Johnson, who commissioned many of his engravings, were connected.

There are, then, plenty of similarities but also many differences between the Moravian hymns and Blake's work, especially the *Songs*.[14] Reading them in tandem reveals several new and important things about both. It tells us something about the historical and material connections between the Moravian church, Catherine Blake, and her son William within the wider context of the eighteenth century. It also tells us something important about the formal points of contact between Anglo-German as well as British hymnody and Blake's poetry at large. Blake and Moravianism introduce a different, and very unusual way of thinking, singing, writing, and knowing into British literary history. If we read them together, in context, they illuminate one another in ways that allow us to gain a wider, more connected understanding of their period.

Notes

1. See Further Reading list for details.
2. See C. Podmore, *The Moravian Church in England, 1728–1760* (Oxford: Clarendon, 1998); R. Rix, *William Blake and the Cultures of Radical Christianity* (Farnham: Ashgate, 2007), pp. 7–24, and M. Farrell, *Blake and the Methodists* (Basingstoke: Palgrave Macmillan, 2016), pp. 30–50.
3. See A. Regier, *Exorbitant Enlightenment: Blake, Hamann, and Anglo-German Constellations* (Oxford: Oxford University Press, 2018).
4. *A Collection of Hymn of the Children of God in All Ages* (London: 1754), p. 336. Many of these more radical hymns were subsequently suppressed. Others, far more conventional, were absorbed into the Methodist canon.

5. See J. Yonan, *Evangelicalism and Enlightenment: The Moravian Experience in England, c. 1750–1800* (Ph.D. diss., University of Oxford, 2006), and P. Peucker, *A Time of Sifting: Mystical Marriage and the Crisis of Moravian Piety in the Eighteenth Century* (Pennsylvania: Pennsylvania State University Press, 2016).
6. She married Blake's father about ten months after her last appearance in the Moravian archive materials. See K. Davies, 'The Lost Moravian History of William Blake's Family', *Literature Compass*, 3.6 (2006), 1297–319 (p. 1307).
7. Quoted in Davies, 'Lost Moravian History', pp. 1308–9.
8. Peucker, *A Time of Sifting*, p. 69.
9. N. R. Knouse, 'Moravian Music: Questions of Identity and Purpose', in N. R. Knouse (ed.), *The Music of the Moravian Church in America* (Rochester, NY: University of Rochester Press, 2008), pp. 252–66 (p. 252).
10. See W. C. Ripley, 'The Influence of the Moravian *Collection of Hymns* on William Blake's Later Mythology', *Huntington Library Quarterly*, 80.3 (2017), 481–98.
11. See J. R. Watson, *The English Hymn: A Critical and Historical Study* (Oxford: Oxford University Press, 1999); M. W. England and J. Sparrow, *Hymns Unbidden: Donne, Herbert, Blake, Emily Dickinson, and the Hymnographers* (New York: New York Public Library, 1966); G. N. Davis, *German Thought and Culture in England 1700–1770: A Preliminary Survey* (Chapel Hill: University of North Carolina Press, 1969).
12. See Farrell, *Blake and the Methodists*.
13. See S. Haggarty and J. Mee, *William Blake: Songs of Innocence and Songs of Experience* (Basingstoke: Palgrave, 2013), p. 133.
14. For a wider analysis of Blake's work in the light of Moravian thought, see M. K. Schuchard, *Why Mrs Blake Cried: William Blake and the Sexual Basis of Spiritual Vision* (London: Century, 2006), and Regier, *Exorbitant Enlightenment*.

CHAPTER 34

Mysticism

Laura Quinney

Was Blake a mystic? The earliest students of Blake, starting with Swinburne, took it for granted that he was. Opinion changed with the appearance of Helen C. White's *Blake's Mysticism* (1927), which argued, in spite of its title, that he was not a mystic proper, and this view was maintained by many major Blake scholars of the later twentieth century, perhaps out of concern to preserve Blake's ascending intellectual reputation. The question of whether or not he was a mystic became entangled with the question of his relationship to esoteric mystical tradition, a relationship explored by early twentieth-century scholars such as S. Foster Damon, William O. Percival, and later Kathleen Raine. In opposition, Northrop Frye declared that Blake was simply a 'Bible-soaked middle-class English Protestant', while Harold Bloom concluded that Blake 'read little with any care besides the Bible and Milton'.[1] The topic seems to have been undergoing a revival recently, however, with the appearance of new monographs on Blake and Boehme.[2] It is not clear that the two questions – of Blake's mysticism and Blake's esotericism – ought to be identified, but that they are is Blake's fault, since he linked himself with Boehme and Swedenborg precisely in so far as they too had 'Visions'. The real issue is what Blake meant by vision. He has been assumed to be a mystic because he said he had visions, but, I will argue, in fact neither his concept of vision nor the character of his visions was mystical.

In what sense might Blake be called a mystic? White agrees that Blake shares some of the 'characteristics' of the mystic – 'dissatisfaction with the ordinary confines of experience' and an 'irrepressible urge to transcend them', a 'positive belief that there is a world of supernal reality' that sometimes 'impinges' on ours, 'the certainty that the properly enlightened human being can in some way pass the limits of the material world and put himself into some effective relation with that world', and the devotion of all his resources to 'the compassing of that goal'. And yet his ultimate goal was not that of the mystic: he did not seek 'profound union with God', nor was he willing to humble his will or subordinate his individuality to that end. White concludes that Blake is better termed "prophetic" and "visionary" than mystic, but strangely and unfortunately, she does not seem to think of him as, primarily, a poet.[3]

Frye at one point insists vividly on the importance of the difference between mystic and poet. In the early pages of *Fearful Symmetry*, he cleanly divides the goal of the artist from that of the mystic:

> [Mysticism] is a form of spiritual communion with God which is by its nature incommunicable to anyone else, and which soars beyond faith into direct apprehension. But to the artist, *qua* artist, this apprehension is not an end in itself but a means to another end, the end of producing his poem.

Yet Frye appears later to have changed his mind. In a 'General Note' on Blake's mysticism that forms the coda of *Fearful Symmetry*, he concedes that Blake may be numbered among the mystics if mysticism is defined more broadly, not merely as the quest for communion, but as the 'effort of vision ... to be conceived neither as a human attempt to reach God nor a divine attempt to reach man, but as the realisation in total experience of the identity of God and Man in which both the human creature and the superhuman Creator disappear'. Such was the aim of Blake's art, Frye maintains – 'as creation designed to destroy *the* Creation' – and with this aim he joins in 'the great speculative Western school which forms a curiously well-integrated tradition at least between Eckhart and Boehme, and which is often called mystical'.[4]

The interpretation of Blake as a mystic has been much encouraged by emphasis on his relation to this tradition, culminating in Raine's scholarship, particularly her exhaustive two-volume study *Blake and Tradition*.[5] Though invaluable as encyclopaedic and suggestive source work, Raine tends to distort Blake's intellectual personality: she treats him as passively influenced by his reading, as highly derivative in his imagery, and as sharing uncritically in the punishing dualism and pessimism of Gnostic and Neoplatonic tradition. Raine quotes Thomas Taylor's account of Plotinus as a view that Blake echoes: "'by thus embracing and adhering to corporeal forms, [the human being] is precipitated, not so much in his body, as in his soul, into profound and horrid darkness'".[6] Works such as *The Marriage of Heaven and Hell* and *The Book of Thel* show that is not Blake's view: he does not think that embodiment spells profound and horrid darkness, but that a certain conception of embodiment does. It is the materialist who dwells in profound and horrid darkness. Though the material and the spiritual world are distinct, that distinction in itself need not cause suffering: suffering in this world is caused, or at least deepened, by subjection of spiritual to material *vision*.

In terms of larger inspiration, E. P. Thompson was right to argue that Blake was heterodox not because he went to school to any of these esoteric sources, but because he maintained the antinomian, humanist spirit of his radical Protestant upbringing. I would add that as an adult he found congenial ideas, logically enough, in the Gnostic, Neoplatonic, and Kabbalistic literature that had, at a distance, helped to shape radical Protestantism, including the Moravian church his mother joined, and the thinking of outliers he admired, such as Boehme and Swedenborg. He rejected the idea of the Creator God, indeed of any 'Nobodaddy', or anthropomorphised male deity ('To Nobodaddy', E 471); he liked the idea of the human as participating in, even constituting, the divine; he resolutely subordinated intelligible to material reality; he was anticlerical and antinomian. He found these and other congenial notions in the various traditions he has been associated with. But complex patterns of inheritance and cross-fertilisation connect them, so that it does not make good sense to hunt down unique sources for his major ideas and images, if indeed it follows that Blake had 'sources' for them. Blake made up his mind early on, and he read rather for inspiration and fellowship than for instruction.[7]

Blake is not a Platonist, a Neoplatonist, a Gnostic, a Behmenist, a Swedenborgian, a Moravian, or a follower of the Hermetic philosophy, but what was it about all these, intertwined as they are, which drew him to them? (And allowed him to borrow freely from them?) What was it about the mystics that he found congenial? The question is not, 'what was it about mysticism in general', because it was precisely the boldness of individual mystics that he liked, and the idea of the individual experience of mysticism. Note that he admired Catholic mystics such as St Teresa as much as Protestant ones such as Boehme (see *Jerusalem* 72: 50, E 227); that he made no distinction indicates that he cared about the religious element of their visions only in the broadest sense of 'religion', meaning: spiritual ambition. He gave his approval to particular ideas in Boehme and Swedenborg, but he admired mystics and visionaries of all kinds for practising what he considered cardinal virtues: intellectual independence, personal authority, and insistence on the priority of spiritual realities. Under intellectual independence might be included antinomianism, anticlericalism, mistrust of organised religion and heterodoxy in general; but even St Teresa, who was orthodox, could count as independent in so far as she pursued her own inspiration, placing the highest value on utterly private, uncountenanced ecstasy. Personal authority means certainty of having such solitary, unmediated contact with immaterial reality. Prioritising that reality means thinking of it as truer than what passes for the 'solid' truth of the material world. For Blake, mysticism brings with it the verve of counter-cultural dissent.

Mysticism to Blake entails a species of rebellion to the extent that it claims validity for interior, unshared, unverifiable experience or conviction in opposition to the common view and the status quo. It is plain enough how his taste for spiritual individualism of this kind comes out of his background and lifelong engagement with radical Protestantism, but it is only because aesthetic vocation came in to complement this taste that Blake was able to extend his enthusiasm to mystics of all kinds. To Blake, mystics were artists too. He assimilated them to himself, rather than the other way around. That is why abjection and bodily self-denial play no important role in what he admires about them.

As we have seen repeatedly in the critical literature, the question of whether or not it is appropriate to call Blake a mystic turns on the question of what he meant by 'vision'. Let us then turn to an examination of how he uses the word. There were, first of all, the 'Visions' that Blake notoriously claimed to have had in person: supernatural appearances that came to him from childhood onward. He had his first vision, he said, when he was eight years old: out walking on Peckham Rye, he looked up and saw 'a tree filled with angels, bright angelic wings bespangling every bough like stars [. . .] Another time, one summer morn, he [saw] the haymakers at work, and amid them angelic figures walking' (Gilchrist 7). The spirit of his brother Robert visited him after his early death. These visions have suggested hallucination to some. But, contrary to popular belief, Blake's visions of this kind – at least those he reported having, or was reported as having had – were not hallucinatory. His nineteenth-century biographer, Alexander Gilchrist, tells an illustrative story about a salon-style conversation:

> 'The other evening,' said Blake, in his usual quiet way, 'taking a walk, I came to a meadow, and at the farther corner of it I saw a fold of lambs. Coming nearer, the ground blushed with flowers; and the wattled cote and its woolly tenants were of an exquisite pastoral beauty. But I looked again, and it proved to be no living flock, but beautiful sculpture.' The lady, thinking this a capital holiday-show for her children, eagerly interposed, 'I beg pardon, Mr. Blake, but *may* I ask *where* you saw this?' '*Here*, madam,' answered Blake, touching his forehead. (Gilchrist 319–20)

Blake liked to startle the bourgeoisie – his common-sensical peers – with shows of visionary enthusiasm, but he never suggested that he failed to distinguish the physical from the imaginative reality. Even when, in the company of his friend John Varley, he sketched portraits of famous dead men he said he saw before him, he showed no signs of succumbing to visionary psychosis, but was instead firmly asserting the priority of imagination.

According to White, the nature of Blake's visions was quite different from the mystics', who sought vision by means of severe self-discipline, including chastity and meditation. They regarded visions merely as 'preliminary challenges and graces' en route to a higher communion.[8] For Blake, vision springs from the creative imagination unique to each person, fuelled by the same energy that fuels love and desire. It is an end in itself. His relation to his own visions is also different from those of St Theresa, Boehme, and Swedenborg in relation to theirs. We might make the distinction, as Frye did in the passage quoted above, in terms of authorial self-consciousness and different modes of truth-value. Blake writes of vision with multiple layers of consciousness. Imagination maintains a distance from unmediated truth and the artist knows it well, glories in it, even; we feel Blake does, while Boehme and Swedenborg and St Theresa doggedly lay claim to truth in a single dimension.

If Blake conceived of his personal visions as aesthetic objects, how much more salient, as we would expect, is the aesthetic dimension of 'vision' as he uses the word in his poems and prose. I distinguish, roughly, seven different meanings of 'vision' in Blake's writing: (1) imagination per se, (2) illusion, (3) grim insight ('prophecy'), (4) joyous insight ('prophecy'), (5) prophetic utterance, (6) Blake's own inspiration, and (7) Blake's poetry and visual art. For Blake every form of vision is imaginative. Even the sight of the eye, 'literal' sight is not literal; really there is no such thing, for 'The Eye altering alters all' ('The Mental Traveller', l. 62, E 485). Hence scepticism about the senses and distinctions between primary and secondary qualities are irrelevant: 'I question not my Corporeal or Vegetative Eye any more than I would Question a Window concerning a Sight I look thro it & not with it' (*Vision of the Last Judgment*, E 566). But when he wants to, Blake distinguishes the imaginative operation of the eye from self-conscious imaginative activity by using vision synonymously with 'Imagination' or 'Inspiration'. A 'Vision' in Blake is never merely a visual image. His word 'Vision' preserves the ambidexterity in the Greek root of 'idea', *eidos*, meaning on the one hand what is seen and on the other what is thought. With regard specifically to Blake's art, no visual image of his fails to suggest an idea, or many, or even competing ones. Consider the provocative power of single images such 'Glad Day' or the 'The Ancient of Days'. A Blakean work of art is *intellectual*. It is in order to make intellectual art, he would say, that he eschews realism. Frye may be exaggerating when he says that Blake's visual art seeks to 'destroy the Creation', but certainly it is the aim of Vision in Blake to counter the relative passivity of the 'Corporeal Eye', which may be influenced by imagination but is not shaping and self-conscious.

Vision in the mystical tradition involves a suspension of the will and (in theory at least) a suspension of individuality. Yet vision as adduced in Blake's writing has a more deliberate nature. It requires an *exercise* of the imagination, and in this way, resembles a work of art. Like a work of art, too, it arises out of an individual imagination exerting its distinctive and unique view. Even in Blake's Heaven, the individual will not disappear into the universal Oversoul, or live in passive harmony with God. The 'Wars of Eternity' will be 'Mental' (*Milton* 31 [34]: 25, E 130); the individual continues to enjoy their own visions – in 'Paradise with its Inhabitants walking up & down in Conversations concerning Mental Delights [...] Conversing with Eternal Realities as they Exist in the Human Imagination' (*Milton* 31 [34]: 25, E 130; 'Preface', *Vision of the Last Judgment*, E 562). Michael Ferber has shrewdly identified 'a Christian transfiguration of the Peripatetics' in this image of heaven: intellectual peers comparing and contrasting their ideas at leisure.[9] The disappearance of the individual into the religious collective, even if it is called 'God', was no part of Blake's aim. A Vision belongs to an individual mind as its own creation. Diversity of perspective is right and necessary, and it is the basis of insight as well as art.

And yet vision is not capricious: 'Vision or Imagination is a Representation of what Eternally Exists. Really and Unchangeably' (ibid., E 554). Iterations may differ, but the substance of a vision is transcendental truth. Yet this honorific definition of Vision does not cover all the senses in which Blake himself uses the word. What of vision as 'illusion' or as 'grim insight'? Do such visions constitute 'a Representation of what Eternally Exists'? In Blake, two kinds of figures have cruel visions: prophets (including Blake himself) because they see the truth and suffering characters because they are deluded. The ever-anxious Urizen tortures himself with 'visions of futurity', his own unfounded fears (*VALA/Four Zoas*, N2, p. 34, l. 7, E 322). But the prophet is justly terrified by the sight of humanity's self-perversion. Blake's own visions can be cruel, and yet it is not (or not always) cruel to him to have them. The autobiographical passage in *Milton* captures this difference:

> For when Los joind with me he took me in his firy whirlwind
> My Vegetated portion was hurried from Lambeths shades
> He set me down in Felphams Vale & prepared a beautiful
> Cottage for me that in three years I might write all these Visions
> To display Natures cruel holiness: the deceits of Natural Religion
> Walking in My Cottage Garden, sudden I beheld
> The Virgin Ololon & address'd her as a Daughter of Beulah.
>
> (36 [40]: 21–7, E 137)

There is an almost comic reversal of affect in these enjambment of 'Visions' and 'To display Natures cruel holiness'. The affect is reversed again when Ololon appears. The passage enacts the division between poet as human being and poet as prophet. The human being William Blake witnesses an epiphany of Ololon; it is a scene of pastoral grace, and Blake receives it gratefully. But for the prophet William Blake inspiration spells indignation, and the Visions of the poem (or some of them) are violent and ambivalent – necessarily so, because they are representations of and responses to cruelty in human culture.

Grim visions are true, but they are not 'Visions of Eternity'. They represent insight into the appalling course of human history. When Los the prophet says, 'I behold the Visions of my deadly sleep of Six Thousand Years', he means that he perceives how the materialism of Western culture has led humanity fatally astray in its conception of itself and its possibilities. This is not an eternal truth; it was not inevitable, and it is not unchangeable. But a vision of something eternal is for Blake necessarily a happy one. It will exalt not for the conventional religious reason (the mystic's reason), that it raises the seer to God or Heaven. Nor will the Socratic reason – that it brings the seer into the realm of permanent truth – wholly explain Blake's view. He has taken Plato's dualism and given it a gay Spinozistic twist: 'the Oak dies as well as the Lettuce but Its Eternal Image & Individuality never dies' (*Vision of the Last Judgment*, E 555). A 'Vision of Eternity' exalts because it keeps company with imperishable being and its joy. For Blake, this kind of being belongs immediately to the human imagination, in and of itself; therefore he is not a mystic.

Notes

1. N. Frye, 'William Blake (I)', in A. Esterhammer (ed.), *Northrop Frye on Milton and Blake* (Toronto: University of Toronto Press, 2005), pp. 266–89 (p. 279); H. Bloom, *Blake's Apocalypse* (New York: Doubleday, 1963), p. 77. For a useful account of the critical history on the topic of Blake and mysticism, see B. Aubrey, *Watchmen of Eternity: Blake's Debt to Jacob Boehme* (Lanham, MD: University Press of America, 1986), pp. 1–11.

2. Aubrey, *Watchmen*, and K. Fischer, *Converse in the Spirit: William Blake, Jacob Boehme, and the Creative Spirit* (Madison, WI: Fairleigh Dickinson University Press, 2004).
3. H. C. White, *The Mysticism of William Blake* (New York: Russell and Russell, 1964), pp. 208, 211, 216.
4. N. Frye, *Fearful Symmetry* (Princeton: Princeton University Press, 1949; repr. 1968), pp. 7, 8, 431–2.
5. See also M. D. Paley, *Energy and Imagination: A Study of the Development of Blake's Thought* (Oxford: Clarendon, 1970), as well as Raine's *Blake and the New Age* (London: George Allen and Unwin, 1979).
6. K. Raine, *Blake and Tradition*, 2 vols. (Princeton: Princeton University Press, 1968), I, 153.
7. As Thompson comments, '[Blake] took each author (even the Old Testament prophets] as his equal, or as something less'. E. P. Thompson, *Witness against the Beast: William Blake and the Moral Law* (New York: New Press, 1993), p. xvi.
8. White, *Mysticism of William Blake*, p. 214.
9. M. Ferber, *The Social Vision of William Blake* (Princeton: Princeton University Press, 1985), p. 207.

CHAPTER 35

Nationalism and Imperialism
Julia M. Wright

Nationalism and imperialism (along with other ideologies of demographic dominance, especially racism) can be mutually reinforcing, most obviously in various instances of twentieth-century fascism, but imperialism predates the emergence of nationalism by a few millennia, and scientific racism slightly post-dates that emergence. Imperialism refers to economically motivated territorial conquest by a central state, and it dates back to the ancient world: two millennia separate the Akkadian Empire from the Roman Empire, and nearly another two millennia separate the founding of the Roman Empire from the British Empire that was partly modelled on it. Nationalism, conversely, defines identity: it posits determining ties between people, land, culture, and language(s) within a historical framework, and it emerged in Europe in the second half of the eighteenth century from Enlightenment thought and the pragmatic need for governments, in the face of ever-larger populations, globalisation, and commerce, to solicit popular emotional support for the nation in principle. While notions of national or regional character had been around for some time (Roman jibes of Greek effeminacy, for instance), the idea of *race* as a biological division within *homo sapiens* was launched in the last quarter of the eighteenth century, with J. F. Blumenbach's division of humanity into a small number of biologically defined 'races' laid out in publications across that period. Scientific racism facilitated the entrenchment of violent social and political practices as well as the consolidation of 'whiteness' over the religious, linguistic, and other differences that had historically divided Europeans. Put broadly, as ideologies that do work, imperialism pursues economic goals by force; nationalism solicits political coordination through culture; and racism automates exclusion and exploitation. Because the ideologies have different objects, they need not be confluent – they sometimes flow together and sometimes apart in political discourse, literature, and other cultural works. Explicitly nationalist, but generally anti-imperialist and anti-racist, William Blake's writings offer a particularly rich body of work for the exploration of some of the tensions between these sometimes mutually reinforcing ideologies.

In the Romantic era, all three of these ideologies were both politically powerful and heavily contested. The impeachment of Warren Hastings (1788–95) by the British parliament for his actions in India was ultimately defeated and did little to question imperialism as such, but it did ask pointed questions about the ethics and efficacy of imperial methods. The lower classes in England, excluded from political participation by property requirements for the vote when nationalism began to hail them as integral parts of the nation, argued for their rights and acted against the military necessary to empire (there were popular songs against impressment, such as John O'Keefe's 'Sweet Poll of Plymouth' [1786], and a spate of mutinies in the 1780s and 1790s, including those on the HMS *Bounty* and the HMS *Hermione*, and, even more seriously, at the anchorages Spithead and the Nore). The abolition movement insisted on a shared humanity as it argued for decades against the slave trade and slavery itself. Though this era ended with the consolidation and then rapid expansion of the British Empire in the so-called Imperial Century (1815–1914), it was a chaotic period in British history – a patchwork of hard-won successes and irreversible defeats. Britain won the Seven Years' War, adding France's Canadian territories to its own, but then lost the American colonies; Britain expanded its empire in India, Australia, and elsewhere, but fought, at enormous cost, wars with the United States and Napoleonic France; and it advanced technologically (the spinning jenny, the Watt steam engine) while still facing food shortages, and related riots, throughout the period.

British imperialism supported trade – the slave trade until 1807, and across the era sugar, tobacco, cotton, opium, and so on – increasing resources and so addressing domestic pressures to provide sufficient food and clothing for the population.[1] For instance, as fabrics shifted from domestic wool to imported cotton, land could be deployed for food production rather than sheep-grazing,[2] while encouraging emigration to the colonies both offset population increases domestically and facilitated control over space imperially. Empire, in other words, was in Blake's time partly a response to the problem of population increases relative to food supply that was detailed in Thomas Malthus's *Essay on the Principle of Population* (1798), and it proceeded in the face of significant material difficulties by drawing on racism and on ideas of England that solicited support for imperial expansion, including definitions of England as a naval power, as a trading nation, and as a defender of Protestant liberty. Blake's invocations of food security, some of which I shall address below, are thus key to understanding his engagement with nationalism and imperialism.

In his early dramatic fragment, 'King Edward the Third' (published 1783), Blake explores these connections between imperial expansion, trade, and domestic demand for food in dialogue involving members of the King's court. The Bishop identifies 'industry', particularly agricultural labour, as the support of both (private) religion and (public) commerce:

> When I sit at my home, a private man,
> My thoughts are on my gardens, and my fields,
> How to employ the hand that lacketh bread.
> If Industry is in my diocese,
> Religion will flourish [...]
> But as I sit in council with my prince,
> My thoughts take in the gen'ral good of the whole,
> And England is the land favour'd by Commerce;
> For Commerce, tho' the child of Agriculture,
> Fosters his parent, who else must sweat and toil,
> And gain but scanty fare. Then, my dear Lord,
> Be England's trade our care; and we, as tradesmen,
> Looking to the gain of this our native land. (2: 21–5, 2: 28–35; E 425)

Commerce increases the food supply, and the military defence of trade protects food from predators likewise; according to Lionel, Duke of Clarence 'the French have fitted out many / Small ships of war, that, like to ravening wolves, / Infest our English seas, devouring all / Our burden'd vessels, spoiling our naval flocks. / The merchants do complain' (2: 65–9; E 426). While the Bishop and Clarence address trade's importance to what we would now call 'food security', Sir John Chandos addresses the land that agriculture requires as the foundation of imperial expansion:

> Teach man to think he's a free agent,
> Give but a slave his liberty, he'll shake
> Off sloth, and build himself a hut, and hedge
> A spot of ground; this he'll defend; 'tis his
> By right of nature: thus set in action,
> He will still move onward to plan conveniences,
> 'Till glory fires his breast to enlarge his castle. (3: 195–201; E 431)

While empire expands on material grounds – 'build[ing]', 'hedg[ing]', 'onward' – being true to the national spirit cannot be measured in roods or troy ounces, and requires stasis rather than movement. In cultural nationalism, cultural conservation rather than economic expansion is at the core – not that individuals necessarily agreed on what that culture was.

While it served imperialism to hail trade and expansion as quintessentially English, Blake was among those to argue for the centrality of the arts. Thus, the battle in the *Notebook* poem 'When England Klopstock Defied' imagines 'English Blake' defeating the German author Klopstock in the field of poetry (l. 6; E 500). 'Klopstock' puts the arts at the centre of national identity and accomplishment, as well as the means by which the nation will be conserved: 'We do not want either Greek or Roman Models if we are but just & true to our own Imaginations' ('Preface to *Milton*' E 95). Susan Matthews has noted that even Blake's early admiration for Greece was as 'a society in which art, the artist and the imagination are rightly honoured'.[3]

Attention to Blake's interest in empire has tended to focus on his American works, *Visions of the Daughters of Albion* and *America*, and his later epics, especially *Jerusalem*. While readings of *Jerusalem* as a text with imperialist resonances disturb the representation of Blake as a radical,[4] the epic imagines a Christian utopia in which ethnic and religious differences are erased, and so is not very different, in these outlines, from the religiously sanctioned imperial projects of the Early Modern era, critiqued, for instance, in Bartolomé De Las Casas' *Short Account of the Devastation of the Indies* (written in 1542 and published a decade later). But this apparent imperialism in Blake is yet complicated by what Molly Anne Rothenberg terms his 'radical scepticism', and particularly his 'refusal of all appeals to authority, the exposure of those appeals as grounded on false or illegitimate premises, and the careful revelation of the strategies by which such appeals are made to appear metaphysically valid – these concerns mark the theoretical project of *Jerusalem*'.[5] This is the allegorical conundrum around which much Blake scholarship pivots: the historical referents of Blake's allegories encourage materialist readings informed by Marxist historiography and its offshoots in New Historicism and post-colonialism (nationalism, imperialism, racism), but Blake's persistent emphasis on interrogating perception (empiricism, scepticism, post-structuralism) undermines any straightforward historicist reading. Blake did not produce scholarly accounts of myth and legend like an antiquarian, or record everyday life like a novelist; as Saree Makdisi points out, imagination and history are not mutually exclusive,[6] and the politics of aesthetics, and the aesthetics of politics, in the era complicate their separation in Blake's texts – as is the case generally in fantasy (arguably a better term for Blake's work than myth, given his creation of an imagined world for satiric purposes, like Jonathan Swift, and his importance to the British tradition of fantasy from William Morris to C. S. Lewis and Mervyn Peake).

In *America*, for instance, Albion's Angel, the Guardian Prince of Albion, and the King of England all invoke George III (indeed, Erdman indexes them as a group, E 500), but they have different functions in the poem. Albion's Angel debates Orc and orders the attack via plague; Albion's Guardian suffers when the plague is forced back to England's shores by fire; and the King of England watches anxiously. The Albion figures are military: the Angel commands 'war-trumpets' (9: 1, E 54) and the other Albion characters are in military camps, from the 'Guardian Prince of Albion [who] burns in his nightly tent' (3: 1, E 52) to 'num'rous hosts, all Albions Angels campd' (13: 13, E 56). The Angel is the imperial offence and the Guardian the national defence, personifying the national boundary and appearing on coastal cliffs (3: 8, E 52). The guardians complicate a reading of *America* as an allegory of the American Revolution. As with Chandos's slave who 'think[s] he's a free agent' in 'King Edward the Third', Blake is addressing control of space. In the opening plates, the Albion figures move outward and send plague to America, but fire causes a reversal. First the 'plagues recoil'd! Then rolld they back with fury' (14: 20, E 56) and pass over the British Isles, nation by nation, city by city, so that the Guardians 'forsook the frontiers' (15: 14, E 57) – and doors open, and gates melt. Blake represents the end of expansion as the undoing of boundaries, an unwinding of the process that Chandos outlines. And again the loss of imperial control over space is specifically a threat to food security: Albion's Angel wails, 'They cannot smite the wheat, nor quench the fatness of the earth. / [...] nor subdue the plough and spade. / [...] They cannot bring the stubbed oak to overgrow the hills' (9: 5–6, 8, E 54), referring to food production, agricultural implements, and the need to clear forested land for agricultural use.

As Jennifer Davis Michael notes of Urizen 'build[ing] a new imperial city' in *VALA / The Four Zoas*, 'war, commerce, and manufacturing are linked together, with slavery' and bound apprenticeships 'to support them all',[7] expanding on the connections in 'King Edward the Third'. Nationalism, for Blake, should lie outside of such violent forms, and he explicitly rejects militarist empire as a contamination of the nation, as when he refers to the leading 'national' poets: 'Shakespeare & Milton were both curbd by the general malady & infection from the silly Greek & Latin slaves of the Sword' (*Milton* pl. 1[i], E 95). 'Curbd' is the operative term here, given wide acknowledgement of Blake's steady opposition to tyranny and constraint. Makdisi discusses 'Blake's elaboration of a form of religious and political freedom that would defy what he called "state religion"' as 'an elaboration of a form of political and cultural freedom from the discourse and practice of imperialism'.⁸ Militarism does not support English freedom but undermines it, in this view. Blake challenged racism as well: Makdisi makes the important point that 'Blake was basically the *only* major poet of the late eighteenth and early nineteenth centuries who categorically refused to dabble in recognisably Orientalised themes or motifs.'⁹ He also rejected racism against Africans in 'The Little Black Boy' and in his anti-slavery statements in *Visions* as well as his work illustrating Stedman's abolitionist *Narrative*. But Blake can sometimes appear to be at a loss when individuals' freedoms are in conflict, as in the controversial Preludium to *America* where the freeing of revolutionary vigour is represented as a rape of Urthona's daughter – 'Urthona', long noted as a suggestive near-homonym of 'earth owner'. Allegorically, the Preludium anticipates the end of property boundaries in the Prophecy proper; literally, it is gendered violence, and implies that revolution will simply reinstate tyranny.

Moreover, some of Blake's ideas, particularly of nation, changed over time. As Michael notes, 'For the first time in his poetry, he makes extensive use of English place names' in *Milton*,[10] grounding the nation in its particular territory as well as its artists. At other moments, we find ourselves in paradox. To celebrate Englishness as commensurate with an originary, shared humanity, or a 'lost immanent unity', is to fall into the universalising of whiteness, so, as is widely noted, the title character of 'The Little Black Boy' looks forward to being 'like' the 'little English boy' when they are both 'round the tent of God' (ll. 22, 28, 24, E 9).[11] Matthews suggests that, in England his whole life, 'Blake has no reason to distinguish a national from a universal identity' and Benedict Anderson's argument that nationalism emerges from diaspora reinforces that view – but the very idea of nationality, as Joep Leerssen argues, depends on differentiation from other nations.[12] To be English is not to be French, or Italian, or Persian or, as 'When Klopstock England Defied' makes clear, German. Moreover, references to Englishness invoke myriad nationalist discourses in which Englishness is Druidic, Saxon, Norman, John Bull, Britannia, or exemplified by champion boxers or military heroes or scientists – all variously intersecting with notions of gender, different sets of core cultural values, and so on. Many of these include nationalist claims to a universally preferable culture, contending that anglicising is civilising. This is the problem of *Jerusalem*'s call to the Jews, the Deists, the Christians, and the Public, all to be resolved into 'harmony' through the power of discourse:

> Thunder of Thought, & flames of fierce desire:
> Even from the depths of Hell his voice I hear,
> Within the unfathomed caverns of my Ear.
> Therefore I print; nor vain my types shall be:
> Heaven, Earth & Hell, henceforth shall live in harmony.
>
> (3: 6–10, E 145)

This passage celebrates the capacity of the imagination to transform human experience, but it also echoes the imperial project of anglicisation, to develop unity (or 'harmony') through the imposition of England's language, culture, and law. 'Therefore I print' in this context is a reminder that the British set up printing presses in colonial spaces to facilitate the anglicising distribution of English materials – Bibles and other religious materials in particular. Like the Preludium to *America*, abstractly, it appears emancipatory; materially, it is the opposite. Such moments necessarily complicate readings of Blake's work, and are part of the tension between his religious and political thought.

Such tensions have also had an impact on the reception of Blake's works, most strikingly in the framing of part of the Preface to *Milton* as an English-nationalist hymn known as 'Jerusalem'. Out of context, it offers a religiously inflected moment of national nostalgia for the verdant countryside before the Industrial Revolution: 'England's pleasant pastures' (l. 4) echo through repetitions of 'green' (ll. 2, 16) and 'pleasant' (l. 16) and the reference to the pastoral commonplace of a lamb (l. 3) (E 9). As Matthews notes, it was the official song of the UK Women's Institute, making it an interesting case with which to close the discussion here.[13] The WI was founded in 1915, at the end of the Imperial Century, to encourage women in rural areas to contribute to the war effort by helping to grow more food. Its current website reports that the first performance of 'Jerusalem' as its anthem took place in 1924 with the Minister of Agriculture in attendance.[14] The WI selection of 'Jerusalem' marks an effort to re-use Blake at a moment when, as in Blake's day, anxiety over empire was ineluctably tied to food insecurity.

Notes

I would like to thank the Social Sciences and Humanities Research Council for its support of my research, and Jane Boyes for her valuable work as a research assistant.

1. For more on empire and food, see R. Biel, 'Food and Imperialism', in I. Ness and Z. Cope (eds.), *The Palgrave Encyclopedia of Imperialism and Anti-Imperialism*, 2 vols. (New York: Palgrave Macmillan, 2016), 1, 1213–19.
2. P. M. Solar, 'The Triumph of Cotton in Europe', Modern and Comparative Seminar, 31 May 2012 (London School of Economics) www.lse.ac.uk/economicHistory/seminars/ModernAndComparative/papers2011–12/Papers/Solar-Textile-fibres-May-12.pdf, p. 7.
3. S. Matthews, '*Jerusalem* and Nationalism', in S. Copley and J. Whale (eds.), *Beyond Romanticism: New Approaches to Texts and Contexts, 1780–1832* (New York: Routledge, 1992), pp. 79–100 (p. 81).
4. See, for example, Matthews, ibid., and J. M. Wright, *Blake, Nationalism, and the Politics of Alienation* (Athens, GA: Ohio University Press, 2004), pp. 135–67.
5. M. A. Rothenberg, *Rethinking Blake's Textuality* (Columbia, SC: University of Missouri Press, 1993), pp. 6, 5.
6. S. Makdisi, *William Blake and the Impossible History of the 1790s* (Chicago: University of Chicago Press, 2003), pp. 1–3.
7. J. D. Michael, *Blake and the City* (Lewisburg, PA: Bucknell University Press, 2006), p. 105.
8. Makdisi, *Impossible History*, p. 205.
9. Ibid., p. 209.
10. Michael, *Blake and the City*, p. 115.
11. Makdisi, *Impossible History*, p. 249.
12. S. Matthews, 'Africa and Utopia: Refusing a "Local Habitation"', in S. Clark and M. Suzuki (eds.), *The Reception of Blake in the Orient* (New York: Continuum, 2006), pp. 104–20 (p. 106); B. Anderson, *The Spectre of Comparisons: Nationalism, Southeast Asia, and the World* (London: Verso, 1998); J. Leerssen, *National Thought in Europe: A Cultural History* (Amsterdam: Amsterdam University Press, 2006); see also J. M. Wright, *Representing the Landscape in Irish Romanticism* (Syracuse, NY: Syracuse University Press, 2014), pp. ix–xxiv.
13. Matthews, '*Jerusalem* and Nationalism', p. 79. For other deployments of the lines, see S. Dent, '"Thou readst white where I readst black": William Blake, the Hymn "Jerusalem", and the Far Right', in M. Crosby, T. Patenaude, and A. Whitehead (eds.), *Re-Envisioning Blake* (Basingstoke: Palgrave Macmillan, 2012), pp. 48–62.
14. 'When and where was Blake's Jerusalem first sung by the WI?', FAQs, The WI, www.thewi.org.uk/faqs/when-and-where-was-blakes-jerusalem-first-sung-by-the-wi

CHAPTER 36

Sex, Sexuality, and Gender

Susan Matthews

In *Jerusalem*, a 'Divine Voice' announces that 'Man in the Resurrection changes his Sexual Garments at will' (51: 61, E 212). But what are 'sexual garments'? Does this phrase refer to gendered clothing, sexed bodies, sexual partners, or to sexualities? Quite apart from questions of context and speaker, of specific meanings accrued by Blake's developing poetic imagination, the word *sexual* (along with *sex* and *gender*) could carry meanings in the Romantic period that are different from – and sometimes opposed to – the meanings they carry in twenty-first century academic discourse. In addition, these words were shifting in meaning during Blake's lifetime. The language Blake used lacks terms which reliably convey the distinction taken for granted in second-wave feminism between *sex* (which categorises the body according to reproductive function) and *gender* (used since about 1945 to describe behaviour culturally associated with the sexed body). Third-wave feminism's assumption that the sexed body is shaped by discourse requires that we understand the ways in which words delimited identities in the world Blake inhabited. Thus the word *sexuality* did not exist in any sense, according to the *OED*, before 1797. The most obvious meaning of *sexual* was 'Characteristic of or peculiar to the female sex; feminine'. The word *gender* (which Blake does not use) could only refer to men and women as a group.[1]

Where they do appear in the Romantic period, therefore, the words *sex, sexuality*, and *gender* are fraught with traps for modern readers. In the long eighteenth century, *the sex* could refer to women, but *sex* could not refer to sexual intercourse or physical contact (a meaning that did not appear until 1900). To be *unsex'd* was not to be lacking in sexual drive or sexless, but to behave in ways that did not conform to the conventions culturally prescribed to the sexed body.[2] Some of the first uses of the word *sexuality*, in the late 1790s, refer to gendered behaviour rather than bodily drives. In a speech at Harvard in 1798, for example, John Thornton Kirkland asked:

whether [American females] are not as free, as lovely, as respectable, and happy, in their present situation in society, as they would be, if their sexuality of character, and employments were done away; and law and custom allowed them to exchange the distaff for the plough; the needle and the pencil for the axe and the hammer.[3]

'[S]exuality of character' here refers to a gendered notion of temperament; 'sexuality [...] of employment' means those jobs (weaving, sewing, and drawing) deemed appropriate to women. Because *sex, sexual,* and *sexuality* can refer to what a modern reader would call gender, especially to the gendered expectations associated with middle- and upper-class women, or to women as a class, and because there is no separate word for gender in the modern sense, it is often unclear which aspects of the cultural (or indeed bodily) construction of sex and gender Blake's work challenges.

The words *sex, sexes, sexual,* and *sexuality* appear for the first time in Blake's surviving writing around 1800, in poetry which is an echo chamber of voices of error and delusion. These words may reflect a new awareness of the gendered division of human experience. From 1800 to 1803 Blake lived in close proximity to the poet William Hayley, whose work explored, celebrated, and, at times, critiqued the period's construction of femininity. Feminine control of temperament was celebrated in Hayley's much republished poem for women, *The Triumphs of Temper* (1781). Blake was engaged to engrave a new set of illustrations for the 1803 edition, but his engraving style fell foul of gendered aesthetic tastes, failing to achieve the requisite softness expected of a poem addressed to women (*BR* 157). In his writing from this period, the words *sex, sexes, sexual,* and *sexuality* refer to an old order of restrictive gender roles. In 'To Tirzah', a late addition to *Songs*, 'The Sexes sprung from Shame & Pride' (l. 5, E 30), and in *Jerusalem* chapter 2, Los claims that 'Humanity knows not of Sex' and laments 'wherefore are Sexes in Beulah?' (44 [30]: 33, E 193). The association of sexuality with Beulah and with Golgonooza may be significant. In *Milton* we are told that Golgonooza, Blake's city of art, cannot be seen 'till you become Mortal & Vegetable in Sexuality' (35 [39]: 24, E 135). In these years, Blake was taking part in the cultured musical and artistic society of Chichester, the walled city close to Felpham. To become 'Mortal & Vegetable in Sexuality' may be to enter a social world whose cultural products reflect a particular model of gendered roles.[4] Certainly Blake benefited from the patronage and sociability of middle- and upper-class women. In the 1780s, his first and only printed collection, *Poetical Sketches*, was supported by Harriet Mathew and her husband. His early illuminated books were found in collections like that of Rebekah Bliss (see further

Chapter 8). Blake produced an extra-illustrated copy of Gray's poems for Ann Flaxman's library, paintings for Mrs Butts, and two works for the Countess of Egremont (shown in his 1809 exhibition). The role of educated women in fostering the arts within polite society and in shaping the field of culture may explain why Los's work in *Jerusalem* chapter 3 includes 'Dividing the Masculine & Feminine' (58: 19, E 208).

The gendering of occupations does not extend to the world of work inhabited, in the same passage, by the Daughters of Los. It is not surprising that Blake's writing should associate women with labour. Blake's wife Catherine, the daughter of a market gardener, illiterate when they married, worked with him, printing and colouring his illuminated books, and continued to print and to sell his work after William's death. And it is the words 'labour' and 'labouring' that the lines from *Jerusalem* emphasise:

> Endless their labour, with bitter food. void of sleep,
> Tho hungry they labour: they rouze themselves anxious
> Hour after hour labouring at the whirling Wheel.   (59: 30–32, E 209)

'Sexuality of character', according to Kirkland, allows an array of 'respectable' and 'happy' feminine occupations. In marked contrast, the daughters of Los in *Jerusalem*, tied to 'the whirling Wheel' are not 'free', neither are they necessarily 'respectable'. In the hostile rhetoric of Hand and Hyle in *Jerusalem* chapter 1, Jerusalem is called 'our Harlot-Sister' (18: 30, E 163). But the poetry consistently challenges categories and labels, offering states of being rather than permanent identities. Apparently simple terms seem to baffle Los when he asks 'What is a Wife & what is a Harlot? What is a Church? & What / Is a Theatre? are they Two & not One? can they Exist Separate?' (57: 8–9, E 207). The poetry rejects the categorisation of women in terms of (what we would now call) sexual identities: an 'outcast' Jerusalem hears a divine voice of pity and forgiveness that tells her 'Every Harlot was once a Virgin' in a passage that challenges the label used by Hand and Hyle (61: 52, E 212). Working-class women do not possess 'sexuality of character' in the sense of respectability. But Blake's work suggests that the forced labour of prostitutes, or the legalised prostitution of a hated marriage, do not define women's potential. Thus in *America*, 'pale religious letchery, seeking Virginity, / May find it in a harlot, and in coarse-clad honesty' (8: 10–11, E 54). The label 'harlot' is made to include 'Virginity' and to parallel 'coarse-clad honesty'. Blake seems to invert the commonly accepted meaning. Instead the line focuses on the hypocritical valuation of 'Virginity' in the customer who hides 'letchery' under religion.[5]

What Blake's writing means by 'sexuality', likewise, can be seen as the creation of culture rather than nature. In the apocalyptic Night the Ninth of *The Four Zoas*, the Eternal Man offers an apparently conventional account of 'the lovely Sex': Ahania will regenerate in the Spring, he says '& all the lovely Sex / From her shall learn obedience & prepare for a wintry grave' (p. 122, ll. 12–13, E 391). Sexual difference, naturalised through the image of plant life, is imagined as existing in Eternity: 'Thus shall the male & female live the life of Eternity.' Taken out of context, these lines could suggest that Blake has shifted towards a socially conservative notion of gender roles. But the Eternal Man speaks in the hope of staving off change and halting revolution. As the Night continues it is clear that stasis is impossible: gendered identities will be changed by the plowing of the land, by the harvest and the vintage that occur at the Last Judgment. The Eternal Man's view of 'the lovely Sex' is partial, shaped by the influence of Urizen, the Prince of Light, which seeks the preservation of the cultural order imagined as nature.

This passage questions the attempt to present the gendered social order as nature. Indeed the word *sexuality* is first detected by the *OED* one year prior to Kirkland's usage, in a reference of 1797 to 'the sexuality of plants'.[6] Books on gardening such as John Hill's *Eden: or, A Compleat Body of Gardening* (1757) had long used Linnaean terms such as 'polygamia' and 'polyandria' to define plant groups.[7] Blake worked as an engraver for the poet and doctor Erasmus Darwin who was fascinated with the sexual taxonomies of the Linnaean system. What was new about Erasmus Darwin's poem *The Loves of the Plants* (1789) was that it used metaphor to represent plant behaviour in terms of human sexual attraction. Thus the following description of plants: 'Thy love, CALLITRICHE, two Virgins share, / Smit with thy starry eye and radian hair.'[8] Neither Linnaeus, nor the botanical texts he inspired, assume a parallel between human and plant behaviour, but Blake, like Darwin, blurs the distinction. When 'The Golden nymph' in *Visions of the Daughters of Albion* tells Oothoon 'pluck thou my flower [. . .] / Another flower shall spring, because the soul of sweet delight / Can never pass away', for instance, readers assume that the reference is not solely to botany (1: 9–11, E 46). Yet Blake goes further than Darwin in also questioning the power of the parallel to constrain and define human behaviour. 'Vegetable' is a strongly negative adjective in Blake's later poetry.

Pornography, literally 'writing about prostitutes', is another word that did not exist in English during Blake's lifetime (though *pornographe* appears in French around the time of the French Revolution). Nevertheless, Blake's interest in the figure of the harlot, and the closeness of his images and text to pornographic and erotic material of his time, suggests that sexually explicit print culture is a relevant context. Phallic worship in ancient religions had been explored by antiquarian William Hamilton, and publicised by Richard Payne Knight in *A Discourse on the Worship of Priapus* (1786), authors who influenced Blake's friend Henry Fuseli. And an interest in erotica is suggested by Blake's work for Fuseli on *Allegory of a Dream of Love* (c. 1790); for Darwin's *Loves of the Plants*; and by the figures that populate the margins of his 1790s illuminated poems. In France, pornography was used to challenge the authority of Church and state under the *ancien régime*.[9] Blake's work, however, suggests a critical reading of pornographic tropes. Rather than using male sexuality to attack authority, Blake's work associates a worship of the phallus with the priest-like power of Urizen. In eternity, 'Embraces are Cominglings: from the Head even to the Feet; / And not a pompous High Priest entering by a Secret Place' (*Jerusalem* 69: 43–4, E 223). Blake's work attacks the ways in which structures of power deform sexual pleasure, creating a world in which a woman can be 'bound / In spells of law to one she loaths' (*Visions of the Daughters of Albion* 5: 21–2, E 49). Perverse sexuality is present as a dark adjunct of power in slavery, colonialism, and class inequality.

But Blake's poetry is clearly not supportive of attempts to control sexual expression. The figures that surround the text in his illuminated books often confuse a reader intent on sexing the body: this is true, for instance, of the central pair of embracing figures that rise from the underground flames on the title-page of *The Marriage of Heaven and Hell*. Obscuring sexual difference, Blake allows a reading of the text as an account of same sex attraction, a theme that emerges explicitly in the relationship of Vala and Jerusalem in *Jerusalem*. There were increased attempts to prosecute pornography after Wilberforce's Proclamation Society was formed in 1787 to spread evangelical ideas of sexual propriety and morality. In Blake's poetry, 'the System of Moral Virtue, named Rahab' is clearly destructive (*Jerusalem* 35 [39]: 10, E 181). The Blake household was clearly not constrained by the new rules of Evangelical propriety. Catherine Blake's only surviving painting (*Agnes, c.* 1800; Fitzwilliam Museum) shows Agnes from Matthew Lewis's 1796 novel *The Monk*, a book that Coleridge attacked in the *Critical Review* of 1797 as one that 'if a parent saw in the hands of a son or daughter he might reasonably turn pale'.[10] Blake's notebook records how one Sunday in August 1807, using their copy of Bysshe's *Art of Poetry* to find their fortune, his wife came up with a passage from Aphra Behn which describes 'His panting breast to hers now joind / They feast on raptures unconfind' (E 696): the new Evangelical view of Sunday and of sexuality would clearly have been uncongenial to this couple for whom erotic culture was entirely appropriate for women.

Although the naturalness of female sexual pleasure would be challenged by Evangelical discourse, Blake's culture offered many ways of imagining an innocent sexuality, from Milton's account of an unfallen sexuality in Eden to the sexual utopia imagined by Blake's friend George Cumberland. In his unpublished prose romance *The Captive of the Castle of Sennaar* (1798), Cumberland describes the island of Sophis where love forms 'the chief link' of society but there is no formal marriage. Any woman 'is at liberty to break or continue this tie, if it be not formed to procure mutual happiness'.[11] *Visions of the Daughters of Albion* offers a glimpse into a world which is both sexual and innocent, a world in which Oothoon can say: 'I loved Theotormon / And I was not ashamed' (iii: 1–2, E 45). But the first word of *Visions* is 'ENSLAV'D' (1: 1, ibid.). This is no African utopia but an American dystopia in which utopian words ('I cry, Love! Love! Love! happy happy Love! free as the mountain wind!') are inevitably rendered deeply ambiguous (7: 16, E 50). Visionary words are placed within contexts of place and time that distort their meaning.

Blake's ability to express sensual pleasure has been linked to his mother's interest in the Moravian community who valued sexuality as a form of spirituality. It is important to remember, however, that there is little evidence that Blake felt a cultish loyalty to a particular sect whether Moravian or Swedenborgian. It was typical of seekers to drop in and out of such communities. Blake's references to female prophets and mystics are revealing. The engraver William Sharp became a devoted follower and supporter of the prophetess Joanna Southcott, an Exeter domestic servant who attracted thousands of followers before her death in 1814. But Blake's notebook verse 'On the Virginity of the Virgin Mary & Johanna Southcott' mockingly questions the passivity required by the idea of virgin birth: 'Whateer is done to her she cannot know' (l. 1, E 501). Rather than celebrating a prophetic voice that reinforced early nineteenth-century sexual morality, Blake's *Jerusalem* presents Mary as an 'Adulteress' (61: 6, E 211). Early eighteenth-century satire had mocked female religious enthusiasm by locating it in the body. Blake's choice of Teresa (of Avila) as one of the figures chosen to guard the gate of Eden facing towards Beulah in *Jerusalem* is telling (72: 50, E 227). It announces his refusal to separate the spiritual from the bodily. Saint Teresa of Avila was the subject of a strikingly erotic sculpture by Bernini, and was discussed by Sir Alexander Crichton in his *Inquiry into the Nature and Origin of Mental*

Derangement (1798), in an account of 'Genius and its Diseases'. Interestingly, Crichton compares the 'dreams of SWEDENBORG' with 'those of a beautiful Spanish lady [...] that lovely, mild, and most uncommon fanaticist St. THERESA'.[12] In choosing Teresa of Avila over Joanna Southcott as a figure of female mysticism, Blake insists on the physicality of spirituality and the power of the imagination.

Whereas doctrinal statements and generalisations within Blake's work emerge from within a culture whose language of sex, sexuality, and gender was shifting and contested, the poetry that Blake created offers instead a multitude of voices, distorted fragments of lost myths variously misremembered. Whether questioning the sexed nature of the body, rejecting labels determined by moral categories, or shifting boundaries between plant, animal and human behaviour, Blake's tendency is to reject the boundaries that fix the meanings of *sex* and *sexuality* in his own time.

Notes

1. 'Sexual, adj. and n.', *OED Online*, Oxford University Press, June 2017, www.oed.com/view/Entry/177084; 'gender, n.', *OED Online*, Oxford University Press, June 2017, www.oed.com/view/Entry/77468.
2. A paradigmatic example is *The Unsex'd Females* (1798), an attack on radical women writers by the anti-Jacobin clergyman Richard Polwhele.
3. J. T. Kirkland, *An Oration Delivered, at the Request of the Society of Phi Beta Kappa, in the Chapel of Harvard College, on the Day of Their Anniversary* (Boston: John Russell, 1798), p. 11.
4. M. D. Paley, 'William Blake and Chichester', in K. Mulhallen (ed.), *Blake in our Time: Essays in Honour of G. E. Bentley* (Toronto: University of Toronto Press, 2010), pp. 215–32 (p. 219).
5. On the figure of the 'harlot' in the early poetry, see S. Matthews, 'Impurity of Diction: The "Harlots Curse" and Dirty Words', in S. Haggarty and J. Mee (eds.), *Blake and Conflict* (Basingstoke: Palgrave, 2009), pp. 65–83.
6. J. Walker, *Elementary Geography* (1797), cited in 'sexuality, n.', *OED Online*, Oxford University Press, June 2017, www.oed.com/view/Entry/177087
7. J. Hill, *Eden: or, A Compleat Body of Gardening* (London: 1757), pp. 63, 66.
8. E. Darwin, *The Botanic Garden, Part II, Containing the Loves of the Plants, A Poem, With Philosophical Notes*, 2 vols. (London: 1790), II, 4.
9. L. Hunt, 'Pornography and the French Revolution', in *The Invention of Pornography, 1500–1800: Obscenity and the Origins of Modernity* (Cambridge, MA: MIT Press, 1993), pp. 301–40 (p. 305).
10. [S. T. Coleridge], 'Review of Matthew G. Lewis, The Monk', *The Critical Review* (February 1797), 194–200.

11. G. Cumberland, *The Captive of the Castle of Sennaar: An African Tale*, ed. G. E. Bentley, Jr (Montreal and London: McGill-Queen's University Press, 1998), pp. 37, 38.
12. A. Crichton, *An Inquiry into the Nature and Origin of Mental Derangement*, 2 vols. (London: Cadell and Davies, 1798) II, 44. In an appendix, Crichton includes an extended account of St Theresa, taken from J. Townsend's *A Journey Through Spain in the Years 1786 and 1787* (London: C. Dilly, 1791).

CHAPTER 37

War and Revolution

Andrew Lincoln

Blake hated war, frequently denounced it, and sometimes wrote as a pacifist. But the Blake who, in his 'Continental' prophecies, imagined the globe swept by violent revolution, saw an obvious connection between war and social transformation.

The American War of Independence (1775–83) began when Blake was seventeen and finished when he was twenty-five. In Britain this period saw a proliferation of newspapers and periodicals, with greater freedom to report, and a new sense of the importance of public opinion. Many Britons sympathised with the Americans, who resisted the British government's attempt to impose taxes (intended to recoup costs of the Seven Years' War of 1756–63). Political caricatures often depicted America as the land of virtue and liberty, England as suffering from corruption and oppression. Dissenters and liberal Anglicans opposed the war, while loyalist Anglicans (including those in America) supported the British government's attempt to quell the rebels by force, as did the Methodist leader John Wesley. Official days of Fast and Humiliation were proclaimed in the King's name, with church services designed to promote the view that rebellion was evil and that war was a punishment from God for national sinfulness. Victories were celebrated with Thanksgiving services. The liturgy of both kinds of service adopted an Old Testament rhetoric of divine wrath. The divisions in public opinion are reflected in verse of the period (much of it printed in periodicals): there is a wide range of poetic protests – against taxes, impressment, military incompetence, the destruction caused by war – and many patriotic poems, including drinking songs, victory celebrations, and protests against American violence.

In Britain writers could usually express sympathies with the rebels or protest against the war more easily than painters could, and might publish anonymously or pseudonymously. Artists who sought to exhibit and sell individual works could not afford to alienate those with money and influence. Painters in Britain known to be sympathetic to the American rebels – including the Americans John Singleton Copley and Benjamin West – usually refrained from expressing such views publicly, and might even paint subjects in support of the British war effort.[1] There were incentives for artists to engage in patriotic commemoration. A public that showed relatively little interest in historical paintings based upon subjects from antiquity might be drawn to one based on a dramatic event from the contemporary wars – as Copley's *Death of Major Pierson* (1783) showed. Engravers could find employment in reproducing patriotic paintings: Richard Earlom and Robert Pollard, for example, both engraved Tilly Kettle's portrait of Admiral Kemperfelt (1782).

The Americans initially saw themselves as defending their rights as British subjects loyal to the crown, but – under the influence of radical pamphlets such as Thomas Paine's *Common Sense* (1776), in which monarchy was 'desacralised' – they came to see themselves as American citizens fighting for an independent Republic.[2] The outcome of the war certainly depended upon actions on the battlefield, but was also decided by the war of ideas, by the contest between alternative visions of the future and beliefs about the authority of tradition.[3] Blake seems to have seen the opposition between libertarian and reactionary views as revelatory, a sign that errors submerged within traditional power structures were being revealed in terms that most people would come to recognise. He saw Paine as a type of prophet, a 'worker of miracles', who could utterly change the way people saw their own possibilities ('Annotations to Watson', E 616).

These ideas emerged slowly in Blake's work. In *Poetical Sketches* (printed privately, in 1783, with the help of friends), the anti-monarchical and anti-war sentiments in his Shakespearean imitations and in the ballad 'Gwin, King of Norway' are distanced and oblique. The two watercolours he exhibited at the Royal Academy in 1784 both treat war in a mode remote from contemporary history. 'War Unchained by an Angel, Fire, Pestilence, and Famine following', now known only from a preliminary sketch (Donald Davidson collection),[4] presents war and its accompanying afflictions as a divine judgement – a view which echoes that of the church. Behind a flying angel Blake depicts, on the right, soldiers rushing with weapons, and on the left, a family in distress. The title evokes the vengeful God of the Old Testament, but also the New Testament book of Revelation, where divine wrath is related to the Last Judgement. This is a connection that for Blake could link the negative effects of war with the positive potential for spiritual transformation – a connection that becomes important but problematic in his work.

The French Revolution, which began in 1789 when Blake was thirty-five, almost certainly strengthened this connection in his thinking, while forcing him to question it. The Revolution was initially welcomed by many Britons, who assumed the outcome would be a French constitutional monarchy like Britain's. But the violent progress of events in France (including the execution of Louis XVI), and the course of the 'revolution debate' in Britain, combined with France's declaration of war in February 1793, generated fierce government reaction. Edmund Burke's conservative warning, *Reflection on the Revolution in France* (1790), provoked a range of radical responses, including the enormously influential *Rights of Man* (1791–2), in which Tom Paine applied his republicanism directly to British politics, and Mary Wollstonecraft's *Rights of Woman* (1792), which offered a fundamental challenge to conventional assumptions about the nature and status of women. Painters with libertarian sympathies, such as James Barry, George Romney, and Henri Fuseli, had recourse to legendary or mythical analogues (e.g. images of Milton's Satan, seen as heroic rebel). As plebeian radicalism began to find a voice, sometimes in the form of millenarian prophecy, the government sought to stifle debate with harsh legal measures, culminating in the two 'Gagging Acts' of 1795. Loyalist Associations and Church and King Clubs also worked to intimidate radicals.[5]

The first book of Blake's incomplete poem, *The French Revolution*, dated 1791, belongs to the early years of hope. Like some other contemporary writers, including Burke and S. T. Coleridge, he turned to the sublime and the Gothic for a language of extremities to portray the momentous significance of the revolution, which was widely seen as an unprecedented occurrence. In suggesting the spiritual significance of the reported political events, he shows the ancient regime as a grotesque existential Bastille; but there are already signs of unease in his presentation of the revolutionaries. For Blake liberty meant the ability to see 'the Infinite in all things' (*There Is No Natural Religion [b]*, E 3). It did not mean simply exchanging the rule of kings for the rule of law. In his poem, a libertarian rhetoric of infinite desire is in tension with the class positions of those who utter it (the liberal aristocrat Orleans, and the liberal cleric Seyes). As the National Assembly constitutes itself as a legislative body in charge of an army, Blake's language assumes ominous signs of petrifaction: 'Like pillars of ancient halls [...] they sat' (*The French Revolution* l. 258, E 297). The text survives only as a proof version of a book that was never published.

The two illuminated 'Prophecies', *America* (1793) and *Europe* (1794), were produced in the context of deepening crisis, and combined enthusiastic optimism with intimations of doubt. 'Illuminated printing' gave Blake control over the production of his works, but did not completely free him from the dangers of expressing radical views. He removed from *America* plates in which 'George the third' was explicitly an agent of oppression; in the final version 'The King of England' appears more ambiguously as a fearful witness of events.[6] The obscurity of Blake's symbolism is often seen as a precautionary measure, but seems essential to his prophetic purpose. He combines the simplified oppositions of popular prints with a huge range of allusions – to history, the Bible, classical literature, English poetry, and the visual arts – producing an idiom that attempts to challenge cultural tradition fundamentally. The visionary perspective works to transform the historical clash of particular material interests into a spiritual conflict between human desire and the powers that seek to repress it. Orc's fierce embrace of the Shadowy daughter of Urthona in the 'Preludium' gives an unsettling view of the consequences of repression. The conflict in the 'Prophecy' between those in America, such as Paine, Franklin, and Washington, and the reactionary government of Britain is the visible manifestation of a deeper conflict between human desire, demonised as Orc, and reactionary fear personified in Albion's Angel. The passions inspired in and by Orc are erotic and anarchic, rejecting all externally imposed restraints. The narrative moves towards a choice between naked human form and the status quo that can now be recognised as subhuman, reptilian. Revolution and war are shown to expose and clarify the errors of tradition, so that they can be recognised and cast off.

This kind of optimism was not repeated in *Europe* (dated 1794). The early war years brought hardship to the labouring classes. Anti-war poetry of the 1790s often focused on the devastation wrought by conflict upon the domestic world, the misery of war-widows, the plight of orphans, ruined cottages.[7] Poets, as usual, had more freedom of expression than painters. When, in 1794, William Hodges exhibited two paintings which contrasted the benefits of peace with the domestic devastation caused by war (*The Effects of Peace* and *The Consequences of War*, 1794), the Duke of York objected to the political tendencies of the pictures; the exhibition soon closed.[8] This context throws light on Blake's recourse in *Europe* to visual depictions of extreme desolation – including fire, famine, and pestilence. But in *Europe* these scenes implicitly pose the question: do the sufferings and destruction inflicted by war and other catastrophes lead to a spiritual awakening, or do they drive people further into superstitious obeisance to repressive, vengeful, warlike conceptions of deity (epitomised in the enthroned, Popish figure shown on plate 11 that bears some resemblance to popular anti-Catholic propaganda)? In the central narrative, Albion's Angel, after his council chamber collapses, retreats into a primitive Druidical mystery religion – perhaps a reflection on the state's recourse to a rhetoric of divine wrath and sinfulness to promote its war effort.

The emphasis on divine wrath in the church's response to war conflicted with the image of Christ the good shepherd, the gentle, loving saviour, and with the sensitivity to beauty and suffering, and the good natured benevolence that were recognised aspects of Christian virtue in the eighteenth century. In *Europe*, the role of a feminised religion of maternal gentleness, beauty, and peace in sustaining the patriarchal barbarism of Albion's angel is explored in Enitharmon's song. In the 'Preludium' the protests of the Shadowy female, a benighted victim of masculine lust, are pacified and repressed by the seductive vision of divinity incarnate as a dependent child.

The continental prophecies are framed by *The Song of Los* (dated 1795) which briefly considers the possibility that revolutionary war might spread liberty across the globe. Such a prospect may have looked increasingly doubtful. During 1797–8 and 1803–5 there were serious threats of a French invasion. In response, the militia and the volunteer movements were greatly expanded across the British Isles and coastal defences were strengthened. Although the major battles were fought abroad, the fabric of British society was becoming increasingly militarised. In August 1803, while Blake was living at Felpham under the patronage of William Hayley, an altercation with a soldier, John Schofield, who had entered his garden led to Blake being charged with, and acquitted of, assault and sedition. If this incident increased his sense of vulnerability as a voice 'crying in the Wilderness' (*All Religions Are One*, E 1), in May 1804 the hopes once inspired by France were further challenged when Napoleon became its emperor.

During these years, Blake worked on his long manuscript poem, *VALA / The Four Zoas* (dated 1797, but composed and revised over several years). This was conceived as a transformation of the martial epic, in which 'strong heroic Verse' would engage in, and promote, 'Intellectual Battle' (N1, p. 3, ll. 2–3, E 300). The original title, *Vala*, is the name of a goddess of love who is characterised by weeping and gentleness, but who presides over universally destructive wars of empire. The narrative ends in a lengthy description of 'The Last Judgment', in which orgiastic violence helps to produce a universal awakening – the ultimate expression in Blake of the liberating potential of violence.

The later illuminated works, *Milton* and *Jerusalem* (both dated 1804), emerge from the experience of seemingly unending war, increasingly served by 'dark Satanic mills', with lethal new technologies, such as

Congreve's rockets and Shrapnel's shells, continuing economic hardship, disrupted trade, high taxes, and accumulating casualties. Blake now associates the problem of war with the Satanic 'selfhood', which fosters self-righteousness and revenge instead of Christian forgiveness, and with the seductive power of Tirzah, the limited conception of material nature. Like some counter-revolutionary writers, including Edmund Burke, Blake now argues that Deism and the influence of classical literature pose a threat to Christianity. Voltaire and Rousseau, who appeared in *The Song of Los* as portents of revolutionary liberation (4: 18, E 68), are now condemned as among the causes of war. John Milton, in attacking the martial values of classical epic in *Paradise Lost*, was still trapped by the narrative form of epic, and by its masculinist mind-set. In *Milton*, the seventeenth-century poet has to descend from eternity and unite with his feminine 'emanation' – and with Blake. The multi-stranded, disruptive prophetic form of Blake's own late epics is implicitly an assault on the mental chains that lie at the root of war. Yet in contrasting corporeal war with mental war, Blake, for all his anti-war sentiments, still apparently saw the possibility of a productive relationship between them ('Preface', pl. 1, E 95). The 'Wine-press' of war is the 'Printing-Press' of Los, Blake's prophet-figure (27 [29]: 8, E 124).

If Blake could oppose war in his privately produced illuminated books, it was more difficult to resist completely the incentives to engage publicly in patriotic celebration. There were many such inducements. In 1795, for example, the government agreed to fund monuments to British heroes of the war, to be erected in Westminster Abbey and St Paul's cathedral. After Nelson's victory at the Battle of the Nile (1798) a competition for a naval monument was announced: Blake engraved three designs by his friend John Flaxman – for a 230-foot high statue of Britannia, to be erected in Greenwich Park. In 1807, in the wake of Nelson's death at Trafalgar (1805), Benjamin West finished an *Apotheosis of Nelson*, while Flaxman began work on a statue of Nelson destined for St Paul's.[9] It is in this context that we need to see the military content of Blake's exhibition of 1809. As an artist and engraver who needed employment, Blake had to find a way of working with the tide of militaristic nationalism. His 'grand Apotheoses of NELSON and PITT', painted 1805–9, were clearly an attempt to do this (see Figs. 7.1 and 7.2). He hoped for 'a national commission to execute these two Pictures on a scale that is suitable to the grandeur of the nation, who is the parent of his heroes' (*Descriptive Catalogue*, E 531). The *Descriptive Catalogue* attempts to dissociate these works in 'Fresco' from the art of ancient Greece, and connect them instead with the art of ancient Asia. The serenity of Blake's two 'heroes' amid the violence of war is in line

War and Revolution 331

with the poetic tradition of British military heroism, but these paintings are no ordinary celebrations of martial valour. In the Nelson picture, the Leviathan (or war by sea) is a monstrous snake that crushes naked bodies ('Nations of the Earth') within its coils, guided by the naked figure of Nelson, who stands above the fallen figure of a black slave. In Pitt, the hero is an angelic, robed figure accompanied by a ploughman and a reaper; the latter drops bodies into the open jaws of the Behemoth (war by land) below Pitt's feet. With their incongruous mixture of serene angelic control and monstrous destruction these pictures may be, as Morton Paley says, 'dark satires of war'.[10] But together they may also show war bringing humanity to a Last Judgement. Nelson and Pitt may be instruments of divine providence (as Blake's Devil would say) 'without knowing it' (*Marriage* pl. 6, E 35).

Blake's exhibition was a commercial failure. In this sense he was unable to capitalise on the opportunities war provided to contemporary painters. But in a less direct sense war did help to sustain his work as an artist. One of his best patrons was Thomas Butts, who bought illuminated books, colour prints, and some major series of paintings – and who worked in the military bureaucracy. It could hardly have escaped Blake's notice that much of his artistic production was partially dependent on funds that had been derived from the office of the Commissary General of Musters.

Notes

1. H. Hoock, *The King's Artists: The Royal Academy of Arts and the Politics of British Culture 1760–1840* (Oxford: Clarendon Press, 2003), pp. 150–64.
2. V. Carretta, *George the Third and the Satirists from Hogarth to Byron* (Athens, GA: University of Georgia Press, 1990), p. 150.
3. See J. E. Bradley, 'The British Public and the American Revolution: Ideology, Interest and Opinion', in H. T. Dickinson (ed.), *Britain and the American Revolution* (London: Longman, 1998), pp. 124–54.
4. The image appears in M. Butlin, 'Note', in 'Five Blakes from a c19th-Century Scottish Collection', *Blake / An Illustrated Quarterly*, 7.1 (1973), 4–8 (p. 4): http://bq.blakearchive.org/7.1.butlin
5. D. Bindman, *The Shadow of the Guillotine* (London: British Museum, 1989), p. 18.
6. D. V. Erdman, *Blake: Prophet against Empire* (Princeton: Princeton University Press, 1977), pp. 152–3.
7. S. Bainbridge, *British Poetry and the Revolutionary and Napoleonic Wars* (Oxford: Oxford University Press, 2003), pp. 40–1.

8. Hoock, *King's Artists*, pp. 191–2.
9. M. Eaves, *The Counter-Arts Conspiracy: Art and Industry in the Age of Blake* (Ithaca, NY: Cornell University Press, 1992), pp. 82–3.
10. M. D. Paley, *Energy and Imagination: A Study of the Development of Blake's Thought* (Oxford: Clarendon Press, 1970), p. 194.

CHAPTER 38

(Without) Sympathy

Steven Goldsmith

Sometime around 1780, perhaps during a stint at the Royal Academy, William Blake drew a back-view pencil sketch of the Belvedere Torso. The art school exercise is common enough, but in this case, the cost-conscious student filled his sketch space with other, unrelated figures, creating a hallucinatory effect: a single right foot, on a sculpture base, seems to materialise directly from the disappearing bottom end of the lightly sketched torso (Fig. 38.1). Within five years, according Martin Butlin's dating, Blake relegated this minor sketch to the back of a more fully developed pen and wash study for a painting of Moses or Aaron (Butlin 112; Fig. 38.2). Again making the best of limited supplies, Blake added a small strip of paper to the original drawing, turned the sheet over, and rotated it ninety degrees. The recto torso-with-foot now subsided into verso, a back-view hidden on the bottom.

Blake remained a lifelong admirer of the Belvedere Torso. His late broadside 'On Homers Poetry' celebrated the ancient fragment as an exemplar of aesthetic unity and originality, and his *Descriptive Catalogue* exempted it from the charge that the Greeks had stolen and perverted Hebraic originals (E 269, 531). A generation after Blake's death Samuel Palmer could still recall how his mentor's 'powers were concentrated in admiration' whenever he spoke of it (*BR* 392). Although faithful to its model, Blake's early sketch provides a stranger view of the antique body than the one he later idealised: a view that is derivative (Blake copied from a plaster cast), segmented without regard to a whole, and – most important – from behind. My proposal is that this inconspicuous sketch initiates a sub-logic of reverse-side embodiment that persists among the human forms comprising Blake's visual corpus, reappearing as a minor but always possible motif: a figure profiled from behind, for whom the back, often in conjunction with the foot but always instead of the face, becomes the distinguishing if generic and non-differentiating feature. As we will see,

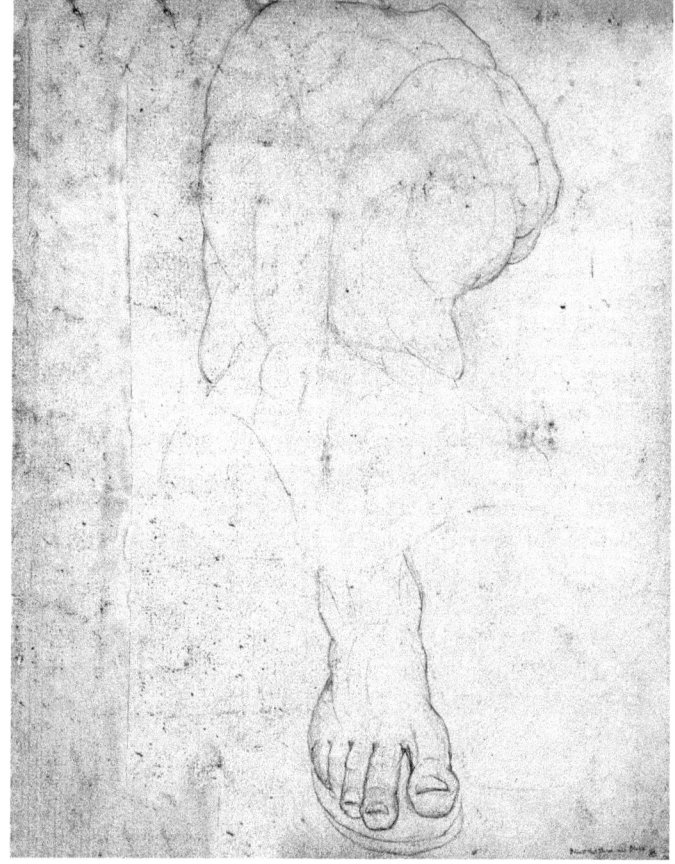

Fig. 38.1: W. Blake, *The Belvedere Torso [verso]*, c. 1779/80, graphite on two joined sheets, Rosenwald Collection, National Gallery, Washington

this *rückenfigur* remains at odds with the period's prevailing norms of identity, social recognition, and, above all, sympathy.

We are accustomed to consider Blake's representation of the liberated human being in terms of a fully revealed frontal form, typically male: one thinks of Jesus resurrected, Milton disrobed, and, most emblematic of all, the image of exuberant youth known as 'Albion rose'. Blake first sketched the latter figure around the same time as the Belvedere Torso drawing, and, moreover, he sketched it twice, in front and back versions, recto/verso on the same sheet of paper (Victoria and Albert Museum; Butlin 73). Together, these seminal drawings suggest that back-view representation

Fig. 38.2: W. Blake, *Moses Staying the Plague (?) [recto]*, c. 1780/85, graphite on two joined sheets, Rosenwald Collection, National Gallery, Washington

involves a principle of completeness: a whole human figure seen from behind need only turn around to reveal its ever present if sometimes hidden face. According to this 360 degree logic, a back-form humanised in this way would belong to the totality of revealed forms Blake invokes towards the end of *Jerusalem* when he declares 'All Human Forms identified' and describes an apocalyptic prosopopoeia that gives a face to *everything*: 'Tree Metal Earth & Stone' (99: 1; E 258). In the end-time, every 'Man stood fourfold', and 'each Four Faces had' (98: 12; E 257), one to point in each cardinal direction. Imagined thus, Blake's resurrected human figure no longer hides its back from observation; it faces forward all around.

The turned away figures I want to trace to Blake's early back-view sketch of the Belvedere Torso represent a minor but persistent challenge, an undertow, as it were, to this desire for fully revealed form and the modes of social relation or communicability it promotes. Rather than representing an incompleteness that might be remedied as soon as one turns to show a face, they affirm the incompleteness of any system of face-to-face identification. Remarkably flexible and various, these reverse figures cannot be reduced to a representation of fallenness, as if embodiment were postlapsarian and back-view embodiment worse, though sometimes they do suggest such a limited state. Blake often shows them in profile, making it difficult to determine whether they are about to reveal themselves or withdraw from attention. More rarely, he shows them departing from us altogether, revealing only the fleshy bottom of a foot as they push off (Fig. 38.3). Even after 'All Human Forms' have been 'identified' in the apocalypse that concludes *Jerusalem*, the book's last, image-only plate (100) still leaves space for a *rückenfigur* of this kind.

Although it may be tempting to consider these rear-view figures as gestures towards a materiality inaccessible to higher cognition, they do not require us to posit some inverse sublimity of flesh and bone, a bottom end of corporeal life inherently unrepresentable and therefore outside the order of signification or culture. In David Wills's *Dorsality*, the back stands for an entanglement of human organism and technologisation operative from the start: at an early evolutionary stage the straightening spine of an upright stance allowed the brain pan to widen while freeing the hands to use tools. For Wills, there is no originary human body apart from such bio-technologisation.[1] The back itself is an internal tool produced by and enabling human development, an idea already familiar from *The Book of Urizen*, where Blake describes the spine, a 'linked infernal chain' (10: 37; E 75), as one of the earliest products of a body formed by neither God nor Nature but by mechanical production. Although they are often strikingly, even eerily beautiful, Blake's back-view figures do not romanticise a bodily life apart from cultural production. They clearly *are* figures, aesthetic extensions of the human, but they also paradoxically indicate that the process of figural extension can never be complete – or completely identified with a face. Within the limits of representation, they invite us to consider what remains of the human figure after prosopopoeia has done its work. Through these back-view forms, 'the human comes into being, again and again, as that which we have yet to know.'[2]

As if it were not strange enough for a foot to dangle directly from a headless torso, without any mediating or organic relation to indicate that these parts belong to *somebody*, perhaps the most disorienting feature of Blake's early sketch is that this anomalous foot faces forward, joining front and rear views, but without reconciling them. While there is no direct correlate to this amalgamation in Blake's later imagery, the figure does bear

Fig. 38.3: W. Blake, *The Angel Rolling the Stone Away from the Sepulchre*, c. 1808, pen and ink and watercolour, Victoria and Albert Museum, London

a striking resemblance to the first and last images of *The Book of Urizen*, Blake's most developed genealogy of embodiment and subject formation. *Urizen* begins and ends in a front view so grotesquely compressed that the titular figure becomes little more than a face pedestalled on a single, precariously aligned foot (WBA copy D, obj. 1, 26). Although the disarticulation of parts is similar, Urizen's face has replaced the back of the

Torso sketch, while the foot, at least on the title page, has become something of a third hand, assisting in the process of textual production by holding open a book from which Urizen copies on either side. Symmetrically framed by its first and last plates, all the contents of *Urizen* lie between self-replicating mirror images of 'face with foot'. *Urizen* is Blake's most suffocating text, governed by a no-exit, all-encompassing logic of fallen development that begins with Mosaic inscription, under the dreaded tablets of law, and ends entangled in the 'Net of Religion' (25: 22; E 82). The human being whose identity comes into existence under the law appears primarily as a face; indeed, he must show his face and be accountable. The law embodies itself as a prosopopoeia that leaves nothing behind.

From early on Blake's figure for this identity between person and law was Moses, whom he began illustrating in a series of pictures contemporaneous with the Torso sketch and already with what would become Urizen's identifying features: a long-bearded face and measured frontal symmetry. Despite his elongated form, 'Moses Receiving the Law' (*c.* 1780; Yale Center for British Art; Butlin 111) clearly anticipates the title plate of *Urizen*. With hindsight, we can now see that the relationship between the Torso sketch and the recto image that eventually displaced it is not quite an accidental one. Almost certainly a scene from the Pentateuch, and most likely a portrait of Moses (only the dark beard has made identification uncertain),[3] the larger, more developed picture (Fig. 38.2) actively reorganises and makes whole the misaligned parts of the earlier sketch (Fig. 38.1). The single right foot of the latter has migrated to the frontal stance of the statuesque, well-balanced Mosaic figure, whose face, by far the most detailed element of the new picture, now becomes the composition's focal point. Meanwhile the back view of the torso gets redistributed to the minor figure in the lower right corner. Whatever scene might be unfolding here, the picture encourages us to imagine a narrative in which this marginal rear-view figure, enabled by the intercession of Moses, might rise, turn, and – like Moses – show his face. To follow the progress from verso sketch to recto painting is like watching disaggregated parts assemble themselves into the personification of a completed human being; it is like watching a brief history of interpellation.

I will not rehearse Althusser's familiar story of the individual, hailed from behind by a policeman, who 'turn[s] around' and by means of 'this mere one-hundred-and-eighty-degree physical conversion [...] becomes a *subject*'.[4] But it is worth remembering that for Althusser, as for Blake, the prototype of 'the ideological recognition function' is Moses, as he turns to answer God's call from the burning bush. Even though Althusser describes interpellation in auditory and linguistic terms, his emphasis on the 'mirror-structure' of ideology suggests that the 180 degree pivot also involves the experience of recognising, and being recognised by, another face. For Blake, these everyday constitutive performances of personhood extend beyond inscription under punitive law. The 'mirror duplication' that Althusser claims 'is constitutive of ideology and enables its functioning' is also a matter of soft power, readily visible in the compulsory kindness required by eighteenth-century norms of sympathy.[5] The commandments Urizen introduces between the first and last plates of his book include 'Laws [...] / Of pity, compassion, forgiveness' (4: 34–5; E 72). If 'the humanistic imperative to conceive others as like subjects' underlies 'a sentimental politics of recognition', as Jacques Khalip suggests,[6] then we can observe this imperative as soon as Adam Smith identifies the mirror effect of shared emotions in *Theory of Moral Sentiments* (1759): 'Grief and joy [...] strongly expressed in the look and gestures of any one, at once affect the spectator with some degree of a like painful or agreeable emotion. A smiling face is, to every body that sees it, a cheerful object; as a sorrowful countenance, on the other hand, is a melancholy one.'[7] Blake condenses this reciprocal structure into a single line from 'The Divine Image': 'Pity, a human face' (l. 10; E 12). Pity takes on the features of a human face, and the face becomes human by expressing pity. Moreover, because 'Pity' toggles between noun and verb, its structure requires that *two* faces be present to one another, the one that expresses pity and the one that is pitied. The problem with this co-facial structure (which precedes any individuals who might occupy it) is that the presiding 'Pity' may be either a spontaneous effusion of benevolent human nature or an abstract personification of the kind ubiquitous in late eighteenth-century poetry. To the extent that Pity is pure convention, producing rather than reflecting human nature, it is as inescapable a mirror structure as the one that frames *The Book of Urizen*. Within that mechanism, whoever shows or sees a face is, in Althusser's terms, 'always-already a subject'.[8]

As scholars have begun to demonstrate, Blake was well versed in the generic expectations sentimentalism placed upon its subjects – subjects whose sympathetic tears were understood to constitute their humanity.[9] 'Moral weeping', writes an anonymous author from 1755, 'is the sign of so noble a passion, that it may be questioned whether those are properly men, who never weep upon any occasion.'[10] Blake mimes, and then troubles, the requirements of face-to-face sympathy in the rhetorical questions that open 'On Anothers Sorrow': 'Can I see anothers woe / And not be in sorrow too. / Can I see anothers grief, / And not seek for kind relief' (ll. 1–4; E 17). Here pity springs forth 'automatically' in both senses of that term: it is a spontaneous, natural response free of deliberation and a social mechanism so habitually engrained as to resist critical reflection. Upon seeing a face of sorrow two consequences immediately follow: one first feels sympathy and then, equally irresistibly, one acts to relieve suffering (or at least seeks to do so). For over a century, sensibility advocates summoned this two-step sequence (first the transfer of emotion from one person to another and then the transfer of emotion into benevolent action) to refute Hobbesean theories of self-interest and to affirm an innate human capacity for compassion. And they did so using a small, programmatic repertoire of words and concepts recycled on any occasion.

Thus a typical theological account of compassion by an early eighteenth-century Anglican preacher, virtually indistinguishable from the language of Latitudinarian clergymen forty years earlier, shares much the same contour as a typical medical account three-quarters of a century later by John Hunter, the London surgeon parodied by Blake in *An Island in the Moon*:

> Richard Fiddes (1720): 'God has implanted in our very Frame and Make, a compassionate Sense of the Suffering and Misfortunes of other People, which disposes us to contribute to their Relief; so that when we see any of our Fellow-Creatures in Circumstances of Distress, we are naturally, I had almost said, mechanically inclined to help them.'[11]
>
> John Hunter (1794): '[O]ne of [sympathy's] chief uses is to excite an active interest in favour of the Distressed, the mind of the spectators taking on nearly the same action with that of the sufferers, and disposing them to give relief or consolation.'[12]

In 'On Anothers Sorrow', Blake estranges the see–feel–act mechanisms of sensibility without disavowing them altogether, using 'sentimental devices to overturn sentiment', as James Chandler nicely puts it.[13] Most importantly, Blake allows the reader to grasp that sentimental paradigms *are* devices, not hardwired facts of nature. In this way 'Pity' becomes available to reconfiguration; one might even imagine a world without it: 'Pity would be no more, / If we did not make somebody Poor' ('The Human Abstract' ll. 1–2; E 27). In 'On Anothers Sorrow', rote emotions subtly give way to more difficult, inarticulate ones. Blake ends his song with the prolonged, unsettling tone of Jesus moaning, a sound one would not know how to translate into readymade feeling or action: 'Till our grief is fled and gone / He [Jesus] does sit by us and moan.' Not fully cooperating with the routines of sympathy, that moan is an acoustic version of Blake's back-view figures; it gestures towards other ways of being human.[14]

Blake calls the desire to undo interpellation 'self-annihilation', and it is this desire to walk away and become impersonal that so often haunts his reverse-side figures. Of course, to avert the face and walk away from the demands of subjectivity is exactly what a subject cannot do. Against the burden of subjection, Blake's back-view figures can only seem wishful. By no means have they already broken free into a post-human landscape; eventually, we understand, they *will* turn and show their faces again. And yet these figures perform a critical function nonetheless; they introduce an element of impersonality that existing modes of identification cannot fully integrate, and they do this in large part by momentarily short-circuiting the comfort of sympathetic recognition.

Consider two possibilities these back-view figures begin to activate. First, they are often frankly erotic, but with an eroticism specific to their self-estrangement and anonymous corporeality. We often have trouble identifying these figures, and even when we feel relatively certain we know who they are, as in the image of Urizen descending through clouds (WBA copy D, obj. 13), their rear views involve a generic, almost interchangeable quality, as if they belonged to no one in particular. It would be difficult to distinguish Urizen's back from Los's, Los's from Milton's, Milton's from Albion's, and so on down the line. One consequence of this non-differentiation from behind is that it opens a space for gender confusion Blake regularly exploited. A somewhat androgynous male runner in *Urizen*, with flames passing between his thighs, becomes a somewhat androgynous female runner in another rendition.[15] Moreover, because Blake followed Michelangelo in rendering every body to some extent a male body, these sites of corporeal indetermination are almost always homoerotic. They invoke modalities of pleasure not easily assimilated into instrumental, procreative sexualities.[16]

In the relentlessly fallen world of *Urizen*, even the most sublimated of these figures retains a hint of reverse-side eroticism. On Plate 25, Urizen re-enacts the scene in Exodus where God grants Moses a passing, partial revelation on Mount Sinai, demonstrating that access to the divine must inevitably be mediated. If, as Anne-Lise François suggests, this biblical scene is best understood as an allegory of inscription under law and language,[17] then Urizen here is a figure for sublimation itself, a possibility Blake sometimes underscored by diminishing the erotic outline of the buttocks and making God's flowing robe more spidery, web-like, and ghostly (WBA copy A; obj. 28):

> Cold he wander'd on high [...]
> A cold shadow follow'd behind him [...]
> Till a Web dark & cold, throughout all
> The tormented element stretch'd
> From the sorrows of Urizens soul. (23: 5–17, E 82)

But conversely, Blake sometimes enhanced the figure's eroticism by making the robe more transparent, allowing Urizen's fleshy back-form to show through (WBA copy G, obj. 23). Depending on the printing, Blake would more or less literalise the lines from Exodus this figure illustrates: 'Thou shalt see my back parts: but my face shall not be seen' (33:23). Moreover, by focusing on this attenuated, backend revelation, Blake accents the contrast within Exodus between this event and another tradition that describes the relationship between God and Moses in terms more conducive to conventions of sympathy: 'And the LORD spoke to Moses face to face, as a man speaketh to his friend' (33:11).

The other thing these figures do is to keep moving forward. They are back-forms mobilised by their feet. Consider the plate in *Milton* (pl. 16 [18], E 110) where Milton reshapes Urizen on the banks of the Arnon River, striding forward through stone tablets of law that fall to either side (Fig. 38.4). Viewers of this plate have noted that the foot shattering the word 'self-hood' at the lower margin corresponds to Milton's hand on the title page, which divides his name in the upper margin: selfhood and name fall away in parallel (WBA copy B, obj. 1).[18] But the title page also suggests that breaking the name represents only a partial step beyond identification, for we still see Milton's half-profiled and immediately recognisable face. This figure may now be nameless but is still Milton. Plate 16 [18] (Fig. 38.4) shows a later stage in the process of self-annihilation; agency shifts from hand to foot, and now the figure shows no face at all.

So what is Milton doing to Urizen's limp, rag-doll face – assuming that this *is* Milton? The closest corresponding text describes Milton as a sculptor, engaged in a 'work on limits' very close to what Foucault would describe as 'a patient labor giving form to our impatience for liberty':[19]

> Silent Milton stood before
> The darkend Urizen; as the sculptor silent stands before
> His forming image; he walks round it patient labouring.
> Thus Milton stood forming bright Urizen. (20: 7–10, E 114)

This labour takes place face to face, but the picture positions us outside the encounter and behind Milton. The fact that the text describes Milton

(Without) Sympathy 343

Fig. 38.4: W. Blake, *Milton a Poem*, Copy B, Plate 15, 1811, relief and white-line etching with hand colouring, Huntington Library and Art Gallery, California

circling Urizen indicates that the 360 degree work of transformation involves shaping Urizen into a whole human being, though it also serves to remind us that Urizen is not all face, that he does indeed have a reverse side. While Milton works to illuminate his fallen, 'darkened' state by giving him human form, there still remains a 'dark end' we cannot see, made visible for us only in the comparable backend of Milton before us. Whatever humanisation is taking place in this scene, and whatever new face is being formed, an anonymous back-form remains, an impersonal embodiment no face can personify completely.

Notes

1. D. Wills, *Dorsality: Thinking Back through Technology and Politics* (Minneapolis, MN: University of Minnesota Press, 2008), pp. 2–23.
2. J. Butler, *Precarious Life: The Powers of Mourning and Violence* (London: Verso, 2004), p. 49.
3. The scene may illustrate Numbers 16:46–50. See *Blake Newsletter*, IX (1975–6), 72.
4. L. Althusser, 'Ideology and Ideological State Apparatuses' [1969], in *Lenin and Philosophy*, trans. B. Brewster (New York: Monthly Review Press, 1971), pp. 127–86 (p. 174).
5. Ibid., pp. 172, 180.
6. J. Khalip, *Anonymous Life: Romanticism and Dispossession* (Stanford, CA: Stanford University Press, 2009), p. 17.
7. A. Smith, *The Theory of Moral Sentiments*, ed. K. Haakonssen (Cambridge: Cambridge University Press, 2002 [1759]), p. 13.
8. Althusser, 'Ideology', p. 176.
9. See S. Goldsmith, *Blake's Agitation: Criticism and the Emotions* (Baltimore: Johns Hopkins University Press, 2013), and J. Chandler, *An Archaeology of Sympathy: The Sentimental Mode in Literature and Cinema* (Chicago: University of Chicago Press, 2013), pp. 269–81.
10. Cited by R. S. Crane, in 'Suggestions toward a Genealogy of the "Man of Feeling"', *ELH*, 1.3 (1934), 205–30 (p. 206).
11. R. Fiddes, *Fifty-Two Practical Discourses on Several Subjects* (London: 1720), p. 112.
12. J. Hunter, *A Treatise on the Blood, Inflammation, and Gun-Shot Wounds* (London: J. Richardson, 1794), p. 6.
13. Chandler, *Archaeology of Sympathy*, p. 275.
14. See chapters 3 and 4 of Goldsmith, *Blake's Agitation*.
15. See the first 'Supplementary Illustration' in W. Blake, *The Urizen Books*, ed. D. Worrall (Princeton: Princeton University Press, 1995), p. 118.
16. See R. Sha, *Perverse Romanticism: Aesthetics and Sexuality in Britain, 1750–1832* (Baltimore, MD: Johns Hopkins University Press, 2009), pp. 183–240, and C. Hobson, *Blake and Homosexuality* (New York: Palgrave, 2000).
17. A.-L. François, *Open Secrets: The Literature of Uncounted Experience* (Stanford, CA: Stanford University Press, 2008), p. 57.
18. See the commentary in W. Blake, *Milton a Poem*, ed. R. N. Essick and J. Viscomi (Princeton: Princeton University Press, 1993), p. 24.
19. M. Foucault, 'What Is Enlightenment?', in P. Rabinow (ed.), *The Foucault Reader*, trans. C. Porter (New York: Pantheon Books, 1984), pp. 32–50 (p. 50).

Further Reading

Introduction

The 'List of Abbreviations' at the beginning of this volume gives details of recommended sources for Blake's texts (Erdman's *Complete Poetry and Prose*) and images (The William Blake Archive, supplemented by Butlin's *Paintings and Drawings*, 2 vols.). W. H. Stevenson (ed.), *Blake: The Complete Poems*, 3rd edn (1971; Harlow: Pearson Education, 2007) is another good source of the poem texts, and contains excellent editorial notes. Likewise excellent is the series of William Blake Trust facsimiles: D. Bindman (gen. ed.), *Blake's Illuminated Books*, 6 vols. (London: William Blake Trust/Tate Gallery; Princeton: William Blake Trust/Princeton University Press, 1991–5, and repr.). Further specialist editions – for example, of Blake's manuscripts – are listed in chapter endnotes, or under the relevant chapter headings below, as are numerous historical editions of Blake's works. Open internet searches will also point you towards images and other useful information held or provided by individual libraries, archives, galleries, museums, and scholarly publications such as the journal *Blake / An Illustrated Quarterly* (blakequarterly.org/index.php/blake).

The 'List of Abbreviations' also indicates which reference works have been most consulted by the authors of this book. Again consulted extensively, and widely recommended, was S. Makdisi, *Blake and the Impossible History of the 1790s* (Chicago: University of Chicago Press, 2003).

Further, recommended, works about Blake include the following:

Eaves, M. (ed.), *The Cambridge Companion to William Blake* (Cambridge: Cambridge University Press, 2003)
Erdman, D. V., *Prophet against Empire*, 3rd edn (1954, 1969, 1977, Princeton: Princeton University Press; New York: Dover, 1991)
Frye, N., *Fearful Symmetry: A Study of William Blake* (1947, 1969; Princeton: Princeton University Press, 1990)
Makdisi, S., *Reading William Blake* (Cambridge: Cambridge University Press, 2015)
Mitchell, W. T. J., *Blake's Composite Art: A Study of the Illuminated Poetry* (Princeton: Princeton University Press, 1978)
Williams, N. M. (ed.), *Palgrave Advances in William Blake Studies* (Basingstoke: Palgrave Macmillan, 2006)

1 Life

Ackroyd, P., *Blake* (London: Sinclair-Stevenson, 1995; New York: Knopf, 1996)
Beer, J., *William Blake: A Literary Life* (London: Palgrave Macmillan, 2005)
Bentley, G. E., Jr, *Blake Records*, 2nd edn (New Haven and London: Yale University Press for the Paul Mellon Centre for Studies in British Art, 2004)
Bentley, G. E., Jr, *The Stranger from Paradise: A Biography of William Blake* (New Haven: Yale University Press, 2001)
Gilchrist, A., *The Life of William Blake, 'Pictor Ignotus'*, 2 vols. (London: Macmillan, 1863, enlarged edition 1880; various reprints subsequently)
Phillips, M., 'No. 13 Hercules Buildings, Lambeth', *British Art Journal*, 5 (2004), 13–21
Ward, A., 'William Blake and the Hagiographers', *Biography and Source Studies*, 1 (1994), 1–24

2 Networks

Haggarty, S., *Blake's Gifts: Poetry and the Politics of Exchange* (Cambridge: Cambridge University Press, 2010)
Harman, G., *Prince of Networks: Bruno Latour and Metaphysics* (Melbourne: Re.press, 2009)
Ingold, T., *Being Alive: Essays on Movement, Knowledge and Description* (Abingdon: Routledge, 2011)
Latour, B., *Reassembling the Social: An Introduction to Actor-Network Theory* (Oxford: Oxford University Press, 2005)
Makdisi, S., *William Blake and the Impossible History of the 1790s* (Chicago: University of Chicago Press, 2003)
Matthews, S., *Blake, Sexuality and Bourgeois Politeness* (Cambridge: Cambridge University Press, 2011)
Mee, J., *Dangerous Enthusiasm: William Blake and the Culture of Radicalism in the 1790s* (Oxford: Oxford University Press, 1992)
Saklofske, J., 'Remediating William Blake: Unbinding the Network Architectures of Blake's Songs', *European Romantic Review*, 22 (2011), 381–8

3 Engraving

Bentley, G. E., Jr, 'Blake's Engravings and His Friendship with Flaxman', *Studies in Bibliography*, 12 (1959), 161–88
'Blake's Heavy Metal: The History, Weight, Uses, Cost, and Makers of His Copper Plates', *University of Toronto Quarterly: A Canadian Journal of the Humanities*, 76.2 (2007), 714–70
Erdman, D. V., 'The Dating of William Blake's Engravings', *Philological Quarterly*, 31 (1952), 337–43

Essick, R. N., 'Blake and the Traditions of Reproductive Engraving', *Blake Studies*, 5.1 (1972), 59–103
The Separate Plates of William Blake (Princeton: Princeton University Press, 1983)
William Blake Printmaker (Princeton: Princeton University Press, 1980)
William Blake's Commercial Book Illustrations (Oxford: Clarendon Press, 1991)
Phillips, M., *William Blake Apprentice and Master* (Oxford: Ashmolean, 2014)
Sung, M.-Y., *William Blake and the Art of Engraving* (London: Pickering and Chatto, 2009)

4 Illuminated Books

Bindman, D. (gen. ed.), *Blake's Illuminated Books*, 6 vols. (London: William Blake Trust/Tate Gallery; Princeton: William Blake Trust/Princeton University Press, 1991–5, and repr.)
Erdman, D. V., *The Illuminated Blake: William Blake's Complete Illuminated Works with a Plate-by-Plate Commentary*, rev. edn (New York: Dover, 1992 [1974])
Viscomi, J., *Blake and the Idea of the Book* (Princeton: Princeton University Press, 1993)

5 Manuscripts

Abbott, R., 'George Eliot, Metre, and the Matter of Ideas: The Yale Poetry Notebook', *ELH*, 82.4 (2015), 1179–211
Allan, D., *Commonplace Books and Reading in Georgian England* (Cambridge: Cambridge University Press, 2010)
Barker-Benfield, B. C., *Shelley's Guitar: An Exhibition of Manuscripts, First Editions and Relics* (Oxford: Bodleian Library, 1992)
Bentley, G. E., Jr, 'The Date of Blake's Pickering Manuscript or the Way of a Poet with Paper', *Studies in Bibliography*, 19 (1966), 232–43
Blair, A., *Too Much to Know: Managing Scholarly Information before the Modern Age* (New Haven, CN: Yale University Press, 2010)
Calè, L., 'Blake, Young, and the Poetics of the Composite Page', *Huntington Library Quarterly*, 80.3 (2017), 453–79
Eaves, M., E. Loy, H. Sidhu, and L. Whitebell, 'Prototyping an Electronic Edition of William Blake's Manuscript of *Vala, or the Four Zoas*: A Progress Report', 19: *Interdisciplinary Studies in the Long Nineteenth Century*, 21 (2015), dx.doi.org/10.16995/ntn.728
Harding, A. J., 'Coleridge's Notebooks and the Case for a Material Hermeneutics of Literature', *Romanticism*, 6.1 (2000), 1–19
Jackson, H. J., *Romantic Readers: The Evidence of Marginalia* (New Haven, CN: Yale University Press, 2005)
Knight, J. T., 'Organizing Manuscript and Print: From Compilatio to Compilation', in T. Johnston and M. Van Dussen (eds.), *The Medieval*

Manuscript Book: Cultural Approaches (Cambridge: Cambridge University Press, 2015), 77–95

Phillips, M., *William Blake: The Creation of the Songs, from Manuscript to Illuminated Printing* (London: British Library, 2000)

Snart, J., *The Torn Book: Unreading William Blake's Marginalia* (Selinsgrove, PA: Susquehanna University Press, 2006)

Van Kleeck, J., 'Editioning William Blake's *VALA/The Four Zoas*', *Editing and Reading Blake, Romantic Circles*, www.rc.umd.edu

6 Book Illustration

Blunt, A., *The Art of William Blake* (London: Oxford University Press, 1959)

Calè, L., 'Blake and the Literary Galleries', in S. Haggarty and J. Mee (eds.), *Blake and Conflict* (Basingstoke: Palgrave Macmillan, 2008), pp. 185–209

Eaves, M., *The Counter-Arts Conspiracy: Art and Industry in the Age of Blake* (Ithaca, NY: Cornell University Press, 1992)

Griffiths, A., 'Book Illustration', in *Print Before Photography: An Introduction to European Printmaking 1550–1820* (London: British Museum, 2016), pp. 181–94

Heppner, C., *Reading Blake's Designs* (Cambridge: Cambridge University Press, 1995)

Mitchell, W. J. T., 'Visible Language: Blake's Art of Writing', in *Picture Theory: Essays on Verbal and Visual Representation* (Chicago: University of Chicago Press, 1994), pp. 111–50

Paley, M. D., The *Traveller in the Evening: The Last Works of William Blake* (Oxford: Oxford University Press, 2003)

Stevens, B., 'The Virgil Woodcuts Out of Scale: Blake's Gigantic, Masculine Pastoral', in H. P. Bruder and T. J. Connolly (eds.), *Blake, Gender, Culture* (London: Pickering and Chatto, 2012), pp. 145–64

7 Painting

Barrell, J., *The Political Theory of Painting from Reynolds to Hazlitt: 'The Body of the Public'* (New Haven, CT, and London: Yale University Press, 1986)

Bindman, D., *Blake as an Artist* (Oxford: Phaidon, 1977)

William Blake, His Art and Times (New Haven, CT: Yale Center for British Art, 1982)

Blunt, A., *The Art of William Blake* (London: Oxford University Press, 1959)

Butlin, M., *William Blake 1757–1827* (London: Tate Gallery, 1990)

Myrone, M., *The Blake Book* (London: Tate Publishing, 2007)

Pressly, N. L., *The Fuseli Circle in Rome: Early Romantic Art of the 1770s* (New Haven, CT: Yale Center for British Art, 1979)

Reynolds, J., *Discourses on Art*, ed. R. N. Wark (New Haven, CN, and London: Yale University Press, 1975, and repr.)

Todd, R., *Tracks in the Snow: Studies in English Science and Art* (London: Gray Walls Press 1946)

8   Early Reception

*Bentley, G. E., Jr, *Blake Books* (Oxford: Clarendon Press, 1977) and its *Supplement* (1995)
  Blake Records, 2nd edn (New Haven, CN, and London: Yale University Press, 2004), noting Appendix I: 'Early Essays on Blake', pp. 561–732
  'William Blake and His Circle', *Blake / An Illustrated Quarterly* (1995–)
  William Blake in the Desolate Market (Montreal, Kingston: McGill-Queen's University Press, 2014)
  (ed.), *William Blake: The Critical Heritage* (London and Boston: Routledge and Kegan Paul, 1975)
Bottrall, M., (ed.), *William Blake, Songs of Innocence and of Experience: A Casebook* (London: Macmillan, 1970)
*Butlin, M., *The Paintings and Drawings of William Blake*, 2 vols. (New Haven, CN: Yale University Press, 1981)
Dorfman, D., *Blake in the Nineteenth Century: His Reception as a Poet from Gilchrist to Yeats* (New Haven, CT: Yale University Press, 1969)
Essick, R. N., 'Blake in the Marketplace', *Blake / An Illustrated Quarterly* (1972–)
The Separate Plates of William Blake: A Catalogue (Princeton: Princeton University Press, 1983)

*These three texts are meticulous in recording provenances. However, to derive data about individual collectors from these books can be very laborious

9   Later Reception

Bertholf, R. J., and A. S. Levitt (eds.), *William Blake and the Moderns* (Albany: SUNY Press, 1982)
Bruder, H. P., and T. Connolly (eds.), *Sexy Blake* (Basingstoke: Palgrave Macmillan, 2013)
Clark, S., and J. Whittaker (eds.), *Blake, Modernity and Popular Culture* (Basingstoke: Palgrave Macmillan, 2007)
Clark, S., T. Connolly, and J. Whittaker (eds.), *Blake 2.0: William Blake in Twentieth-Century Art, Music, Culture* (Basingstoke: Palgrave Macmillan, 2012)
Crosby, M., T. Patenaude, and A. Whitehead (eds.), *Re-envisioning Blake* (Basingstoke: Palgrave Macmillan, 2012)
Dent, S., and J. Whittaker, *Radical Blake: Influence and Afterlife from 1827* (Basingstoke: Palgrave Macmillan, 2002)
Eisenman, S. F., *William Blake and the Age of Aquarius* (Princeton: Princeton University Press, 2017)

Goode, M., 'Blakespotting', *PMLA*, 121.3 (2006), 769–86
Larrissy, E., *Blake and Modern Literature* (Basingstoke: Palgrave Macmillan, 2006)

10 Editing and Editions

Eaves, M., 'Crafting Editorial Settlements', *RoN: Romanticism on the Net* [now *RaVon*], www.ron.umontreal.ca/, University of Montreal, issues 41–2 (February–May 2006), www.erudit.org/revue/ron/2006/v/n41–42/013150ar.html
    'The Editorial Void: Notes toward a Study of Oblivion', *Huntington Library Quarterly*, 80.3 (2017), 517–38
    'Graphicality: Multimedia Fables for "Textual" Critics', in E. B. Loizeaux and N. Fraistat (eds.), *Textual Studies in the Late Age of Print* (Madison: University of Wisconsin Press, 2002), pp. 99–122
    'National Arts and Disruptive Technologies in Blake's Prospectus of 1793', in S. Clark and D. Worrall (eds.), *Blake, Nation and Empire* (London: Palgrave, 2006), pp. 119–35
    'Picture Problems: X-editing Images 1992–2010', *Digital Humanities Quarterly*, 3.3 (summer 2009), digitalhumanities.org/dhq/vol/3/3/000052/000052.html
Grant, J. E., 'Blake in the Future', *Romantic Texts, Romantic Times: Homage to David V. Erdman*, special issue of *Studies in Romanticism*, 21.3 (Fall 1982), 436–43
Kraus, K., '"Once, Only Imagined": An Interview with Morris Eaves, Robert N. Essick, and Joseph Viscomi on the Past, Present, and Future of Blake Studies', *Studies in Romanticism*, 41 (2002), 143–99. [Published online by Romantic Circles.]

11 Comedy

Bakhtin, M., 'Carnival Ambivalence', in P. Morris (ed.), *The Bakhtin Reader* (London: Edward Arnold, 1994), pp. 194–244
    'Discourse in the Novel', in M. Holquist (ed.), *Dialogic Imagination: Four Essays*, trans. C. Emerson and M. Holquist (Austin: University of Texas Press, 1981), pp. 259–422
Beattie, J., 'On Laughter and Ludicrous Composition', in *Essays* (London and Edinburgh, 1778), pp. 321–486
England, M., 'The Satiric Blake: Apprenticeship at the Haymarket?', in W. K. Wimsatt (ed.), *Literary Criticism: Idea and Act. The English Institute 1939–1972. Selected Essays* (Berkeley, CA: University of California Press, 1974)
Erasmus, D., *Praise of Folly; and, Letter to Maarten Van Dorp, 1515* (Harmondsworth: Penguin, 1993)
Hutcheon, L., *A Theory of Parody: The Teachings of Twentieth-Century Art Forms* (New York: Methuen, 1985)
Rawlinson, N., *William Blake's Comic Vision* (Basingstoke: Palgrave Macmillan, 2003)
Rose, M. A., *Parody: Ancient, Modern and Post-Modern* (Cambridge: Cambridge University Press, 1993)

Weinbrot, H. D., *Menippean Satire Reconsidered: From Antiquity to the Eighteenth Century* (Baltimore, MD: Johns Hopkins University Press, 2005)

12 Prophecy

Balfour, I., *The Rhetoric of Romantic Prophecy* (Stanford, CA: Stanford University Press, 2002)
Bundock, C., *Romantic Prophecy and the Resistance to Historicism* (Toronto: University of Toronto Press, 2016)
Marks, H., 'On Prophetic Stammering', *Yale Journal of Criticism*, 1.1 (1987), 1–20
Mee, J., *Dangerous Enthusiasm: William Blake and the Culture of Radicalism in the 1790s* (Oxford: Clarendon Press, 1992)
Smith, O., *Romantic Women Writers, Revolution, and Prophecy* (Cambridge: Cambridge University Press, 2013)
Tucker, H., *Epic: Britain's Heroic Muse 1790–1900* (Oxford: Oxford University Press, 2008)

13 Rhythm

Fox, S., *Poetic Form in Blake's 'Milton'* (Princeton: Princeton University Press, 1976)
Frye, N., *Fearful Symmetry: A Study of William Blake* (Princeton: Princeton University Press, 1947)
Gleckner, R. F., *Blake's Prelude: 'Poetical Sketches'* (Baltimore, MD: Johns Hopkins University Press, 1982)
Hollander, J., 'Romantic Verse Form and the Metrical Contract', in *Vision and Resonance: Two Senses of Poetic Form* (New York: Oxford University Press, 1975), pp. 187–211
Kumbier, W., 'Blake's Epic Verse', *Studies in Romanticism*, 17 (1978), 163–92
Lowery, M. R., *Windows of the Morning: A Critical Study of William Blake's 'Poetical Sketches' 1783* (New Haven, CT: Yale University Press, 1940)
Ostriker, A., *Vision and Verse in William Blake* (Madison, WI: University of Wisconsin Press, 1965)
Paley, M. D., *William Blake's 'Jerusalem'* (Oxford: Clarendon Press, 1983)
Saintsbury, G., *History of English Prosody*, 3 vols. (London: Macmillan, 1906)
Wolfson, S. J., 'Blake's Language in Poetic Form', in M. Eaves (ed.), *The Cambridge Companion to William Blake* (Cambridge: Cambridge University Press, 2003), pp. 63–84

14 Songs

Dugaw, D., 'Popular Marketing of "Old Ballads": 18th-Century Antiquarianism Reconsidered', *Eighteenth Century Studies*, 21 (1987), 71–90

Friedman, A. B., *The Ballad Revival: Studies in the Influence of Popular on Sophisticated Poetry* (Chicago: Chicago University Press, 1961)
Fumerton, P., A. Guerini, and K. McAbee (eds.), *Ballads and Broadsides in Britain, 1500–1800* (Farnham: Ashgate, 2010)
McLane, M., *Balladeering, Minstrelsy, and the Making of British Romantic Poetry* (Cambridge: Cambridge University Press, 2008)
Newman, I., 'Civilizing Taste: "Sandman Joe", the Bawdy Ballad and Metropolitan Improvement', *Eighteenth-Century Studies*, 48.4 (2015), 437–56
Newman, S., *Ballad Collection, Lyric, and the Canon: The Call of the Popular from the Restoration to the New Criticism* (Philadelphia, PA: University of Pennsylvania Press, 2007)
Perry, R. (ed.), *The Eighteenth Century, Special Issue: Ballads and Songs in the Eighteenth Century*, 47.2 (2006)
Stewart, S., 'Scandals of the Ballad', *Representations*, 32 (1990), 134–56
Watson, J. R., *The English Hymn: A Critical and Historical Study* (Oxford: Oxford University Press, 1999)

15 Sound

Anderson, E. R., *A Grammar of Iconism* (Madison, NJ: Fairleigh Dickinson University Press, 1998)
Essick, R. N., *William Blake and the Language of Adam* (Oxford: Clarendon Press, 1989)
Jarvis, S., 'Thinking in Verse', in J. Chandler and M. McLane (eds.), *The Cambridge Companion to Romantic Poetry* (Cambridge: Cambridge University Press, 2008), pp. 98–116
Mitchell, W. J. T., 'Chaosthetics: Blake's Sense of Form', *Huntington Library Quarterly*, 58.3/4 (1995), 441–58
Ostriker, A., *Vision and Verse in William Blake* (Madison, WI: University of Wisconsin Press, 1965), ch. 6, pp. 79–91
Prynne, J. H., *Stars, Tigers and the Shape of Words* (London: Birkbeck College, 1993)
Stewart, S., *Poetry and the Fate of the Senses* (London: Chicago University Press, 2002), ch. 2, pp. 59–105
Wolfson, S. J., *Formal Charges: The Shaping of Poetry in British Romanticism* (Stanford: Stanford University Press, 1997), ch. 2, pp. 31–62

16 Sublimity

Baulch, D., 'Reflective Aesthetics and the Last Judgment: Blake's Sublime Aesthetic and Kant's Third Critique', *European Romantic Review*, 12.2 (Spring 2001), 198–205
Burke, E., *A Philosophical Enquiry into the Origin of Our Ideas of the Sublime and Beautiful*, ed. J. T. Boulton (Notre Dame and London: University of Notre Dame Press, 1958)

De Luca, V. A., *Words of Eternity: Blake and the Poetics of the Sublime* (Princeton: Princeton University Press, 1991)
Kant, I., *Critique of Judgement*, trans. J. C. Meredith (Oxford: Clarendon Press, 1952)
Longinus, D., *On the Sublime*, trans. W. Smith (London: S. Cornish, 1739)
Lyotard, J.-F., *Lessons on the Analytic of the Sublime*, trans. E. Rottenberg (Stanford: Stanford University Press, 1994)
Otto, P., *Blake's Critique of Transcendence: Love, Jealousy, and the Sublime in The Four Zoas* (Oxford: Oxford University Press, 2000)
Vine, S., 'Blake's Material Sublime', *Studies in Romanticism*, 41 (Summer 2002), 237–57

17 System, Myth, and Symbol

Ault, D., 'Re-Visioning the Four Zoas', in N. Hilton and T. Vogler (eds.), *Unnam'd Forms: Blake and Textuality* (Berkeley and Los Angeles, CA: University of California Press, 1986), pp. 105–40
Coleridge, S. T., 'Definition of Symbol and Allegory', from *The Statesman's Manual*, in R. J. White (ed.), *Lay Sermons* (Princeton: Princeton University Press, 1972), pp. 28–31. Vol. 6 of *The Collected Works of Samuel Taylor Coleridge*, 16 vols. (1969–2001)
Damon, S. D., *A Blake Dictionary: The Ideas and Symbols of William Blake* (Providence: Brown University Press, 1965; rev. M. Eaves and repr., Hanover, NH: Dartmouth College Press / University Press of New England, 2013)
Damrosch, L., *Symbol and Truth in Blake's Myth* (Princeton: Princeton University Press, 1980)
Ellis, E. J., and W. B. Yeats, 'The Symbolic System', in E. J. Ellis and W. B. Yeats (eds.), *The Works of William Blake, Poetic, Symbolic and Critical*, 3 vols. (London: Bernard Quaritch, 1893), pp. 233–420
Halmi, N., *The Genealogy of the Romantic Symbol* (Oxford: Oxford University Press, 2007)
Hegel, G. W. F., *Aesthetics: Lectures in Fine Art*, trans. T. M. Knox, 2 vols. (Oxford: Clarendon, 1970)
Kant, I., 'The Architectonic of Pure Reason', in P. Guyer and A. Wood (eds.), *Critique of Pure Reason*, trans. P. Guyer and A. Wood (Cambridge: Cambridge University Press, 1998), pp. 691–701
Rajan, T., '(Dis)Figuring the System: Vision, History, and Trauma in Blake's Lambeth Books', *William Blake: Images and Texts, Huntington Library Quarterly*, 58.3/4 (1995), 383–411
  'Blake's Body without Organs: The Autogenesis of the System in the Lambeth Books', *European Romantic Review*, 26.3 (2015), 357–66
Schelling, F., 'On the Nature of Philosophy as Science' (1823), trans. M. Bullock, in R. Bübner (ed.), *German Idealist Philosophy* (Harmondsworth: Penguin, 1997), pp. 210–43

The Philosophy of Art, trans. D. Stott (Minneapolis: University of Minnesota Press, 1989)

18 The Bible

Erdman, D. V. (ed.), *Blake and His Bibles* (West Cornwall, CT: Locust Hill Press, 1990)
Rix, R., *William Blake and the Cultures of Radical Christianity* (Farnham: Ashgate, 2007)
Rowland, C., *Blake and the Bible* (New Haven, CT: Yale University Press, 2010)
Tannenbaum, L., *Biblical Tradition in Blake's Early Prophecies: The Great Code of Art* (Princeton: Princeton University Press, 1982, and repr.)

19 Chaucer, Spenser, and Shakespeare

[Anon.], *William Blake's Heads of the Poets* (Manchester: Manchester City Art Galleries, 1969)
Adams, H., *William Blake on His Poetry and Painting: A Study of 'A Descriptive Catalogue'* (Jefferson, NC: McFarland, 2011)
Myrone, M. (ed.), *Seen in My Vision: A Descriptive Catalogue of Pictures* (London: Tate, 2009)
Pace, C., 'Blake and Chaucer: "Infinite Variety of Character"', *Art History*, 3 (1980), 388–409

20 Milton

Behrendt, S. C., *The Moment of Explosion: Blake and the Illustration of Milton* (Lincoln, NE: University of Nebraska Press, 1983)
Bolton, B., '"A Garment Dipped in Blood": Ololon and Problems of Gender in Blake's *Milton*', *Studies in Romanticism*, 36 (1997), 61–101
Fox, S., *Poetic Form in Blake's* Milton (Princeton: Princeton University Press, 1976)
Johnson, M. L., '*Milton* and Its Contexts', in M. Eaves (ed.), *The Cambridge Companion to William Blake* (Cambridge: Cambridge University Press, 2003), pp. 231–50.
Lewalksi, B., *The Life of John Milton: A Critical Biography*, rev. edn (Oxford: Blackwell, 2003)
Marks, C., 'Writings of the Left Hand: Blake Forges a New Political Aesthetic', *Huntington Library Quarterly*, 74.1 (2011), 43–70
Rosso, G. A., *The Religion of Empire: Political Theology in Blake's Prophetic Symbolism* (Columbus, OH: Ohio State University Press, 2016)

Von Maltzhahn, N., 'Milton's Readers', in D. Danielson (ed.), *The Cambridge Companion to Milton*, 2nd edn (Cambridge: Cambridge University Press, 1999), pp. 236–52

Wittreich, J. A., 'Opening the Seals: Blake's Epics and the Milton Tradition', in S. Curran and J. A. Wittreich (eds.), *Blake's Sublime Allegory: Essays on the Four Zoas, Milton, Jerusalem*, ed. (Madison, WI: University of Wisconsin Press, 1973), pp. 23–58

Zwierlein, A.-J., *Majestic Milton: British Imperial Expansion and Transformations of Paradise Lost, 1667–1837* (Münster: LIT, 2001)

21 The Eighteenth Century and Romanticism

Abrams, M. H., 'English Romanticism: The Spirit of the Age', in H. Bloom (ed.), *Romanticism and Consciousness: Essays in Criticism* (New York: Norton, 1970), pp. 90–119

Bloom, H., 'The Internalization of Quest-Romance', in H. Bloom (ed.), *Romanticism and Consciousness: Essays in Criticism* (New York: Norton, 1970), pp. 3–24

Butler, M., *Mapping Mythologies: Countercurrents in Eighteenth-Century British Poetry and Cultural History* (Cambridge: Cambridge University Press, 2015)

Duff, D., *Romanticism and the Uses of Genre* (Oxford: Oxford University Press, 2009)

Folkenflik, R., 'Macpherson, Chatterton, Blake and the Great Age of Literary Forgery', *Centennial Review*, 18.4 (1974), 378–91

Gleckner, R. F., *Blake's Prelude: Poetical Sketches* (Baltimore, MD: Johns Hopkins University Press, 1982)

Groom, N. (ed.), *Thomas Chatterton and Romantic Culture* (Basingstoke: Macmillan, 1999)

Lowery, M. R., *Windows of the Morning: A Critical Study of William Blake's Poetical Sketches, 1783* (New Haven: Yale University Press, 1940)

Moore, D. (ed.), *Ossian and Ossianism*, 4 vols. (London: Routledge, 2004)

Simpson, D., 'Blake and Romanticism', in M. Eaves (ed.), *The Cambridge Companion to William Blake* (Cambridge: Cambridge University Press, 2003), pp. 169–88

22 Byron

Ferber, M., *The Social Vision of William Blake* (Princeton: Princeton University Press, 1985)

Green, M. J. A., 'Voices in the Wilderness: Satire and Sacrifice in Blake and Byron', *The Byron Journal*, 36.2 (2003), 117–29

Hopps, G., 'Introduction', in G. Hopps (ed.), *Byron's Ghosts: The Spectral, the Spiritual, and the Supernatural* (Liverpool: University of Liverpool Press, 2013), pp. 8–18

Mann, P., 'Apocalypse and Recuperation: Blake and the Maw of Commerce', *English Literary History*, 52.1 (1985), 1–32

McGann, J., 'Blake and Byron; or, Art and Imagination after the Second Fall', *Christianity and Literature*, 66.4 (2017), 609–30

McKeever, K. E., 'Naming the Name of the Prophet: William Blake's Reading of Byron's Cain. A Mystery', *Studies in Romanticism*, 34.4 (1995), 615–36

Paley, M. D., *The Traveller in the Evening* (New York: Oxford University Press, 2003), pp. 8–19, 53–100

Shears, J., '"In One We Shall Be Slower": Byron, Retribution, and Forgiveness', *Christianity and Literature*, 66.2 (2017), 193–212

Smith, S., 'Milton's Theology of the Cross: Substitution and Satisfaction in Christ's Atonement', *Christianity and Literature*, 63.1 (2013), 5–25

23 Pre-Raphaelites and Aesthetes

Dorfman, D., *Blake in the Nineteenth Century: His Reception as a Poet from Gilchrist to Yeats* (New Haven, CT: Yale University Press, 1969)

Gilchrist, A., *Life of William Blake, 'Pictor Ignotus'*, 2 vols. (London: Macmillan, 1863)

Helsinger, E., *Poetry and the Pre-Raphaelite Arts: Dante Gabriel Rossetti and William Morris* (New Haven, CT: Yale University Press, 2008)

Poetry and the Thought of Song in Nineteenth-Century Britain (Charlottesville, VA: University of Virginia Press, 2015)

Rossetti, C., *Goblin Market and Other Poems* (London: Macmillan, 1862, 1865)

Sing-Song: A Nursery Rhyme Book, illus. A. Hughes (London: Macmillan, 1915) (Manuscript illus. Rossetti available at www.bl.uk/collection-items/manuscript-of-sing-song-a-collection-of-nursery-rhymes-by-christina-rossetti)

Rossetti, D. G., *Dante Gabriel Rossetti: Collected Poetry and Prose*, ed. J. McGann (New Haven: Yale University Press, 2003). (See also The Rossetti Archive, ed. McGann, at www.rossettiarchive.org/, which contains most of Rossetti's pictorial, poetic, and prose work.)

Swinburne, A. C., *William Blake: A Critical Essay* (London: John Camden Hotten, 1868)

Trodd, C., *Visions of Blake: William Blake in the Art World 1830–1930* (Liverpool: Liverpool University Press, 2012)

24 Yeats, Eliot, and Auden

Bertholf, R. J., and A. S. Levitt (eds.), *William Blake and the Moderns* (Albany, NY: SUNY Press, 1982)

Clark, S., and J. Whittaker (eds.), *Blake, Modernity and Popular Culture* (Basingstoke: Palgrave Macmillan, 2007)
Dent, S., and J. Whitaker, *Radical Blake: Influence and Afterlife from 1827* (Basingstoke: Palgrave Macmillan, 2002)
Larrissy, E., *Blake and Modern Literature* (Basingstoke: Palgrave Macmillan, 2006)
Quinn, 'K., Blake and the New Age', *Virginia Quarterly Review*, 13.2 (1937), 271–85

25 Whitman, Crane, and the Beats

Elliot, C., 'William Blake and America: Freedom and Violence in the Atlantic World', *Comparative American Studies*, 7.3 (2009), 209–24
Freedman, L., 'Walt Whitman and William Blake: The Prophet-Artist and Democratic Thought', in D. Maudlin and R. Peel (eds.), *Transatlantic Traffic and (Mis)Translations* (New Hampshire: University of New Hampshire Press, 2013), pp. 133–53
  William Blake and the Myth of America: From the Abolitionists to the Counterculture (Oxford: Oxford University Press, 2018)
Kripal, J. J., 'Reality against Society: William Blake, Antinomianism and the American Counterculture', *Common Knowledge*, 13.1 (2007), 98–112
Otto, P., '"Rouze Up O Young Men of the New Age!" William Blake, Theodore Roszak and the Counter Culture of the 1960s–1970s', in S. Clark, T. Connolly, and J. Whittaker (eds.), *Blake 2.0: William Blake in Twentieth-Century Music and Culture* (Basingstoke: Palgrave Macmillan, 2012), pp. 27–41
Pease, D., 'Blake, Whitman, Crane: The Hand of Fire', in R. J. Bertholf and A. S. Levitt (eds.), *William Blake and the Moderns* (Albany: State University of New York, 1982), pp. 15–38
  'Blake, Crane, Whitman and Modernism: A Poetics of Pure Possibility', *PMLA*, 96.1 (1981), 64–85
Schmidgall, G., *Containing Multitudes: Walt Whitman and the British Literary Tradition* (Oxford: Oxford University Press, 2014)

26 Animals

Baine, R. M., and M. R. Baine, *The Scattered Portions: William Blake's Biological Symbolism* (Athens, GA: Distributed by the Author, 1986)
Bleakley, A., *The Animalizing Imagination: Totemism, Textuality and Ecocriticism* (Basingstoke: Macmillan; New York: St Martin's Press, 2000)
Bruder, H. P., and T. Connolly (eds.), *Beastly Blake, Palgrave Studies in Animals and Literature* (Basingstoke: Palgrave Macmillan, 2018)
Derrida, J., *The Animal That Therefore I Am*, ed. M-L Mallet, trans. D. Wills (New York: Fordham University Press, 2008)
Fosso, K., '"Feet of Beasts": Tracking the Animal in Blake', *European Romantic Review*, 25.2 (2014), 113–38
Haraway, D. J., *When Species Meet* (Minneapolis: University of Minnesota Press, 2008)

Heymans, P., *Animality in British Romanticism: The Aesthetics of Species* (New York: Routledge, 2012)
Pedley, C., 'Blake's Tiger and the Discourse of Natural History', *Blake / An Illustrated Quarterly*, 24.1 (1990), 238–45
Perkins, D., *Romanticism and Animal Rights* (Cambridge: Cambridge University Press, 2003)
Schwartz, J. A., *Worm Work: Recasting Romanticism* (Minneapolis: University of Minnesota Press, 2012)
Thomas, K., *Man and the Natural World: Changing Attitudes in England 1500–1800* (London: Allen Lane, 1983; rpt. New York: Oxford University Press, 1996)

27 Antiquarianism

Bryant, J., *A New System, or, Analysis of Ancient Mythology*, 3 vols. (London: 1774–6)
De Luca, V. A., *Words of Eternity: Blake and the Poetics of the Sublime* (Princeton: Princeton University Press, 1991)
Heringman, N., and C. B. Lake (eds.), *Romantic Antiquarianism. Romantic Circles Praxis Series* (University of Maryland, 2014), www.rc.umd.edu/praxis/antiquarianism
Hungerford, E., *Shores of Darkness* (New York: Columbia University Press, 1941)
Momigliano, A., *The Classical Foundations of Modern Historiography* (Berkeley, CA: University of California Press, 1990)
Pearce, S., *Visions of Antiquity: The Society of Antiquaries of London, 1707–2007* (London: Society of Antiquaries of London, 2007)
Raine, K., *Blake and Tradition*, 2 vols. (Princeton: Princeton University Press, 1968)
Ritson, J., *A Select Collection of English Songs*, 3 vols. (London: Joseph Johnson, 1783)
Schnapp, A. (ed.), *World Antiquarianism: Comparative Perspectives* (Los Angeles: Getty Research Institute, 2013)
Stukeley, W., *Abury: A Temple of the British Druids* (1743; New York: Garland, 1984)
Sweet, R., *Antiquaries: The Discovery of the Past in Eighteenth-Century Britain* (London: Hambledon and London, 2004)

28 Education and Childhood

Ferber, M., 'Not for the Kiddies', *Academe*, 87.4 (2001), 50–2
Heather, G., *Vision and Disenchantment: Blake's Songs and Wordsworth's Lyrical Ballads* (Cambridge: Cambridge University Press, 1983)
Grenby, M. O., *The Child Reader, 1700–1840* (Cambridge: Cambridge University Press, 2011)

Kennedy, T. C., 'From Anna Barbauld's *Hymns in Prose* to William *Blake's Songs of Innocence and of Experience*', *Philological Quarterly*, 77.4 (1998), 359–77
Leader, Z., *Reading Blake's Songs* (Boston, London, and Henley: Routledge & Kegan Paul, 1981)
O'Malley, A., *The Making of the Modern Child: Children's Literature and Childhood in the Late Eighteenth Century* (New York: Routledge, 2003)
Richardson, A., *Literature, Education, and Romanticism: Reading as Social Practice 1780–1832* (Cambridge: Cambridge University Press, 1994)
Rowland, A. W., *Romanticism and Childhood: The Infantilization of British Literary Culture* (Cambridge: Cambridge University Press, 2012)
Ruwe, D., *British Children's Poetry in the Romantic Era: Verse, Riddle, and Rhyme* (Basingstoke: Palgrave Macmillan, 2014)
Wakely-Mulroney, K., and L. Joy (eds.), *The Aesthetics of Children's Poetry: A Study of Children's Verse in English* (London: Routledge, 2017)
Williams, N. M., *Ideology and Utopia in the Poetry of William Blake* (Cambridge: Cambridge University Press, 1998)

29 Empiricism

Ault, D., *Visionary Physics: Blake's Response to Newton* (Chicago: University of Chicago Press, 1974)
Clark, S. H., 'Blake's *Milton* as Empiricist Epic: "Weaving the Woof of Locke"', *Studies in Romanticism*, 36 (1997), 457–82
Cooper, A. M., *William Blake and the Productions of Time* (Farnham: Ashgate, 2013)
Glausser, W., *Locke and Blake: A Conversation across the Eighteenth Century* (Gainesville, FL: University Press of Florida, 1998)
Green, M. J. A., *Visionary Materialism in the Early Works of William Blake: The Intersection of Enthusiasm and Empiricism* (Basingstoke: Palgrave Macmillan, 2005)
Jarvis, S., 'Blake's Spiritual Body', in R. Wilson (ed.), *The Meaning of 'Life' in Romantic Poetry and Poetics* (New York: Routledge, 2009), pp. 13–32
Peterfreund, S., *William Blake in a Newtonian World: Essays on Literature as Art and Science* (Norman, OK: University of Oklahoma Press, 1998)
White, H., 'Blake's Resolution to the War Between Science and Philosophy', *Blake / An Illustrated Quarterly*, 39.3 (2005–6), 108–25

30 Life Sciences

Engelstein, S., *Anxious Anatomy: The Conception of the Human Form in Literary and Naturalist Discourse* (Albany: State University of New York Press, 2008)
Gigante, D., *Life: Organic Form and Romanticism* (New Haven: Yale University Press, 2009)

Goldstein, A. J., *Sweet Science: Romantic Materialism and the New Logics of Life* (Chicago: University of Chicago Press, 2017)
Lenoir, T., *The Strategy of Life: Teleology and Mechanics in Nineteenth-Century German Biology* (Chicago: University of Chicago Press, 1982)
McLane, M., *Romanticism and the Human Sciences: Poetry, Population, and the Discourse of the Species* (Cambridge: Cambridge University Press, 2000)
Mitchell, R., *Experimental Life: Vitalism in Romantic Science and Literature* (Baltimore: Johns Hopkins University Press, 2013)
Richardson, A., *British Romanticism and the Science of the Mind* (Cambridge: Cambridge University Press, 2001)
Riskin, J., *The Restless Clock: A History of the Centuries-Long Argument over What Makes Living Things Tick* (Chicago: University of Chicago Press, 2015)
Tweedy, R., *The God of the Left Hemisphere: Blake, Bolte Taylor and the Myth of Creation* (London: Karnac Books, 2013)
Youngquist, P., *Monstrosities: Bodies and British Romanticism* (Minneapolis: University of Minnesota Press, 2003)

31 London

German, L., and J. Rees, *A People's History of London* (London: Verso, 2012)
Linebaugh, P., *The London Hanged: Crime and Civil Society in the Eighteenth Century* (Cambridge: Cambridge University Press, 1993)
Makdisi, S., *Making England Western: Occidentalism, Race and Imperial Culture* (Chicago: University of Chicago Press, 2014)
Nead, L., *Victorian Babylon: People, Streets and Images in Nineteenth-Century London* (New Haven, CN: Yale University Press, 2011)
Porter, R., *London: A Social History* (London: Penguin, 1994)
Rasmussen, S. E., *London: The Unique City* (Cambridge, MA: MIT Press, 1984)
Sheppard, F., *London 1800–1870: The Infernal Wen* (Berkeley: University of California Press, 1971)
Sinclair, I. (ed.), *London: City of Disappearances* (London: Penguin, 2007)
Stedman Jones, G., *Outcast London: A Study in the Relationship between Classes in Victorian Society* (New York: Pantheon, 1984)
White, J., *London in the Nineteenth Century* (London: Vintage, 2008)
Whitfield, P., *London: A Life in Maps* (London: British Library, 2006)

32 Money

Baucom, I., *Specters of the Atlantic* (Durham, NC: Duke University Press, 2005)
Cobbett, W., *Paper against Gold and Glory against Prosperity*, 2 vols. (London: J. M'Creery, 1815)
Crosby, M., 'The Bank Restriction Act (1797) and Banknote Forgery', *BRANCH: Britain, Representation and Nineteenth-Century History*, ed.

D. F. Felluga. www.branchcollective.org/?ps_articles=mark-crosby-the-bank-restriction-act-1797-and-banknote-forgery
Dick, A., *Romanticism and the Gold Standard: Money, Literature, and Economic Debate in Britain 1790–1830* (New York: Palgrave Macmillan, 2013)
Finn, M. C., *The Character of Credit: Personal Debt in English Culture, 1740–1914* (Cambridge: Cambridge University Press, 2003)
Ricardo, D., 'The High Price of Bullion a Proof of the Depreciation of Bank Notes', in J. R. McCulloch (ed.), *A Select Collection of Scarce and Valuable Tracts on Paper Currency and Banking* (London, 1856; repr., New York: Augustus M. Kelley, 1966), pp. 361–401
Rowlinson, M., *Real Money and Romanticism* (Cambridge: Cambridge University Press, 2010)
Simmel, G., *The Philosophy of Money*, trans. T. Bottomore and D. Frisby, ed. D. Frisby, 2nd edn (London and New York: Routledge, 1990)
Valenze, D. M., *The Social Life of Money in the English Past* (New York: Cambridge University Press, 2006)

33 Moravianism

Davies, K., 'The Lost Moravian History of William Blake's Family', *Literature Compass*, 3.6 (2006), 1297–319
'William Blake's Mother: A New Identification', *Blake / An Illustrated Quarterly*, 33.2 (1999), 36–50
Davies, K., and M. K. Schuchard, 'Recovering the Lost Moravian History of William Blake's Family', *Blake / An Illustrated Quarterly*, 38.1 (2004), 36–43
Peucker, P., *A Time of Sifting: Mystical Marriage and the Crisis of Moravian Piety in the Eighteenth Century* (Pennsylvania: Pennsylvania State University Press, 2016)
Podmore, C., *The Moravian Church in England, 1728–1760* (Oxford: Clarendon, 1998)
Regier, A., Exorbitant Enlightenment: Blake, Hamann, and Anglo-German Constellations (Oxford: Oxford University Press, 2018)
Schuchard, M. K., *Why Mrs Blake Cried: William Blake and the Sexual Basis of Spiritual Vision* (London: Century 2006)

34 Mysticism

Altizer, T. J., *The New Apocalypse: The Radical Christian Vision of William Blake* (East Lansing, MI: Michigan State University Press, 1967)
Bellin, H. F., and D. Ruhl (eds.), *Blake and Swedenborg: Opposition Is True Friendship – An Anthology* (New York: Swedenborg Foundation, 1985)
Hanegraaff, W., *Western Esotericism: A Guide for the Perplexed* (London: Bloomsbury, 2013)
Harper, G. M., *The Neoplatonism of William Blake* (London: Oxford University Press, 1961)

Hill, C., *The World Turned Upside Down: Radical Ideas during the English Revolution* (London: Penguin, 1984)
Louth, A., *The Origins of the Christian Mystical Tradition: From Plato to Denys* (Oxford: Oxford University Press, 1981)
McGinn, B., *The Presence of God: A History of Western Christian Mysticism*, 6 vols. (New York: Crossroad, 1991–2017)
Nuttall, A. D., *The Alternative Trinity: Gnostic Heresy in Marlowe, Milton and Blake* (Oxford: Oxford University Press, 1998)
Spector, S. A., *Wonders Divine: The Development of Blake's Kabbalistic Myth* (Lewisburg: Bucknell University Press, 2001)

35 Nationalism and Imperialism

Bindman, D., *Mind-Forg'd Manacles: William Blake and Slavery* (London: Hayward Gallery, 2007)
Clark, S., and D. Worrall (eds.), *Blake, Nation, and Empire* (New York: Palgrave Macmillan, 2006)
Colley, L., *Britons: Forging the Nation, 1707–1837* (New Haven, CT: Yale University Press, 1992)
Erle, S., 'Representing Race: The Meaning of Colour and Line in William Blake's 1790s Bodies', in S. Clark and M. Suzuki (eds.), *The Reception of Blake in the Orient* (New York: Continuum, 2006), pp. 87–103
Ford, T. J. '"Jerusalem Is Scattered Abroad": Blake's Ottoman Geographies', *Studies in Romanticism*, 47.4 (2008), 529–48
Fulford, T., and P. J. Kitson (eds.), *Romanticism and Colonialism: Writing and Empire, 1780–1830* (Cambridge: Cambridge University Press, 2005)
Janowitz, A., *England's Ruins: Poetic Purpose and the National Landscape* (Cambridge, MA: Blackwell, 1990)
Welch, D. M., 'Essence, Gender, Race: William Blake's *Visions of the Daughters of Albion*', *Studies in Romanticism*, 49.1 (2010), 105–31
Wright, J. M., '"Greek & Latin Slaves of the Sword": Rejecting the Imperial Nation in Blake's *Milton*', in E. Sauer and B. Rajan (eds.), *Milton and the Imperial Vision* (Pittsburgh, PA: Duquesne University Press, 1999), pp. 255–72

36 Sex, Sexuality, and Gender

Binhammer, K., 'The Sex Panic of the 1790s', *Journal of the History of Sexuality*, 6 (1996), 409–34
  'Thinking Gender with Sexuality in 1790s' Feminist Thought', *Feminist Studies*, 28.3 (2002), 667–90.
Bruder, H. P., *William Blake and the Daughters of Albion* (Basingstoke: Macmillan, 1997)
Darnton, R., *The Forbidden Best-Sellers of Pre-Revolutionary France* (London: Fontana Press, 1997)

Essick, R. N., 'William Blake's "Female Will" and its Biographical Context', *SEL: Studies in English Literature, 1500–1900*, 31.4 (1991), 615–30
Harvey, K., *Reading Sex in the Eighteenth Century: Bodies and Gender in English Erotic Culture* (Cambridge: Cambridge University Press, 2004)
Hobson, C. Z., *Blake and Homosexuality* (New York and Basingstoke: Palgrave, 2000)
Laqueur, T., *Making Sex: Body and Gender from the Greeks to Freud* (Cambridge, MA: Harvard University Press, 1990)
Matthews, S., *Blake, Sexuality and Bourgeois Politeness* (Cambridge: Cambridge University Press, 2011)
Schuchard, M. K., *Why Mrs Blake Cried: William Blake and the Sexual Basis of Spiritual Vision* (London: Century, 2006)

37 War and Revolution

Conway, S., *The British Isles and the War of American Independence* (Oxford: Oxford University Press, 2000)
Forrest, A., K. Hagemann, and J. Rendall (eds.), *Soldiers, Citizens and Civilians: Experiences and Perceptions of the Revolutionary and Napoleonic Wars, 1790–1820* (Basingstoke: Palgrave, 2009)
Kennedy, C., *Narratives of the Revolutionary and Napoleonic Wars: Military and Civilian Experience in the Britain and Ireland* (Basingstoke: Palgrave, 2013)

38 (Without) Sympathy

Berlant, L., *Compassion: The Culture and Politics of an Emotion* (New York: Routledge, 2004)
Butler, J., *Giving an Account of Oneself* (New York: Fordham University Press, 2005)
Cameron, S., *Impersonality: Seven Essays* (Chicago: University of Chicago Press, 2007)
Das, V., 'Language and Body: Transactions in the Construction of Pain', in A. Kleinman, V. Das, and M. Lock (eds.), *Social Suffering* (Berkeley and Los Angeles: University of California Press, 1997), pp. 67–92
Derrida, J., *Politics of Friendship*, trans. G. Collins (London: Verso, 1997)
Hartman, G., 'The Sympathy Paradox: Poetry, Feeling, and Modern Cultural Morality', in *The Fateful Question of Culture* (New York: Columbia University Press, 1997), pp. 141–64
Menely, T., *The Animal Claim: Sensibility and Creaturely Voice* (Chicago: University of Chicago Press, 2015)
Nussbaum, M., *Upheavals of Thought: The Intelligence of Emotions* (Cambridge: Cambridge University Press, 2001)
Pinch, A., *Strange Fits of Passion: Epistemologies of Emotion, Hume to Austen* (Stanford: Stanford University Press, 1996)
Smock, A., *What Is There to Say?* (Lincoln: University of Nebraska Press, 2003)

Index

abolition, 310 *See also* slavery
Adam, 10, 189, 205–6, 207, 251
Aders, C. (Charles, husband of Eliza), 82–3, 84
Aders, E. (wife of Charles), 18, 79, 81, 82–3, 84
Aestheticism, 216
Albion, 11, 152, 174, 249, 251, 275 *See also* Englishness
allegory, 12, 58, 64, 71, 75, 118, 151, 155, 156, 174, 175, 178, 181, 251, 312, 313, 314
Althusser, L., 338–9
America *See also* Blake, W.: works: *America, Visions of the Daughters of Albion*
    American Revolution, 117, 185, 313
    American War of Independence, 325–6
    Blake's reception in, 97, 227
    Native Americans, 156, 250
androgyny, 321, 341
Anglicanism, 7, 131–2, 184, 188, 294, 325, 340
Anglo-German relations, 81, 167, 192, 293–4, 298–9, 314
animal rights, 239, 240–1
animal-based materials, 241
annotation, 44, 48–9, 50–1
    books annotated by Blake, 52, 108, 192 *See also* Blake, W.: works
anthropocentrism, 237
anthropology, 156, 161, 250–1
antinomianism, 2, 186, 201, 303
antiquarianism, 132–3, 137, 192, 195, 245–52
    practical, 247, 249, 252
    Society of Antiquaries, 24, 247, 248, 250, 252
    syncretism, 245, 246, 249, 251
apocalypticism, 11, 118, 176, 184–5, 186, 187, 188, 189, 335, 336
    apocalyptic literature, 116, 117, 197
apprentices, 39 *See also* Blake, W.: apprenticeship; Owen, T.; Parker, J.
archaism, 194, 196 *See also* Gothicism; Medievalism

Arianism, 191, 201
artisans, 2, 4, 9, 251, 280 *See also* Blake, W.: as an engraver
atonement, 202, 204–5, 206, 209
Auden, W. H., 173, 219–20, 225
audience, 1 *See also* Blake, W.: audience within his lifetime
Austin, S., 80
autographs, 51

Bacon, F., 262, 264, 274
ballads, 127, 129, 134, 135, 137, 140, 250
Bank Restriction Act, 286–8
banking industry, 287
banknotes, 287, 290
Barbauld, A. L., 239, 244, 257
bards, 144, 184, 194–5, 232, 233
Barlow, J., 197
Basire, J., 8, 9, 23, 27, 28, 30, 33, 245, 246, 250, 271, 272, 283
the Beats, 89, 90, 231, 232 *See also* Burroughs, W.; Ginsberg, A.; Kerouac, J.
Belvedere Torso, 333 *See also* Blake, W.: works
Berkeley, G., 262, 268, 269
the Bible, 64–6, 68, 71, 108, 125, 160, 165, 171, 184, 196, 201, 239, 249, 301, 315
    biblical prophecy, 113–19, 144 *See also* Elijah; Ezekiel; Isaiah; Moses
    as poetry, 113–15, 165, 167–70 *See also* Lowth, R.
bibliomancy, 50, 321–2
bills of exchange, 287, 288, 289
biographies of Blake, 2, 7–14, 79, 83, 95–6, 97, 192, 211–12, 252 *See also* Gilchrist, A. (husband of Anne)
Blake, C. (*née* Boucher), 8–9, 13, 36, 80, 271, 273, 319, 321–2
Blake, C. (William's mother), 293, 294, 295, 296, 297, 298
Blair, R. *See* Blake, W.: works, illustrations to Blair's *Grave*

364

Index

Blake, W.
  apprenticeship, 8, 23, 25, 33, 35, 121, 175, 252, 283
  as a book illustrator, 23, 25, 79
  as a painter, 70, 71–3, 75–6, 97
  as a prophet, 97, 215, 229, 231
  as an engraver, 7, 16, 23, 70, 75, 97
  audience within his lifetime, 1, 19, 46, 48, 79, 94–6, 97, 98, 134–5, 192–3, 198, 255
  autodidacticism, 2, 4, 170 *See also* Blake, W: education
  baptism, 7
  cause of death, 13
  childlikeness, 212, 215
  children, 10
  contrariety, 2, 15–16
  destruction of works, 13, 43
  education, 8 *See also* Blake, W.: apprenticeship; autodidacticism
  enthusiasm, 18, 50, 79, 304, 327
  exhibitions, 12, 28, 38, 74, 76, 319, 330, 331 *See also* exhibition culture
  finances, 9, 23, 27–8, 37, 49, 70, 77, 286, 288–9, 290
  heterodoxy, 303
  Irishness, imputed, 220
  language-learning, 170
  madness, imputed, 12, 79, 197, 198, 273
  marriage, 9
  pet cat, 241–2
  residences, 109, 273, 283–4
  trial for sedition, 7, 11–12, 188
  works
    Albion Rose, 185, 187, 334
    All Religions Are One, 36, 41, 82
    America, 53, 114, 117, 126, 156–7, 186, 187, 195, 227, 233, 237, 275, 312, 313, 314, 315, 319, 327–8
    The Ancient Britons, 72–3, 245
    annotations to Berkeley's *Siris*, 268
    annotations to Lavater's *Aphorisms*, 48, 51, 263, 273, 287
    annotations to Reynolds's *Discourses*, 49, 74, 147–51
    annotations to Watson's *Apology for the Bible*, 114–15, 165–6
    annotations to Wordsworth's *Poems*, 48, 198
    [annotations to] Wordsworth's *Recluse*, 198
    As if an Angel, 179, 181–1
    'Auguries of Innocence', 8, 46
    autograph in Upcott's album, 51
    Belvedere Torso, 333–4, 335
    Book of Ahania, 34, 37, 126, 159 *See also* Blake, W.: works: Urizen books
    Book of Los, 37, 126, 159–60 *See also* Blake, W.: works: Urizen books
    Book of Thel, 41, 53, 80, 124–5, 211, 249, 254, 302
    Book of Urizen, 10, 36, 40, 96, 126, 157–60, 239, 275, 336–8, 339, 341–2 *See also* Blake, W.: works: Urizen books; Urizen
    Characters in Spenser's 'Faerie Queene', 176–8
    Chaucer's Canterbury Pilgrims, 25, 28–30, 33, 71, 74, 81, 174–6
    Descriptive Catalogue, 12, 71, 72, 75, 174, 175, 192, 193, 245, 249, 330, 333
    drafts, 45, 46–7, 48, 95
    'The Ecchoing Green', 141–2, 144
    Europe, 109, 110–11, 126, 135, 155, 156, 157, 159, 275, 327, 328–9
    'The Everlasting Gospel', 165
    'Fair Elenor', 120
    'The Fly', 237, 243
    For Children: The Gates of Paradise, 41, 174, 255
    The French Revolution, 16, 35, 126, 327
    Genesis, 44, 45
    Ghost of Abel, 200–1, 202, 207–8
    'Gwin, King of Norway', 120, 195, 326
    'Holy Thursday' (*Experience*), 133–4
    'Holy Thursday' (*Innocence*), 133, 134
    ['Holy Thursday'] (*Island*), 130–2
    illustrations to Blair's *Grave*, 59–61, 68, 80, 214
    illustrations to Dante's *Commedia*, 27, 33, 66–8
    illustrations to Gray's *Poems*, 57, 176, 195, 289, 319
    illustrations to the Book of Job, 13, 27, 32–3, 52, 61–6, 68, 80, 81, 174, 211, 289
    illustrations to Thornton's *Pastorals of Virgil*, 27, 30–2, 33
    illustrations to Wollstonecraft's *Original Stories*, 254
    illustrations to Young's *Night Thoughts*, 28, 49, 54, 57–8, 61, 80, 187, 214
    'Introduction' to *Innocence*, 65, 259, 297
    Island in the Moon, 15, 44, 45, 47, 48, 105–7, 111, 122–3, 130–2, 133, 195, 272, 274–5, 286
    Jerusalem, 11, 38, 61, 74, 96, 117, 126, 135, 139–40, 152, 155, 160, 188, 202, 239–40, 245, 251, 275, 277, 282, 312, 314–15, 319, 321, 322, 329–30, 335, 336 *See also* 'Jerusalem' (hymn)
    Joseph of Arimathea, 25, 252
    'King Edward the Third', 120, 193, 311–12, 313
    'The Lamb', 237, 242
    Laocoön, 167–8, 249–50

366   Index

Blake, W. (cont.)
   Large and *Small Book of Designs*, 40
   ['Laughing Song'] 'Song 2nd by a Youn[g] Shepherd', 47, 121–2
   letters, 44, 48
   'London', 280, 282
   'Mad Song', 120, 121, 194
   Marriage of Heaven and Hell, 10, 18, 39–40, 108, 112, 115, 116, 143, 170, 185, 186, 195–6, 206, 223–4, 225, 237–8, 242, 263, 321
   'The Mental Traveller', 220
   Michael Foretells the Crucifixion, 189
   Milton, 12, 38, 91, 110, 113, 117–19, 126–7, 135, 143, 151–2, 155, 160, 185, 188, 202, 206–7, 223, 238–9, 243, 250, 252, 267–8, 275, 289, 306–7, 314, 329–30, 334, 342–4
   Moses Staying the Plague, 338
   notebooks, 43, 46, 53 *See also* Blake, W.: works: Notebook
   Notebook, 44, 45, 46–7, 50, 95, 99, 123, 124, 211, 223
   ['Nurses Song'] (*Island*), 122–3
   'On Anothers Sorrow', 339–41
   On Homers Poetry [and] *On Virgil*, 38, 39, 192, 333 *See also* 'Living Form'
   Pickering Manuscript, 46, 47
   Pity, 181
   Poetical Sketches, 15, 47, 82, 120–1, 129, 132, 141, 142, 185, 193–6, 211, 213, 254, 257
   (Prospectus, October 1793) 'To the Public', 56–7, 94–5, 288
   'Public Address', 44, 74
   'Samson', 196
   The Sea of Time and Space (the Arlington Court Picture), 82
   'The Sick Rose', 108
   sketchbooks, 32, 44, 46, 52, 61, 66
   'Song' ['Fresh from the dewy hill'], 142
   'Song' ['My silks and fine array'], 120–1, 142
   Song of Los, 99, 126, 156, 159, 179, 264, 329, 330
   Songs (joint), 9–10, 82, 96–7, 123–4, 129, 132–3, 134, 141, 197, 211, 216, 220, 237, 250, 254, 256, 257–8, 259, 297
   Songs of Experience, 47, 109, 195, 216, 250, 289
   Songs of Innocence, 19, 35, 36, 38, 41, 47, 82, 107, 121, 198, 256, 258–9, 275, 289
   Spiritual Form of Nelson, 71–2, 74, 75, 245, 249, 331
   Spiritual Form of Pitt, 71–2, 74, 75, 245, 331
   'Spring', 259, 295–7
   tempera, 70, 74, 75 *See also* Blake, W.: works: *Spiritual Form of Nelson*, *Spiritual Form of Pitt*
   There Is No Natural Religion, 36, 41, 82, 135, 167
   Tiriel, 44, 45, 46, 124, 125
   'The Tyger', 81, 265
   Urizen books, 156, 157
   VALA/The Four Zoas, 44, 45, 46, 53, 57–8, 98, 99, 100, 126, 139, 142–3, 155, 188, 313
   'Vision of the Last Judgment', 44
   Visions of the Daughters of Albion, 10, 53, 126, 196, 237, 263, 264, 312, 320, 321, 322
blank verse, 120, 121, 123, 126, 139
Bliss, R., 79, 80–1, 318
blood, 159, 241, 272, 273, 274
Boehme, J., 11, 170, 301, 302, 303, 305
   Behmenist, 303
Boydell, J., 27, 28, 46, 72, 290
Boyle, D., 136
brain, 73, 158, 273, 274, 336
Bryant, J., 245, 246, 249, 251
Burke, E., 49, 131, 147–8, 185–6, 327, 330
Burroughs, W., 89, 90, 231
Butts, E. (wife of Thomas), 82, 319
Butts, T. (husband of Elizabeth), 13, 17, 70, 80, 149, 151, 331
Byron, G. G., 192, 193, 198, 200–8
Bysshe, E., 50, 321

Carter, A., 90
Carter, J., 246, 247, 250
Cary, J., 88
Catholicism, 303
   anti-Catholicism, 329
cell theory, 270
Chatterton, T., 120, 132, 193, 195–6, 248
Chaucer, G., 174, 182, 192 *See also* Blake, W.: works: *Chaucer's Canterbury Pilgrims*
Chichester, 17, 318
Chichester, J. P. (husband of Susannah), 82
Chichester, S. (wife of John), 79, 82–3
children, 36, 130–1, 132, 133–4, 242, 254–9, 294, 295, 296–8 *See also* Blake, W.: childlikeness, children; namby-pamby
children's literature, 124, 254–9 *See also* nursery rhymes
Christ, 61, 168, 185, 187, 188, 189, 201–2, 205, 223, 242, 294–5
Christianity, 115–16, 166, 169, 173, 187, 188, 204, 219–20, 223, 224, 249, 293, 297, 306, 312, 329, 330 *See also* the Bible
church attendance, 105, 165
classicism, 128, 144, 167–8, 170, 173, 175, 179, 249, 251, 330 *See also* neoclassicism
coin, 286–7, 288, 289, 291 *See also* guineas; Quid
Coleridge, S. T., 9, 18, 82, 95, 141, 156, 167, 168, 169, 170, 197, 239, 271, 272, 274, 321, 327

Index

colonialism *See* imperialism
colour printing, 10, 28, 34, 37, 38, 41, 74, 75, 290
    See also printmaking; relief etching
commonplacing *See* note-taking
composite art, 1, 4, 10, 43, 56, 57, 95, 132, 213, 214, 254, 259
contraries, 10, 90, 91, 108, 111, 143, 185, 186, 220, 224 *See also* Blake, W.: contrariety
Cope, J., 92
counter-culture, 87–90, 227, 232, 304
Crane, H., 229–31, 232
creation, 17, 19, 20, 64–6, 150, 302
the Creation, 157, 167, 302, 306 *See also* sensation: five senses
Cromek, R. H., 28, 48, 59
Cumberland, G., 17, 20, 322
Cunningham, A., 79, 96, 211, 215

D'Hancarville, P.-F. H., Baron, 246, 247, 249, 252
Damon, S. F., 14, 87, 155, 156, 301
Dante, 212, 213–14, 221, 222 *See also* Blake, W.: works: illustrations to Dante's *Commedia*
Darwin, E., 197, 239, 251, 271, 275, 320, 321
Deism, 166, 330
Deleuze, G., 158, 161, 267
democracy, 115, 184, 227, 228, 229, 230, 232–3
Denman, M., 82
Dissent, 4, 7, 13, 50, 79, 80, 184, 325
division of labour, 56 *See also* engraving: copy engraving
dolnik, 121–3, 124, 125, 127
drawing, 1, 8, 33, 47, 49, 55 *See also* the Sketch
drug-taking, 88–9
Dylan, B., 89

Edgeworth, M., and R. L., 259
editing, 94
    electronic editing, 100 *See also* William Blake Archive
education, 201, 202, 222, 254–9 *See also* apprentices; Blake, W.: education
electricity, in medical use, 273–4
Elijah, 200, 204, 208, 209 *See also* the Bible: biblical prophecy
Eliot, G., 84
Eliot, T. S., 4, 109, 219, 220, 221–3, 229–30, 231
Ellis, E. J., 220 *See also* Yeats, W. B.
Emin, T., 91
empire, 66, 185, 187, 279, 329 *See also* imperialism
Englishness, 312, 314–15 *See also* nationalism
engraving, 23–33, 36, 38, 46, 56, 64, 247 *See also* Blake, W.: as an engraver, apprenticeship; relief etching

banknote engraving, 290
copy engraving, 23, 24–5, 27, 33, 56, 68, 290
intaglio, 24, 32, 34, 37, 288, 290
line engraving, 24, 25–7, 28, 30, 32–3
repoussage, 33
woodcuts, 30–2
Enlightenment, 2, 152, 201, 202, 203
enthusiasm, 322 *See also* Blake, W.: enthusiasm
epic, 139, 329, 330 *See also* prophecy: as genre or mode
Erdman, D. V., 87, 174
    Complete Poetry & Prose of William Blake, xxi, 35, 44, 45, 52, 98
eroticism, 293, 294–5, 296, 320–2, 328, 341–2
    homoeroticism, 321, 341
esotericism, 174, 220, 251, 301, 303
Evangelicalism, 165, 169, 185, 188, 321–2
Eve, 189, 203–4, 205
exhibition culture *See also* lending and sharing books; Blake, W.: exhibitions
    in Blake's lifetime, 12, 71, 328
    in recent history, 70, 91
extra-illustration, 20, 57, 68, 69, 319
Ezekiel, 8, 18, 28, 115, 116, 118–19

the Fall, 167, 203, 322, 336, 338, 343
fantasy, 312
Felpham, 11, 109, 188, 283
femininity, 318
Flaxman, A. (Nancy, wife of John), 82, 319
Flaxman, J. (husband of Ann (Nancy)), 13, 81, 175, 330
food security, 310, 313, 315
Foote, S., 107
forgiveness, 110, 203–5, 207, 209, 330, 339
fourteeners, 122, 125, 128
freedom, 136, 227, 313–14
French invasion, threat of, 329
French Revolution, 9, 152, 156, 185–6, 197, 201, 203, 327 *See also* Blake, W.: works: *The French Revolution*
    Jacobin terror, 187
fresco, 71, 74–5
Fuseli, H., 13, 16, 51, 175, 255, 299, 321, 327
Fyre, N., 14, 87, 127, 155, 192, 263, 301, 302, 305

genres
    mixing of, 196 *See also* heteroglossia
George III, 313, 328 *See also* regicide
Gilchrist, A. (husband of Anne), 13, 50–1, 54, 79, 97, 211–12, 213, 258
Gilchrist, Anne (wife of Alexander), 79, 97, 216
Ginsberg, A., 88, 89–90, 231–3
Gnosticism, 10, 302, 303

Gormley, A., 90
the Gothic, 327 *See also* Gothicism
Gothicism, 175, 195, 246, 250, 251, 252, 253 *See also* medievalism
'Gothic' form, 202, 266
guineas, 287, 288–9, 291, 292

handwriting, 43, 49–51, 53, 96 *See also* mirror writing
harlot, 280, 319, 320–1
Harris, T., 91
Hartley, T., 274
Haworth, E. F., 80
Hazlitt, W., 79, 197
Hegel, G. W. F., 159, 167
Herder, J. G., 167, 170, 179
heteroglossia, 107
history, 2, 114, 245, 247–8, 312 *See also* antiquarianism
history painting, 72, 148
Homer, 250
Horovitz, A., 90
horses, 241
  Bruno the pony, 241
humanism, 243, 303, 339
Hunt, L., 12, 192, 193, 274
Hunt, R., 12, 73, 192, 274
Hunter, A. H. (wife of John), 271
Hunter, J. (husband of Anne), 271–3, 340
Hunter, W., 271
hunting, 240 *See also* animal rights
Huxley, A., 88–9
hymns, 123, 131–2, 242 *See also* 'Jerusalem' (hymn)
  Moravian hymns, 129, 294–5, 296, 297–9

ideology, 94, 151–2, 338–9
illuminated books, 1, 2, 9, 12, 23, 27, 30, 35–41, 43, 44, 47, 56, 70, 95, 192, 219, 291 *See also* Blake, W.: works; illuminated printing; illustration
  as 'virtual networks', 20
  edition printing, 36–7, 38
  lack of uniformity between copies, 290
  sequencing of pages, 19, 39–40, 41, 68
illuminated printing, 27–8, 41, 47, 56–7, 74, 94–5, 213, 328 *See also* illuminated books; printmaking; relief etching
illustration, 10, 56, 174, 189, 247 *See also* extra-illustration
  book illustration, 27, 28, 35, 38, 46, 56–68, 132–3, 258–9 *See also* Blake, W., works
imperialism, 188, 201, 249, 309–15 *See also* empire
inspiration, 18, 113, 117–18, 150, 151–2, 157, 188, 189, 305 *See also* prophecy; vision

intaglio, *See* engraving
Ireland, 152 *See also* Blake, W.: Irishness, imputed
  Irish culture, 194–5, 221
Iremonger, E., 80
irony, 109
Isaiah, 8, 18, 115, 116, 167

Jarman, D., 90
'Jena' Romantics, 170
'Jerusalem' (hymn), 87, 90, 135–6, 315 *See also* Blake, W., *Jerusalem*
Johnson, J., 16, 17, 27, 28, 37, 271, 299
  circle of, 16, 21, 186, 192
juvenilia, 193 *See also* Blake, W.: works: *Poetical Sketches*

Kabbalism, 220, 303
Kant, I., 147, 151, 153, 155, 158, 170, 171, 201
Keats, J., 15, 141, 219
Kerouac, J., 89, 231–2

lambs *See* Blake, W.: works: 'The Lamb'
lending and sharing books, 48, 80, 82, 83–4, 211, 231
letterpress, 35, 44, 46, 56, 57–8, 60–1, 64, 95, 96–7, 286, 288, 290
letter-writing, 48 *See also* Blake, W.: works: letters
Lewis, C. S., 312
life force (*vis viva*), 270–1 *See also* organism
Linnaeus, C., 239, 320
Linnell, J. (husband of Mary Ann), 13, 17–18, 30, 32, 33, 66, 81, 82, 84
Linnell, M. A. (wife of John), 82, 129, 137
literalism, 28, 58, 118–19, 134, 169, 174, 178, 181, 182, 201, 305, 314, 342
'Living form', 266, 268 *See also* Gothicism: 'Gothic' form
Locke, J., 107, 148, 240, 259, 262–3, 274
London, 7, 91, 92, 129, 130–1, 135, 222, 241, 252, 277–84, 293, 298, 299 *See also* Blake, W.: residences; works: 'London'; Thames
  2012 Olympics, 136
  Cries of London, 130 *See also* street cries
  Nash's Regent Street project, 281, 284
  Soho, 7, 71, 281, 283–4
  St Paul's Cathedral, 131, 133, 134, 165, 330 *See also* Blake, W.: works: 'Holy Thursday'
Longinus, 148, 149–51, 153
Los, 156, 159–60, 207, 277, 307 *See also* Blake, W.: works: *Book of Los, Song of Los*
Lowth, R., 114–15, 119, 144, 154, 167, 170
Lunar Society, 274, 275
lyric, 50, 139, 141, 144, 194, 212, 213, 214, 219 *See also* songs

Macpherson, J., 132, 248 *See also* Ossian
Malkin, B. H., 178, 192, 194, 198, 252, 258
Malthus, T. R., 310 *See also* food security; population
marginalia *See* annotation
marriage, 319, 322 *See also* Blake, W.: marriage
masculinity, 58, 159, 330
materialism, 198, 262, 265, 271, 288, 289, 291, 301, 303–4, 336
  materials of Blake's art, 50, 68, 237, 241
  matter and spirit, 213–14, 216, 302–3
Mathew, A. S. (husband of Harriet), 15, 82, 257, 271
Mathew, H. (their daughter), 82
Mathew, H. (wife of Anthony), 15, 82, 271
Mathews salon, 15, 16, 82, 271
medicine *See* electricity, in medical use; surgery
Medievalism, 9, 56, 120, 196, 214, 246, 248 *See also* Gothic
meshworks, 19
Methodism, 50, 165, 185, 293, 298, 299 *See also* the Wesleys; Whitefield, J.
Milton, J., 8, 49, 58, 91, 113, 115, 126, 173, 178, 184–9, 196, 214, 263, 301, 322, 327 *See also* Blake, W.: works: *Milton*
mirror writing, 36 *See also* handwriting
Monckton Milnes, R., 83–4
Moravianism, 50, 170, 303 *See also* hymns: Moravian hymns
Morris, W., 213, 214, 217, 312
Morrison, J., 88, 89
Moses, 113, 166, 338–9, 341, 342 *See also* the Bible: biblical prophecy; Blake, works: *Moses Staying the Plague*
motion, scientific theories of, 268
multilingualism, 293, 298–9 *See also* Anglo-German relations; Blake, W.: language learning
muses, 110, 157, 188, 189
museums *See* exhibition culture
mysticism, 8, 79, 82–3, 170, 220, 227, 229, 232, 237, 301–7, 323
myth, 2, 7, 11, 14, 45, 109–10, 114, 139, 140, 155–61, 174, 175, 185, 188, 193, 215–16, 217, 219, 220, 221, 222, 245–6, 247, 249, 251, 265, 312, 327
mythology, allegory, and schematism, 156
myths vs mythology, 155

namby-pamby, 256, 257–8
nationalism, 75, 136, 188, 245, 309–15, 331
natural history, 239, 250, 271 *See also* Darwin, E.; Linnaeus, C.
neoclassicism, 148, 149, 194, 247, 249–50 *See also* classicism

Neoplatonism, 249, 253, 302–3
nerves, 158, 270, 273, 274
Newbery, J., 258
Newton, I., 3, 10, 262, 264–6, 267, 268, 269
note-taking, 46, 49, 50 *See also* annotation
nursery rhymes, 122, 127, 140, 143, 215, 255–6 *See also* children: children's literature

Ofili, C., 91
Okri, B., 91
Ololon, 109, 188, 306–7
Orc, 156, 157, 159, 181, 185, 187, 188, 255, 328
organism, 158, 270, 336 *See also* life force (*vis viva*); 'Living Form'
  dis-organisation, 158, 160, 336
Ossian, 125, 140, 196 *See also* Macpherson, J.
Owen, T., 27–8

Pacific, 250
pacifism, 184, 187, 188, 189, 325
Paine, T., 165–6, 326, 327, 328
paper, 19, 32, 33, 43, 49, 75, 287
  paper currency, 287–8, 289, 290 *See also* banknotes
parallelism, 114, 143, 196
Parker, J., 27
parody, 18, 58, 107, 108–9
patriotism, 249, 325, 326, 330
patronage, 15, 17, 37, 48, 70, 74, 82, 108, 288, 290, 318 *See also* Butts, T.; Cumberland, G.; Hayley, W.; Johnson, J.; Linnell, J.; Mathew, A.S.; Matthew, H.
Peake, M., 312
Percy, T., 82, 120, 133, 137, 194–5, 213, 215
the Picturesque, 49, 149
pity, 132, 159, 339–41
Platonism, 253, 303, 307
polite culture, 2, 16, 79, 130, 319
Pope, A., 110, 140, 142, 143, 194
popular culture
  in Blake's lifetime, 107, 122, 123, 124, 129, 132, 133, 135, 246, 249, 250, 310, 328 *See also* ballads; nursery rhymes; street cries
  in recent history, 87, 89, 92, 98, 136
population, 249, 278, 279, 281, 309, 310 *See also* food security
pornography, 320–1
poverty, 132, 133–4, 277–8, 279–80 *See also* Blake, W.: finances
Pre-Raphaelitism, 90, 211–17, 220 *See also* Morris, W.; the Rossettis
Priestley, J., 37, 274–5
primitivism, 156, 250, 251, 252
print culture, 47–8, 68
printmaking, 1, 23, 25–7, 35, 38–9, 41, 70, 74, 290

prophecy, 8, 107, 113–19, 144, 155, 184, 185, 186, 188, 189, 195, 196, 216, 227, 229, 230, 232–3, 302, 305, 307, 323, 326, 327, 328 *See also* the Bible: biblical prophecy; Blake, W.: as a prophet
as genre or mode, 115, 116, 117, 119
mock-prophetic, 110–11
prostitution *See* harlots
Protestantism, 115, 293, 301, 303, 304, 310
Pullman, P., 91

Quid, 286, 291

racism, 309–10, 314
Rahab, 188, 321
Raine, K., 174, 301, 302–3
Read, H., 88
Reason, 10, 58, 106, 151, 152, 157, 186, 203, 237
rationalism, 2, 4, 143, 184, 186, 202, 262
regicide, 184, 187 *See also* George III
relief etching, 9, 23, 27, 30–2, 34, 35, 36, 37, 56, 94–5, 290 *See also* illuminated printing
repoussage, *See* engraving
republicanism, 185, 188, 217, 227–8, 326, 327
revision, 44, 45, 47 *See also* Blake, W.: drafts; engraving: repoussage
revolution *See* America: American Revolution; French Revolution; regicide; violence
Reynolds, J., 8, 74–5, 147–51, 153 *See also* Blake, W.: works: annotations to Reynolds's *Discourses*
rhyme, 125, 126, 139–46, 214, 257 *See also* nursery rhyme
Ritson, J., 129, 132, 239, 250
Robinson, H. C., 9, 18, 48, 80, 81, 192, 198, 289
Robinson, M., 197
Rossetti, C., 214–15
Rossetti, D. G., 46, 83, 97, 211–14, 215, 216
Rossetti, W. M., 83, 97–8, 100, 211, 212
Rossetti Manuscript, 46
Rousseau, J.-J., 250, 254–5, 258, 330
Royal Academy, 8, 70, 71, 249, 271
Royal Society, 24, 250, 262, 275
rückenfigur, 333–6
Rushdie, S., 91

Samson, 184–5, 187, 188, 196
satire, 106, 107, 109, 110
Schelling, F., 155, 156
Schlegel, F., 169–70
Schleiermacher, F., 170
school, 122, 131, 133, 167, 258–9 *See also* education
Scolfield, J., 12 *See also* Blake, W.: trial for sedition

scribal culture, 47–9
sensation, 168, 170, 259, 262–8, 274
aesthetic, 149, 151, 152, 153
five senses, 134, 259, 262, 263–4, 268, 305–6
sensibility, 270, 273–4
sensuality, 58, 231, 296, 322 *See also* eroticism
sensibility, 339–41
Shakespeare, W., 120–1, 181–2, 183, 193, 313
Shelley, P. B., 146, 216, 219
Sinclair, I., 90, 277
the Sketch, 49, 193, 334–5 *See also* Blake, W.: works: sketchbooks
sketching *See* drawing
slavery, 169, 187, 310, 311, 313, 314, 321, 322, 331
the Slave Trade, 28, 310
Smith, A., 339
Smith, C., 16, 197
Smith, J. T., 15
songs, 106, 120, 124, 127, 129–37, 179, 194, 213, 214–15, 217, 250, 271, 294, 295, 297–8, 310, 325 *See also* hymns; nursery rhymes; Blake, W.: works
sound and sense, 145, 156
sound effect, 140
Southcott, J., 323
Spenser, E., 141, 176–8, 182
Stedman, J. G., 16, 314
Stothard, T., 27, 28, 71
street cries, 130, 280
Stukeley, W., 245, 249, 251
the Sublime, 7, 49, 114, 147–52, 327
surgery, 272
Swedenborg, E., 108, 196, 293, 301, 303, 305
Swedenborgianism, 8, 39, 79, 83, 96, 303, 322
Swedenborgians, 80, 82, 97
Swinburne, A. C., 45, 50, 51, 83, 84, 97, 98, 141, 144, 211, 212, 214, 217, 227, 228, 232, 301
symbol, 155, 156, 159
symbolism, 174, 178, 181, 219, 221, 242, 328 *See also* literalism
symbolisme, 221
system, 155, 157, 158, 159–60, 161

Tatham, F., 13, 23, 43, 80, 95–6
Tennyson, A., 84, 219
Teresa of Avila, 303, 305, 323
Thames, 9, 13, 131, 281–2, 283, 284
things, 18–19, 243, 268, 290–1
Thompson, E. P., 4, 303, 308
trade, 287, 310, 330
Transcendentalists, 97
Tulk, C. A. (husband of Susannah), 82, 97
Tulk, S. (wife of Charles), 82
Twiss, R., 37, 80

Upcott, W., 51
Urizen, 19, 64, 66, 157–60, 186, 188, 224, 264, 306, 313, 320, 321, 337, 338, 339, 342–4 *See also* Blake, W.: works: *Book of Urizen*, Urizen books

Varley, D. (wife of John), 82
Varley, J. (husband of Devalle), 52, 305
violence, 134, 166, 184, 186, 187, 188, 200–1, 206, 210, 307, 309, 313, 314, 325, 327, 329, 330 *See also* pacifism; regicide
virginity, 119, 254, 319, 322
Viscomi, J., 19, 37–8, 41, 47, 55, 99, 291
vision, 2, 8, 9, 12, 15, 88, 89, 91, 107, 108, 109, 110–11, 115, 135–6, 168, 186, 188, 189, 196, 198, 204–5, 208, 212, 213, 215, 216, 220, 227, 229, 230, 231, 265, 273, 301, 302, 303, 306–7, 322, 328
vitalism, 271, 272, 274
Voltaire, 330

Walpole, H., 246, 247, 248
watercolour, 9, 28, 32, 33, 36, 57, 70, 71, 74, 75, 241 *See also* fresco

Watts, I., 18, 50, 124, 131, 215, 256–7
Wesleys, the, 131, 170, 244, 293
  Wesley, C., 242
  Wesley, J., 298, 325
White, H. C., 301–2, 305
Whitefield, G., 107
Whitman, W., 217, 227, 230, 231, 232, 233
Wilkinson, J. J. G., 82, 96–7
William Blake Archive, xxi, 20, 44–5, 100, 291
wit, 107, 109, 110
Wollstonecraft, M., 16, 254, 327
Women's Institute, 315
Wordsworth, M. (wife of William), 48
Wordsworth, W. (husband of Mary), 7, 9, 18, 48, 81, 95, 100, 168, 170, 192, 194, 197, 198, 248, 280

Yeats, W. B., 98, 155, 181, 219, 220
Young, E. *See* Blake, W.: works: illustrations to Young's *Night Thoughts*

Zinzendorf, N. L. von, 293 *See also* Moravianism

For EU product safety concerns, contact us at Calle de José Abascal, 56–1°, 28003 Madrid, Spain or eugpsr@cambridge.org.

www.ingramcontent.com/pod-product-compliance
Ingram Content Group UK Ltd.
Pitfield, Milton Keynes, MK11 3LW, UK
UKHW022240220326
469255UK00018B/276